Contemporary Islamist Perspectives
on International Relations

This book is part of the Peter Lang Regional Studies list.
Every volume is peer reviewed and meets
the highest quality standards for content and production.

PETER LANG
New York • Bern • Berlin
Brussels • Vienna • Oxford • Warsaw

Sami E. Baroudi

Contemporary Islamist Perspectives on International Relations

Mainstream Voices from the Sunni and Shii Arab World

PETER LANG
New York • Bern • Berlin
Brussels • Vienna • Oxford • Warsaw

Library of Congress Control Number: 2021949049

Bibliographic information published by **Die Deutsche Nationalbibliothek**.
Die Deutsche Nationalbibliothek lists this publication in the "Deutsche Nationalbibliografie"; detailed bibliographic data are available on the Internet at http://dnb.d-nb.de/.

ISBN 978-1-4331-9357-6 (hardcover)
ISBN 978-1-4331-9378-1 (ebook pdf)
ISBN 978-1-4331-9379-8 (epub)
DOI 10.3726/b19175

© 2022 Peter Lang Publishing, Inc., New York
80 Broad Street, 5th floor, New York, NY 10004
www.peterlang.com

All rights reserved.
Reprint or reproduction, even partially, in all forms such as microfilm, xerography, microfiche, microcard, and offset strictly prohibited.

To the memory of my mother Minerva Baroudi and my aunt Aida Baroudi

Contents

	Preface	ix
1	Introduction: The Moderate-Reformist (Mainstream) Strand of Political Islam	1
2	The Founding Generation: Jamal al-Din al-Afghani, Muhammad 'Abduh and Rashid Rida	33
3	The Second Generation: Mahmoud Shaltut and Muhammad Abu Zahra	63
4	The Second Generation: Muhammad al-Bahi	101
5	The Third Generation: Yusuf al-Qaradawi	133
6	The Third Generation: Wahbah al-Zuhaili	189
7	The Third Generation: Muhammad Hussein Fadlallah	217

8   Conclusion: The Mainstream Islamists Within Their Ideational
    and Historical Milieus   259

    Bibliography   283
    Index   297

Preface

This book has been in the works for several years. Many hurdles had to be overcome before the writing process could be brought to a fruitful conclusion. Although I have published scholarly articles on most of the scholar sheikhs examined here, for this work I decided to analyze afresh the works by each scholar sheikh; instead of going back and reworking (or rehashing) my own past writings on the subject. The reading of the international relations discourses of the six turbaned scholars examined here represents my own comprehension of their thought and is not necessarily in line with how other researchers understood their views. Despite the relatively narrow focus of this book—being primarily concerned with perspectives on international relations—I had to immerse myself in the totality of the oeuvres of the selected authors in order to comprehend their worldviews which undoubtedly shaped their analyses of international relations. A principal challenge throughout has been to maintain a middle of the way (or *wasati*) approach to the views of the surveyed authors; avoiding both extremes of identifying with these views and assailing them. Thus, while I consistently strove to identify the tensions, and indeed internal contradictions, in the international relations discourse of each examined scholar sheikh, I never intended this work to be a critique of their views, or indeed of political Islam. My approach to political Islam, within whose broad parameters this study lies, is to treat it as a powerful, albeit not hegemonic, current within Islam. Islam is definitely broader than political Islam; but there is nothing wrong, odd, or un-Islamic, about the incessant attempts of scores of Islamic scholars and arguably millions of lay Muslims worldwide to Islamize the political sphere, including the realm of international relations.

Political Islam is a social reality whose multiple facets warrant careful examination; irrespective of whether we personally agree, or disagree, with the Islamization of politics and more broadly of society. As a broad and diverse field of study, political Islam has tended to focus inter alia on the histories, organizations and ideologies of both popular Islamist movements, such as the Muslim Brotherhood, and radical Islamist ones, in particular al-Qaeda and its offspring the Islamic State in Iraq and al-Sham (ISIS).

It has also addressed at length the relationship between Islam and important political phenomena such as democratization, human rights, women rights, and violent extremism. Understandably, the literature also abounds with studies on the life and thought of prominent radical Islamist thinkers, such as Sayyid Qutb, Osama bin Laden, Ayman al-Zawahiri, and Abu Muhammad al-Maqdisi (just to name a prominent few).

But despite some notable exceptions, there have not been many academic studies, especially in English, on Islam and international relations. This book's principal contribution to the field of political Islam lies in offering a close examination of the international relations' views of a select number of prominent moderate-reformist Arab scholar sheikhs, who are referred to here as mainstream. My reading of the discourses of the six scholar sheikhs aims at identifying the principal elements of this moderate-reformist (mainstream) perspective on international relations. I also seek to trace the origins of this perspective and shed light on its evolution over three generations of scholar sheikhs. Last but not least, I situate the examined discourses on international relations within their ideational and historical settings and elaborate on the principal differences between the mainstream perspective and the radical one, arguing that political Islam encompasses both camps.

While this work falls primarily within the broad field of political Islam, it also significantly intersects with the even broader field of International Relations (IR). The study seeks to contribute, even if modestly, to both burgeoning fields of study. Its contribution to IR lies in demonstrating the usefulness of the field's principal concepts and theories for analyzing non-Western, in this case Islamist, perspectives on international relations. Stated otherwise, I maintain that the standard concepts and theories of IR, despite their Western origins, can be intelligently applied to analyze how non-Western thinkers conceptualize international relations. One thus need not invent a new lexicon of IR and come up with new theories to comprehend how non-Western thinkers conceptualize international relations.

The book further contends that—while anchored in the Quran, the Sunna, and the Islamic tradition—the discourses of mainstream Islamists reflect the major historic developments that impacted the Arab and broader Islamic worlds since the latter part of the 19th century. It further argues that, despite their distinctive Islamic character, these discourses center on themes that are at the core of the IR discipline (such as power, independence, interdependence, sovereignty, international conflict, war, and peace), rendering it worthwhile to compare the views of each of the six scholar sheikhs to the basic tenets of the two principal traditions of theorizing on international relations: realism and liberal internationalism.

Throughout the writing process, I benefited from the unfailing support of my home institution, the Lebanese American University (LAU) and its libraries, despite the very dire conditions in Lebanon over the past few years. My friend and LAU colleague Dr. Vahid Behmardi was a constant source of encouragement and a superb translator of difficult passages from Arabic to English. Ms. Samira al-Shami and Ms. Hala Nasreddine provided valuable editorial assistance. I would also like to thank the editorial team at Peter Lang for their major support.

When I started the writing process, my mother Minerva and my aunt Aida, my immediate family and main source of emotional support, were with me, albeit in failing health. Losing both of them in 2019 left a void in my heart that was only exacerbated by the upheaval and socioeconomic deterioration that my country Lebanon has been witnessing since 2019 and by the COVID 19 pandemic. I myself caught the COVID 19 virus around New Year Eve 2021 but made a full recovery following a short stay at the LAU Medical Center where I received excellent treatment. While adding to the stress, working on this manuscript gave me focus and helped me deal with my personal loss and with the turmoil in my beloved country Lebanon and indeed in the world.

1

Introduction: The Moderate-Reformist (Mainstream) Strand of Political Islam

Aim of the Book

Much has been written on radical Islamist groups and movements, such as al-Qaeda[1] and more recently the Islamic State in Iraq and Syria (ISIS).[2] Similarly, studies on the political thought of radical Islamist figures such as Abu Muhammad al-Maqdisi,[3] Ayman al-Zawahiri,[4] Sayyid Qutb,[5] and Osama bin Laden[6] have proliferated. In contrast, scant attention has been paid to the political and social thought of moderate-reformist contemporary Islamist scholars, referred to here as mainstream. The aim of this work is to help fill this gap by examining an important, albeit understudied, dimension of the political and social thought of moderate-reformist Islamists, namely their conceptualizations of international relations. It provides a close, critical reading of the international relations discourses of six contemporary scholar sheikhs from the Sunni and Shia Arab world of the 20th and early 21st centuries. Four of these scholar sheikhs are Sunni Egyptians who received their education at al-Azhar and/or maintained a long-term affiliation with the institution. They are Mahmoud Shaltut (1893–1963), Muhammad Abu Zahra (1897–1974), Muhammad al-Bahi (1905–1982), and Yusuf al-Qaradawi (1926–). The fifth is the Sunni Syrian Sheikh Wahbah al-Zuhaili (1932–2015) who also studied at al-Azhar before pursuing a doctorate in jurisprudence at the University of Cairo. He functioned as a university professor and a practicing cleric in his native Syria. Finally, there is Sayyid Muhammad Hussein Fadlallah (also written Fadlullah) (1935–2010) a renowned Lebanese Shia cleric, who received his religious training at al-Hawza in Najaf, Iraq, the Shia equivalent of al-Azhar. The reasons for the focus on these six Islamist scholars are briefly addressed below.

The Choice of the Authors

While each of the six scholar sheikhs noted is renowned in the Arab and broader Muslim worlds, their perspectives, especially on international relations, have received scant attention from Western and Arab academics alike. That is why a principal aim of this book is to highlight the insights on contemporary international relations that these scholar sheikhs represent, driven in part by an urge to identify the multiple ways in which religion influences contemporary political and social reality in the Arab world, especially popular perceptions of the major powers, primarily the United States, and more generally views on international relations. In the introductory chapter of a popular graduate textbook on international relations, Burchill and Linklater underscore that religion, among other factors such as language, culture, and ethnicity, is one of "a few of the factors that shape world-views" about international relations.[7]

Equally important, as noted above, each of the six scholars received extensive and rigorous religious training at two of the most renowned religious-educational institutions in the Muslim World, primarily al-Azhar in Egypt and al-Hawza in al-Najaf, Iraq. In the words of Sheikh Sobhi al-Mahmassani – a moderate Lebanese Sunni cleric and author – each of the six scholars has met the "conditions of juristic fulfillment" (*shurut al-kifaya al-shar'iya*).[8] Their religious backgrounds shaped their worldviews on political and social issues, including international relations, while lending credibility, especially among Muslims, to their massive discourses, which relied extensively on the Quran, the Sunna, and the opinions of classic and post-classic Muslim jurists.

The oral and written discourses of religious scholars, such as the ones included here, undoubtedly constitute a principal medium through which religious ideas influence public opinion, politics, and society. For decades, the Arab public has been subjected to a plethora of conflicting ideas about the meaning of Islam and the role it should play in Arab politics and societies. While Western literature has generally focused on the radical Islamists, this book contends that the

Introduction: The Moderate-Reformist (Mainstream) | 3

differing perspectives of mainstream Islamists, such as the ones examined here, represented an equally important and competing source of influence on the Arab public. Both radical and mainstream Islamists start from the premise that Islam is a comprehensive way of life and that there can be no separation between religion and politics under Islam, but they arrive at strikingly different conclusions about how Islam should shape politics.

This book argues that the mainstream Islamists, despite their differences, share a common outlook on international relations, characterized by the following features. First, it posits peace rather than war as the norm, or guiding principle, in international relations, and more specifically in relations with non-Muslim states. Second, it encourages dialog and cooperation with non-Muslim states, as long as the resulting interactions are mutually beneficial and do not form guises to dominate Muslims. Third, it categorically rejects the use of violence to impose Islam on non-Muslims. Fourth, it presents jihad in the context of defending Muslim lands, lives, and freedoms, particularly the freedom to practice and call peacefully for Islam. Fifth, it advocates a peaceful and incremental approach to achieving Islamic unity, which need not take the form of a caliphate.

Furthermore, each of these six scholar sheikhs actively disseminated his views to wide audiences, including non-Muslims, employing varied traditional and novel means—lengthy manuscripts, fatwas (religious verdicts), Friday Sermons, and, in the cases of Qaradawi and Fadlallah, broadcast media, and the Internet. They were all embodiments of the public intellectual, deliberately reaching out beyond the confines of the pulpit and the gates of the academy to inform and educate mass audiences transcending national, linguistic, and even sectarian boundaries, with Bahi, Abu Zahra, and Zuhaili university professors at state institutions. Their discourses help shed light on the role of public intellectuals in structuring political debates in the Arab world. Broadly speaking, Islamist scholars constitute one wing of the Arab intelligentsia, the other being the more secular Arab nationalist thinkers.[9]

Islamist thinkers are heterogeneous in that they propagate varying views on the role of Islam in politics, but while there are significant differences between them, this book follows the commonly drawn distinction between moderate and radical Islamists.[10] It focuses on the first group for the following three reasons: First, as argued, they have been understudied in comparison to radical Islamists. Second, their perspectives on international relations are far more nuanced and sophisticated than those of radical Islamists, thus providing a richer understanding of the diversity within political Islam. Third, their perspectives on international relations, especially on armed conflict and relations with non-Muslims, have had a greater influence on Arab decision-makers and the Arab public than those of radical Islamists, as will be further addressed in the concluding chapter.

In addition, all six figures subscribed to an institutional view of Islam, underscoring the indispensable role of religious institutions, such as al-Azhar[11] and al-Hawza, in serving as deliberative forums among religious scholars and as authoritative bodies interpreting Islam to the general public and propagating its "true" message. A few examples follow. During his tenure as Sheikh al-Azhar, Shaltut defended its autonomy from both state and societal figures, while playing an important role in modernizing the institution. Not a product of al-Azhar himself, still Abu Zahra's first teaching assignment was at al-Azhar, and he would return later to serve in its prestigious Islamic Research Academy (*majma' al-buhuth al-Islamiya*). In addition, Qaradawi's strong informal ties to the Muslim Brotherhood did not diminish his advocacy for an independent al-Azhar. Thus, throughout his long career as a scholar and activist for Islamic causes, he staunchly defended the autonomy of al-Azhar from both the state and influential societal figures. Similarly, Fadlallah, while ideologically close to Hezbollah and to the Islamic Republic of Iran, did not want either to dominate al-Hawza or other Shia religious-educational centers, such as Qum. Equally important—and capitalizing on his role as the exclusive agent (*wakil*) in Lebanon of his former mentor in Najaf, Grand Ayatollah Abu al-Qassem al-Khoei—Fadlallah established a dense nexus of religious, educational, philanthropic, and media institutions, whose independence he carefully guarded against undue influence from both Tehran and Hezbollah. These institutions, still functioning after his death, are being currently led by his sons and are likely to be the most enduring aspect of his legacy.

As the chapters on Qaradawi and Fadlallah, treated here as members of the third generation, demonstrate, each worked tirelessly to institutionalize his vision of Islam, viewing himself as part of a community of religious scholars that transcended the boundaries of nationality and indeed sect. Thus, while taking great pride in belonging to al-Azhar and al-Hawza, respectively, both Qaradawi and Fadlallah shunned formal ties to political movements with which they had undeniable ideological affinities (the Muslim Brotherhood and Hezbollah, respectively). Such formal affiliations would have undermined their standing as independent scholars, as well as their roles in the religious institutions they revered, al-Azhar and al-Hawza. This commitment to institutions, and more broadly to an institutionalized form of Islam, can be traced back to the first generation of moderate-reformist scholars, such as Muhammad 'Abduh and Rashid Rida. Mahmoud

Haddad describes Rida as follows: "While his ideal exposition stressed that Islam had no religious hierarchy comparable to Christianity, he was, in fact, calling for a similar Muslim religious institution that would reinterpret the *sharia* and commit all Muslims to one modern unified interpretation of its edicts."[12] This dual commitment to religious institutions and institutionalized, or structured, Islam is one of several demarcation lines that separate the moderate-reformist Islamist scholars considered here from the radical Islamists. The commitment to religious institutions and to an institutionalized form of islam can, however, go hand in hand with a commitment to reform and to revisit certain aspects of the Islamic tradition. In line with Muhammad Qassim Zaman, I seek to demonstrate that "traditionally educated religious scholars," such as the six scholar sheikhs surveyed here, can be "vigorous critics of specific aspects of that [Islamic] tradition and by, the same token, important contributors to the debate on reform in Muslim societies."[13] In this regard, the appellation "reformers" applies to each of the six scholar sheikhs examined here.

Finally, each of the six scholar sheikhs devoted considerable attention to the analysis of both theoretical and practical issues in contemporary international relations, undoubtedly emanating from a number of historical realities, particularly 1) the legacy of colonialism, which spread to most Muslim lands, 2) the division of the Muslim world into multiple and often rival entities or states, 3) the proliferation of economic, political, military, and cultural ties with non-Muslim countries, and 4) the major disparities in power between the nascent majority-Muslim states, overwhelmingly developing countries, and the more developed states, whether these were part of the US-led Western camp or the Soviet-led Eastern camp. The ideological division of the developed world and the concomitant Cold War were mainly felt by members of the second and third generations of scholar sheikhs. The international relations discourses of Qaradawi, Fadlallah, and to a lesser extent, Zuhaili (the three representing the third generation) include multiple references to the post-Cold War era and the emergence of US ascendancy.

The impact of these historic realities appears as early as the discourses of Jamal al-Din al-Afghani, Muhammad 'Abduh and Rashid Rida, treated here as representing the first, or founding, generation of contemporary mainstream Islamists. Subsequent historic realities, especially the rival ideological camps of the developed world competing for support throughout the developing world, and the eventual triumph of the first camp, the Western, as of 1989, as well as the ideas of the founding reformist scholars, shaped the discourses of subsequent generations of Islamists. In this work, Shaltut, Abu Zahra, and Bahi represent the second generation of moderate-reformist Islamists, while Qaradawi, Zuhaili and Fadlallah stand for the third generation.

While this book is about the international relations' discourses of members of the second and third generations, the first substantive chapter is devoted to the political thought of the founding generation since I seek to situate the ideas of the six scholar sheikhs within their proper historic and ideational contexts. For this reason, following a chronological order from the founding generation to the second generation and finally to the third generation, I place major emphasis on demonstrating the continuity of thought from one generation to the next.

For thematic unity, the analysis of the discourses of these scholars revolves largely around four principal questions. First, what is the nature of international relations and what are its underpinning principles? Second, what is the prevalent relationship between the West and the Muslim world and how is it to be restructured? Third, what is Jihad and what are its purposes? Fourth, how is Islamic unity to be achieved and what form should it take? These are fairly complex and difficult questions, especially since they comprise both descriptive and prescriptive dimensions. However, given the varied concerns of the selected scholar sheikhs, there will be some variation in the international relations topics discussed in each case. Chapter 4 on Bahi, for example, provides a detailed analysis of his critiques of capitalism and socialism, both as ideologies and as political systems. These critiques, which find echoes in the discourses of the other scholar sheikhs, are pivotal for his construct of international relations and his understanding of the role of the Muslim world on the global stage. The remainder of this introductory chapter addresses three interrelated issues. It situates this inquiry within the context of the growing literature on political Islam, introduces the terms used and the study's methodology, and provides an outline of ensuing chapters.

The Many Variants of Political Islam or Islamism

Since this book is a study on political Islam, the thorny question of what political Islam is must be tackled. In line with Mohammed Ayoob, Khaled Hroub, Peter Mandaville, and Faiz Sheikh, among others, I use the terms political Islam and Islamism interchangeably.[14] Admittedly, either term has had negative connotations, especially among many Westerners and secularists, who regard political Islam as a deviation from spiritual Islam, which, similarly to Christianity, focuses on the individual's relation with God while leaving worldly matters to be decided by humans. Charles Hirschkind captures this negative attitude when he observes,

"The term 'political Islam' has been adopted by many scholars in order to identify this seemingly unprecedented intrusion of Islamic religion into the secular domain of politics."[15]

In light of what she depicts as a "terrain of stereotypes and fearmongering" that "dominates mainstream (Western) debates on the Middle East and Politics," Jillian Schwedler notes that "we might do well to abandon altogether the idea that 'political Islam' represents a tangible object of study."[16] In her seminal work on secularism in international relations, Elizabeth Hurd analyzes the source of this Western bias, underscoring that "Political Islam is interpreted by secular analysts as epiphenomenal, as a divergence and/or infringement on neutral secular politics."[17] This negative view of Islamism is by no means restricted to Westerners, as a number of Arab secularists subscribe to it. Bassam Tibi, for example, writes, "To engage in a distinction between Islamism and Islam and to criticize Islamist movements and their ideology is in no way an expression of Islamophobia."[18]

While agreeing that this Western-secular construct of political Islam is biased, I take issue with the suggestion of casting aside the notion of political Islam. As Khaled Hroub notes, political Islam has proved itself to be "more resilient than previously thought... reproducing itself in novel, expansive forms, and reaching out to new geographical areas."[19] Accordingly, and "despite the problem of defining what political Islam stands for,"[20] the notion of political Islam, mercuric as it may be, represents an indispensable first step in the journey to contextualize the discourses of the scholars examined here.

The literature offers numerous, often conflicting, conceptualizations of political Islam and Islamism. Equating political Islam with "Islamic fundamentalism," John Esposito underscores the debate among "governments, policy makers and experts" on whether it is a "multifaceted and diverse phenomenon or a uniformly clear and present danger to be consistently and persistently repressed or eradicated." Esposito clearly leans toward the first view, noting that the "varieties of Islamic activist groups and experiences are a testimony to the flexibility of Islam, and of political Islam in particular."[21]

Ayoob notes that the departure point for "adherents to political Islam" is their belief that "Islam as a body of faith has something important to say about how politics and society should be ordered in the contemporary Muslim world and implemented in some fashion."[22] Rather interestingly, Ayoob refers to two respected Western academics, Graham Fuller and Greg Burton, as "adherents to political Islam." Casting aside these broad and "friendly" interpretations, Ayoob defines political Islam as "a form of instrumentalization of Islam by individuals, groups and organizations." As for its foundations, he quotes Guilain

Denoeux who notes that political Islam rests on "reappropriated, reinvented concepts borrowed from the Islamic tradition."[23] While pristine, Ayoob's definition is somewhat problematic on two principal grounds. First, it is rather ideological, reflecting an *a priori* critical stance toward political Islam. Second, the term "instrumentalization" implies that Islamists strategically employ Islamic notions for political advantage. In my viewpoint, Islam, or more precisely the Islamic tradition broadly construed, is not an external resource that Islamists selectively and deliberately draw on, but their principal heuristic for comprehending and communicating political and social reality. The sources Islamists draw on are not just well used texts sitting on their bookshelves, but are internalized sets of concepts and beliefs, deeply embedded in their psyches and at the core of their thought processes. To his credit, though, Ayoob brings into focus the diversity within political Islam, as reflected in his book's title *The Many Faces of Political Islam* and his powerful rebuttal of the "myth of the Islamic monolith."[24]

Clearly, we need to examine the literature further to identify less subjective and more neutral conceptualizations of Islamism. For Mandaville, political Islam is a broad sphere created by the intersection of politics and religion, especially in Muslim-majority countries.[25] This broad construction of political Islam or Islamism emanates from an equally broad understanding of Islam itself. He writes, "Islam should always be considered in relation to how it is understood and experienced in specific contexts and circumstances... Embodied within the very idea of a tradition is the notion that this tradition has boundaries – but these... are always open to contestation and negotiation."[26]

For Andrew March, "political Islam is a modern movement that asserts the obligation of Muslims to manage their political affairs according to some interpretation of Islamic law."[27] Michelle Browers is more succinct, defining Islamism as "an ideological understanding of Islam that actively seeks to apply Islamic precepts to all spheres of life."[28] Likewise, Sheri Berman defines Islamism as "the belief that Islam should guide social and political as well as personal life."[29] In his Introduction to *Political Islam: A Critical Reader*, Frédéric Volpi notes that the "terms 'political Islam' and 'Islamism' will be used interchangeably."[30] He proceeds to define the two terms as such, "Political Islam is defined primarily as a construct that refers to what individuals in a particular socio-historical context think about the political and the religious." On the other hand, "Islamism refers to the political dynamics generated by the activities of those people who believe that Islam has something crucial to say about how society should be organized, and who seek to implement this idea as a matter of priority."[31]

Introduction: The Moderate-Reformist (Mainstream) | 9

The emphasis on the normative element within political Islam leads Faiz Sheikh to stress one important manifestation of political Islam, namely "Normative Political Islam," which emphasizes "the pursuit of politics that adheres to Islamic norms and values."[32] Given the preponderance of the normative element in the international relations discourses of the scholar sheikhs that this book analyzes, Faiz Sheikh's notion of "Normative Political Islam" is very pertinent. Thus, one may speak of "Normative International Relations," advocated by the scholar sheikhs examined here. This "Normative International Relations" can be seen primarily in the distinction that mainstream Islamists, and indeed all Islamists, draw between relations among Muslim states, seen as matters that are internal to the one Muslim *umma*, and relations between Muslim and non-Muslim states, which constitute the proper purview of international relations. Sheikh's definition of *umma* as "a community of believers who are bound by the laws of that community irrespective of territorial boundaries" is also relevant for the purposes of this study.[33]

The growing literature focusing primarily on Islamist movements tends to be cognizant of the heterogeneity of these movements. Based on his "understanding of socio-religious movements" in the Middle East, Asef Bayat "discards monolithic and totalizing narratives" of these movements.[34] John Esposito sees in the "varieties of Islamic groups and experiences" a "testimony to the flexibility of Islam, and of political Islam in particular."[35] Similarly, Nathan Brown notes that, "Islamist actors with different missions follow different paths."[36] In a recent introductory text on Islamism, Tarek Osman underscores that "Islamism is a multifaceted and complicated movement, which has had different worldviews, references, leaders and advocates, and whose constituencies have varied hugely over the past two centuries."[37] After discussing the historic context within which Islamism emerged, simultaneously as a way of distinguishing majority-Muslim societies from the West and as a response to the presumed failure of Kemalist westernization projects from Mustafa Kamal Ataturk, Bobby Sayyid defines Islamists as "those who use Islamic metaphors to narrate their political projects."[38]

Looking at the period since the 1970s, Salwa Ismail underscores the "diversity of actors, modes of action and, to some extent, objectives" within "Islamist politics." She classifies "Islamist actors" into militants, conservatives and moderates, based largely on "particular social origins and modes of action."[39] Wael Hallaq distinguishes between two strands within contemporary Islam, the modernists and Islamists, primarily based on their stances on jihad.[40] The modernists, whose beliefs he traces back to the Indian religious reformer Sir Sayyid Ahmad Khan (1817–1898), view jihad in the context of defending the Islamic state against external attack and not as a means of forcing Islam on others.[41] The Islamists, on the other hand, view jihad as a legitimate offensive means for spreading the Islamic message.[42] While fully agreeing with Hallaq's identification of Rashid Rida and Mahmoud Shaltut as modernists, I question his exclusion of these modernists from the Islamist category and his limitation of the latter to radical Islamists. Although my disagreement with Hallaq may be purely semantic, it is pivotal to reiterate that, for me, what Hallaq calls the modernists are at the core of political Islam and are as Islamist as are the radicals.

The classification of Thomas Hegghammer is more useful. Hegghammer distinguishes between five rather conflicting strands of political Islam: 1) state-oriented, 2) nation-oriented, 3) *umma*-oriented, 4) morality-oriented, and 5) sectarian Islam.[43] This typology refers to the principal preoccupations, or rationales, of different Islamist movements. State-oriented Islam, for example, focuses on reforming existing states along Islamic lines, principally by changing the laws to conform to the Islamic *sharia*; nation-oriented Islam revolves around the liberation of dominated Muslim people, such as in Palestine and Myanmar; morality-oriented Islam, on the other hand, aims at educating society on the teachings of Islam.[44]

Many works simply distinguish between radical and mainstream Islamist movements, while aware of the differences within each category. After defining Islamist movements as "those that believe Islam or Islamic law should play a central role in political life and explicitly organize around those goals in the public arena," Shadi Hamid argues that, "though they now find themselves eclipsed by radicals, the most politically influential Islamist groups have generally been of the mainstream and nonviolent variety."[45] A few paragraphs later, though, he seems to revert to generalizations by identifying opposition to liberalism as a defining characteristic of all Islamists.

One must caution, though, that even within the same Islamist movement there can be considerable diversity, tension, and disagreement. Informed by her extensive research on the Muslim Brotherhood, Carrie Rosefsky Wickham argues that Islamist movements "are not monolithic entities whose members think and act in lockstep."[46] She reiterates this point later by noting that, "Islamist leaders within the same country, and even within the same group, have come to assume very different positions on such 'meta issues' as the definition of Sharia rule, as well as on various policy matters of the day."[47]

To sum up, political Islam is too broad, diverse, and internally inconsistent to be viewed as a single ideology or perspective. Conceptualized here instead as a range of often contending perspectives on politics and the state, including international relations, these perspectives are held by individuals or groups that are informed by the Islamic tradition, which encompasses the following sources, in descending order of importance: the Quran, the Sunna of the Prophet Muhammad, the sayings and practices of the first four caliphs (the righteously guided caliphs in the Sunni tradition), and the opinions of classic, post-classic, and contemporary jurisprudents (*fuqaha'*) and scholars (*'ulama*). Even focusing exclusively on the contemporary era, we encounter scores of thinkers and movements who draw on these four sources to articulate quite divergent stances in the realms of politics, social relations, and international relations.

What best characterizes political Islam is its inclusive heterogeneity despite the common sources in the Islamic religious tradition that its adherents draw on. Writing about the uses of religion in public argument in the context of Western societies, Andrew March notes: "It is acknowledged that there are many ways of using religion in public argument. Not all religious arguments take the same form or are delivered in the same way."[48] March's observation applies quite well to political Islam.

Informed by Edward Said's seminal work, *Orientalism*[49], a number of postcolonial scholars, particularly Talal Asad[50] and Samira Haj,[51] question the validity of viewing the Islamic tradition through the Western liberal–secular lens. They argue, instead, for construing the Islamic tradition of theorizing, which undoubtedly encompasses political Islam, as a discursive tradition, "consisting of historically evolving discourses embodied in the practices and institutions of communities."[52] While I appreciate the merits of this view, I do not subscribe to it on two principal grounds. First, it views traditions of theorizing, in this case the Islamic and liberal traditions, as completely independent of each other, which is inaccurate. Second, it discourages comparative analyses of the views of Islamists and non-Islamists on pertinent contemporary issues, including issues of international relations.

In this work, I opt for a broader, constructivist-informed understanding of political Islam, which forms an integral component of the Islamic tradition, viewing it as a loose system of intersubjective meanings shared by its many, often at odds, adherents. While Islamism can be viewed as a frame of mind, or as a hermeneutic tool, it is best compared to a language system that Islamists have internalized and converse in to say some very different things. The language analogy also implies that some Islamists are more proficient in the language than others. The Islamists studied in this book are all highly proficient in the language of political Islam, due to their rigorous religious training, high scholastic aptitude (they all distinguished themselves from their peers from a very young age), and eagerness to comprehend and internalize the teachings of Islam before seeking to apply them to the political universe. The same cannot be said of most of the radical Islamists, who are less steeped in the Islamic tradition and less likely to view it holistically.

Terminology

This book is, thus, a lengthy inquiry into one variant of political Islam that I refer to as the moderate-reformist, or mainstream, strand. Clearly, there exist other appellations to this variant of contemporary political Islam. Uriya Shavit refers to some of the scholar sheikhs examined here and to others of a similar orientation as "modernist-apologists" because, in his view, their principal preoccupation is to demonstrate that Islam is not just compatible with modern sciences and with Western forms of government, including representative democracy, but is indeed superior to them.[53] While Shavit argues his case rather effectively, I still find the term "apologetic" objectionable on two grounds. First, it does not capture the extent to which contemporary Islamists, especially those writing on international relations, are ready to embrace prevalent Western notions about international peace, state sovereignty, international law, and the sanctity of international treaties. Second, the term apologetic is somewhat pejorative (although this is not the intention of Shavit), and it underestimates the novel elements in the thought of contemporary mainstream Islamists. Somewhat less importantly, I also avoid using the term modernist, which Shavit employs, referring myself to this school of thought as the "moderate reformist school," in order to stay clear of the discussion of what constitutes modernity. Instead of modern, this book uses the more neutral term "contemporary," hence its title "Contemporary Islamist Perspectives on International Relations."

Although the terms moderate, reformist, and mainstream, repeated throughout the text, have been extensively used in the literature, it is necessary to specify their meanings in the context of this study. Moderate is clearly a relative term, which is best understood in the context of its opposite, extreme. Despite the diversity within each category of Islamists, it still makes sense to distinguish between them based on how moderate or extreme their stances are. The term "moderate" translates to Arabic as either *mu'tadil* (from *i'tidal* which means moderation) or *wasati* (adjective *wasatiya*). *I'tidal* refers primarily to eschewing extreme positions without abandoning essential beliefs, and it also denotes a preference for incremental and peaceful change over a radical, violent one. The other, the widely used concept of *wasatiya*, entails adopting a middle-ground position that avoids both *tashdid* (excessiveness) and *tafrit* (laxity) in interpreting Islam. For the scholars covered in this work, Islam itself is viewed as a religion of *wasatiya* and Muslims are often depicted as a *wasati* people (*umma wasat*). A further discussion of *wasatiya*, and its implications for international relations, will be referred to in Chapter 5 on Qaradawi, given his extensive treatment and utilization of the term.

Reformist (*islahi* in Arabic) connotes an openness to change, a belief that change is both desirable and unavoidable. All the sheikhs surveyed in this work view Islam as a dynamic religion that is capable of self-renewal in light of changes in the material, the political and socioeconomic, and ideational domains. In contrast to *salafi* thinkers, reformists do not view religious renewal (*al-tajdid fi al-Din*) as a bad innovation (*bid'a sayi'a*), but as a pressing need in order to ensure that Islam remains at the core of the life of Muslim communities. Qaradawi, for example, repeatedly quotes the Prophetic Hadith that "God sends someone to renew the religion at the head of every century."[54] This spirit of *tajdid* can be traced back to the thought of the founding generation of the moderate-reformist strand, especially Muhammad 'Abduh. To quote Mark Sedgwick, "Muhammad 'Abduh did implicitly promote a new variety of exegesis: that of defying *taqlid*, both in the technical legal sense of refusing to follow a single *madhhab* and in the more general sense of refusing to be bound by tradition, by precedent and custom, of reading the Qur'an anew, ignoring previous interpretation."[55]

Undoubtedly, reformists acknowledge that Islam is founded on immutable pillars, namely that God is One, Muhammad is His Messenger, the Quran is the Word of God, and Muslims form one *umma* (community), united by a common creed (*'aqidat al-Tawhid*), and by common practices, such as prayer, fasting, and alms giving (*zakat*). These beliefs, however, do not translate into an unchangeable Islamic posture throughout the centuries. From this reformist perspective, Islam signifies a constantly expanding body of knowledge that provides answers to pertinent questions. Reflecting the immutable foundations of Islam and informed by Islamic tradition, such answers must also take into account the lived realities of Muslim individuals and groups, realities that clearly change across time and space. Arguably, one of the most contentious, albeit central, claims of this work is that the moderate-reformist current represents the mainstream, or hegemonic, interpretation of Islam amongst Islamists and lay Muslims.

Given its focus on moderate-reformist Islamists, this book devotes only limited space to the discourses of radical Islamists. Nevertheless, and due to the frequent references to radical Islamists and to radical Islam, it is pivotal that

I outline how I define radical Islamists (*al-Islamiyyin al-Mutatarifiin*). Radical Islamists subscribe, albeit to varying degrees, to a number of basic tenets discussed below.

To start with, radical Islamists question the legitimacy of existing regimes in much of the Arab and Islamic worlds on the grounds of their being un-Islamic. Equally important, they endorse the use of violence to bring about regime change and establish Islamic, *sharia*-based states, a sanctioning of violence that does not emanate from an intrinsic preference for violent change; instead, it reflects a belief, harnessed by decades of harassment and violent confrontations with regimes, that existing non-Islamic systems of rule are too entrenched and too violent themselves to be changed by peaceful means.

Moreover, radical Islamists adopt an expansive view of jihad, viewing jihad as *al-Farida al-Gha'iba* (the often forgotten duty of all capable Muslims), and the principal means to achieve a wide range of goals, including spreading the Islamic message and establishing the *sharia* state. Clearly, mainstream Islamists also embrace jihad but conceive of it in a more constricted way than the radicals do. The ensuing chapters elaborate on the differences between the mainstream and radical Islamists on the meaning and purposes of jihad.

Finally, radical Islamists adopt a more confrontational stance toward non-Muslims than their moderate counterparts do. In the realm of international relations, this more confrontational stance translates into deep skepticism about the intentions of non-Muslim states toward Muslims; an ensuing rejection of dialog and cooperation with non-Muslims; adherence to the traditional binary division of the world into the abode of war (*dar al-harb*) and the abode of peace (*dar al-silm*), the latter including only Islamic lands; and the belief that war, rather than peace, is the norm in the relationship between Muslim and non-Muslim states.

It is in this realm of international relations that the differences between the moderate and the radical Islamists are most pronounced. On the whole, mainstream Islamists are confident of the ability of Muslim societies to both adapt to and incrementally change prevalent international realities, principally 1) the international distribution of power; 2) dominant international practices, such as the uses of force and of diplomacy; 3) institutions, such as the United Nations; and 4) rules, norms, and conventions, as especially embodied in international law. Mainstream Islamists do not view international relations as a zero-sum game. They seek peaceful coexistence, dialog, and cooperation with non-Muslim societies as long as these relationships are established from positions of strength; do not infringe on the independence and sovereignty of Muslim societies, especially their right to apply the *sharia* and to work with each other in the pursuit of greater political, economic, and cultural unity; are reciprocal and mutually beneficial; and are aligned with Islamic principles, as enunciated in the *sharia*.

Above all, perhaps the scholar sheikhs studied here, and others of the moderate-reformist tradition, viewed themselves as conveyers of the "civilizing" message of Islam to humanity. Stopping way short of seeking to convert non-Muslims to Islam, they argued that Islam, both as a religion and a civilization, had something to teach humanity in its entirety, especially in terms of regulating interpersonal and intergroup relations, including the conduct of international relations.

As for radical Islam, the literature abounds with terms that are often associated with it. Radical Islamists are often depicted as salafi-jihadists and as *takfiris*. Since the focus of this text precludes a detailed treatment of these important, albeit contentious, notions, I restrict myself here to basic constructs of these terms, since they appear frequently throughout the book. Salafism is generally associated with a yearning to restore the original unity, purity, and vibrancy of the Muslim *umma*, allegedly found under the moral and political leadership of the Prophet and the first four caliphs, who are seen as *al-salaf al-salih* (the righteous forefathers or righteous ancestors).[56] Clearly, not all salafis are, to use the words of Byman and Polk, "salafi-militants" who embrace "an extreme interpretation of Islam [and] who want to use violence to unite Muslims under religious rule."[57] Many salafis are quietist, indeed apolitical, as is the case with the Saudi Wahhabis. Ayoob captures this diversity within salafism when he notes, "Salafism is diverse enough to accommodate both the highly political – and therefore ideologically malleable – Muslim Brotherhood and the more literalist, rigid and less overly political tendencies evidenced in the Gulf and Saudi Arabia."[58] The only problem with Ayoob's view is that he generally conflates the part, salafis, with the whole, political Islam. However, a detailed discussion of the variations and mutations of salafism is beyond the remit of this work.[59]

By convention, the compound term salafi-jihadists, the same as salafi- militants, refers to those individuals and groups who advocate the use of violence, including terrorism, to promote their diverse agendas, which include 1) destabilizing existing "un-Islamic regimes"; 2) signaling their ability to fight back the West, the far enemy, by targeting its interests and its civilians, 3) inflicting harm on religious minorities, including the Shia, in order to drive them out of predominantly Sunni areas; 4) weakening, or eliminating, other radical Islamist groups; and 5) consolidating their hold over areas they militarily control, the case with ISIS before its annihilation.

Again, by convention, the term salafi-jihadist is reserved for Sunni groups although several Shia groups, for example, Hezbollah, do resort to religiously legitimated violence. Because of their penchant to resort to *takfir* (excommunication) of the regimes and groups they oppose, these militant Sunni groups (and their ideologues) are often depicted as *takfiris*. The term *takfiri* clearly applies to al-Qaeda, ISIS, and the previously active *jama'at al-tabligh wa al-hijra* in Egypt. It does not apply, though, to other salafi-jihadist groups, such as Hamas and the Islamic Jihad in Palestine, which do not declare non-Muslims to be unbelievers and do not resort to excommunicating other Islamist groups. While it recognizes the diversity within each of reformist-moderate and radical Islam, this book is premised on maintaining the basic distinction between them, focusing on the first group.

Methodology

This book provides a detailed and critical treatment of the international relations writings of a select number of contemporary authors who invariably come from a religious background, hence the terms scholar sheikhs or turbaned scholars, and who have all chosen to apply their knowledge of Islam to address issues of international relations, whether in their fatwas, Friday Sermons, short articles, or (most importantly for my purposes) in full-fledged scholarly books. It is worth reiterating here that, in order to maintain thematic unity and consistency, I examine the answers of the surveyed scholar sheikhs to the common set of four questions discussed above. I rely exclusively on published material whose attribution to the six scholar sheikhs is beyond questioning. While I have no reason to doubt that the public statements of these scholar sheikhs also reflect their private views, this work is not about their private beliefs, but exclusively about their public discourse.

The reason I stress this point is that there exists a general tendency, including in the Islamic world, to question the sincerity of moderate Islamists, claiming that their discourse is primarily aimed at assuaging Western and secular concerns about political Islam. The contention is that there is no substantial difference between the agendas of moderate and radical Islamists since both groups seek to bring about an Islamic or *sharia* state that would, inter alia, apply the Islamic penal code and shield majority-Muslim societies from undue Western and secular influences, such as traditional banking practices, treatment of religious minorities, relations between the sexes, and above all, separation of religion from politics.

Introduction: *The Moderate-Reformist (Mainstream)* | 17

Moderate Islamists, according to this argument, are simply more shrewd, or more deceitful, than their radical counterparts. They conceal their true beliefs and motives, primarily an unwavering belief in and commitment to establishing a strong Islamic state by any means, behind a moderate, well-polished discourse in order to win support, both within and outside the Islamic world, for their program to quietly render Islamic the body politic and society. However, the Western-secular claim that moderate Islamists resort to double-talk cannot be substantiated and invokes images of orientalism and even Islamophobia.

Most importantly, this claim is not consequential for my work because very few have had access to the private views of the scholar sheikhs discussed here. Their relevance and influence, within the Arab and Islamic worlds and beyond, emanate from their public discourses and the other activities, primarily charitable, that they undertook in public. With the possible exception of al-Afghani from the first generation, allegedly engaged in many covert activities, there is no evidence whatsoever that these scholar sheikhs belonged to secret societies or established private channels through which they communicated exclusively with their core supporters and presumably conveyed to them messages different from their public discourses.

This book lies at the intersection of two flourishing and diverse bodies of literature, the literature on political Islam and that on international relations. While making ample references to this literature, it relies first and foremost on primary sources, namely the Arabic published works of the six scholar sheikhs. A principal aim of this book is to apply theoretical insights from the discipline of International Relations (IR) to shed light on the discourses of contemporary mainstream Islamists. Stated more precisely, this book investigates the extent to which the international relations discourses of these scholar sheikhs are compatible with Western notions, especially those that emanate from the realist and the liberal internationalist (liberal institutionalist) perspectives on IR, the two most influential paradigms in the IR field. In the conclusion, I argue that, while drawing on the Islamic tradition, our scholar sheikhs generally independently arrive at conclusions about international relations that are comparable to those of Western scholars writing in the realist and liberal international schools of IR.

Introducing IR perspectives into the study of a particular aspect of political Islam is in line with Bayat's important observation that Islamism is not "something particular and unique which cannot be analyzed by the conventional social science perspectives."[60] This book is largely predicated on two interconnected convictions: an outright rejection of "Islamic Exceptionalism," or for that matter "Arab Exceptionalism," and a firm belief that notions that are at the core of the discipline of IR – such as peace, the many types of war, neutrality, diplomacy, reciprocity, the state, state sovereignty, nonintervention, and international law – have significant traveling capacity, i.e., they have applicability outside the Western context within which they emerged. Stated more precisely, these notions, despite their base in Western history and enlightenment thought, can be used to analyze the discourses of scholars from non-Western backgrounds, in this case contemporary Islamists. In this respect, I take issue with the claim of a growing number of IR scholars, especially ones from the developing world, that the discipline of IR is too Western-centered to take proper account of the experiences of non-Western societies.[61] I maintain that our IR lexicon, with some calibration, is quite sufficient to capture the thought of contemporary Islamists, including the most sophisticated ones, such as the six scholar sheikhs this work examines.

Based on a close and critical reading of the public discourses of the six scholar sheikhs, I argue that, while offering major insights into contemporary international relations, all six scholar sheikhs invariably fall short of developing original and internally consistent IR theories. At best, they reinterpret the Islamic tradition so as to render it more aligned with prevalent Western international conceptions, especially regarding sovereignty, rights and duties of states, diplomacy, conduct of war, international law—especially international humanitarian law—and international organizations. As Shavit notes, this failure, seen primarily in internal contradictions and lingering ambiguities, mirrors the failure of the moderate-reformists, modernist-apologists in Shavit's parlance, to advance an internally consistent revelation-based theory of governance for Muslim societies.[62]

This point should not be pushed too far, though. Even prominent Western IR scholars, such as Kenneth Waltz[63] and John Mearsheimer,[64] have succeeded in advancing parsimonious and internally consistent theories of international relations only by invoking at least two draconian assumptions. The first assumption views the state as a rational and unitary actor with considerable autonomy from society and the competing domestic groups that comprise it. The second assumption depicts the international system as anarchic in structure, characterized by self-help and defined by the distribution of power. While elegant, their theories of structural realism and offensive realism, respectively, fail to capture numerous emphases in international relations and have been subjected to intense criticism, even refutation, from other IR scholars.[65]

International relations may simply be too diverse, too complex, and too intersubjective to allow for parsimonious theories with major explanatory power. Thus, the perspectives on international relations of our six scholars, despite their inconsistencies and limitations, merit close investigation based on both primary sources and on the well-developed lexicon of IR. In sum, it becomes possible to justify a dispassionate and critical inquiry into the international relations discourses of a carefully selected group of influential non-Western intellectuals in order to understand how their views relate to our prevalent IR paradigms, mainly those of realism and liberal internationalism.

Clearly, it falls beyond the remit of this work to discuss in any detail these two leading traditions of theorizing about international relations. Nevertheless, it is useful to highlight the principal tenets of each tradition, or school. Broadly speaking, realism, which encompasses more than one variant,[66] depicts the international system as anarchic and the states as "self-regarding autonomous units."[67] Realists emphasize the competetive, indeed conflictual, nature of international politics, driven by the fears of states for their security. The concerns of states for their own security, indeed survival, in an anarchic, self-help, international system trigger arms races that diminish the security of states, hence the security dilemma that realists explain in detail.[68] The preservation of international order (or world order), a key concern for most realists, hinges primarily on the operations of the balance of power. There are important differences among realists, however, regarding how the balance of power exactly operates,[69] and whether certain distributions of power are more conducive than others to a stable international order.[70]

Liberal internationalists, sometimes referred to as liberal institutionalists, on the other hand, point to the key role that international institutions, broadly construed, play in mitigating international anarchy, managing international conflict and facilitating cooperation among states in mutually beneficial areas.[71] They view international politics as a mixed nonzero-sum game or set of games involving both conflict and cooperation. Liberals believe that humans and states are capable of overcoming their fear of each other primarily by establishing formal institutions or less formal international regimes that serve as venues for preventing the escalation of conflict and for fostering cooperation on a range of issues, where interests converge.[72] Moreover, liberal internationalists underscore the role that international law, including international humanitarian law, and prevalent international norms and conventions, e.g., the Geneva Conventions on the treatment of prisoners of war,[73] play in influencing state conduct and ameliorating the consequences of international anarchy. Finally, liberal internationalists draw on the writings of liberal classic political economists, such as Adam Smith and David Ricardo, to argue that free trade in goods and services and unhindered movement of capital across national boundaries contribute to global prosperity and global peace. Nevertheless, liberal internationalists recognize that states and multilateral bodies, such as the International Monetary Fund, the World Bank, and the World Trade Organization, have a pivotal role to play in the multilateral management of the global economy.[74]

For liberal internationalists, the combined forces of globalization and democratization have heightened the need for multilateral management or indeed international governance of the world economy, while rendering such governance more feasible.[75] In a recent work, Mearsheimer, a renowned realist succinctly states the core claim of liberal institutionalism. Mearsheimer writes, "Liberal institutionalism claims that states that join international institutions are more likely to cooperate with each other, because they will be constrained by the organization's rules, which is almost always in their long-term interest to obey."[76]

To recapitulate, this book analyzes both the textual and contextual features of the writings of well-known contemporary Arab scholar sheikhs, with these four overlapping goals in mind, namely to 1) shed light on their conceptualizations of the principal theoretical and substantive issues in contemporary international relations; 2) identify the similarities and differences in their perspectives on international relations and compare these perspectives to those of the radical Islamists; 3) situate their discourses within their proper ideational and historical contexts; and 4) relate these discourses to prevalent Western notions and theories about international relations that are at the core of the discipline of IR.

Map of the Book

This book comprises six chapters in a chronological order and a conclusion. Each chapter opens with a biographic sketch that presents the life experiences of the scholar sheikh(s) the chapter covers. In line with Seyyed Vali Reza Nasr who writes, "the biography is the context for the ideology,"[77] I underscore the need to relate the ideas of the surveyed scholar sheikhs to their life experiences. Chapter 2 examines the political thought of the three members of the founding generation: al-Afghani, 'Abduh, and Rida. Although these three sheikhs did not dwell at length on issues of international relations, their views on relations with the non-Muslim, especially Western, world, the purposes of jihad and the paths to Islamic unity provided the basis for the better structured and more detailed treatment of members of the second and third generations whose discourses on international relations are discussed here. Since the lives and thought of these three fairly well-known early figures have been well covered in the literature, Chapter 2 will focus primarily on their views on international relations, which have received

Introduction: The Moderate-Reformist (Mainstream) | 21

less attention, in order to demonstrate how these views helped shape the thought of subsequent moderate-reformist scholar sheikhs.

The ensuing two chapters are devoted to the international relations discourses of Shaltut and Abu Zahra (Chapter 3) and Bahi (Chapter 4). Shaltut, probably the most renowned of the three figures, served as Sheikh of al-Azhar from 1958 until his death in 1963, and was well-known for his subtle criticisms of Wahhabism and his respectful attitude toward the Shia, evident in his call for treating the Ja'fari school, to which Twelver Shias adhere, as a *mazhhab* (legal school) of the same validity as the four commonly recognized mazhhabs of Sunni Islam. Moreover, Abu Zahra and Bahi were well-respected scholar sheikhs and public intellectuals, who achieved significant renown within Islamist circles and among the broader Arab public. While Chapter 3 briefly considers Shaltut's somewhat *avant-gardiste* views, at least from a mainstream Sunni perspective, on sectarian differences within Islam, it focuses primarily on his discourse on international relations, especially his views on jihad as conveyed in his short but influential track *al-Qital fi al-Quran* (Fighting in the Light of the Quran). The chapter then discusses the far more extensive discourse of Abu Zahra, as primarily conveyed in his three principal works on international relations: *al-'Alaqat al-Duwaliya fi al-Islam* (International Relations in Islam),[78] *Nazhariyat al-Harb fi al-Islam* (Theory of War in Islam),[79] and *al-Wihda al-Islamiya* (Islamic Unity).[80]

The lengthy treatment Chapter 3 accords Abu Zahra results from the fact that despite his prominence in the Islamic world, which earned him the appellation "Imam of his Era," his texts on international relations have received scant attention from Arab and non-Arab academics alike. More importantly, Abu Zahra's views—especially on the centrality of peace in relation to non-Muslim states, the defensive purposes of jihad and the need for a peaceful and incremental approach to the restoration of Islamic unity—represent the hallmarks of the mainstream Islamist perspective on international relations. Equally important, the chapter reveals the many tensions and ambiguities in Abu Zahra's international relations discourse, especially regarding the pivotal notion of the "Islamic state," since these tensions and ambiguities continued to manifest themselves in the discourses of subsequent Islamists. Finally, Chapter 3 will underscore Abu Zahra's influence on the international relations discourses of subsequent Islamists, particularly Zuhaili and Qaradawi, who draw largely on his works on this topic.

Chapter 4 provides a detailed and critical reading of the international relations discourse of another prominent Azharite scholar sheikh, Muhammad al-Bahi, hereafter referred to as Bahi. Bahi has received scant treatment in the Western academic literature despite the popularity of his discourse in Arab Islamist and

Arab nationalist circles, and the influence of his ideas on members of the third generation, particularly Qaradawi, with whom he had a close personal and intellectual relationship. With a doctorate in philosophy from Germany, Bahi's familiarity with Western ideas and ideologies, for example, materialism, liberalism, capitalism, and socialism, surpasses that of the other five scholar sheikhs covered here. Thus, while in substance, Bahi's discourse on international relations bears a major resemblance to the discourses of Qaradawi and Fadlallah, his treatment of international relations is more theoretical, reflecting his philosophical background.

Chapters 5, 6, and 7 are devoted to the writings of the three representatives of the third generation, Qaradawi, Zuhaili, and Fadlallah, respectively. Undoubtedly, Qaradawi is one of the best known contemporary Islamists in the Muslim world and beyond, due to the proliferation of his writings and his effective utilization of the broadcast media and the Internet to convey a fairly consistent message that emphasizes the *wasatiya* of Islam and its pertinence to address all political and social problems facing the Muslim *umma*. While Qaradawi has received more attention from academics than the other scholar sheikhs did for these understandable reasons,[81] his extensive discourse on international relations has not been subjected to the thorough and critical reading found in Chapter 5. Focusing on a number of published works by Qaradawi, especially his works on the jurisprudence of *wasatiya*,[82] relations with the West[83] and Jihad,[84] the chapter highlights his many insights into contemporary international relations, especially his emphasis on the centrality of peace and dialog in relations with the non-Muslim world, the defensive purposes of jihad, and the categorical rejection of violence as a means to advance the Islamist agenda domestically as well as to bring about the cherished goal of all Islamists, namely Islamic unity.

Chapter 6, on Zuhaili, examines his views on international relations, especially as conveyed in his three principal works on the subject: *Athar al-Harb* (Effects of War)[85], *Al-'Alaqat al-Duwaliya fi al-Islam* (International Relations in Islam),[86] and *Al-Qanun al-Duwali al-Insani wa Huquq al-Insan* (International Humanitarian Law and Human Rights).[87] While Zuhaili did not achieve the same renown as Qaradawi and Fadlallah, who became household names, his treatment of international relations is arguably one of the most detailed and rigorous treatments of the subject by a contemporary Islamist. Zuhaili is also one of a few contemporary Islamists whose treatment of international relations was included in a selection of essays that was published by the International Committee of the Red Cross.[88] Still, the chapter argues that Zuhaili's discourse suffers from the same tensions and ambiguities that afflicted the discourses of earlier Islamists, particularly Abu Zahra.

Sayyid Fadlallah's is the only voice from the Shia part of the Arab world to be considered in this inquiry into contemporary Islamists. While the Shias are a minority in the Arab world, they constitute the majority in Iraq and Bahrain and are at parity with the Sunnis in Lebanon. Developments such as the Lebanese war (1975–1989), the 1979 Iranian revolution, the defeat of Saddam Hussein in the 1991 war over Kuwait and his ultimate downfall in 2003, and lately the eruption of the Arab Spring in 2011, emboldened Arab Shias, propelling them to the center of the political arena. Fadlallah's discourse, especially his emphasis on the dynamic nature of Islam (*al-Islam al-Haraki*), embodies this greater Shia activism. Fadlallah's views on international relations are more radical than those of his Sunni counterparts are, mirroring, albeit to a limited extent, the revolutionary rhetoric of the Islamic Republic of Iran. Nevertheless, a close reading of his international relations discourse reveals many similarities with the discourses of his mainstream Sunni counterparts, in particular Bahi and Qaradawi.

As will be clarified in the ensuing chapters, both Qaradawi and Fadlallah subscribe to a largely realist reading of international relations. Zuhaili's international relations discourse, on the other hand, represents a complex, although somewhat chaotic, blend of realism and liberal institutionalism. On the other hand, the scholar sheikhs of the second generation—Shaltut, Abu Zahra, and Bahi—are more normative in their approach and are primarily concerned with demonstrating Islam's compatibility with, indeed its superiority to, Western notions about international relations. To a limited extent, they fit Shavit's depiction of modernist-apologists. The above distinctions between generations should not be pushed too far, though. All six scholar sheikhs approach international relations from a largely normative-ethical-legalistic standpoint that is primarily informed by their readings of the Islamic tradition. However, in the case of members of the third generation, this normative-ethical-legalist approach is balanced by a largely realist view of international relations (more visible in the discourses of Qaradawi and Fadlallah) and a keen interest in reflecting on and theorizing about prevalent international realities, especially the Arab-Israeli conflict, relations of the Muslim world with the non-Muslim West, and the implications of the end of the Cold War and the emergence of American hegemony.

Again, at the risk of overstating the case, the "other," mainly the West, occupies a more prominent place in the discourses of the scholar sheikhs who belong to the third generation. Members of this third generation are engaged with the West in multiple, complex, and often conflicting ways. They clearly seek to understand the West, although not on its own terms, as well as to dialog and cooperate with it, while simultaneously warning about and struggling against its alleged political, economic, and cultural encroachments on majority Muslim societies.

The principal distinction amongst mainstream Islamists that this book draws, though, lies between Bahi, Qaradawi, and Fadlallah, on the one hand, and Shaltut, Abu Zahra, and Zuhaili, on the other. It is argued that the first three scholar sheikhs are close in their views to the "Western" realist school of IR, while Shaltut, Abu Zahra and especially Zuhaili are close to the "Western" liberal-internationalist approach to IR. Drawing on Khaled Hroub's important distinction between "contextualization" and "ideologisation" as far as treatments of Islamist movements,[89] this book obviously adopts the contextualization approach. The concluding chapter is thus predicated on the notion that all systems of ideas are simultaneously products of prior ideas, or responses to them, and experienced historic realities. Accordingly, it reads the discourses of the six scholar sheikhs against the backdrop of the centuries-old, rich, and diverse, Islamic tradition, which has always allocated significant emphasis to relations with non-Muslim societies, but as of the late 19th century has got more preoccupied with these relations. This reflected the heightened and largely asymmetrical ties with these non-Muslim, primarily Western, societies. Last but not least, the concluding chapter also reads these discourses as ideational responses to the historic realties of colonialism, which, according to Islamists, conquered and fragmented the Islamic world, including its Arab core; and paved the way for its continued political, economic, and cultural subjugation even after the achievement of political independence.

Conclusion

This introductory chapter laid out the book's purpose and justified the selection of authors, while situating the study within the flourishing literature on political Islam, or Islamism. It also clarified the meanings of the main terms adopted by the book, spelled out the methodology used, and introduced the topics of the ensuing chapters. The following chapter is devoted to the thought of the founding generation of moderate reformers. Chapters 3–7 provide a detailed analysis of the international relations discourses of the six scholar sheikhs chosen for this study. Chapter 8 (conclusion) reiterates the book's principal argument and situates the discourses of the six scholar sheikhs within their appropriate ideational and historic settings.

Notes

1 For academic works on al-Qaeda, see Francois Burgat, *Islamism in the Shadow of Al-Qaeda* (Austin, TX: The University of Texas Press, 2010); Jason Burke, *Al-Qaeda: The True Story of Radical Islam* (London: I. B. Tauris & Co, 2003); and Barak Mendelsohn, *The al-Qaeda Franchise: The Expansion of al-Qaeda and its Consequences* (Oxford: Oxford University Press, 2016). Works targeting a less academic readership include Brian Fishman, *The Master Plan: ISIS, al-Qaeda and the Jihadist Strategy for Final Victory* (Yale University Books, 2016).
2 Works on ISIS are numerous ranging from the academic to the sensational. For academic works, see Abdel Bari Atwan, *The Digital Caliphate* (Oakland, CA: California University Press, 2015); Fawaz Gerges, *ISIS: A History* (Princeton and Oxford: Princeton University Press, 2016); Roxanne L. Euben, "Spectacles of Sovereignty in Digital Time: ISIS Executions, Visual Rhetoric and Sovereign Power," *Perspectives on Politics* 15, no. 4 (2017): 1007–1033; and Sami E. Baroudi, "On origins: Arab Intellectuals' Debates on the ideational Sources of ISIS," *Middle East Journal* 74, no. 2 (Summer 2020). https://doi.org/10.3751/74.2.13. Sensational works include: Erick Stakelbeck, *ISIS Exposed: Beheadings, Slavery and the Hellish Reality of Radical Islam* (Washington, DC: Regnery Publishing, 2015); William McCants, *The ISIS Apocalypse: The History, Strategy and Doomsday Vision of the Islamic State* (New York: St. Martin's Press, 2015); and Yonah Alexander and Dean Alexander, *The Islamic State: Combatting the Caliphate without Borders* (Lanham, Boulder, New York, London: Lexington Books, 2015).
3 Joas Wagemakers, *A Quietist Jihadi: The Ideology and Influence of Abu Muhammad al-Maqdisi* (Cambridge: Cambridge University Press, 2012). See also Joas Wagemakers, "The Transformation of a Radical Concept: al-wala' wa al-bara' in the Ideology of Abu Muhammad al-Maqdisi," in *Global Salafism: Islam's New Religious Movement*, ed. Roel Meijer (Oxford: Oxford University Press, 2013), 81–106.
4 See Laura Mansfield, *His own Words: A Translation of the Writings of Dr. Ayman al Zawahiri* (Old Tappan: TLG Publications, 2006); Daniel Lav, *Radical Islam and the Revival of Medieval Ideology* (New York: Cambridge University Press, 2012), 170, 199, 201; and Lawrence Pintak, *Reflections in a Bloodshot Lens: America, Islam and the War of Ideas* (London: Pluto Press, 2006), 60, 108, 124, 285.
5 James Toth, *Sayyid Qutb: The Life and Legacy of a Radical Islamic Intellectual* (Oxford: Oxford University Press, 2013).
6 Jonathan Randal, *Osama: The Making of a Terrorist* (London and New York: I.B. Tauris, 2004); and Michael Scheuer, *Osama Bin Laden* (Oxford: Oxford University Press, 2011).
7 Scott Burchill and Andrew Linklater, "Introduction," in *Theories of International Relations*, eds. Scott Burchill and Andrew Linklater, 5th ed. (New York: Palgrave Macmillan, 2013), 18.

26 | Contemporary Islamist Perspectives on International Relations

8 Sobhi al-Mahmassani, *Arkan Huquq al-Insan fi al-Islam* (The Pillars of Human Rights in Islam) (Beirut: Dar al-'Ilm lil-Malyeen, 1979), 124.
9 For works on the international relations discourses of these more secular Arab thinkers, see Sami E. Baroudi, "Countering US Hegemony: The Discourse of Salim al-Hoss and other Arab Intellectuals," *Middle Eastern Studies* 44, no. 1 (January 2008), 105–29; and Sami E. Baroudi and Jennifer Skulte-Ouaiss, "Mohamed Hassanein Heikal on the United States: The Critical Discourse of a Leading Arab Intellectual," *Middle Eastern Studies* 50, no. 1 (2015), 93–114.
10 See Ahmad S. Moussali, *The Islamic Quest for Democracy, Pluralism and Human Rights* (Gainesville: University Press of Florida, 2001), 160.
11 While autonomous, al-Azhar, to quote Nathan Brown is a central "element in the state-religion complex" in Egypt. Nathan Brown, *Post Revolutionary al-Azhar*, The Carnegie Papers, Middle East September 2011 (Washington, DC: Carnegie Endowment for International Peace, 2011), 4. https://carnegieendowment.org/files/al_azhar.pdf.
12 Mahmoud Haddad, "Arab Religious Nationalism in the Colonial Era: Rereading Rashid Rida's Ideas on the Caliphate," *Journal of the American Oriental Society* 117, no. 2 (1997): 253–77, 254.
13 Muhammad Zaman, *Modern Islamic Thought in a Radical Age: Religious Authority and Internal Criticism* (Cambridge, Cambridge University Press, 2012), 2.
14 Mohammed Ayoub, *The Many Faces of Political Islam: Religion and Politics in the Muslim World* (Ann Arbor: The University of Michigan Press, 2008), 2; Khaled Hroub, "Introduction," in *Political Islam: Context versus Ideology*, ed. Khaled Hroub (London: SAQI in association with London Middle East Institute, SOAS, 2010), 1–3; Peter Mandaville, *Islam and Politics*, 2nd ed., (London and New York: Routledge, 2014), 1–2; and Faiz Sheikh, *Islam and International Relations: Exploring Community and the Limits of Universalism* (London and New York: Rowman & Littlefield, 2016), 18. See also Katerina Dalacoura, *Islamist Terrorism and Democracy in the Middle East* (Cambridge: Cambridge University Press, 2011).
15 Charles Hirschkind, "What is Political Islam," in *Political Islam: A Critical Reader*, ed. Frédéric Volpi (London and New York: Routledge, 2011), 13.
16 Jillian Schwedler, "Studying Political Islam," *International Journal of Middle East Studies* 43, no. 1 (2011): 135–37; 135.
17 Elizabeth Hurd, *The Politics of Secularism in International Relations* (Princeton: Princeton University Press, 2008), 118.
18 Bassam Tibi, *The Sharia State: Arab Spring and Democratization* (New York: Routledge, 2013), 44.
19 Khaled Hroub, "Introduction," 2.
20 Sheikh, *Islam and International Relations*, 22.
21 John Esposito, "Introduction," in *Political Islam: Revolution, Radicalization, or Reform?*, ed. John Esposito (Boulder, CO: Lynne Rienner Publisher, Inc., 1997), 4.

22 Mohammed Ayoob, *The Many Faces of Political Islam* (Michigan: University of Michigan Press, 2008), 2.
23 Guilain Denoeux, "The Forgotten Swamp: Navigating Political Islam," *Middle East Policy* 9, no. 2 (2002), 56–81, 61.
24 Ayoob, *The Many Faces of Political Islam*, 14–17.
25 Mandaville, *Islam and Politics*, 1–2.
26 Mandaville, *Islam and Politics*, 5.
27 Andrew F. March, "Taking People As They Are: Islam As a 'Realistic Utopia' in the Political Theory of Sayyid Qutb," *American Political Science Review* 104, no. 1 (2010): 189–206, 189.
28 Michelle Browers, *Political Ideology in the Arab world: Accommodation and Transformation* (Cambridge: Cambridge University Press, 2009), 17.
29 Sheri Berman, "Islamism, Revolution, and Civil Society," *Perspectives on Politics* 1, Issue, 2 (2003): 257–72, 257.
30 Frédéric Volpi, "Introduction," in *Political Islam*, ed. Frédéric Volpi, 1.
31 Volpi, "Introduction," 1.
32 Sheikh, *Islam and International Relations*, 27.
33 Sheikh, *Islam and International Relations*, 29.
34 Asef Bayat, "Islamism and Social Movement Theory," *Third World Quarterly* 26, no. 6 (2005): 891–908, 892.
35 Esposito, "Introduction," 4.
36 Nathan J. Brown, *When Victory Is Not an Option: Islamist Movements in Arab Politics* (Ithaca: Cornell University, 2012), 4.
37 Tarek Osman, *Islamism: What It Means for the Middle East and the World* (New Haven: Yale University Press, 2016), xviii.
38 Bobby Sayyid, *A Fundamental Fear: Eurocentrism and the Emergence of Islamism* (London and New York: Zed Books, 1997), 157.
39 Salwa Ismail, "Being Muslim: Islam, Islamism and Identity Politics," in *Political Islam*, ed. Volpi, 17.
40 Wael Hallaq, *Shari'a, Theory, Practice, Transformation* (Camridge, Cambridge University Press, 2009), 324–41.
41 Hallaq, *Shari'a*, 336–37.
42 Hallaq, *Shari'a*, 338–41.
43 Thomas Hegghammer, "Jihadi-Salafis or Revolutionaries? On Religion and Politics in the Study of Militant Islamism," in *Global Salafism: Islam New Religious Movement*, ed. Roel Meijer (Oxford: Oxford University Press, 2013), 244–66, 258–9.
44 Hegghammer, "Jihadi-Salafis or Revolutionaries?", 244–66, 258–9.
45 Shadi Hamid, *Islamic Exceptionalism: How the Struggle over Islam is Reshaping the World* (New York: St. Martin's Press, 2016), 6.
46 Carrie Rosefsky Wickham, *The Muslim Brotherhood: Evolution of an Islamist Movement* (Princeton and Oxford: Princeton University Press, 2013), 2.

47 Rosefsky Wickham, *The Muslim Brotherhood*, 14.
48 Andrew F. March, "Rethinking Religious Reasons in Public Justification," *American Political Science Review* 107, no. 2 (2013): 523–39, 525.
49 Edward Said, *Orientalism* (New York: Pantheon, 1978).
50 Talal Asad, "The Idea of an Anthropology of Islam," Occasional Papers Series (Washington, DC: Georgetown University, Center for Contemporary Arab Studies, 1986), 14.
51 Samira Haj, *Reconfiguring Islamic Tradition: Reform, Rationality, and Modernity* (Stanford, CA: Stanford University Press, 2009), esp. 4–5.
52 Haj, *Reconfiguring Islamic Tradition*, 6.
53 Uriya Shavit, *Scientific and Political Freedom in Islam: A Critical Reading of the Modernist-Apologetic School* (London and New York: Routledge, 2017).
54 Yusuf Qaradawi, *Ummatna Bayn Qarnayn* (Our Umma between two Centuries) (Cairo, Dar al-Shuruq, 2000), 10.
55 Mark Sedgwick, *Makers of the Muslim World: Muhammad 'Abduh* (Oxford: Oneworld Publications, 2010), 100.
56 See Ayoob, *The Many Faces of Political Islam*, 116–17.
57 Daniel L. Byman and Kenneth M. Pollack, "Iraq's Long Term Impact on Jihadist Terrorism," *The Annals of the American Academy of Political and Social Science* 618 (2008), 55–68, 55.
58 Ayoob, *The Many Faces of Political Islam*, 116.
59 For studies on salafism, see Marc Lynch, "Islam Divided between Salafi-Jihad and the Ikhwan," *Studies in Conflict and Terrorism* 33, no. 6 (2010): 469, https://doi.org/10.1080/10576101003752622; Gilles Kepel, *Jihad: The Trails of Political Islam*, trans. Anthony F. Roberts (Cambridge, MA: Belknap Press, 2002); Daniel Lav, *Radical Islam and the Revival of Medieval Theology* (Cambridge: Cambridge University Press, 2012), 120–200; Madawi Al-Rasheed, "The Local and the Global in Saudi Salafi-Jihadi Discourse," in *Global Salafism: Islam's New Religious Movement*, ed. Roel Meijer (Oxford: Oxford University Press, 2013), 301–20.
60 Bayat, "Islamism and Social Movement Theory," 892.
61 See, in particular, Amitav Acharya, *Rethinking Power, Institutions and Ideas in World Politics: Whose IR?* (London and New York: Routledge, 2014); and Imad Mansour, "A Global South Perspective on International Relations Theory," *International Studies Perspectives* 18, Issue 1 (2017), 2–3, https://doi.org/10.1093/isp/ekw010.
62 See, in particular, Shavit's chapter "Islam and Democracy," in *Scientific and Political Freedom in Islam*, ed. Shavit, 107–64.
63 Kenneth Waltz, *Theory of International Politics* (Reading, MA: Addison-Wesley, 1979); and Waltz, "The Emerging Structure of International Politics," *International Security* 18, no. 2 (1993), 44–79.
64 John Mearsheimer, *The Tragedy of Great Power Politics* (New York and London: W.W. Norton & Company, 2001).

Introduction: *The Moderate-Reformist (Mainstream)* | 29

65 For a refutation of structural realism from a constructivist perspective, see Alexander Wendt, "Anarchy is What States Make of It: The Social Construction of Power Politics," *International Organization* 46, no. 2 (1992), 391–425.
66 There is considerable diversity within the realist tradition. The main distinction is between classic realism, associated with such luminaries as Hans Morgenthau, Henry Kissinger, George Kennan, Nicolas Spykman (among many others), and structural realism, whose best known advocates are Kenneth Waltz and John Mearsheimer. Seminal works within the Realist school include: Hans Morgenthau, *Politics Among Nations, The Struggle for Power and Peace* (7th ed.), (McGraw-Hill Education, 2005); Henry Kissinger, *A World Restored: The Politics of Conservatism in a Revolutionary Age* (New York: Grosset & Dunlap, 1964) and *Diplomacy* (New York: Simon and Schuster, 1994); Nicholas Spykman, *America's Strategy in World Politics: The United States and the Balance of Power* (Oxford and New York: Routledge, 2007) (originally published by Harcourt, Brace and Company in 1942); George Kennan, *American Diplomacy* (Sixtieth-Anniversary Expanded Edition with introduction by John Mearsheimer) (Chicago: Chicago University Press, 2012).
67 See, for example, Richard J. Harknett and Hasan B. Yalcin, "The Struggle for Autonomy: A Realist Structural Theory of International Relations," *International Studies Review* 14, no. 4 (2012), 499–521.
68 Summaries about the basic tenets of Realism abound. See, for example, Jack Donnely, "Realism," in *Theories of International Relations*, ed. Scottt Burchill et al. (4th ed.), (New York: Palgrave MacMillan, 2009), 32–56.
69 Broadly speaking, classic realists emphasize the role that status quo powers (such as Great Britain during the 18th and 19th centuries) play in the preservation of the balance of power. See, for example, Henry Kissinger, *Diplomacy* (New York: Simon and Schuster, 1994). Structural realists, on the other hand, contend that the balance of power emerges spontaneously as a result of the quest of each of the major powers to expand its power. See, in particular, Waltz, *Theory of International Politics* and Mearsheimer, *The Tragedy of Great Power Politics*.
70 This discussion revolves primarily on whether stable international orders are based on bipolar, or multipolar, distributions of power. Waltz is the principal advocate of the view that a bipolar international order (characterized by the presence of two major powers) is more stable than a multipolar order. See, in particular, Kenneth Waltz, *Theory of International Politics*. Morton Kaplan, on the other hand, associates stability with a multipolar international order, dominated by four-five major powers. Kaplan, *System and Process in International Politics* (New York: John Wiley, 1957).
71 Literature on liberal internationalism, or liberal institutionalism, sometimes also referred to as neoliberalism, abounds. Some of the best works in this tradition have been written by G. John Ikenberry. See, in particular, Ikenberry, *Liberal Leviathan: The Origins, Crisis and Transformation of the American World Order* (Princeton: Princeton University Press, 2011); Ikenberry, *After Victory: Institutions,*

Strategic Restraint, and the Rebuilding of Order after Major Wars (Princeton: Princeton University Press, 2012); and *A World Safe for Democracy: Liberal Internationalism and the Crises of Global Order* (New Haven: Yale University Press, 2020). For a summary of the tenets of liberal internationalism, see Beate Jahn, *Liberal Internationalism: Theory, History, and Practice* (London: Palgrave MacMillan, 2013). For a review of the thought of prominent advocates see, for example, Per Hammarlund, *Liberal Internationalism and the Decline of the State: The Thought of Richard Cobden, David Mitrany, and Kenchi Ohmae* (London: Palgrave MacMillan, 2005). For the origins of this school and its relation to the ideas of US President Woodrow Wilson, see Tony Smith, *Why Wilson Matters: The Origin of American Liberal Internationalism and Its Crisis Today* (Princeton: Princeton University Press, 2017). For a realist critique of liberal internationalism, see, for example, John Mearsheimer, *The Great Delusion: Liberal Dreams and International Realities* (New Haven: Yale University Press, 2018).

72 Tang argues that only offensive realists contend that states cannot overcome their fears of each other. All other approaches to international relations, including classic realism, recognize that states can work together through international institutions to provide some security assurances to each other and thus mitigate the problem of fear. Shiping Tang, "Fear in International Relations: Two Positions," *International Studies Review* 10, Issue 3 (2008): 451–71. https://doi.org/10.1111/j.1468-2486.2008.00800.x.

73 The discourse of Zuhaili (Chapter 6) has multiple references to and analyses of the Geneva Conventions, especially regarding the treatment of civilians and of prisoners of war. For the text of "The Third Geneva Convention Relative to the Treatment of Prisoners of War," see David Kinsella and Craiq Carr, eds., *The Morality of War: A Reader* (Boulder and London: Lynne Rienner Publishers, 2007), 221–29.

74 Liberal internationalism is the hegemonic theory in the study of international political economy (IPE). Works on IPE that utilize the insights of the liberal internationalist perspective include Robert Gilpin, *The Political Economy of International Relations* (Princeton, N.J.: Princeton University Press, 1987), Robert Gilpin, *Global Political Economy: Understanding the International Economic Order* (Princeton, N.J.: Princeton University Press, 2001); Daniel Drezner, *All Politics is Global: Explaining International Regulatory Regimes* (Princeton, N.J.: Princeton University Press, 2007). One of the most popular IPE texts is written mainly from a liberal internationalist perspective. Joan Spero and Jeffrey Hart, *The Politics of International Economic Relations* (7th ed.), (Belmont, CA: Wadworth Cengage Learning, 2010).

75 See, for example, Jagdish Bhagwati, *In Defense of Globalization* (Oxford: Oxford University Press, 2004), 221–64.

76 Mearsheimer, *The Great Delusion: Liberal Dreams and International Realities* 6.

77 Seyyed Vali Reza Nasr, *Mawdudi and the Making of Islamic Revivalism* (New York and Oxford: Oxford University Press, 1996), 4.

78 Muhammad Abu Zahra, *al -'Alaqat al-Duwaliya fi al-Islam* (Cairo: Dar al-Fikr al-Arabi, 1995), First published in 1964.
79 Muhammad Abu Zahra, *Nazhariyat al-Harb fi al-Islam* (Cairo: Wizarat al-Awqaf, al-Majlis al-A'la lil-Shu'oun al-Islamiya, 2008). First published as an article in al-Majala al-Masriya lil-Qanun al-Duwali, 1958.
80 Muhammad Abu Zahra, *al-Wihda al-Islamiya* (Cairo: Dar al-Fikr al-'Arabi, 2011). First published by Cairo: Dar al-Jihad in 1958.
81 For Qaradawi's fame, see, especially, "The World's Top 20 Public Intellectuals," *Foreign Policy*, no. 167 (2008): 54–57. For academic works on Qaradawi, see, especially, Bettina Graf and Jakob Skovaard-Peterson, eds. *Global Mufti: The Phenomenon of Yusuf Qaradawi* (New York: Columbia University Press, 2009); Bettina Graf, *Sheikh Yusuf al-Qaradawi in Cyberspace* (Die Welt des Islams, New Series, 47, Issue 3/4, Islam and Societal Norms: Approaches to Modern Muslim Intellectual History (2007), 403–421; Zaman, *Modern Islamic Thought*, especially 271–314; Sami E. Baroudi, "Sheikh Yusuf Qaradawi on International Relations: The Discourse of a Leading Islamist Scholar (1926–)," *Middle Eastern Studies* 50, no. 1 (2014): 2–36; Sami E. Baroudi, "The Islamic Realism of Sheikh Yusuf Qaradawi (1926–) and Sayyid Muhammad Hussein Fadlullah (1935–2010)," *British Journal of Middle Eastern Studies* 43, no. 1 (2016): 94–114; and Paul Berman, Jeffrey Herf and Marc Lynch, "Islamism Unveiled: From Berlin to Cairo and Back Again," *Foreign Affairs* 89, no. 5 (September/October 2010): 144–50.
82 Yusuf Qaradawi, *Fiqh al-Wasatiya al-Islamiya: Ma'alem wa Manarat* (The Jurisprudence of the Islamic Moderate and Balanced Approach: Landmarks and Signposts) (Cairo: Dar al-Shuruq, 2010).
83 Yusuf Qaradawi, *Nahnu wa al-Gharb* (Us and the West) (2005). https://www.al-qaradawi.net/node/5041, accessed 12 April 2012.
84 Yusuf Qaradawi, *Fiqh al-Jihad: Dirasa Muqarina li-Ahkamih wa Falsfatih fi Daou' al-Qur'an wa al-Sunna* (The Jurisprudence of Jihad: A Comparative Study of its Rules and Philosophy in Light of the Qur'an and the Sunna), Vols. 1 & 2 (Cairo: Maktabat Wahba, 2009).
85 Wahbah al-Zuhaili, *Athar al-Harb: Dirasa Fiqhiya Muqarina* (4th ed.) (Damascus: Dar al-Fikr, 2009). This study relies on the fourth edition of *Athar al-Harb*, which includes some new material, especially on the distinction between jihad and terrorism. The work's core argument has not changed since the first edition appeared in early 1963.
86 Wahbah al-Zuhaili, *Al-'Alaqat al-Duwaliya fi al-Islam: Muqarana bil-Qanun al-Duwali al-Hadith* (Damascus: Dar al-Fikr, 2011).
87 Wahbah al-Zuhaili, *Al-Qanun al-Duwali al-Insani wa Huquq al-Insan: Dirasa Muqarina* (Damascus: Dar al-Fikr, 2012).

88 A link to Zuhaili's article can be found at: Wahbah al-Zuhaili, "al-Islam wa al-Qanun al-Dawli" (Islam and International Law), *ICRC* (2005). https://www.icrc.org/ar/doc/resources/documents/article/review/review-858-p269.htm, accessed 12 April 2012.

89 Hroub writes: "If 'contextualisation' offers flexible approaches to the understanding of Islamism where the specificities of each context and case are given primacy, 'ideologisation' offers an opposite approach heavily reliant on 'textual' rather than 'contextual' interpretation of the phenomenon". What Hroub says about Islamist movements applies as well to Islamist thought. Hroub, "Introduction," in *Political Islam: Context versus Ideology*, ed. Hroub, 16.

2

The Founding Generation: Jamal al-Din al-Afghani, Muhammad 'Abduh, and Rashid Rida

Introduction

Determining the origins of the moderate-reformist, or mainstream, strand of political Islam is a complex task. One could conceivably start the discussion with the perspective of the Egyptian Sheikh Rifaʻa Badawi Rafiʻ al-Tahtawi (1801–1873), who can be considered the first contemporary Muslim religious reformer of some renown.[1] Tahtawi's contact with the West, mainly with France, prompted him to seek reform in the Muslim world, especially in education. However, in the words of Myriam Salama-Carr, Tahtawi was more of a "translator, essayist and educationalist"[2] than an analyst of political and social conditions, including international relations. Still, Tahtawi exhibited a mixed response to and deep reflections on his contacts with Europe, early indicators of the influence that the West would exert on the discourses of subsequent Islamists. As Hourani notes: "Tahtawi lived and worked in a happy interlude of history, when the religious tensions between Islam and Christendom were relaxed and had not yet been replaced by the new political tension between east and west."[3] International conditions then changed, and not for the better, especially with renewed British and French colonial pursuits in the latter part of the 19th century, impacting most of the Muslim world. However, reverting in time to Tahtawi is contentious since it is difficult to establish a direct link between his thought and the discourses of the six scholar sheikhs covered in this text. It is, thus, preferable to start this narrative a few decades later with Sayyid Jamal al-Din al-Afghani, an influential figure in the discourses among them, especially as far as their views of the West and their conceptualization of Islamic unity.

Prior to introducing the three central figures of the founding generation, it is necessary to identify the aims and organization of this chapter and briefly revisit the issue of terminology discussed in Chapter 1. To begin, the purpose of this chapter is not to add to the substantive body of work on al-Afghani (referred to as Afghani), 'Abduh and Rida; for as Shavit notes, "Since the 1920s, al-Afghani, 'Abduh and their immediate successors have received much scholarly attention."[4] Instead, the chapter aims to highlight the influence these three foundational figures exercised on the international relations discourses of members of the second and third generations of moderate-reformist Islamists, an influence evinced in both their ideas and modes of argumentation.

It is equally important to clarify why the chapter avoids two terms that abound in the literature in reference to these founding figures, namely salafism and modernism. As Esposito,[5] Haykel,[6] 'Imara,[7] Maher,[8] Meijer,[9] Shavit,[10] and Wagemakers,[11] among others, point out, all three figures regarded themselves as salafis, in that their quest was to restore Islam to its initial energy during the days of the Prophet and the rightly guided first four caliphs. However, especially since the appearance of al-Qaeda, the term Salafism has become almost totally associated with either Wahhabism or with militant figures and movements seeking to overthrow existing regimes and advocating violence against the West. In terms of both ideals and tactics, today's salafis have little similarity to the founding generation of moderate-reformers, even if the latter also identified themselves as salafis. As Wagemakers notes:

> Just as contemporary Salafism should not be equated entirely with Wahhabism, it should also not be confused with the late nineteenth and early twentieth-century movement often referred to as Salafism. This modernist trend... did indeed try to move Islam back into the direction of the *salaf* but with a completely different objective. Whereas contemporary Salafis try to emulate the predecessors to purify Islam and revert to its supposedly original and true form, al-Afghani, 'Abduh, Rida and others did so in order to rid Islam of the centuries of legal and historical baggage that had, in their view, turned it into a rigid religion unit for modern times.[12]

In a similar vein, Haykel clarifies that the "legacy of Ibn Taymiyya, and his use of the term Salafi, should not be conflated or confused with the Salafi ideas associated with the late nineteenth century reformist scholars . . . al-Afghani, .. 'Abduh and the early views of . . . Rida."[13] Moreover, while harboring fewer reservations regarding the term modernist, I do not use it; I adhere instead to the terminology discussed in Chapter 1, namely the terms moderate-reformist and mainstream to depict members of all three generations.

Afghani: Anti-Colonialism, Constitutionalism, and the Quest for Islamic Unity

The literature portrays Afghani as a mysterious, fiery, autocratic, itinerant, and charismatic figure, as well as an agitator par excellence. Albert Hourani draws attention to Afghani's "troubled career and endless wanderings,"[14] reiterating Gordon Blunt's depiction of him as a "wild man of genius."[15] Ayoob is less flattering, noting that Afghani "himself was a bundle of contradictions."[16] In one of the best studies on the life and thought of Afghani, Nikki Keddie describes him as "one of the outstanding figures of nineteenth century Islamic history."[17] She observes that little is known about Afghani's first twenty-seven years of life and that, while he presented himself as a Sunni from Afghanistan, most accounts note that he was born a Shia in Iran.[18] Adding to the mystery is Afghani's membership in the Free Masons secret society, to which he introduced the young Muhammad 'Abduh, among other members of the Egyptian political, economic, and intellectual elite.[19] As the recently deceased Muhammad 'Imara points out, Afghani organized a secret society of his own while in exile, al-'urwa al-wuthqa (the firmest bond), which, according to 'Imara, was both a periodical and a secret society.[20] Afghani's first lieutenant in both enterprises was none other than 'Abduh. 'Imara adds that, at Afghani's behest, 'Abduh, in exile with Afghani, illicitly entered Sudan and Egypt to report on the Mehdi revolt in Sudan and public sentiment in Egypt regarding the recent British occupation.[21]

While acknowledging his indebtedness to Afghani's ideas on Islamic unity, Abu Zahra praises him as *hakim al-Islam* (the wise man of Islam), the "first to issue the clarion call for Islamic unity in our epoch and the rejuvenator of intellectual awareness in all the land of Islam."[22] Bahi, another admirer of Afghani from Abu Zahra's generation, paints a romantic image of his travels, noting that he "journeyed first throughout India, Egypt, Hejaz, Iran, Iraq, and

Istanbul in the lands of the East, before setting off to London, Paris, Munich, and St. Petersburg in the lands of the West."[23] Bahi also defends Afghani against charges that he was shallow and spiteful toward Europe and Christianity.[24] Although Bahi's defense of Afghani is rather weak, focusing on the motives of his critics rather than challenging the substance of their criticism, his passionate defense reflects the high esteem with which most Islamists, both moderate and extreme, hold Afghani, especially regarding his anti-colonial stance and calls for Islamic unity.

Abu Zahra's and Bahi's views notwithstanding, there is near consensus among researchers that Afghani was not a deep thinker and that he did not do much writing, leaving that task largely to his pupil 'Abduh. On his own, Afghani is credited with a single manuscript, which 'Abduh, assisted by a follower of Afghani by the name of 'Aref Effendi Abu Trab, translated into Arabic from the original Persian under the title, *al-Radd 'ala al-Dahriyyin* (Refutation of the Materialists).[25] Despite its polemical style and limited relevance to conditions in the Arab world, written in the context of the political and ideational developments in the Indian subcontinent, the piece became a staple in the repertoire of contemporary Arab Islamists.[26] Its association with the renowned figures of 'Abduh and Afghani in the Arab world added to its significance.

In his seminal work on the origins of contemporary Arab thought, Hourani describes Afghani as "eloquent, knew many languages, was fond of talking endlessly to his friends and was a stirring public orator. But he did not like writing and wrote little."[27] Hourani provides further insights into Afghani's thought that are worth reiterating. To start with, his "thought was not exclusively political,"[28] evidenced, among other considerations, by the fact that the only published work attributed solely to Afghani was not a political tract. Second, and more importantly, Afghani viewed Islam as both a revealed religion, indeed the truest of all religions, and a civilization. Hourani, thus, writes that for Afghani "Islam was not just a religion but also a civilization."[29] Hourani sees in this view of Islam as a civilization the influence of the renowned French 19th-century eminent historian Francois Guizot.[30] Capturing the essence of Afghani's worldview, Hourani notes: "In its great days, the *umma* had all the necessary attributes of a flourishing civilization: social development, individual development, belief in reason, unity and solidarity; later it lost them."[31] Reiterating Hourani's important argument, Esposito writes, "Afghani stressed that Islam was more than just a religion in the Western sense of the term. It was a religion and civilization. Moreover, Islam was an ideology, supplying the raison d'être of for Muslims both as individuals and as a sociopolitical community."[32]

Third, and perhaps most importantly, Afghani believed that religion and science were compatible, and, more broadly, that reason does not and cannot contradict revelation. Despite his opposition to Europe and his insistence on restoring Islam to the golden age of the Prophet and the righteous caliphs, Afghani was not a traditionalist. As Esposito notes, for Afghani "Islam was no simple imitation of the past or complacent passivity, but rather the religion of reason and action."[33] Subsequent Islamists, starting with Rida, were more political in their discourses than Afghani and definitely 'Abduh. They, however, retained Afghani and 'Abduh's view of Islam as both a religion and a civilization, and indeed as the principal bond tying members of the *umma*, irrespectively of ethnicity or nationality. They also retained the assertion that revelation and reason are paths to the same absolute truth. All mainstream Islamists emphasize the centrality of reason for ordering human relations, including international relations. The scholar sheikhs of the third generation, in particular, underscore the need for dispassionate and rational analysis of international conditions (principally by the *wulat al-amr*) before taking any major decisions regarding war and peace. In brief, major decisions about international relations could not be made exclusively by turning to the revealed text; these decisions required *ijtihad* as well as rational analysis of where the public interest (*al-maslaha al-'amma*) of the Muslims lay.

As for Afghani's great lasting influence over multiple audiences in the Arab world and beyond, it emanated in no small part from his strong personality, command of the sacred text, considerable knowledge of Islamic philosophy, and undeniable oratorical skills. More importantly, though, his appeal and legacy also stemmed from the simplicity, consistency, and potency of the message he delivered, revolving around three intrinsic themes: resistance to colonial rule and more generally to European influence in the Muslim, and more broadly non-Western, world; opposition to despotic rule in the Muslim world on the ground that it violated *shura* (the consultation principle) and treated the population as subjects or even slaves of the rulers; and insistence on the immediate need for Islamic unity as the only way to rejuvenate the *umma* and solve its internal problems as well as free it from Western occupation, domination, and exploitation. The centrality of these three political themes in the discourses of subsequent mainstream Islamists of the second and third generations warrants a brief treatment of each.

Resistance to Colonialism and European Domination

Afghani's angry and defiant message ought to be read primarily as an Islamic response to Western encroachment on the Muslim world. The late 19th century saw a renewed wave of European imperialism and a scramble for colonies that left only small swaths of Asia and Africa politically independent.[34] Hourani captures the spirit of the age when he writes: "Al-Afghani lived in the age when European power suddenly became as wide as the world."[35] As Raquibuz Zaman notes, it fell upon Afghani to issue "clarion calls to all Muslims to wake up and face the dangers of western expansionism."[36] Afghani's anti-colonial stance is arguably best captured by the title Keddie chose for her anthology of his political and religious discourses, *An Islamic Response to Imperialism*.[37] As Keddie, Hourani, 'Imara and Qadri Qal'aji, among others, demonstrate, repelling British and more generally European colonialism in India, Egypt, and other parts of the Muslim world took precedence over other goals in Afghani's rather direct political agenda. Afghani, thus, enjoined India's Muslims to join hands with the Hindu population in the common fight against British colonial rule.[38] Afghani had a firsthand encounter with British imperialism in Afghanistan, India, and Egypt, where he traveled from 1871 until 1879. As Qal'aji points out, British authorities were directly or indirectly implicated in evicting him out of all three countries.[39] That partly explains why most of his anti-colonial polemics was directed against Britain, although he did make a few references to French colonialism in North Africa.[40] As John Kelsay notes, Afghani argued that, "The first task before the Muslims was to free themselves from British dominance."[41]

Afghani's condemnation of and opposition to European colonialism, however, did not translate into outright rejection of European concepts and European institutions. Afghani, thus, had no qualms when it came to the Muslim world benefiting from Europe's scientific and technical achievements, even selectively adopting some European institutions, particularly parliaments.[42] This emphasis on distinguishing between resisiting Western colonialism and neocolonialism, on the one hand, and borrowing selectively from the West, on the other, became a hallmark of the discourses of subsequent mainstream Islamists. Always in haste, inclined to clandestine activities, and heavily embroiled in the politics of the day, Afghani never articulated an internally consistent, thorough view of Europe or the West. His resentment of European powers went hand in hand with his admiration of Western scientific and technical achievements. Roy Jackson captures this point well when he notes, "What al-Afghani saw as virtues in the Western world, those of rationality, science and patriotism, he saw as the same virtues as the essence of Islam."[43]

Here it is worth noting that Afghani disassociated European advancement from Christianity, maintaining that Europe advanced despite and not because of Christianity. Hourani sums up Afghani's stance on this matter by noting that the latter argued:

> The Christian peoples grew strong because the Church grew up within the walls of the Roman Empire and incorporated its pagan beliefs and virtues; the Muslim peoples grew weak because the truth of Islam was corrupted by successive waves of falsity. Christians are strong because they are not really Christian; Muslims are weak because they are not really Muslim.[44]

Afghani's complex and ambivalent relationship with Europe, and more generally the West, came to characterize the discourses of mainstream Islamists of the second and third generations. With the end of World War II, colonialism gave way to neocolonialism. Neocolonialism, manifesting itself primarily in asymmetric economic, cultural, and political ties with the former colonizers (and with the emergent superpowers, the United States and the former Soviet Union), was condemned in equally strong language as the original colonialism was, especially in the discourse of Bahi, Qaradawi, and Fadlallah. Equally important, the United States, which overtook Great Britain as the leading Western power by the end of World War II, also replaced it as the bête noire in the international relations discourses of contemporary Islamists, whether radical or mainstream. As the subsequent chapters point out, though, the political demonization of the United States and the West at no point translated into denying their scientific and technological achievements. It also did not translate into outright calls for declaring jihad against the West.

Opposition to Despotic Rule

While clearly not an advocate of Western democracy, Afghani sincerely believed that despotism in the Muslim world weakened the *umma* and facilitated Western domination of Muslim political communities. However, just as Afghani failed in formulating an internally consistent theory about the West, he also failed in articulating even a semblance of a theory of governance for Muslim societies. It is clearly estblished that Afghani's fortunes were always closely tied to his relationships to powerful figures, such as Khedive Ismail of Egypt; Naser al-Din Qajar, Shah of Iran; and Sultan 'Abdul Hamid of the Ottoman Empire. The apparent paradox between Afghani's close, though always brief, association with absolute rulers and his principled, undoubtedly genuine opposition to despotic rule can be resolved if we adopt, as Afghani probably did, Aristotle's distinction between the organization of government and the purposes of government. For Aristotle, and thus Afghani, there was nothing inherently immoral about absolute rule if the ruler, in Aristotle's terminology the monarch, ruled in the interests of the ruled. Despotic rule only occurred when the ruler ruled in his own interest or in the interest of foreign powers, rather than in the interest of the ruled, in this case the *umma*.

Afghani was, thus, on good terms, even if briefly, with absolute rulers when he thought that they had the interest of the *umma* in mind. He quickly parted company with them when he lost faith in their intention to seek the political unity of the *umma* and to rid it of European occupation and domination. Afghani strongly believed in the principle of the *shura*, namely that rulers ought to consult with the wise men of the community and indeed with the entire population on political matters,[45] although he was vague, as most Islamists are, on the mechanisms of achieving that.

Afghani's discourse on governance is rather problematic on at least two related grounds. First, he does not properly define what constitutes the body politic; Is it the entire Muslim *umma* or smaller groups, such as Egypt or India, that comprise both Muslims and non-Muslims? Moreover, Afghani does not provide an internally consistent answer to what constitutes the best form of government. He does not object to absolute rule as long as the ruler has the right intentions and the power to act on them, but, simultaneously, he calls for popular rule, as embodied in his famous call for "Egypt to be governed by its people" through "popular participation in proper constitutional governance."[46] As 'Imara notes, Afghani goes a step further by calling for the establishment of parliamentary life in Egypt, insisting on the independence of parliament from the ruler and from foreign powers.[47] While such bold assertions endeared Afghani to the masses and earned him the reputation of a revolutionary, they undoubtedly contributed to his fall from grace with the powerful rulers who had once protected and funded him. In his final years, Afghani was the virtual prisoner of Ottoman Sultan 'Abdul Hamid in Istanbul, although Hourani notes that he was treated honorably,[48] but there are rumors that he did not die of natural causes.[49] It becomes clear, though, that Afghani's many inconsistencies on matters pertaining to the internal governance of the *umma* can be partly attributed to the secondary importance he assigned to this issue, for his overriding concern was to free the *umma* of foreign domination.[50]

Pan-Islamism and the Unification of the Umma

Despite the importance of his anti-colonial stance and his support for *shura* and indeed constitutional rule, Afghani is best noted for his advocacy of Islamic unity as the sure path for rejuvenating the *umma*. As Bahi notes, Aghani called for "ending the enmity between Sunnis and Shias in order to bring together the two principal political powers within the Islamic Wolrd at the time: the authority of Iran and that of Constantople."[51] While clearly anchored in religious text, especially the verses that refer to the Muslims as one *umma*—specifically 2:143, "Thus We have appointed you a median *umma* . . ." and 3:110, "You are the best *umma* ever brought forth among mankind. . ." and 21:92, "This then is your *umma*, a single *umma*. . ."—Afghani's call for Islamic unity also rested on practical political grounds, primarily that only by acting in unison can Muslim rulers and the Muslim public resist Western occupation and domination.

Part of Afghani's legacy to Islamists of subsequent generations emanated from his construct of pan-Islamism as a form of nationalism, where the religious bond replaced the ethnic bond.[52] It must be noted that Afghani lived at a time when European nationalism was at its zenith. French nationalism, given a major boost by Napoleon Bonaparte's reforms and conquests, had survived his downfall and exile. It remained a powerful force in the 19th century, ensuring the preservation of French independence despite the defeat of 1815, and contributing to France's unabated economic, intellectual, and technological advancement then and to its renewed quest for colonies.

Equally important, rising nationalist sentiments had culminated in the unification of Italy and Germany in 1871 and their almost immediate formation as imperial powers joining the European push for colonies and domination. These transformative developments—and the earlier success of American nationalism in gaining independence from British rule—were not amiss on Afghani, in exile in Europe between 1883 and 1889, first living in Paris then moving to various European capitals and ending in St Petersburg.[53] Stated briefly, pan-Islamism, as a contemporary ideology that began with Afghani before becoming a principal theme in the discourses of mainstream Islamists, must be viewed first and foremost as a response to European and American nationalism.

Muhammad 'Abduh and the Pursuit of Religious, Social and Political Reforms

As Keddie notes, "Afghani's main influence may be traced in a line going back chiefly to two men, his Egyptian disciple Muhammad Abduh, and the latter's follower Rashid Rida."[54] Unlike Afghani, who came to the Arab world from another country and whose origins and early years were shrouded in mystery, 'Abduh was born in the Nile Delta, in the heart of rural Egypt, to a "family of modest means," as Malcolm Kerr notes.[55] Hourani observes:

> His ['Abduh's] origin was very different from that of al-Afghani. Al-Afghani came from some distant place not to be determined with certainty, and passed like a meteor from one country to another; 'Abduh was firmly rooted in an ordinary family of the country where his main work was to be done.[56]

While 'Abduh's upbringing and education were not exceptional,[57] his career was truly spectacular, with his legacy enduring for over a century now. 'Abduh began his intellectual journey in the shadow of Afghani, whom he met in 1872, when 'Abduh was 23 and Afghani 33 years of age. 'Abduh was Afghani's most devoted disciple until the latter was expelled from Egypt in 1879.[58] Later in life, especially after he returned from exile to permanently settle in Egypt in 1889, 'Abduh distanced himself from his former mentor both physically and intellectually, developing a personal approach to questions of religious, social and political reforms. As Hourani points out, 'Abduh "was to become a more systematic thinker than his master and have a more lasting influence on the Muslim mind, not only in Egypt but far beyond."[59] While more methodical in his thinking than Afghani, 'Abduh, as Kerr demonstrates, did not exhibit clarity and consistency in his discourse.[60] For that reason, the tensions and inconsistencies in 'Abduh's views were transmitted to his closest disciple, Rida.

Three interconnected themes in 'Abduh's thought were to resonate in the discourses of subsequent mainstream Islamists: 'Abduh's insistence on the compatibility of reason and revelation, at the core of his reformist theology; his emphasis on the need for wide-ranging reforms in the political, social and especially educational realms in order to rejuvenate political communities; and his construct of Europe and more generally the West.

'Abduh's Reformist Theology: The Compatibility of Reason and Revelation

A great deal has been written on 'Abduh's approach to religious reform, particularly his contribution to the development of the mainstream Islamist argument that there is no contradiction between revelation and human reason and that human reason, when properly applied, is capable of comprehending religious as well as other truths. While this argument originated in the teachings of Afghani, 'Abduh was the one to thoroughly develop it and give it its established form.

Subsequent mainstream Islamists embraced, indeed internalized, this argument, making it the basis for their theorizing on political and social issues.

While criticisms of this mainstream Islamist claim of the compatibility of revelation and reason abound, the claim was pivotal for launching serious inquiries by subsequent Islamists into political, legal and social issues, including issues of international relations. Since this book focuses on the implications of this mainstream position for theorizing about international relations, it is necessary to summarize 'Abduh's stance on this pivotal matter and briefly present the critiques of his position, mainly by Kerr and other Western academics.[61] Despite the passage of years, and the critiques of post-colonial writers inspired by Edward Said's work on Orientalism,[62] Kerr's work retains its salience both in terms of fairly presenting as well as critiquing 'Abduh's position on religious matter, i.e., 'Abduh's theology. Kerr writes:

> One of 'Abduh's most constantly stressed themes in his theological and apologetic writings is the essential harmony of reason, revelation, and individual moral temperament. When properly expressed and understood, there can be no conflict between them, although the fact that men often understand them in distorted form leads them to suppose that there are contradictions.[63]

Based on 'Abduh's principal theological work, *Risalat al-Tawhid*, Kerr further notes that for 'Abduh, "Reason and revelation are different paths to truth and fulfill different functions, but cannot contradict each other."[64] The basic tenet of Kerr's argument is that 'Abduh, like most Sunni *'ulama*, adhered to the Ash'arite doctrine that God did not detach Himself from the world after creating it, but that things happen in this world because God wills them to happen. His will, rather than nature itself, regulates all the laws that govern the universe, including the *Sunnan* (plural of *Sunna*) that regulate human interactions.[65] Thus, in the footsteps of Afghani, whose principal text on the subject, refutation of the materialists, he translated into Arabic, 'Abduh rejects naturalist, or materialist, explanations of physical as well as social phenomena. In this regard, he embodies the traditional Sunni view of the cosmos, that it is governed by God's laws (*Sunnan Allah*), which Kerr translates as God's custom, rather than by natural laws.[66] Nevertheless, as Kerr clarifies, what was novel in 'Abduh's theology was his insistence that human reason, when properly applied, is capable of discovering *Sunnan Allah* and other religious truths.[67]

'Abduh's belief in human reason surpassed that of early and medieval jurists who discouraged rational inquiries into the existence and attributes of God and into related thorny religious matters, such as the creation of the Quran. Kerr attributes this rationalist tendency in 'Abduh's thought primarily to his comprehension of the Mu'tazilite stance that rejected predestination in favor of free will, while placing faith in human reason, without himself fully subscribing to it. Kerr, as well as Keddie, also see in 'Abduh's rationalism the influence of his mentor Afghani who, given his Persian-Shia background, was quite familiar with the rational philosophy of Ibn Sina (Avicenna).[68] While not a specialist on theological questions herself, Keddie provides a succinct summary of the difference between the Mu'tazilite and Ash'arite stances in the context of her discussion of the theological views of Afghani and 'Abduh.[69] She writes:

> Mu'tazilism believes in free will of humans, while Ash'arism says everything that occurs is willed by God. While both free will and predestination have in various places and times been used to support activism, it would seem that in modern Islam Ash'arite predestination was associated with a nonactivist clinging to old ways, while an implicit Mu'tazilite belief in free will was more characteristic of activists and reformers.[70]

As Kerr demonstrates, however, 'Abduh faces an intellectual dilemma when trying to explain why humans cannot rely solely on reason and also need revelation, offering competing and partial explanations that revolve around the deficiency of human reason, which is often clouded by selfish desires or by limited understanding; and humans' intrinsic need for spiritual guidance, which only revelation can provide through God-sent prophets and messengers. 'Abduh also fails to specify the exact relationship between reason and revelation. Is reason of equal standing to revelation, or is it simply a handmaiden to revelation, helping humans better understand revealed truths? 'Abduh's position is that while human reason may not understand all religious truths, there is nothing in Islam, when properly understood as the Islam of the Salaf, that contradicts reason. However, despite the numerous problems in 'Abduh's theology, his insistence on the compatibility of revelation and reason was to play a pivotal role in encouraging subsequent Islamists, such as the six scholar sheikhs examined here, to resort extensively to rational arguments combined with ample references to the Islamic tradition in their inquiries into international relations. This argumentation style, blending rational arguments with references to pertinent Quranic verses and prophetic *hadiths*, undoubtedly constitutes a significant component of 'Abduh's legacy since it was embraced by subsequent mainstream Islamists.

Rejuvenating the Umma through Political and Social Reforms

'Abduh's legacy as a reformer, however, resulted from his reformist stance on political and social issues as it did from his theology. 'Imara distinguishes at least three phases in the evolution of 'Abduh's thought on political and social issues. In the initial phase, and despite the influence of the more revolutionary Afghani, 'Abduh adopted a cautious incremental stance on issues of political and social reform, emphasizing that Egyptian society as well as other Eastern societies were not equipped to vest authority in the still largely uneducated public.[71] Rather interestingly, and in light of Afghani's self-proclaimed origin, 'Abduh uses the example of the Afghans, noting that "it would take centuries of progress in the realms of the dissipation of scientific knowledge, cultivation of the minds and reigning in private desires before public awareness can emerge in that land." Only then, "would what is good for America be also good for the Afghans," he clarifies.[72]

'Abduh's rejection of large-scale emulation of European institutions and practices was not, however, grounded in religion. Afghani, and especially 'Abduh, did not claim that Islam was incompatible with the then emerging democratic trend in Europe and America. 'Abduh had nothing but praise for the American political system, whose basic features he seems to have well understood.[73] He, however, genuinely believed that the Egyptian people, and more generally the people of the East, were not ready to exercise the powers that such a system vested in them, and not because of their religion.[74] In a sense, 'Abduh unwittingly adopted the stance of the Orientalists who maintained that non-Europeans had to be educated on how to participate in political democracy before they were given the opportunity to do so.

'Imara identifies a second more revolutionary phase in 'Abduh's intellectual journey that started with the 'Urabi revolt in 1881.[75] 'Imara argues that 'Abduh reluctantly embraced the 'Urabi movement agenda that revolved around introducing constitutional limits to the powers of the Khedive, undermining the role of the Turkish-Circassian officers and functionaries who dominated the higher echelons of the army and bureaucracy and reigning in growing European influence over Egyptian finances and affairs.[76] 'Imara maintains that this revolutionary phase in 'Abduh's career abruptly ended with the defeat of 'Urabi at the hands of the British in December 1882, and the ensuing brief imprisonment and then exile of 'Abduh.[77]

During his rather long exile 'Abduh briefly renewed his ties with Afghani, staying with him in Paris between late 1883 (or early 1884) and 1885, where they collaborated in publishing *al-'urwa al-wuthqa* and also engaged in covert action aiming at undermining British rule in Egypt and Sudan.[78] It is evident, though, that by the time 'Abduh left to Beirut, then under Ottoman rule, from Paris in 1885, he had given up not only on political activism but also on writing on politics, devoting himself entirely to educational work and to formulating his own understanding of the Islamic religion. The lectures that he delivered at *al-Madrassa al-Sultaniya* in Beirut formed the bases of his principal theological work, *Risalat al-Tawhid* (Essay on Theology).[79]

It is evident that 'Abduh's eventual return to Egypt in 1889 was negotiated with the British. The clemency he received from the khedive, at the behest of British authorities, was conditional on his relinquishing political activism. As 'Imara notes: "When [Lord] Cromer became convinced that 'Abduh would not work in politics and would restrict his activities to educational, cultural and intellectual work, he used his influence to obtain him a pardon from khedive Tawfiq."[80]

The third phase in 'Abduh's intellectual journey either started during his relatively long sojourn in Beirut as of 1885 or, more lilkely, upon his return to Egypt. This third and final phase was characterized by the abandonment of the revolutionaly ideals and tactics that he reluctantly embraced around the time of the 'Urabi revolt. Clearly, 'Abduh was at the height of his career and of his influence in the years that followed his return to Egypt, where he held a number of important government positions, culminating in his appointment in 1899 as Mufti of the Egyptian realm. The mature 'Abduh reverted to his initial incremental stance, established cordial ties with the British, and disavowed political activism, focusing instead on educational and legal reform as well as on religious and intellectual renewal. As 'Imara points out, 'Abduh made a full circle: starting out as a reformer (phase one), then briefly adopting the revolutionary tactics of his mentor, Afghani (phase two), before reverting to his initial reformist stance (phase three).[81]

'Abduh's eventual abandonment of politics as a means of effecting change was prompted by both pragmatic considerations and the realization that educational and legal reforms, as well as the pursuit of religious and intellectual renewal, constituted more effective long-term means to bring about the desired changes. Despite his forays into political writings at different stages in his rich career, 'Abduh never developed a consistent political philosophy. Clearly, he was a critic of despotic rule, as can be seen, for instance, from the opening sentence of one of his early editorials in the Egyptian Gazette. 'Abduh wrote that the country "is content and its affairs are set right when the stature of the law is raised in it, its status is elevated and is respected first by those who govern and then by those who are governed."[82]

'Abduh, however, did not articulate an alternative to despotism beyond general references to the centrality of *shura* in Islam and to the *sharia* as providing restraints on the arbitrary powers of rulers. In one of his last public statements, 'Abduh conveyed this ambivalence about the best form of government. In January 1905, 'Abduh addressed the Egyptian officers stationed in Sudan, as such:

> O Officers of the Army! You have accomplished in Sudan, in the best possible manner, what has been commissioned to you. The aspects of civilization which you have implemented, and which I have witnessed, make me wish – in spite of my inclination towards civil order and the constitution – the Egyptian government becomes a military government; and then perhaps it would enjoy, through you, the progress which Sudan has made.[83]

There are two problems with 'Abduh's stance on politics that need to be briefly addressed. First, 'Abduh in line with Afghani, and arguably under the influence by Aristotelian political philosophy, did not take a clear position on the legitimacy of rule by one person or by a few when the one or the few are acting in the public interest. Equally important, he did not address the thorny issue of where sovereignty lies in an Islamic unit of rule. Does it lie with the ruler, with the ruled, or with God, as all radical Islamists maintain? While attentive to the needs of those ruled and to the importance of involving them in the affairs of the state, 'Abduh steered clear of espousing the doctrine of popular sovereignty. He accomplished this stance by falling back on cultural, rather than religious, arguments, namely that the population in Eastern societies are not ready for direct rule. Most studies on 'Abduh demonstrate that his ingenuity lay in his remarkable ability to avoid thorny, divisive questions, which he knew had no answer in religion.

Although writing more fully on political issues than 'Abduh, subsequent mainstream Islamists also failed to provide clear answers to these pivotal questions, despite their importance for constructing any systematic political theory. Nevertheless, despite its ambiguities and latent tensions, 'Abduh's discourse on governance paved the way for more detailed, although not necessarily more systematic, inquiries into questions of governance by subsequent scholar sheikhs. 'Abduh's views on Europe and the West also formed part of his legacy, proving to be more positive than those of earlier or subsequent Islamists.

'Abduh's Openness toward Europe and the West

'Abduh was among the first contemporary Islamists to have sustained an intellectual as well as a political relationship with Europe. He was also one of a few contemporary scholar sheikhs to have mastered a European language, French. As Keddie notes, Europe played a "dual role" in the thought of Afghani and 'Abduh as both a "threat and a model."[84] However, unlike Afghani, who maintained a defiant stance toward the British throughout, 'Abduh reconciled himself to the reality of the British thinly disguised occupation of Egypt. As Jackson notes: "'Abduh saw colonial rule as a necessary evil at least until Egypt could stand on its own two feet and become a modern state."[85]

'Abduh's accommodation of British rule over Egypt undoubtedly contributed to his rift with Afghani, which lasted till the former's death. Indeed, as noted, 'Abduh's eventual return to Egypt in 1899 was negotiated by the British. By and large, 'Abduh lived up to his side of the bargain, withdrawing from the political arena and focusing instead on issues of legal and educational reforms, as well as reforming the curriculum and organization of al-Azhar.

'Abduh's intellectual engagement with Europe was more significant and more sustained than his political engagement with the European continent. It started at a young age, even before he taught himself French and spent time in Europe. It became more intense during 'Abduh's mature years, as 'Abduh translated many European works and made a number of trips to Europe, including a visit to the renowned yet controversial British author, Herbert Spencer. For 'Abduh, selective borrowing from Europe, whether in the scientific and technical fields or in the organizational and political realms, was essential for the rejuvenation of the Muslim world. As Hourani notes, 'Abduh was "convinced that the Muslim nations could not become strong and prosperous until they acquired from Europe the sciences which were the product of its activity of mind, and they could do this without abandoning Islam."[86] 'Abduh also had no qualms about engaging with European philosophy, notwithstanding the close link between philosophy and religion, of which he was quite aware.

In summary, 'Abduh adopted a middle ground regarding the dominant currents of Europe, whether naturalism, evolution, individualism, or a secular approach to politics and society, neither wholeheartedly embracing them nor categorically rejecting them. He did not feel that these systems of ideas threatened the Islamic religion or Islamic identity. This spirit of positive engagement with European thought spared 'Abduh the fate of some subsequent Islamists, including his disciple Rida, who became preoccupied with defending Islam against

Western criticism. Still, it is true that ʿAbduh did occasionally resort to apologetic rhetoric, engaging in polemical writings against Western and Christian Arab secular critics of Islam, primarily Ernest Renan and Farah Antoun.[87]

These controversial texts, however, constituted only a fraction of his oeuvre, and did not distract from his grand project of demonstrating Islam's compatibility with science and reason, and his embrace of serious intellectual dialog with Europe. Clearly, ʿAbduh, in line with Afghani and most contemporary Islamists, yearned to restore Islam to the initial purity that allegedly prevailed during Islam's golden age, and, in this regard, he was a Salafi. ʿAbduh, however, did not conceive of Islam as a self-contained system of ideals that should be sheltered from outside influences.[88] His openness to dialog with non-Islamic systems of ideas, although guarded, became a hallmark of the discourses of the subsequent mainstream Islamists studied here. Samira Haj effectively argues that ʿAbduh embraced a *wasati* (middle ground) stance toward both European thought and the Islamic tradition. She attributes this *wasati* stance to the influence of the renowned medieval theologian and jurist Abu al-Hamid ibn Muhammad al-Ghazali on ʿAbduh's thought.[89] While Haj's depiction of ʿAbduh as a *wasati* is quite fair, it must be noted that ʿAbduh did not identify himself as a *wasati*; nor did he openly advocate *al-wasatiya* as the proper approach to Islam.

Finally, ʿAbduh's break with certain facets of the Islamic tradition, especially his rejection of *taqlid*, and his concomitant embrace of certain elements of Western thought led some of his Western admirers and Egyptian critics—such as Lord Cromer and the Khedive Abbas Hilmi, with whom ʿAbduh had a disagreement in his final years—to claim that he was an agnostic or, in the harsh words attributed to the Khedive, "the enemy of religion... the enemy of the Muslims."[90] This depiction of ʿAbduh is quite unfair; and, as Hourani, Kerr, Sedgwick, and others note, is based on flimsy evidence. Samira Haj comes closer to the truth, when she notes, "Engaging Western discourses, however, did not make ʿAbduh a lesser Muslim nor necessarily a liberal."[91]

Rashid Rida: The Reluctant Reformer

Roy Jackson writes that the "Lebanon-born Muhammad Rashid Rida forms a trinity with Jamal al-Din al-Afghani and Muhammad Abduh as the great synthesizers of modern Islam and the founding intellectual fathers of the salafi movement."[92] Despite this praise, Rida was the least original and most traditional of the three founding figures. His legacy as a reluctant reformer who increasingly sought to embrace Islam's traditional values, nevertheless, had a significant impact on the discourses of subsequent mainstream Islamists, as well as on the thought of Hassan al-Banna, the founder the Muslim Brotherhood.[93] Moreover, just as 'Abduh began his intellectual journey in the shadow of Afghani, Rida started his in that of 'Abduh. However, while 'Abduh severed his political and personal ties to Afghani after 1899, his association with Rida lasted until his death. In addition to persuading 'Abduh to make regular contributions to his recently founded journal *al-Manar*, Rida played a major role in preserving 'Abduh's legacy by completing his biography, which 'Abduh died before finishing, and collecting and publishing his writings. In addition to being 'Abduh's biographer, Rida was his "most trusted friend."[94] In his later years, however, Rida shifted from the stance and methodology of 'Abduh, while never acknowledging this shift, thus preserving the narrative of a continuous Islamic revivalist tradition extending from Afghani to 'Abduh and to Rida.

This narrative, which can be described as a foundational myth of continuity, was pivotal for anchoring the discourses of subsequent mainstream Islamists on a bedrock of core assumptions, regarding the compatibility of reason and revelation; the permissibility, actually the necessity, of incorporating from the West, especially in the scientific and technical fields; the centrality of *ijtihad* for reviving Islam to restore its centrality in the life of the *umma*; and the need for thorough political, legal, and social reforms, ones that should be anchored in a reinterpreted *sharia*.

Born in 1865 in the town of Qalamoun, near Tripoli in what is today North Lebanon,[95] Rida shared a similar family background with "Abduh," except for the claim of descent from the Prophet Muhammad through his grandson Imam Hussein, a claim Rida did not allude to much.[96] While Rida's father, Ali, was the sheikh of his home town and the Imam of its mosque, his religious education, though extensive, was less formal and not undertaken at prestigious institutions, such as the Ahmadi mosque in Tanta or al-Azhar. Most accounts note that the young Rida was impressed by both Muhammad 'Abduh, at the time in exile in nearby Beirut, and Jamal al-Din al-Afghani. Rida corresponded with Afghani in his Paris exile, and he managed to meet twice with 'Abduh on the latter's short trips to Tripoli. Yet it was only after Rida migrated to Egypt in 1897 that he established a close personal and professional relationship with 'Abduh, lasting till the latter's death.[97] *Al-Manar*, which Rida founded shortly after arriving in Egypt, became a platform for disseminating the reformist views of 'Abduh, with Rida even doing some writing on behalf of 'Abduh.[98] A challenge facing researchers on Rida is how to distinguish his thought from that of 'Abduh, especially since the former sought to conceal any differences between his ideas and those of his mentor. An even more perplexing challenge pertains to the fluidity of Rida's thought and his shifting positions on key issues, such as the nature of the caliphate and its role in the life of the Muslim *umma*.[99]

It is beyond the aims of this discussion to engage in a comparative analysis of the thought of 'Abduh and Rida, or to dwell on the ambiguities and inherent tensions in the thought of Rida. What I seek is to identify key aspects of his thought that influenced subsequent mainstream Islamists, three of which warrant further attention: 1) Rida's critical, and at times hostile, stance toward Europe and the West, which was only reinforced by the conduct of the Western allies during World War I and in its immediate aftermath; 2) his emphasis on restoring Islamic unity, by resurrecting the institution of the caliphate; and 3) his gradual embrace of a traditionalist interpretation of Islam that quietly eliminated most of the innovative elements in the thought of 'Abduh.

Rida's Critical Stance toward Europe and the West

Rida's views of Europe and the West were closer to those of Afghani than 'Abduh's. While 'Abduh eventually reconciled himself to the British protectorate over Egypt, Rida's personal disposition, as well his awareness of the increased European meddling in Muslim affairs, placed him on a collision course with Europe and the West. What initially drew the young Rida to Afghani and 'Abduh, at the time when both were forced to flee Egypt for political reasons, was their perceived stance as champions of a political project that revolved around rejuvenating the Muslim *umma* in order to resist European encroachment. Also, in the early 20th century, a confluence of factors reinforced Rida's negative stance toward Europe and the West. For one, Rida was critical of the work of European and American backed missionary groups. While Rida did not fear that these groups would succeed in converting many Muslims to Christianity, what really worried him was that their influence could cause many Muslims to doubt the comprehensiveness of the Islamic message and to seek ways to supplant Islam with European ideas and habits, thus becoming increasingly westernized in their modes of thinking and conduct.

Rida was equally critical of the growing discourse—championed by some European thinkers and politicians as well as by a few westernized, especially Christian, Arab intellectuals, such as Farah Antoun and Shibli Shmayyel— which blamed the backwardness of Muslim societies and people on their rigid adherence to Islam and their rejection of "modern" European notions of secularizing the state and relegating religion to the private sphere. Not only did Rida categorically reject these ideas as utterly unsuitable to Muslim societies, he was also adamant that their propagation served the European project of shattering the Muslim *umma*'s unity by turning it away from its religion, thus removing the last obstacle to its domination and exploitation. British and French conduct during World War I and in its immediate aftermath served only to reinforce Rida's hostility toward the European project, especially for the Arab world.

Although residing in British-dominated Egypt, Rida tacitly supported the Ottoman Empire, since he regarded it as the only remaining independent major Islamic power.[100] This pro-Ottoman stance probably explains why the British authorities in Egypt kept Rida under surveillance during the war years. World War I undoubtedly caused Rida considerable distress for he was neither confident that the declining Ottoman Empire would be able to prevail nor did he endorse its repressive policies in the Arab provinces, especially since the young Turks came to power in 1907–1908. However, Rida did not join the cause of the Arab nationalists, who pinned their hopes on the revolt of Sharif Hussein of Mecca, primarily because he viewed Hussein and his sons as accomplices of the British.[101]

In the immediate years following the Great War, roughly 1919–1921, Rida became heavily embroiled in Syrian politics, first as the President of the Syrian National Congress in 1920, and later as a member of the Syrian-Palestinian delegation that traveled to Geneva in 1921 to protest before the League of Nations the imposition of French and British mandates over Syria and Palestine, respectively.[102] This rather ineffectual immersion into Levantine politics only reinforced Rida's resentment toward the French, and especially toward the British, whom he believed lured the Arabs to revolt against their Muslim brethren, the Turks, with false promises of independence, and subsequently betrayed them to the Zionists in Palestine and the French in Syria.[103]

Although Rida harbored apprehensions about Christianity, his opposition to the West was rooted in political rather than religious causes.[104] It was the West's colonial project, rather than its adherence to Christianity, nominal as that might have been, that infuriated him. Stated otherwise, Rida did not frame the conflict between the Muslim world and the West in religious terms, but primarily in political, and to a lesser extent cultural, terms. In line with Rida, none of the six scholar sheikhs, discussed in the ensuing chapters, viewed Christianity as the principal reason behind Western efforts to dominate the Muslim world. Bahi and Qaradawi did, however, dwell at length on the lingering "crusader" element in Western policy toward the Muslim world, while making a number of references to Western support of Christian missionaries in the Muslim world. Fadlallah's position, on the other hand, closely mirrored that of Rida. As will be seen in the chapter on Fadlallah, he argued that Western policy toward the Muslim world was driven by material interests and had little to do with the West's "forgotten Christian past."

Despite his apprehensions about the West, at no point in his long career did Rida specifically advocate jihad against any Western country, including Britain and France, to drive them out of the Middle East and other parts of the Muslim world; nor did he condone acts of violence against Western interests, Westernized Muslims who criticized the *sharia*, or Arab Christian intellectuals who often criticized Muslims for rejecting the separation of religion from the state. Rida, however, did respond to the latter two groups with equally forceful polemics. Rida's confrontation with the West, and its perceived local allies, the Westernized Muslims and local Christians, was, thus, a rhetorical one and did not translate itself into the realm of praxis.

At the theoretical level, which is central to this study, Rida distinguished between defensive jihad, which he approved of in theory, and offensive jihad that aimed at invading the lands of others and/or forcefully converting them to Islam, which he categorically rejected, on the ground that there can be no compulsion in religion. Without exception, all the scholar sheikhs covered in this book adhered to this distinction, a distinction that can be partly attributed to the legacy of Rida and, undoubtedly, 'Abduh's.

Rida's Political Project: Resurrecting the Caliphate

Rida wrote more prolifically on political subjects and was more immersed in the politics of his day than his mentor 'Abduh ever was or wished to be. While 'Abduh, as quoted by none other than Rida, stated that "whatever politics penetrates it corrupts,"[105] the young Rida once observed that the chief ailment from which the Muslim *umma* suffered was that its "'*ulama* knew little about politics, while its' political leaders knew little about religion."[106] Rida was an early champion of the contemporary Islamist doctrine that religion and politics cannot be separated in Islam. References to Islam as providing both "spiritual guidance" and a "civilizing social policy" abound in Rida's discourse.[107] While 'Abduh probably subscribed to this view too, he consciously refrained from purporting a religiously-informed reading of politics. Rida, on the other hand, was a pioneer among contemporary Islamists in maintaining such a reading, which largely explains the endurance of his legacy.

The resurrection of the institution of the caliphate was at the core of Rida's political project. While this is not the place to review Rida's conceptualization of the caliphate, addressed by other researchers, two observations are in order. To start with, as argued by Mahmoud Haddad, Rida's views on the caliphate changed with time, largely a result of changed historic circumstances.[108] Equally importantly, as emphasized by Mahmoud Haddad, Hourani, and Kerr, at no point in time did Rida articulate an internally consistent theory of the caliphate. His construct of the caliphate suffered from certain ambiguities and latent tensions that emanated from at least four sources.[109] First, Rida did not specify the exact responsibilities of the caliph in the religious and temporal domains. That is, would the caliph be primarily responsible for interpreting the meaning of the *sharia*, leaving it to others to derive specific laws from it and then implement them, or should his office also be vested with legislative powers as well as the means to enforce the implementation of the *sharia*-derived laws in the various Muslim societies? Second, Rida was equally unclear with respect to the role of *shura* (consultation) in the proposed caliphate.[110] Was the caliph obligated to follow the advice provided by *ahl al-'aqd wa al-hal* (individuals endowed with power and authority), or did he merely have to solicit their advice and then make his own judgment based on his own *ijtihad*? Third, Rida failed to delineate the relationship between the caliph and existing Muslim rulers. Should the caliph have formal authority over these rulers, or would his role be confined to settling disputes among them and fostering cooperation? Fourth, was the caliphate simply an office, an institution, or was it the epicenter of the universal Islamic state? While Rida grappled with these thorny questions, he failed to provide satisfactory answers to any of them. Undoubtedly, the ambiguities in his construct of the caliphate, and the growing awareness of the difficulties associated with resurrecting even a weak form of the caliphate, encouraged subsequent mainstream Islamists to quietly abandon the notion of the caliphate altogether.

Finally, Rida held a largely instrumental view of the caliphate. Rida's ultimate goal was to restore the political, socioeconomic and cultural unity of the *umma*, after it became fragmented as a result of a myriad of forces, particularly: 1) colonialism, 2) the growth of "secular" nationalism, such as Egyptian nationalism and Arab nationalism, 3) the growing internal divisions within the *umma*, such as those between Sunnis and Shia, and 4) the breakup of the Ottoman Empire and formal dissolution of the caliphate. Thus, despite the centrality of the caliphate to Rida's political project, it was a means to an end, the chief, indeed indispensable, instrument for reviving the unity of the *umma*, conceived along material lines, whether political, socioeconomic, or cultural lines. While, as noted, subsequent

Islamists phased out the notion of the caliphate, they subscribed to Rida's quest for restoring the political, socioeconomic and linguistic unity of the *umma*. The ensuing chapters explore their blueprints for restoring such coveted unity.

Rida's Growing Conservatism

There is general consensus among researchers that Rida became increasingly drawn to conservative interpretations of Islam in the period following 'Abduh's death in 1905, partly reflected in his ultimate embrace of the Hanbali School of jurisprudence (from Ibn Hanbal, who died in 854), which was more strict than the Hanafi school (From Abu Hanifa, who died in 767) that was predominant in Egypt and to which 'Abduh belonged.[111] Concurrently, Rida had a change of heart about Wahhabism, which he earlier criticized, but in later years came to endorse.[112] What attracted Rida to Wahhabism, and to the new kingdom of Saudi Arabia with which it became identified, was its emphasis on the strict enforcement of *sharia* law. At that stage, Rida had come to fully embrace the conservative view that Islam was a "religion of 'sovereignty and politics and government' and Islamic law could not be reformed unless the Islamic polity is remade."[113] Similarly, Rida's discourse grew more apologetic and more polemical as Rida became preoccupied with demonstrating that Islam represented a comprehensive, self-sufficient system of ethics and social conduct that was superior to any other system. This conservative bent was to become an integral component of Rida's legacy, and influenced the discourses of subsequent Sunni mainstream Islamists.

Thus, it can be concluded that Rida's thought comprised a complex, though internally inconsistent, blend of reformism and conservatism. On the one hand, he argued in favor of the compatibility of reason and revelation; the importance of dialog with non-Muslims, albeit this dialog frequently degenerated to polemics; the permissibility of borrowing from the West in the scientific and technological fields; the necessity of *ijtihad*, without clearly spelling out who was entitled to engage in *ijtihad*; and the need to balance the power of the ruler with that of the representatives of the *umma*. However, most significant for the purpose of this study, Rida was an early champion of the doctrine of defensive jihad.

On the other hand, Rida grew increasingly drawn to rigid interpretations of Islam, namely Hanbalism and Wahhabism.[114] He also became more forceful in advancing the thesis that there can be no separation between religion, law, and politics in Islam, as well as more adamant in insisting on enforcing the *sharia* as the surest way to reform Muslim polities and societies. In brief, his blueprint for reform became increasingly centered on reviving the thought and practices of the *salaf,* the righteous forefathers, whom he primarily defined as the first generation of Muslims.

Conclusion

This chapter provided an overview of the political and social thought of the three main founders of the moderate-reformist, mainstream, strand in political Islam, as a prelude to a discussion of how subsequent generations of moderate-reformist scholar sheikhs built on their ideas to provide a mainstream Islamist perspective on international relations. It is true that Afghani, 'Abduh and Rida did not address issues of international relations at any length. Nevertheless, their views on the possibility, indeed desirability, of peace in relations between Muslim and non-Muslim states, as long as this peace was not a guise for the domination and exploitation of Muslims; the defensive purposes of jihad; and the impermissibility of coercing non-Muslims to embrace Islam became hallmarks of the discourses of subsequent mainstream Islamists.

Writing against the backdrop of the decline and then the demise of the Ottoman Empire and the intensified European intervention in the Muslim world, the three scholar sheikhs of the first generation had to grapple with the subject of Islamic unity. Of the three, only Rida lived to see the collapse of the Ottoman Empire and the division of its remaining Arab territories. In his later years, Rida was preoccupied with devising schemes for restoring Islamic unity by resurrecting the institution of the caliphate. While subsequent mainstream Islamists shared his preoccupation with rebuilding Islamic unity, they gradually moved away from the idea of the caliphate, *de facto,* if not *de jure.*

Notes

1 For studies of Tahtawi, see Albert Hourani, *Arabic Thought in the Liberal Age: 1798–1939* (Cambridge: Cambridge University Press, 1983) (First published in 1962), 67–83; Muhammad 'Imara, *Rifa'a al-Tahtawi: Ra'id al-Tanwir fi al-'Asr al-Hadith* (Rifa'a al-Tahtawi: The Pioneer of Enlightenment in the Modern Period) (Cairo: Dar al-Shuruq, 2009); and Qadri Qal'aji, *Thalatha min A'lam al-Huriya: Jamal al-Din al-Afghani, Muhammad 'Abduh and Sa'd Zaghlul* (Three Luminaries for Freedom: Jamal al-Din al-Afghani, Muhammad 'Abduh, and Sa'd Zaghlul) (Beirut: Sharikat al-Matbou'at lil-Nashr wa al-Tawzi', 1994), 3–150.

2 Myriam Salama-Carr, "Negotiating Conflict: Rifā'a Rāfi' al-TahTāwī and the Translation of the 'Other' in Nineteenth-century Egypt," *Social Semiotics* 17, no. 2 (2007): 213–27. Doi: https://doi.org/10.1080/10350330701311496, 213.
3 Hourani, *Arabic Thought*, 81.
4 Shavit, *Scientific and Political Freedom in Islam*, 2.
5 John Esposito, *Islam and Politics* (4th ed.) (Syracuse, NY: Syracuse University Press, 1984), 50.
6 Bernard Haykel, "On the Nature of Salafi Thought and Action," in *Global Salafism*, ed. Meijer, 33–51, 45. Haykel uses the term "enlightened salafis" to refer to the three figures.
7 Muhammad 'Imara, *al-A'mal al-Kamila lil-Imam al-Sheikh Muhammad 'Abduh* (The Complete Works of the Imam Sheikh Muhammad 'Abduh) (Cairo: Dar al-Shuruq, 1993).
8 Shiraz Maher, *Salafi-Jihadism: The History of an Idea* (Oxford and New York: Oxford University Press, 2016), 50.
9 Roel Meijer, "Salafism, Doctrine and Practice," in *Political Islam*, ed. Hroub, 37–60, 45; and "Introduction," in *Global Salafism*, ed. Meijer, 1–32, 7.
10 Shavit, *Scientific and Political Freedom in Islam*, 12.
11 Wagemakers, *A Quietist Jihadi*, 5–7.
12 Wagemakers, *A Quietist Jihadi*, 6–7.
13 Haykel, "On the Nature of Salafi Thought and Action," 45.
14 Hourani, *Arabic Thought*, 116.
15 Hourani, *Arabic Thought*, 112.
16 Ayoob, *Many Faces of Political Islam*, 133.
17 Nikki Keddie, *Sayyid Jamal al-Din "al-Afghani": A Political Biography* (Berkeley: University of California Press, 1972), 2. See also Keddie, *An Islamic Response to Imperialism: Political and Religious Writings of Sayyid Jamal ad-Din "al-Afghani"* (Berkeley: Berkeley University Press, 1983). First published in 1968; and Keddie, "Sayyid Jamal al-Din al-Afghani," in *Pioneers of Islamic Revival*, ed. Ali Rahnema (London: Zed Books, 1994), 11–29.
18 Keddie, *Sayyid Jamal al-Din al-Afghani*, 10–36. In addition to Keddie's works, the section on Afghani is based on the following works: Hourani, *Arabic Thought*, esp. 103–129; Esposito, *Islam and Politics*, 48–50; and Qal'aji, *Thalatha min A'lam al-Huriya*, 9–122.
19 P. J. Vatikiotis, *The History of Modern Egypt from Muhammad Ali to Mubarak* (4th ed.) (Baltimore: The Johns Hopkins University Press, 1991), 136; 'Imara, *al-A'mal al-Kamila*, 26.
20 'Imara, *al-A'mal al-Kamila*, 73–76.
21 'Imara, *al-A'mal al-Kamila*, 28–29.
22 Abu Zahra, *al-Wihda al-Islamiya*, 245.
23 Bahi, *al-Fikr al-Islami al-Hadith*, 75.

24 Bahi, *al-Fikr al-Islami al-Hadith*, esp. 76–77.
25 'Imara, *al-A'mal al-Kamila*, 31. Since 'Abduh did not know Persian, the translation must have been drafted by Abu Trab, with 'Abduh putting it in its final form. Keddie, *An Islamic Response to Imperialism*, x.
26 Keddie, *An Islamic Response to Imperialism*, provides one of the most sophisticated treatments of the piece, as well as a translation from the original Persian, 130–74.
27 Hourani, *Arabic Thought*, 112.
28 Hourani, *Arabic Thought*, 113.
29 Hourani, *Arabic Thought*, 114.
30 Hourani, *Arabic Thought*, 114.
31 Hourani, *Arabic Thought*, 115.
32 Esposito, *Islam and Politics*, 50.
33 Esposito, *Islam and Politics*, 50.
34 For the influence of these developments on Afghani, see Roy Jackson, *Mawlana Mawdudi and Political Islam: Authority and the Islamic State* (London and New York: Routledge, 2011), 101–02.
35 Hourani, *Arabic Thought*, 113.
36 M. Raquibuz Zaman, "Islamic Perspectives on Territorial Boundaries and Autonomy," in *Islamic Political Ethics: Civil Society, Pluralism and Conflict*, ed. Suhail Hashmi (Princeton: Princeton University Press, 2002), 79–101, 89.
37 Keddie, *An Islamic Response to Imperialism*.
38 Ayoob, *Many Faces of Political Islam*, 134; Keddie, *An Islamic Response to Imperialism*, esp. 55–60.
39 Qal'aji, *Thalatha min A'lam al-Huriya*, 122–23.
40 Keddie, *An Islamic Response to Imperialism*, 12, 20, 24 and Keddie, "Sayyid Jamal al-Din al-Afghani," 18–19.
41 John Kelsay, *Arguing the Just war in Islam* (Cambridge, Massachusetts and London: Harvard University Press, 2007), 79.
42 Keddie, *An Islamic Response to Imperialism*, esp. 40–42; and Jackson, *Mawlana Mawdudi*, 102–03.
43 Jackson, *Mawlana Mawdudi*, 102.
44 Hourani, *Arabic Thought*, 129.
45 Bahi, *al-Fikr al-Islami al-Hadith*, 82.
46 'Imara, *al-A'mal al-Kamila*, 40.
47 'Imara, *al-A'mal al-Kamila lil-Imam al-Sheikh Muhammad 'Abduh*, 39–42.
48 Hourani, *Arabic Thought*, 112.
49 Qal'aji, *Thalatha min A'lam al-Huriya*, 122–23.
50 Bahi, *al-Fikr al-Islami al-Hadith*, esp. 78–81.
51 Bahi, *al-Fikr al-Islami al-Hadith*, 83.
52 See, inter alia, Bahi, *al-Fikr al-Islami al-Hadith*, esp. 78–82.
53 There is some ambiguity regarding the dates of Afghani's stay in Europe. What we know is that he had a relatively long sojourn in Paris, starting in 1879, and

The Founding Generation: Jamal Al-Din al-Afghani | 59

then he moved around various European capitals, ending in St. Petersburg between 1887 and 1889. For Afghani's travels, see, inter alia, Keddie, *An Islamic Response to Imperialism*, 14–33; Keddie, "Sayyid Jamal al-Din al-Afghani," esp. 12–13 and Bahi, *al-Fikr al-Islami al-Hadith*, 75.

54 Keddie, "Sayyid Jamal al-Din al-Afhani," 25.
55 Malcolm H. Kerr, *Islamic Reform: The Political and legal Theories of Muhammad 'Abduh and Rashid Rida* (Berkeley and Los Angeles: Berkeley University Press, 1966), 103–52, 104. In addition to the excellent study by Kerr, the section on 'Abduh is mainly based on Hourani, *Arabic Thought*, 130–60; Mark Sedgwick, *Makers of the Muslim World: Muhammad 'Abduh* (Oxford: Oneworld Publications, 2010); 'Imara, *al-A'mal al-Kamila*; and Qal'aji, *Thalatha min A'lam al-Huriya*, 151–315.
56 Hourani, *Arabic Thought*, 130.
57 It is worth noting, though, that unlike boys his age (and some of the scholar sheikhs discussed in this book) 'Abduh did not attend the local kuttab, but learned reading and writing and started memorizing the Quran at home. At the age of 14 years, he was sent to the Ahmadi mosque in Tanta (which Abu Zahra also attended) and then continued his education at al-Azhar, receiving his *'alimiya* degree in 1877. He then taught for a short while at al-Azhar. See Sedgwick, *Makers of the Muslim World*, 1–14.
58 Sedgwick, *Makers of the Muslim World*, 8–14.
59 Hourani, *Arabic Thought*, 130.
60 Kerr, *Islamic Reform*, esp. 151–52.
61 Shavit, *Scientific and Political Freedom*, esp. 20–27. Bahi's brief discussion of the relationship between revelation and reason in the thought of 'Abduh is in line with Kerr's treatment. Bahi, *al-Fikr al-Islami al-Hadith*, 150–61.
62 Haj acknowledges the influence of Said, but maintains that her critique is more extensive. See, in particular, Haj, *Reconfiguring Islamic Tradition*, 2–3.
63 Kerr, *Islamic Reform*, 109.
64 Kerr, *Islamic Reform*, esp. 107–10.
65 Kerr, *Islamic Reform*, 111–13.
66 Kerr, *Islamic Reform*, 120.
67 kerr, *Islamic Reform*, 126.
68 Keddie, *An Islamic Response to Imperialism*, 9–11.
69 Keddie, *An Islamic Response to Imperialism*, xiii.
70 Keddie, *An Islamic response to Imperialism*, xv.
71 'Imara, *al-A'mal al-Kamila*, 48–49.
72 'Imara, *al-A'mal al-Kamila*, 49.
73 'Imara, *al-A'mal al-Kamila*, 49.
74 'Imara, *al-A'mal al-Kamila*, 49; Yvonne Haddad, "Muhammad Abduh: Pioneer of Islamic Reform," in *Pioneers of Islamic Revival*, ed. Ali Rahnema (London: Zed Books, 1994), 30–63, 7–38.
75 For the 'Urabi revolt see P. J. Vatikiotis, *The Modern History of Egypt* (New York and Washington: Frederick A. Praeger publishers, 1969), 126–75.

76 'Imara, *al-A'mal al-Kamila*, 49–50.
77 'Imara, *al-A'mal al-Kamila*, 27–28.
78 'Imara, *al-A'mal al-Kamila*, 28–29.
79 The literature on this rather short work is rather extensive. See, in particular, Hourani, *Arabic Thought*, esp. 145–47, Sedgwick, *Makers of the Muslim World*, esp. 63–70.
80 'Imara, *al-A'mal al-Kamila*, 32.
81 'Imara, *al-A'mal al-Kamila*, 22, 37–84.
82 *AL-Waqa'i' al-Misriyya* (the Egyptian Gazette), No. 952, October 1880; reprinted in 'Imara, *al-A'mal al-Kamila*, 303–11, 303.
83 Imara, *al-A'mal al-Kamila*, 54.
84 Keddie, *An Islamic Response to Imperialism*, xvi.
85 Jackson, *Mawlana Mawdudi*, 104.
86 Hourani, *Arabic Thought*, 151.
87 Hourani, *Arabic Thought*, esp. 140–44.
88 Yvonne Haddad, "Muhammad Abduh," esp. 42–43.
89 Haj, *Reconfiguring Islamic Tradition*, 86–90.
90 See especially Sedgwick, *Makers of the Muslim World*, 113–14.
91 Haj, *Reconfiguring Islamic Tradition*, 27.
92 Jackson, *Mawlana Mawdudi*, 105.
93 This section on Rida is primarily based on the following English sources: Hourani, *Arabic Thought*, 222–44; Kerr, *Islamic Reform*, 153–208; Simon A. Wood, *Christian Criticisms, Islamic Proofs: Rashid Rida's Modernist Defence of Islam* (Oxford: Oneworld Publications, 2007); Mahmoud Haddad, "Arab Religious Nationalism in the Colonial Era: Rereading Rashid Rida's Ideas on the Caliphate," 253–77; Eliezer Tauber, "Three Approaches, One Idea: Religion and State in the Thought of 'Abd al-Rahman al-Kawakibi, Najib 'Azuri and Rashid Rida," *British Journal of Middle Eastern Studies* 21, no. 2 (1994): 190–98; Daniel A. Stolz, "By Virtue of Your Knowledge: Scientific Materialism and the Fatwas of Rashid Rida," *Bulletin of SOAS* 75, no. 2 (2012): 223–47; and Zaman, *Modern Islamic Thought*. Two Arabic sources were also highly useful. Al-Amir Shakib Arslan, *al-Sayyid Rashid Rida aw Ikha' Arba'in Sanna* (Sayyed Rashid Rida: The Brotherhood of Forty Years, Vols. 1–3) (Mukhtara, Mount Lebanon: al-dar al-Taqadummuua, 2010; introduction by Wajih Kawtharani) and Rashid Rida, *al-Khilafa* (the Caliphate) (Cairo: Mu'assat Hindawi lil-Ta'lim wa al-Thaqafa, 2012; book was first published in 1923).
94 Haj, *Reconfiguring Islamic Tradition*, 102.
95 Wood, *Christian Criticisms, Islamic Proofs*, 23–24; Tauber, "Three Approaches, One Idea," 195; Zaman, *Modern islamic Thought*, 4.
96 Arslan, *al-Sayyid Rashid Rida*, Vol. 1, 24–25, 93.

97 Sedgwick, *Makers of the Muslim World*, 88–91; Mahmoud Haddad, "Arab Religious Nationalism in the Colonial Era: Rereading Rashid Rida's Ideas on the Caliphate," 253–77; Eliezer Tauber, "Three Approaches, One Idea: Religion and State in the Thought of 'Abd al-Rahman al-Kawakibi, Najib 'Azuri and Rashid Rida," *British Journal of Middle Eastern Studies* 21, no. 2 (1994): 190–98; and Daniel A. Stolz, "By Virtue of Your Knowledge: Scientific Materialism and the Fatwas of Rashid Rida," *Bulletin of SOAS* 75, no. 2 (2012): 223–47.
98 Wood, *Christian Criticisms, Islamic Proofs*, 26–27; Tauber, "Three Approaches, One Idea," 195; Arslan, *Al-Sayyid Rashid Rida*, Vol. 1, 40–41.
99 For this fluidity, see, for example, Mahmoud Haddad, "Arab Religious Nationalism" esp. 253–54.
100 Mahmoud Haddad, "Arab Religious Nationalism," 256.
101 Mahmoud Haddad, "Arab Religious Nationalism," 264–65.
102 Hourani, *Arabic Thought*, 226–27; Arslan, *Al-Sayyid Rashid Rida*, Vol. 1, 128–32.
103 Arslan, *Al-Sayyid Rashid Rida*, Vol. 1, 131–35.
104 For Rida's views on Christianity, see Wood, *Christian Criticisms, Islamic Proofs*, esp. 35–47.
105 Mahmoud Haddad, "Arab Religious Nationalism," 264–65.
106 Arslan, *al-Sayyid Rashid Rida*, Vol. 1, 91.
107 Rida, *al-Khilafa*, 9.
108 Mahmoud Haddad, "Arab Religious Nationalism."
109 While in line with the aforementioned secondary sources on Rida, this section on Rida's construct of the caliphate largely reflects my own reading of Rida's principal work on the subject, *al-Khilafa* (the Caliphate).
110 For Rida's discussion of *al-shura* see *al-khilafa*, esp. 17–35.
111 Hourani, *Arabic Thought*, 239, Haj, *Reconfiguring Islamic Tradition*, 150; and Zaman, *Modern Islamic Thought*, 11.
112 Wood, Christian *Criticisms, Islamic Proofs*, 28–29.
113 Hourani, *Arabic Thought*, 239.
114 Hourani, *Arabic Thought*, 231–33, 239.

3

The Second Generation: Mahmoud Shaltut and Muhammad Abu Zahra

Introduction

The first of two chapters on the contributions of the scholar sheikhs of the second generation, this chapter examines the international relations discourses of Sheikhs Mahmoud Shaltut and Muhammad Abu Zahra, while the subsequent chapter is devoted to the discourse of a slightly younger associate, Sheikh Muhammad al-Bahi. Whereas all six scholar sheikhs examined in this book share a great deal in terms of their outlooks on international relations, the views and arguments of Shaltut and Abu Zahra are so similar, actually almost identical, that it makes perfect sense to consider them jointly. Beginning with short biographies of the two, the chapter then discusses their principal arguments with regard to the underpinning principles of international relations and the relations between Muslims and non-Muslims; the purposes of jihad, the rules of fighting in Islam, and the importance of military preparedness; and the road to Islamic unity.

Shaltut and Abu Zahra: Brief Biographies

Mahmoud Muhammad Shaltut was born in a small town in the Bahira governorate in the delta of Egypt.[1] Having memorized the Quran by the age of

13, he began studying at an al-Azhar affiliated religious school in Alexandria. He continued his religious studies at al-Azhar in Cairo, receiving his 'alimiyya degree in 1918. In 1919, he took part in the popular revolt against the British, returning in the same year to teach in Alexandria, where he stayed until around 1927. The following year, he was "promoted" to teach at al-Azhar, at the behest of its reformist head, Sheikh Muhammad Mustafa al-Maraghi, the Sheikh of al-Azhar between 1928 and 1929 and between 1935 and 1945.[2] Shaltut's fortunes were closely tied to those of Sheikh al-Maraghi; when al-Maraghi was forced to resign from the leadership of al-Azhar in 1929 as a result of a dispute with King Fouad, Shaltut, and other *ulama* who backed al-Maraghi were suspended from teaching at al-Azhar.[3] Away from al-Azhar between October 1931 and February 1935, Shaltut worked as a lawyer for the *sharia* courts, with the famous sheikh, 'Ali 'Abd al-Raziq, who was permanently removed from al-Azhar for publishing his highly controversial *al-Islam wa Usul al-Hukm*.[4] After the conflict between the authorities and the *ulama* was resolved, Shaltut returned to al-Azhar, where, in May 1935, al-Maraghi was reappointed as its Sheikh. Shaltut's career quickly advanced after 1935, with al-Maraghi appointing him as director of the *sharia* department at al-Azhar in 1937, and four years later, he became the youngest member of al-Azhar highest body, the Council of Leading *'Ulama (Hay'at Kibar al-'Ulama)*.

As of the mid 1930s and until his appointment as Sheikh of al-Azhar in 1958, Shaltut was at the center of Egypt's religious life, both within and outside the walls of al-Azhar. He lectured extensively on jurisprudence (first at al-Azhar and, as of 1950, at Cairo University as well), contributed numerous editorials to Islamic papers, wrote short treatises, answered questions on juristic matters on the radio, presented at local and international conferences on behalf of al-Azhar, and served on scores of prestigious committees. His multiple engagements, as well as the very broad range of the juristic matters he was interested in, suggest why he failed to produce book-length manuscripts on specific topics.

Shaltut had a close professional and personal relationship with the leading sheikhs of his time, particularly al-Maraghi; Mustafa 'Abd al-Raziq, brother of 'Ali 'Abd al-Razeq, and Sheikh al-Azhar between 1945 and 1947; and 'Abd al-Majid Saleem, sheikh al-Azhar between 1950 and 1951 and then in 1952. All three sheikhs were pupils of 'Abduh and followed his reformist path. Thus, while Shaltut himself did not study with 'Abduh, he developed a strong intellectual bond with some of his most prominent pupils.

The multiple achievements of Shaltut, including the recognition of his name, his good rapport with the leading *'ulama* and his conciliatory character, all contributed to the career path that eventually placed him at the helm of al-Azhar in 1958. After the passage of law 103 on the reorganization of al-Azhar, covered in detail in Chapter 4, Shaltut became its first Sheikh to go by the title of the Grand Imam (*al-Imam al-Akbar*).[5] However, Shaltut's appetite for reform seems to have waned after 1958, for despite being Sheikh al-Azhar, he was not involved in drawing up Law 103. After its passage, he began quarreling with his former protégé, Sheikh Muhammad al-Bahi, over its implementation.

The conflict between these two prominent sheikhs was largely over respective jurisdiction. As the founding director of al-Azhar University, appointed to the post by President Jamal (Gamal) Abdel Nasser (hereafter Nasser) and not by Shaltut, Bahi sought institutional autonomy from the mother organization, but Shaltut was reluctant to grant him free reign in managing the teaching duties and ranks of the *'ulama*. The relationship grew more acrimonious after Bahi became Minister of Religious Endowments and the Affairs of al-Azhar. Bahi believed that, in accordance with law 103, the Grand Imam should focus on articulating al-Azhar's stance on pivotal issues facing Egypt and the Muslim *umma* and on spreading the message of Islam, while delegating administrative and financial duties to a competent staff. However, Shaltut felt that the more junior Bahi was using his authority as Minister to undermine the role of Sheikh al-Azhar. A rigid bureaucrat, Bahi objected, in particular, to Shaltut's reliance on his relatives, his in-laws according to Bahi and Qaradawi,[6] to manage the office of Sheikh al-Azhar. Shaltut was to carry his grudge against Bahi to the grave.

The conflict between Shaltut and Bahi had nothing to do with ideology as both scholar sheikhs were mainstream Islamists who believed in reforming Islam from within, opposed socialism and materialism, embraced peaceful coexistence with non-Muslims, and subscribed to a defensive view of jihad and an incremental peaceful path to Islamic unity. Equally important, both believed that the two Great Wars of the 20th century and the ensuing Cold War emanated from the limitations and the tensions of materialist ideologies.

Stylistically, Bahi's writings were influenced by European philosophy and reflected significant familiarity with the political and socioeconomic systems in the capitalist West and socialist East, whereas Shaltut's discourse was far more traditional, as he relied primarily on the Quran to back his original arguments about contemporary affairs. Shaltut is best remembered for his bold, accommodating stance toward the Shias, recognizing in a controversial fatwa that Twelver Shiism (Imami Shiism) represented a *mazhhab* (a juristic school), in Islam that was on a par with the four Sunni-recognized juristic schools.[7] While the weight of the evidence suggests that Shaltut did issue such a fatwa, a few prominent

Sunni sheikhs, including Sheikh Qaradawi who was close to Shaltut, dispute its existence.[8] However, what is worth emphasizing is that Shaltut embraced the idea of bringing Sunnis and Shias closer together in the hope of restoring the unity of the Muslim *umma*.[9] Unlike several sheikhs who only paid lip service to the notion, Shaltut did engage in a number of initiatives to bring about such a rapprochement.

Shaltut was also criticized by hardline Islamists for his conciliatory attitude toward Christians and Jews. For Shaltut, the People of the Book, mainly Jews and Christians, who followed their own scriptures, were not unbelievers (*kufar*), even if they rejected the call to Islam for whatever reason. At the risk of oversimplifying, Shaltut restricts the term *kufar* to those who deny the existence of God and the afterlife. The obvious corollary of the above is that since Jews and Christians believe in God and in the afterlife, they are not *kufar*. Building on this logic, Qaradawi notes that Jews and Christians are *kufar* in a relative, rather than an absolute, sense. Their *kufr* is relative because they only reject the message of Islam, without rejecting God's existence and the afterlife.[10]

Abu Zahra was born on March 29, 1898 in *al-Mahallah al-Kubra*, a large town in the *Gharbieh* province in Lower Egypt, a province from which Qaradawi also hailed.[11] He memorized the Quran at the local *kuttab* and then studied at the school of al-Ahmadi mosque in Tanta. In 1916, he ranked first among applicants to the Cairo-based Institute for Training Sharia Judges (*Madrasat al-Qada' al-Shar'i*), from which he graduated in 1924.[12] Three more years of formal education followed at the equally renowned *Dar al-'Ulum*. Abu Zahra did not study at al-Azhar, but his first teaching assignment was at its Faculty of Theology (*Kuliyat Usul al-Din*). A few years younger than Shaltut, Abu Zahra came from the same Egyptian provincial milieu. Abu Zahra's career at Cairo University mirrored that of Shaltut at al-Azhar, with each ending up as the head of the *sharia* department at his respective institution. While Shaltut eventually became the Grand Imam of al-Azhar, Abu Zahra was appointed in 1962 to al-Azhar's highest body. The two scholar sheikhs were to cross paths on multiple occasions. Both Shaltut and Abu Zahra were *sharia* specialists, as were Qaradawi and Zuhaili after them, but while their views on international relations were very similar, they did not see eye to eye on every issue.

In a widely reported incident, Abu Zahra publicly challenged Shaltut's fatwa on the lawfulness of dealing with conventional banks that paid and charged interest rates.[13] Abu Zahra argued that Shaltut's fatwa legitimated financial transactions that constituted modern forms of usury (*riba*).[14] Abu Zahra went on to publish a manuscript on the prohibition of usury in Islam, in which he criticized Shaltut for his lenient attitude toward the operations of conventional banks without directly naming him.[15] While Shaltut was the first Sheikh al-Azhar to be granted the title of Grand Imam, Abu Zahra's admirers and fellow sheikhs bestowed on him the title of the Imam of his era (*Imam 'asruh*). Qaradawi writes that the renowned Islamist thinker and former member of the Muslim Brotherhood, Sheikh Muhammad al-Ghazali, made this comment on Abu Zahra's books on the four Imams, "Only an Imam is to fit to write about another Imam."[16]

It was at Cairo University that Abu Zahra spent most of his academic career. There, he taught oration (*khutba*) and Islamic law (*sharia*), eventually becoming the head of the *sharia* department.[17] After he retired from teaching in 1958, he was appointed to the prestigious Islamic Research Academy (*Majmaʿ al-Buhuth al-Islamiyya*) at al-Azhar in 1962, a position he held until his death in 1974.[18] Abu Zahra wrote over forty books and essays.[19] While his writings covered a broad range of issues, he is mainly remembered for his eight books on prominent classic and post-classic Muslim jurisprudents, four of which focused on the lives and thought of the founders of the four principal legal schools in Sunni Islam (Imams Malik, Abu-Hanifa, al-Shafiʿ, and ibn-Hanbal),[20] while the other four dealt with Ibn Taymiyya,[21] Ibn-Hazm,[22] and the Shia Imams Zaid Ibn-ʿAli[23] and his brother Jaʿfar al-Sadiq.[24] Abu Zahra's detailed and respectful treatment of the opinions of prominent Shia Imams attest to his recognition of the Shias as an integral part of the Muslim *umma*.[25]

Abu Zahra's stance toward the Shias coincides with that of Shaltut. Both Shaltut and Abu Zahra passed away prior to the 1978 Islamic revolution in Iran, and so did not live to witness the revolution's generally adverse repercussions on Sunni–Shia relations. Zuhaili and even more so Qaradawi, of the third generation, adopted a more critical stance toward the Shias. Their criticisms, however, mainly focused on alleged attempts by the Shias to spread their *mazhhab* among Sunnis (see Chapter 6 on Zuhaili). Of the five Sunni scholar Sheikhs examined in this work, Qaradawi stands out as sometimes a harsh critic of Shiism, but even Qaradawi acknowledges, without any equivocation, that the Shias constitute an integral part of the Muslim *umma*.

The Underpinning Principles of International Relations

Peace is the basic principle (*al-asl*) or the principal condition (*al-hala al-asliya*) in the relations between Muslim and non-Muslim societies, while war is the exception. This simple statement captures the essence of Abu Zahra and Shaltut's construct of international relations, with the works of the two scholar sheikhs including ample references to this key claim. In the few pages devoted to international relations in his book, *Islam: Doctrine and Sharia*, Shaltut refers to peace as the guiding principle, or principal condition, in international relations at least three times.[26] Similarly, Abu Zahra's *International Relations in Islam* includes a section demonstrating that peace is the original condition in relations with non-Muslims. Abu Zahra argues that "Islam affirms that peace is one of the principles of relations between states." He goes on to argue that Islam "respects the right of every state to exist and its rights to be the master of its own affairs and to defend its territory and its sovereignty."[27] Abu Zahra further clarifies this position by stating that "undoubtedly in Islam war is not the principal condition (*al-hala al-asliya*) in international relations."[28] Abu Zahra and Shaltut anchor the assertion that peace is the basic principle in several Quranic verses, particularly 2:208 and 4:90.[29]

While all the scholar sheikhs reviewed in this text emphasize the centrality of peace to international relations, this theme is far more dominant in the discourses of Shaltut, Abu Zahra, and Zuhaili. Bahi, Qaradawi, and Fadlallah, on the other hand, are more skeptical about the prospects of preserving international peace over the long haul. As will be argued further in the conclusion, the first three scholar sheikhs are closer in their views to the liberal-institutionalist (or liberal internationalist) school of IR, while the latter three are closer to realism in their outlook. These comparisons are important for a better contextualization of the international relations perspectives of mainstream Islamists, by relating them to the dominant paradigms in the IR field. They should not be over-emphasized, though, especially since none of the six scholar sheikhs, including the German-educated Bahi, consciously engages with any of the Western academic perspectives on IR.

What is the purview of international relations? How is international peace to be preserved or restored after war, bearing in mind that in the views of Shaltut and Abu Zahra, peace is the basic principle, or principal existing condition, in relations between human societies?[30] What are the requisites of international peace? This following section focuses on how Shaltut and Abu Zahra address these pivotal, interrelated questions.

The Purview of International Relations

At the outset, it is essential to clarify one key concept. For Shaltut, Abu Zahra, and the other contemporary mainstream Islamists, international relations pertain to relations between Muslim and non-Muslim societies, while relations among Muslim societies themselves are viewed as internal matters that concern the one Muslim *umma* alone. The latter, thus, lie outside the proper purview of international relations. Anchoring their argument in Quranic verse 49:9,[31] Abu Zahra and Shaltut maintain that the Quran provides the mechanisms for resolving armed conflicts among Muslims, first through mediation, and then through force against the aggressor if mediation fails.[32] What is quintessential is that all contemporary Islamists, whether mainstream or radical, deny non-Muslim states or groups any pretext to intervene in conflicts among Muslims.

Mainstream Islamists acknowledge, *de facto* albeit not *de jure*, the division of the Muslim world into several independent states. Nevertheless, in their international relations discourses, they adhere to the notion of a single Muslim *umma* represented by one Islamic government or state, whose existence is assumed for the sake of argument, rather than proven. Stated otherwise, the principal unit of analysis for contemporary mainstream Islamists is the one Islamic society or Islamic state. Thus, while the terms "Islamic state" and "Islamic society" in the singular permeate their discourses, we rarely encounter them in the plural, i.e., as "Islamic states" and "Islamic societies." Shaltut, for example, does not hesitate to depict the Muslim community that the Prophet founded in Medina as a "state with an international presence," although he is cognizant that the term "state" entered use later.[33] Shaltut, Abu Zahra, and contemporary Islamists employ a range of plural terms such as *aqalim* or *aqtar* (Muslim provinces); *wulat al-amr* (literally those in charge); *ru'asa'* (heads of state or government) to connote the various Muslim states and their governments. This enables them to avoid the detested term "Islamic states."

In a nutshell, the rules that govern relations among Muslims are different than those that govern relations between Muslims and non-Muslims. Muslims are, thus, obliged to come to the aid of fellow Muslims if attacked, but are not required to do that with non-Muslims, unless they have a mutual defense agreement with them. Shaltut and Abu Zahra's treatment of intra-Muslim relations will be discussed later in this chapter in the section on Islamic unity.

Preserving International Peace

Writing against the backdrop of two devastating world wars and a raging Cold War, while aware of the weaknesses of the newly independent Muslim states, Shaltut and Abu Zahra project a strong aversion to war and a keen interest in preserving international peace. Their discourses include several references to the destruction caused by World War I and World War II and to the dangers to humanity that the then ongoing conflict between the two nuclear superpowers posed. Shaltut, for example, criticizes the "development of new weapons that were designed, by the oppressive powers, for demolition and destruction and for terrorizing humanity (*tarwi'al-insaniya*)." He calls on Muslims to unite in order to protect themselves, and the world, from the prevalent international "foolhardiness (*taysh*) that is extinguishing peace and security, while ravishing virtues (*al-fada'el*) and true religiosity (*al-tadayun al-haq*)."[34]

In a similar vein, Abu Zahra laments the absence of international justice, reprimanding the "major powers for acquiescing to one another's oppression of the weak states."[35] For Abu Zahra, the "law of the jungle" seems to govern the relations between states: "every state transgresses against every other state, except when prevented by its own weakness or by the existence of a non-aggression pact."[36] The two scholar sheikhs anchor this unequivocal embrace of international peace in the Quran and the Sunna, quoting literally all Quranic verses that reject coercion in religion, while calling for peace, dialog, and cooperation with non-Muslims. Since the verses they quote are also referred to by all subsequent mainstream Islamists, the most recurrent of these verses are cited in an endnote.[37]

The first section of Shaltut's most quoted short work, *Fighting in the Light of the Quran*, refutes the notion that Islam historically spread through the sword, i.e., through violence. Noting that it is not permissible to coerce non-Muslims into embracing Islam,[38] Shaltut argues that the appeal of Islam emanates from its simplicity, rationality, and perfect agreement with human nature.[39] Instead of requiring coercion or violence to spread, Islam's principal driver is the forcefulness of its message. Shaltut maintains throughout that the Prophet Muhammad sought peace even with the unbelievers, polytheists, of Arabia and fought them only in order to repel their aggression against the nascent Muslim community and defend the right of Muslims to practice their religion freely.[40] Shaltut also briefly refers to the special bond between the Prophet and his uncle Abi Taleb, who protected him from the harm of Quraysh and acted as his emissary to the polytheists, without ever embracing Islam.[41]

Based on brief interpretations of the Quranic verses noted above, Shaltut arrives at five pivotal conclusions regarding Islam, peace, and freedom of religion.[42] First, the message of Islam, clear and in line with human nature, does not require any coercion to spread.[43] Second, the *sharia*, "whose source is the Quran" and can only be in agreement with God's law for the universe (*sunnat Allah al-kawniya*), leaves it up to the individual to believe or to disbelieve. Third, the *sharia*, similar to previous religious laws, does not permit the use of coercion to impose religion.[44] Shaltut emphasizes that, "There is not a single verse in the Holy Quran that shows or indicates that the purpose of fighting in Islam is to coerce people to embrace it."[45] Elsewhere, he writes that the teachings of Islam "affirm the principle of freedom of belief; and that no human has the authority to impose a certain belief on another human."[46] Fourth, the Prophet was called upon to teach and to warn (*tabligh wa-indhar*) and not to ensure that people believe. Fifth, and most importantly, since the Quran does not recognize the belief of those who are coerced into believing, it is not logical to force people to believe.

Abu Zahra is equally adamant that there can be no coercion in religion, citing the same verses as Shaltut and providing examples from the practices of the Prophet and the first four rightly guided caliphs. Guided by these Quranic verses, Abu Zahra, thus, writes, "These are clear Quranic texts that prove beyond doubt that the wars of the Prophet and of his fine companions after him were brought about by the need to repel aggression; they did not aim at imposing a particular view or religion."[47] Abu Zahra reiterates this assertion again and again, noting that the Prophet objected when a Muslim sought to force some of his children to embrace Islam.[48] More importantly, Abu Zahra, in line with Shaltut, underscores that the Prophet did not fight to coerce others into embracing "his religion," but fought to defend freedom of belief (*huriyat al-i'tiqad*), which is one of the core principles of Islam. Abu Zahra adds that the Prophet fought the Romans (*al-Roum*) not because they were Christian but because they engaged in aggression against Muslims and persecuted subjects who embraced Islam of their own free will.[49]

In summary, the Quran, as interpreted by Shaltut and Abu Zahra, instructs Muslims to respect the religious freedom of non-Muslims and to seek peace and collaboration with them as long as the latter do not attack or threaten to attack Muslims, or forcefully seek to turn them away from Islam. Shaltut and Abu Zahra's contention, unchallenged by any mainstream Islamist, that the respect for religious freedom is a pillar of national and international peace is highly compatible with prevalent "liberal" understandings of the requisites of peace. Abu Zahra, for example, writes that "Islam is keen on preserving the freedoms of the weak, especially their religious freedom." He goes on to emphasize that, "Preserving religious freedom is the chief reason why Muslims fight non-Muslims."[50] Abu Zahra also writes, "Islam is the religion of individual freedom, freedom of thought and freedom of religion."[51] Abu Zahra and Shaltut, thus, embody the mainstream Islamist view that while Islam is universal in scope, calling on all humans to embrace its teachings of their own free volition, Islam is not an imperial religion that seeks material conquest by the sword.[52]

Shaltut addresses issues of international relations in other shorter, lesser-known, tracts that found their way into the two main collections of his work, *al-Islam: 'Aqida wa Sharia* and *Min Tawjihat al-Islam*. The first compendium includes a chapter that is simply titled "International Relations in Islam." It addresses, somewhat briefly, a range of issues in contemporary international relations, with a particular focus on the preservation of international peace. Shaltut commences the chapter by noting that the dawning of Islam ushered a new era in human history and human relations. In colorful language, Shaltut writes, "The light radiating from the rising sun of Islam awakened the human soul, revived human consciousness and provided the individual with guidance to what is good and what is right."[53]

In the same vein, Abu Zahra draws a sharp distinction between conditions in Arabia and the world prior to the dawn of Islam on the one hand, and the teachings of the Quran and the *Sunnah* of the Prophet on the other. Abu Zahra writes that prior to Islam, the "law of the jungle" prevailed in the "relations amongst states and tribes, for every state transgressed against others."[54] Quoting Quranic verses 2:208 and 8:61, Abu Zahra adds that "Islam came to enlighten the world" as it emphasized that "the general principle in relations among states... is peace as stated in the Quran and practiced by the Prophet."[55]

Shaltut, Abu Zahra and mainstream Islamists in general adopt a broad construal of peace, which entails dialog and collaboration, in addition to nonaggression. Based on Quranic verse 5: 2, "join hands in virtue and piety, but join not hands in sin and aggression," Abu Zahra observes that "collaboration is a general principle" in Islam. He, however, cautions that the aim of collaboration should be the promotion of virtue and the public good, and not the fostering of aggression against third parties.[56] Abu Zahra and Shaltut see in the alliance that Prophet Muhammad made with the Jews of Medina an early example of international cooperation, noting that it was the Jews who violated the terms of this alliance by plotting with the polytheist enemies of the Prophet.[57]

Shaltut further notes that Islam proclaimed the unity of humanity, declaring that all human beings are "united in their servitude to the One Lord and united in their descent from the same father [Adam]."[58] In another place, Shaltut writes that the "*sharia* was revealed to Muhammad to serve as the foundation of a universal human edifice that would contribute to the advancement of all of humanity without regard to ethnicity, color or religion."[59] Abu Zahra develops the argument one step further, noting that, according to Islam, all of humanity forms one *umma*. Thus, in his *al-Mujtama' al-Insani fi Dhil al-Islam*, Abu Zahra writes that Islam "regards the whole of humanity as forming one *umma*, without any distinction between one sect or another or one color or another; for all are God's creation and all are descendants of Adam who was from clay."[60] He reiterates this assertion in *al-'Alaqat al-Duwaliya fi al-Islam*, anchoring it in at least three Quranic verses, 2:213, 7:189, and 49:13.[61]

Shaltut's second compendium, *From the Guidance of Islam*, includes equally unequivocal statements on the centrality of peace in human relations. Shaltut states that those who reject the call for peace reject God's guidance. "God wants His worshipers to preserve peace, to call for peace and to spread peace," Shaltut asserts.[62] He also writes that the "Quran was revealed with the aim of reforming the World, and guiding [humans] to the right path, the path of security and peace and of buttressing truth and justice."[63] Elaborating on the meaning of peace, Shaltut stresses that peace should be based on the establishment of justice and freedom in relations between states and should be backed with sufficient power to deter potential aggressors, as called for in verse 8:60 "Prepare against them whatever force and war cavalry you can gather to frighten therewith the enemy of God and your enemy."[64]

Abu Zahra shares this view, emphasizing that unless peace is predicated on justice and freedom, it is a hollow peace.[65] In *al-Mujtama'al-Insani fi Dhil al-islam*, Abu Zahra treats international justice as one of the three branches of justice; the other two being legal justice, i.e., equality before the law and social justice.[66] Abu Zahra thus maintains that establishing the principle of peaceful international relations hinges on establishing other, equally important principles, particularly justice, virtue, tolerance, and the respect of the freedom and independence of all states.[67] In the realm of international relations, justice exists primarily in reciprocal treatment (*al-mu'amala bi al-mithl*) and honoring one's commitments (*al-wafa' bi al-'ahd*).[68]

In one reference, Shaltut describes the type of peace he advocates as armed peace (*al-salam al-musalah*).[69] Although he rarely employs this term that he coined, Shaltut was a strong advocate of military preparedness. Shaltut and Abu Zahra's texts on international relations make ample reference to the necessity of preparing for the eventuality of war, but without provoking one. Their discourses on power and military preparedness are covered below in the section on war and jihad. As will be seen, the scholar sheikhs of the third generation write extensively on the subject of military preparedness, especially in the work on war by Zuhaili or on jihad by Qaradawi and Fadlullah.

Abu Zahra and Shaltut's insistence that peace, rather than war, forms *al-asl* (the basic principle) in relations with non-Muslims leads them to challenge the classic binary division of the world, made by many early and medieval Muslim jurists, into the abode of Islam (*dar al-Islam*), or the abode of peace (*dar al-Salam*), and the abode of war (*dar al-harb*). Giving more thought to the matter than Shaltut, Abu Zahra subscribes to the notion of a single abode of Islam (same as abode of peace), noting that there is a consensus that *dar al-Islam* is the state, in the singular, where authority is vested with Muslims and where strength and power belong to Muslims (*takun al-min'a wa al-quwa fiha lil-Muslimin*).[70] He, however, objects to treating all other territories as forming a uniform and singular abode of war. The binary division of abode of Islam versus abode of war assumes that war, rather than peace, is *al-asl* (the basic principle) or norm in relations with non-Muslims, contrary to Abu Zahra and Shaltut's thesis that peace is the basic principle in such relations.

Drawing on his rich understanding of the views of classic jurists, Abu Zahra turns to the opinions of three prominent classic jurists, Abu Hanifa, Muhammad bin Hassan al-Shaybani,[71] and Imam al-Shafi'i. He contends that the three prominent jurists differentiated between two types of non-Muslim states: states with which Muslims did not have nonaggression pacts, or expected aggression from; and states with which nonaggression pacts existed, or from which aggression was not expected.[72] The latter were clearly not part of the abode of war and constituted a third abode, the abode of covenant or treaty (*dar al-'ahd*). Rather ingeniously, Abu Zahra thus resurrects the classic notion of *dar al-'ahd* to legitimize peaceful and collaborative relations with the overwhelming majority of non-Muslim states.

Most importantly, Abu Zahra notes, though in passing, that since the overwhelming majority of Muslim states joined the United Nations, all non-Muslim states that ratified the UN Charter automatically became part of *dar al-'ahd*.[73] Moreover, he writes that any non-Muslim country that safeguards the lives and properties of Muslims is not part of the abode of war.[74] Treading in the footsteps of Abu Zahra, and building on the notion of *dar al-'ahd*, Qaradawi and particularly Zuhaili provide detailed discussions of relations with different categories of non-Muslim states. As will be argued in Chapter 6, the most radical view on this pivotal matter of how the world is organized was articulated by Zuhaili, who notes that, in light of the growing connectedness of the world, the whole world has become one abode.

It is essential to situate Abu Zahra and Shaltut's emphasis on the centrality of peace in international relations in the context of their broader understanding of the "human condition" (to borrow a term from Hannah Arendt.)[75] A recurrent theme in the discourses of Shaltut and Abu Zahra is that while humanity is one, it is defined by its diversity. Shaltut, for example, refers to Muslims as a community among communities (*jama'a min al-jama'at*).⁷⁶ Abu Zahra has more to say on human diversity, treating it as one of God's universal or cosmic laws (*min sunnan Allah*), as conveyed in Quranic verses 2:213 and 30:22. Guided by these verses, Abu Zahra maintains that God intended the division of humanity into distinct groups and nations so that people would communicate and cooperate for mutual benefit.⁷⁷ For the two scholar sheikhs, international peace emanates from the embrace of human diversity, the recognition of the rights and duties of each nation, and the renunciation of attempts to coerce others into submitting to the will of a particular group or to adopt its convictions, religious or otherwise.

The association between peace and freedom of the state, i.e., freedom from foreign rule and foreign dictation, permeates the discourses of other mainstream Islamists. Bahi, for example, as covered in Chapter 4, predicates international peace, *inter alia*, on respecting the right of Muslim societies to reject both capitalism and socialism as organizational principles and to mold their political and socioeconomic systems on Islam. While mainstream Islamists reject imposing the *sharia* on non-Muslims, they insist, in the same breath, on the freedom of Muslim societies to adopt the *sharia* in organizing their internal affairs. However, the scholar sheikhs examined in this work avoid addressing the thorny question, even if only hypothetically, of what to do if a majority of Muslims, in a majority-Muslim society, reject Islamic rule that is based on the *sharia*. The idea of Muslims willfully rejecting Islamic rule was so alien to the thinking of mainstream Islamists that they refused to even entertain it. Radical Islamists, on the other hand, are more internally consistent since they view most Muslims today to be living under conditions of *jahiliya* (ignorance of Islam). Radical Islamists do not shy away from advocating the use of force to impose Islamic governance and the rule of the *sharia*.

The Requisites of International Peace

Abu Zahra and Shaltut are aware that international peace requires conscious action on the part of those groups that desire its preservation, with bilateral or multilateral treaties constituting the most obvious instrument of preserving it. Abu Zahra thus writes, "The path to the stabilization of international peace lies in security and non-aggression pacts."⁷⁸ Abu Zahra provides more detail, noting that, "Since peace is the original condition, treaties exist either to end a temporary war (*harb 'arida*), and thus return to the condition of perpetual peace, or to affirm peace and strengthen its pillars."⁷⁹ Abu Zahra and Shaltut insist that it is both permissible and desirable for Muslims to enter into treaties with non-Muslims that aim at prohibiting aggression and facilitating exchanges, such as the economic and cultural. Shaltut puts it succinctly by noting, "It is permissible for Muslims to establish as many treaties as they deem fit with non-Muslims, as long as the aim is to maintain the original condition of peace, or to return to peace after ending a war either temporarily or permanently." Shaltut adds that "joint defense agreements directed at repelling a common enemy" are also permissible.[80]

Qaradawi and especially Zuhaili were to follow the same logic as Abu Zahra's and Shaltut's in discussing in significant detail the history of international treaties in Islam and their role in the organization of relations with non-Muslims. Abu Zahra and Shaltut can, thus, be regarded as the pioneers in articulating the mainstream Islamist view on international treaties. Their perspective emphasizes at least seven principal points.[81] First, it is both permissible and desirable for Muslim societies to enter into treaties with non-Muslim societies, whether limited in time or permanent, as long as these treaties do not violate any precept of the *sharia*. In this regard, Shaltut quotes the following prophetic hadith to underscore that no treaty can include a provision that violates the content of the Quran, "Any stipulation that is not in the Book of God [the Quran] is invalid."[82] Second, treaties should aim at the promotion of peace, security and justice, and not be alliances of the strong against the weak. Third, the terms of international treaties should be made public, i.e., treaties should not have secret clauses. Fourth, treaties which focus on security matters should serve defensive, rather than offensive, purposes. Fifth, all international treaties are to be based on reciprocity and mutual benefit, while safeguarding the independence and freedom of the contracting parties. Sixth, negotiating and implementing international treaties are the prerogative of the *wulat al-amr*, literally those in charge of government, in a Muslim society. Seventh, Muslims must honor the terms of treaties as long as the other side is honoring them. Abu Zahra, for example, devotes a section of his *International Relations in Islam* to the subject of honoring one's vows.[83]

Despite their support for international treaties, Abu Zahra and Shaltut do not view them as sufficient for the preservation of international peace. Non-Muslim states cannot be entirely trusted because of the vicissitude of human nature, the history of colonialism, the hegemony of materialist ideologies in both the capitalistic and socialist camps, and the lingering desire on the part of major powers to suppress Islam and dominate Muslim people politically, economically, and, above all, culturally. Accordingly, the strength of Muslim societies individually and collectively represents the best guarantor of international peace.

Shaltut, Abu Zahra, and all subsequent mainstream Islamists maintain that Muslim societies must build their individual power base, as well as coordinate their military strategies, foreign policy, and economic relations, not only to defend themselves but also to preserve international peace by deterring potential aggressors. Without having read Hobbes's *The Leviathan*, and without necessarily embracing his view of human nature, mainstream Islamists subscribe to the Hobbesian notion that "Covenants, without the sword, are but words and of no strength to secure a man at all."[84] As will be seen, Abu Zahra and Shaltut are firm believers in deterrence that requires possessing a sufficient power base.

On War, Jihad, and Military Preparedness

Abu Zahra writes, "War is the most detestable thing (*abghad al-ashya'*) for the soul of the believer; for the essence of war lies in destroying the human soul and it is not easy for the believer to destroy what God Almighty has built [i.e., the human soul]"[85] Despite their aversion toward war, Shaltut and Abu Zahra, in line with mainstream Islamists, do not deny its necessity under certain circumstances. For Shaltut, "War is just a remedy to a perversion (*'ilajan li-shuzhuzh*) that could not be cured through wise counsel and gentle exhortation."[86] Just as Shaltut and Abu Zahra literally quote all the Quranic verses on the centrality of peace, dialog, and collaboration in international relations, they cite virtually all the Quranic verses that pertain to war. These verses are identified in an endnote; in much of the ensuing discussion on war in this and subsequent chapters, reference will only be made to the verse number.[87]

This section examines Shaltut and Abu Zahra's views on war and jihad, focusing on three key questions. What are the legitimate reasons for fighting in Islam, i.e., What are the purposes of jihad? What are the rules of war, or how are wars to be fought and how do wars end? How can aggression be deterred and peace preserved through military preparedness? At this point, it must be noted that Abu Zahra and Shaltut's discourses on war are highly normative, indeed legalistic. They address the subject of war with the aim of discerning what Islam permits and prohibits with regard to war, i.e., the lawful and the prohibited in war, while not approaching the subject as historians or political scientists who seek to uncover whether the wars Muslims fought over the centuries were any different, in reality, from the wars of other nations.

The Purposes of Fighting

Shaltut and Abu Zahra identify two legitimate purposes for fighting in Islam, or for jihad: repelling an actual, or imminent, attack on Muslims, and protecting the freedom of Muslims, particularly their freedom of belief. Abu Zahra thus writes, "The basic principle (*al-asl*) in international relations is peace; that is until there is an actual attack on the Islamic state, or an attempt is made to forcefully turn Muslims away from their religion. In these cases, war becomes a necessity (*daroura*) dictated by the law of self-defense and of defending one's belief and one's religious freedom."[88] Thus, Abu Zahra maintains that the Prophet Muhammad fought for only two reasons. First, he fought against the polytheists because they drove many Muslims out of Mecca and persecuted those who remained there, seeking then to annihilate the Muslims in Medina in order to "uproot the call for Islam and wipe it off the face of the earth."[89] Second, the Prophet, toward the end of his life, fought the kings (*muluk*) of Persia and Byzantium, who plotted against him and more importantly "persecuted their subjects who chose to embrace Islam of their own free will."[90]

Based on short interpretations of verses 22:40–41 and 2:194, Shaltut arrives at the same conclusion, noting that the "principles embodied in these verses [demonstrate] in the clearest terms that Muslims were commanded to fight because of the aggression that befell them, because they were driven from their homes, and due to the attempts to turn them away from what they believed in."[91] He makes the same point when summarizing the purposes of fighting, emphasizing that "the reason for fighting, as indicated in the above verses, is restricted to repelling aggression (*rad al-'idwan*), and defending the right to call for Islam and the freedom of religion."[92]

The slightly younger Azharite scholar, Sheikh Sayyid Sabiq (1915–2000), makes exactly the same point in his popular three-volume work *Fiqh al-Sunna* (*The Jurisprudence of the Sunna*). In line with Shaltut and Abu Zahra, Sabiq is unequivocal in arguing that in Islam "the general principle is peace, while war is the exception."[93] Regarding the centrality of peace to the message of Islam, Sabiq argues, "Peace is one of the principles that Islam has deeply rooted in the souls of Muslims. Hence, peace has become part of their entity, and a doctrine in their beliefs."[94] A few lines later, he notes that Islam emphasizes a "relationship of peace and security" (*'alaqat salam wa aman*), whether in "relations among Muslims, or in relations between Muslims and others."[95] Drawing on the same Quranic verses that Shaltut and Abu Zahra (and similarly Qaradawi and Zuhaili of the third generation) quote, Sabiq emphasizes that Islam justifies war only under two conditions: self-defense, defending "one's life, honor, property, and homeland against aggression," and defending the freedom of peacefully calling for Islam.[96] Accordingly, Muslims are enjoined to remain at peace, as long as these two basic freedoms are not denied. Equally important, and in line with Abu Zahra and Shaltut, Sabiq emphasizes that all the wars that the Prophet Muhammad fought were defensive wars that "had nothing of aggression in them" (*lays fiha shay'a min al-'udwan*).[97] Sabiq's view on peace is, thus, nearly identical to that of Abu Zahra and Shaltut.

Despite the relative brevity of their discourses on war, in comparison with those of the scholar sheikhs of the third generation, Shaltut and Abu Zahra (as well as Sabiq) were forerunners among contemporary mainstream Islamists in weaving a coherent narrative out of the many Quranic verses on war, a narrative emphasizing that the Quran authorized fighting for defensive purposes only, whether physical defense or as defense of freedom of belief, and not as a means of spreading the message of Islam or, even worse, of conquering others for worldly gains. In one of many renditions of the same idea, Abu Zahra notes that the purpose of "fighting in Islam is to repel aggression (*daf' al-i'tida'*), and not to get others to follow a certain belief."[98] Shaltut clarifies that "when the Quran authorized fighting, it disassociated it from the motives of greed, domination and humiliation of the weak; and sought it as a path to peace and tranquility and the anchoring of human life on the precepts of justice and equality."[99] Quoting verse 28:83, "There stands the abode of the Hereafter, which we have assigned to those who do not seek exaltation on earth, or corruption. The final outcome belongs to the pious," Sayyid Sabiq contends that Islam prohibited wars that were prompted by "expansion, domination, and the hegemony of the strong."[100] In the same context, the aforementioned Sabiq quotes two further verses that rarely appear in the discourses of the other mainstream scholar sheikhs, contending that these verses prohibit wars that are triggered by motives of revenge and aggression[101] and wars that merely aim at wreaking havoc and causing destruction.[102]

In the discourses of Abu Zahra and Shaltut, as in Sabiq's, we find the basic elements of the mainstream Islamist thesis that the only war Islam authorizes is the just war, or "a war of virtue" (*harb al-fadeela*), in the parlance of Abu Zahra.[103] The first, and most fundamental, condition for a war to be just is that it ought to be fought for a just purpose or cause. Subsequent mainstream Islamists expanded on this core thesis that Islam only authorizes just wars, but its essence was laid out in the writings of Abu Zahra, Shaltut and Sabiq.

The Rules of War

Even when fighting for a just cause, war ought to be conducted in accordance to certain rules of warfare that are derived from the Quran and the Sunna, Shaltut and Abu Zahra maintain. Here I list these rules as identified by the two scholar sheikhs, deferring more elaborate treatment to the chapters on Qaradawi and Zuhaili, who address these rules in significant detail. At the outset, it must be noted that Shaltut and especially Abu Zahra view war as a highly regulated, and indeed political, activity involving organized forces on both sides. Abu Zahra emphasizes that wars are fought between governments and their organized armies and not between people.[104]

Wars have limited aims, repelling attack and protecting freedom of religion. The notion of total war that is fought until the annihilation of the enemy, or one's own annihilation, is anathema to Shaltut, Abu Zahra and mainstream Islamists. For Abu Zahra, the "Purpose of war is not to annihilate the enemy but to prevent aggression."[105] To paraphrase the renowned political theorist Hannah Arendt, the "justification for war" (repelling aggression and protecting freedom of religion) "constitutes its political limitation."[106] Abu Zahra even maintains that trade may continue with an enemy state, except in material that can be used in the war effort.[107] Since Abu Zahra gives more thought than Shaltut to the rules of war, this section is primarily based on his views as articulated in *International Relations in Islam* and *Theory of War in Islam*. Abu Zahra identifies at least seven rules of fighting that subsequent Islamists adopted and significantly expanded on.

First, before battle, the enemy should be offered the choice of embracing Islam, or paying the *jizya* (poll tax), as a sign of fealty to the Muslims; only if both options are rejected should fighting ensue. Second, it is preferable, although not necessary, for the Muslim side to wait until the enemy delivers the first blow and be the first to shed blood. Abu Zahra bases this rule on the instructions that the Prophet gave to the commanders of Muslim forces.[108] Third, the killing of noncombatants is not permitted. Abu Zahra, Shaltut, and all subsequent mainstream Islamists, emphasize that children, women, ordinary workers (*'umal*), monks, and priests should not be harmed in war as long as they are not directly involved in combat or, in the case of monks and priests, are providing counsel to the enemy combatants and exhorting them to keep on fighting.[109] Fourth, the destruction of civilian property, which Abu Zahra cites from the Islamic tradition as the demolishing of houses and the cutting down of trees, ought to be kept to a minimum and only be permitted when necessary from a military point of view.[110] Fifth, prisoners of war ought to be dealt with humanely and released after the cessation of hostilities, either in exchange for Muslim prisoners or as a show of mercy, as called for in Quranic verse 47:4: "When you encounter the unbelievers, blows to necks it shall be until, once you have routed them, you are to tighten their fetters. Thereafter, it is either gracious bestowal of freedom or holding them to ransom, until war has laid down its burdens."[111] Shaltut makes exactly the same point.[112] Sixth, the mutilation of the fallen bodies of enemy combatants is strictly prohibited even if the enemy mutilates the corpses of fallen Muslims. Abu Zahra maintains that although relations with non-Muslims, in times of peace and war, are governed by reciprocity, adherence to virtue forbids Muslims from engaging in heinous acts (i.e., the mutilation of bodies), even when the enemy does so.[113] Seventh, if at any point during battle, the enemy declares its embrace of Islam, or its willingness to pay the *jizya*, then hostilities will cease.

Abu Zahra acknowledges that after the death of the Prophet and the end of the reign of the rightly guided caliphs, Muslim armies did not scrupulously observe these rules. He attributes this laxity to three factors: the insufficient knowledge of the *sharia*; the excessive cruelty of the enemies of the Muslims, which prompted retaliation; and the incorporation into the expanding Islamic state and Muslim armies of certain ethnicities; he was to name the Mongols and the Turkmans that had a rough character.[114]

Deterrence and Peace

Despite their aversion to war, mainstream Islamists are firm believers in deterrence as a principal means of preventing aggression and preserving peace. Shaltut allocates a significant portion of his short treatise on war, *Fighting in the Light of the Quran*, to the interrelated topics of military preparedness and deterrence, with the former as a perquisite to the latter. Abu Zahra, Shaltut, and all subsequent mainstream Islamists contend that weakness invites aggression. The "Islamic state" must, thus, build its power base in order to ward off attack, but if attacked be ready to fight and repel aggression.

Shaltut identifies three features of military preparedness. The first element is strengthening the morale of the population (*taqwiyat al-rouh al-maʿnawiya lil-umma*), by reinforcing belief in God and in the justice of one's cause, and by combatting defeatist elements in society who spread rumors and weaken morale.[115] Shaltut literally invokes all the Quranic verses exhorting believers to demonstrate their readiness to sacrifice comfort, wealth and, if necessary, their lives, to defend themselves and their religious freedom. The second element of military preparedness revolves around building the material power base of society, especially its industry and its military capabilities. For Shaltut, military power consists of numbers of combatants (*al-'adad*), and war equipment (*al-'ida*), including military and transportation equipment and provisions.[116] To underscore the centrality of military preparedness, Shaltut quotes two Quranic verses: 8:60, "Prepare for them whatever force and war cavalry you can gather to frighten therewith the enemy of God and your enemy" and 4:102, "The unbelievers long for you to be negligent with your weapons and equipment, and thus would attack you in one rush." While verse 8:60 is standard in the repertoire of Islamists, few mainstream Islamists focus on verse 4:102, which Shaltut interprets as a clear warning to the Muslims to remain constantly vigilant and attentive to every move of the enemy.[117]

The third element of military preparedness is effective planning for the contingency of war. Shaltut extrapolates from the Quranic verses that refer to iron to underscore the centraliy of industry to the strength of the military—namely, verses 57:25: "And we sent down iron in which there is great strength and benefits to mankind" and 34:10–11: "Upon David We bestowed of our grace... And we made iron soft for his benefit and said to him: Make coats of mail and fashion their links in right measure." Shaltut specifically refers to the importance of iron for the development of land, naval and aerial capabilities, and, more generally, the capabilities of the *umma*.[118] Quite succinct, Shaltut's "modern" interpretation of the Quranic references to iron anticipated the more detailed treatments of the scholar sheikhs of the third generation, all of whom underscored the necessity of industry and of modern technology in military effectiveness.

Shaltut also briefly addresses the interrelated questions of military service, army discipline, and military doctrine, positing that all able-bodied men should have some military training. He is traditional in exempting from military service the young, the old, the infirm, and the very poor, who need to work. Shaltut is adamant that the sons of rulers, the holders of advanced university degree, and those who recite the Quran should not be exempt from military service.[119] He equally emphasizes the importance of military discipline, punishment of deserters, secrecy with regard to military matters, and obedience to the orders of commanders, while exhorting troops to fight in close impenetrable lines, as in cited in Quranic verse 61:4: "God loves those who fight in his cause in a battle-line, like an edifice, impenetrable."[120] The level of military mobilization, whether partial or full, would be determined by the *wulat al-amr* based on their assessment of the level of danger.[121] Finally, Shaltut underscores that verse 39:123, "O believers fight the unbelievers near you and let them find you harsh," outlines the military doctrine for Muslims; fight the nearest enemy first, and then move to the more distant.[122]. Briefly, Abu Zahra and Shaltut embody the mainstream Islamist distinction between being prepared for war and being aggressors, with Muslims ready for war at all times, but not provoking a war.

The Road to Islamic Unity

As with their views on the defensive purposes of fighting in Islam, Abu Zahra and Shaltut were trendsetters in separating the notion of Islamic unity from that of the caliphate. Knowledgeable about the many obstacles that would prevent resurrecting the institution of the caliphate, Shaltut and more so Abu Zahra thought of alternative, more practical, means of restoring Islamic unity. Since Islamic unity is a recurrent theme in the discourses of Abu Zahra, Shaltut and subsequent mainstream Islamists, it is important to clarify at the outset that for these mainstream Islamists, just as peace is the principle, or norm, in relations with non-Muslims, unity is the basic principle, *al-asl*, in relations among Muslims. Given that Islamists of all shades, by definition, reject the separation of religion and politics, they cannot but assume that the religious unity of the Muslims, established by the Quran and the Sunna, has profound political and socioeconomic implications.

The current political division among Muslims is, thus, seen as a deviation from the norm, irrespective of its duration. That means the division of Muslims into distinct, and sometimes rival, states should not become the norm or be acknowledged *de jure*, irrespectively of the passage of time. More seriously, Islamists of various shades see this disunity as a deviation from the Quranic stipulation that the Muslims constitute one *umma*, invariably translated into English as nation or community, as stated in several Quranic verses, such as verses 2:143, "Thus We have appointed you a median nation.", 3:110, "You are the best community ever brought forth among mankind." and 21:92, "This then is your *umma*, a single *umma*." Abu Zahra argues that Islamic unity is an established truth (*haqiqa thabita*), according to Quranic texts and the Prophet.[123]

Shaltut reads in verse 49:10, "The believers are indeed brothers, so make peace among your brothers, and fear God" an injunction to the "governing body" of the Muslim *umma*, whose existence he simply assumes to settle all political disputes among Muslims first through mediation and, if that fails, through the use force against the aggressors until they accept peace. Shaltut adds that, "Preserving the unity of the *umma* and preventing its disintegration, as well as preserving the religious brotherhood (*al-ukhuwa al-diniya*), are matters of religious faith (*min shu'oun al-Iman*)."[124] Shaltut also notes that Islam "regards Muslims as one *umma*, possessing all the ingredients to form what people later on came to refer to as a state," with this "imagined" unified Islamic state characterized by "grandeur, glory, and power," as Shaltut boasts.[125] Shaltut identifies and briefly discusses four pillars of his envisioned Islamic state: the brotherhood of believers, or religious brotherhood; the social solidarity among all members of the *umma*; the principle of *shura*, consultation, as the basis of good governance (*al-hukm al-salih*); and justice, whether in the government's dealings with the population, people's dealings with each other, or the Islamic state's relationships with other states and noncitizens.[126] The discourses of Abu Zahra, particularly in his text, *Human Society in the Shadow of Islam*, Bahi (Chapter 4) and the mainstream Islamists of the third generation (Chapters 5–7) elaborate on these principles and their centrality to managing the affairs of the Muslim *umma*.

The Realization and Subsequent Loss of Islamic Unity

Like all Islamic thinkers, Abu Zahra and Shaltut maintain that Islamic unity was first achieved by the Prophet Muhammad when he molded the immigrants from Mecca and the fresh converts to Islam from Medina, the *ansar*, into a single community under his religious and political leadership.[127] The notion that the Prophet played a dual role as a spiritual and as a political leader is not unique to Islamists, such as Shaltut, Abu Zahra and Qaradawi. The Western academic Kenneth Cragg makes the same point. Cragg, thus, writes, "Muhammad's whole *Sirah* had yielded a religio-political amalgam as the founding theme of Islam."[128] For Shaltut, the Prophet's migration (*hijra*) to Medina was the landmark event that founded the Muslim *umma*, a community led by the Prophet, the first interpreter of the Quran in both spiritual and temporal matters and guided by the Quran as its principal source of legislation. Shaltut goes on to note that upon its inception, the Muslim *umma* established an "international presence" (*wujud duwali*) by entering into non-aggression pacts with neighboring communities.[129]

This initial "Islamic state," a term that permeates the discourses of contemporary Islamists, was founded on three principles: first, complete obedience and allegiance to the Prophet Muhammad, who forged and led the Muslim *umma* and defended it against all external and internal threats; second, the brotherhood of Muslims, irrespective of status, wealth, clan, tribal origins, or ethnicity[130]; and third, the Quran that provided spiritual guidance and constituted the principal source of legislation on all temporal matters, i.e., the *sharia*. In the same vein, the prominent Tunisian Islamist scholar and activist, Sheikh Rashid al-Ghannushi, underscores that "the Islamic state which materialized in Medina during the reign of the Prophet [PBUH] and his rightly guided successors" possessed the four principal attributes of statehood: population (that included Muslims, Jews and polytheists), territory, authority, and legal system.[131] However, for most Islamists, this initial unity of the *umma* began to disintegrate after the end of the reign of the first four rightly guided caliphs.

Abu Zahra, who as aforementioned gave more thought to the matter of Islamic unity than Shaltut, contends that in order to restore Islamic unity in the contemporary era, we must first come to grips with the historic causes of division among Muslims.[132] In this regard, he presents a convincing account of the growing fragmentation of the Islamic community over the centuries, while offering a sound analysis of the causes and consequences of these divisions. To start with, he acknowledges that faint signs of division appeared even during the life of the Prophet, as manifested in the scheming of the hypocrites (*al-munafiqin*) to slander the Prophet and to saw discord between the emigrants from Quraysh and the local clans of Medina.[133]

These concealed divisions surfaced almost immediately following the death of the Prophet, revealed by the refusal of Saʻd ibn ʻUbadah, a leading figure among the *ansar* (literally supporters; but referring to the Medina converts to Islam), to offer the traditional oath of allegiance (*bayʻa*), to either Abu Bakr or Umar.[134] More serious examples of the growing fissures in the body of the *umma*, which Abu Zahra recounts, included the wars of Abu Bakr against the apostate Arab tribes; the murder of the third caliph, Othman ('Uthman), following a bitter conflict among opposing factions within the still young Muslim community; and the conflicts of the fourth caliph Ali, whom Abu Zahra reverentially refers to as the Imam of Right Guidance (*Imam al-Huda*), with the *wali* of Syria, Muawiyah, and later with the *Khawarej*.[135]

The fragmentation of the Muslim *umma* was further accelerated by the expansion in the territories of the Islamic state; the addition of many non-Arab peoples, with their own languages, cultures and traditions; and, particularly, the switch from a caliphate to dynastic rule (*mulk*), under the Umayyad and later the Abbasid dynasties, whose legitimacy was rejected by many Muslims, especially the Shias.[136] For Abu Zahra, the erosion of Islamic unity cannot be attributed to a single factor, but to a combination of religious, demographic, linguistic, and political ones.

Restoring (Reviving) Islamic Unity

Abu Zahra's detailed account of Islamic divisions is primarily designed to draw appropriate lessons from history in order to reestablish Islamic unity in the contemporary era on firmer grounds.[137] Writing against the backdrop of a colonial legacy that exacerbated the divisions and the weaknesses of the *umma*, the recent memory of two devastating world wars, and aware of the power disparities between the capitalist West and the socialist East, on the one hand, and the Muslim world, on the other, Abu Zahra emphasized that Islamic unity can be restored only through peaceful means and in an incremental fashion.

Abu Zahra's vision of Islamic unity was influenced by his reading of the renowned Indo-Pakistani Islamist intellectual and activist, Sayyed Abu al-A'la Mawdudi (1903–1979), who devoted considerable attention to the subject of reviving Islamic unity.[138] An equally important influence was Afghani, whom Abu Zahra credits with introducing the concept of the "Universal Islamic League" (*Jami'a Islamiya 'Alamiya*), which he borrowed.[139] Abu Zahra showers praise on Afghani, describing him as a great reformer who sought to awaken the Muslim *umma* from its long slumber.[140] For Abu Zahra, restoring the unity of the *umma*, "after a long division" should constitute the paramount goal of all Muslims. This goal is to be pursued, though, gradually and exclusively by peaceful means, namely through rousing Muslims to live their Islam.[141] With great passion, he writes:

> Islamic unity is our objective, and every Muslim should make it his own goal. The one who does not believe that Muslims are one single nation, he has, indeed, opposed the texts of the Quran and has joined those who have exerted sedition towards God and His Prophet, and He has said: 'Whoso defies the Messenger after right guidance has become clear to him, and follows a path other than that of the believers, We assign to him a master he chose to obey, and scorch him in hell – and what a wretched place to end!' [4:115].We became divided among ourselves in the past and, consequently, the wolves of earth had ravished us, we became despised, and scattered into pieces. If the abominable racialism had divided us, the Quran brings us together now to a unity which should have existed long ago. If personal desires of the rulers, and their passion for domination had made us go astray in the past, we should gather in the shade of Islam and its unifying force.[142]

While the first step toward this noble goal was achieved with the freeing of Muslim countries from the yoke of colonial rule, the road ahead remained a long and hard one, Abu Zahra notes.[143] The most immediate obstacle resulted from the desire of the rulers of most Muslim countries to give priority to political, economic and cultural ties to non-Muslim countries, dating back to the colonial era, over ties to other Muslim countries.[144] Abu Zahra sounds confident that this obstacle can be surmounted by a combination of popular pressure in support of Islamic unity and a change of heart among rulers as they start seeing the benefits of a closer relationship with fellow Muslim countries. Without offering a clear roadmap for achieving Islamic unity, Abu Zahra does identify what he believes to be the principal changes in the political, economic, cultural, and above all religious realms that are required in order to bring about this unity.

In the realm of politics and security, Abu Zahra calls on Muslim countries to refrain altogether from waging, or even threatening, war against one another, and from joining military alliances with non-Muslim countries that are directed against a Muslim state.[145] Abu Zahra rejects military alliances between Muslim and non-Muslim countries, fearing that they would draw Muslim countries into fighting unjust wars that do not serve their interests. As aforementioned though, he supports non-aggression pacts and long-term peace treaties.[146] If war should ever erupt among Muslim states, every effort should be made to resolve it peacefully. If this is not possible, then Muslim states may use force against the aggressor Muslim state, as stipulated in Qur'anic verse 49:9.[147] What is of paramount importance to Abu Zahra and other mainstream Islamists is to deny non-Muslim countries any pretext to interfere in the internal affairs of the Muslim *umma*.

In line with Shaltut and other Islamists, Abu Zahra draws a clear distinction between relations among Muslim states and relations between Muslim and non-Muslim states. Clearly, there is a strong idealist-normative, indeed utopian, streak in Abu Zahra and Shaltut's discourses on relations among Muslim states. The Kantian/Liberal notion of "pacific realm" or "zone of peace,"[148] as well as the more recent, albeit similar, concept of "security community" or "no-war zone,"[149] best capture the two scholar sheikhs' construct of how relations amongst Muslim states should be. It is highly unlikely, though, that they were aware of these Western-inspired academic notions.

In the economic sphere, Abu Zahra advocates removing trade barriers among Muslim states, in order for the different Islamic regions to benefit from each other's surplus production.[150] While discussing in some length the role that trade historically played in connecting the various Muslim regions, Abu Zahra does not properly explain the concept of "surplus" (*al-fa'ed*). One can assume that Abu Zahra also implies the issue of free movement of capital (and not just the movement of goods), although he does not address it. Most importantly, Abu Zahra maintains that Muslims should be able to migrate to any Muslim country in quest of employment or economic opportunities.[151] However, Abu Zahra's discussion of the economic dimension of Islamic unity is rather brief, and general, compared, for example, to Bahi's (Chapter 4). Still, neither Abu Zahra nor Bahi, who provides more details on the envisioned economic relations among Muslim states, seem to appreciate how difficult it would be for Muslim countries to reorient their trade and economic relations from their former colonizers, and from the non-Muslim world in general, in order to give priority to enhancing their trade and other economic ties with Muslim states.

In the domain of culture, Abu Zahra argues for reviving the Arabic language as the lingua franca of the Muslim *umma*, maintaining that when Islamic power was at its peak, Arabic was the dominant language in the expanding Islamic state, including its non-Arab provinces. The decline of Arabic, as of the late Abbasid period, resulted from the rise of local languages among the non-Arabs, mainly Turkish and Persian, and the shift away from classical to colloquial Arabic in the Arab provinces. Restoring the Arabic language to its former dominant position is, thus, clearly one ingredient of reviving the Islamic power and the unity of the *umma*.

Clearly, though, a change in the hearts and minds of Muslims themselves is the change most needed to surmount the material obstacles to Islamic unity. For Abu Zahra, only if Muslims truly embrace Islam and accept to live by its laws, would they be able to make headway toward reuniting the Muslim *umma* after its long divisions.[152] Efforts at reviving Islamic unity will, thus, be fruitless unless they are embedded in a larger project of reviving Islam as a religion and as a way of life. This inexorable link between restoring the unity of the *umma* and reviving the Islamic religion is underscored in the discourses of nearly all contemporary reformist Islamists, from al-Afghani and 'Abduh (founding generation) to Abu Zahra, Shaltut and Bahi (second generation) to Qaradawi and Zuhaili (third generation).

Abu Zahra is ambivalent regarding the ultimate goal of the Islamic (re)unification project. He oscillates between two possible endpoints: the restoration of the caliphate (the grand imamate as he sometimes calls it[153]) and the formation of an Islamic League (*Jami'a Islamiya*).[154] However, although Abu Zahra at no point explicitly repudiates the notion of restoring the caliphate, he does not insist on it as a condition for realizing Islamic unity.[155] Arguably, the most original idea in *al-Wihda al-Islamiya* lies in providing a vision, vague though it may be, for realizing Islamic unity that does not necessarily revolve around a universal caliphate.

While a clean break with the notion of restoring the caliphate could have strengthened Abu Zahra's argument, his main problem lies in the equally vague notion of the Islamic League. Clearly what he envisions goes well beyond what historian Friedrich Meinecke calls a "heteronymy, a system of multiple relationships of normative obligations that cut across national boundaries."[156] Briefly, Abu Zahra is too short on specifics regarding the Islamic League, not making it entirely clear how it would be different from the caliphate. Outlined more clearly, his notion of the Islamic League remains as under-theorized as are the notions of the Islamic State and the caliphate in his own writings and in the writings of other contemporary Islamists. To sum up, while moving the discussion on Islamic unity beyond the caliphate, Abu Zahra's alternative—the Islamic league—is equally fraught with ambiguities.

Conclusion

In the discourses of Abu Zahra and Shaltut, we encounter all the elements of the mainstream Islamist view on international relations. These elements include an embrace of human diversity, including religious diversity, within the context of the unity of humanity; a strong preference for peace, dialog and collaboration with non-Muslims on the bases of reciprocity, mutual respect, and mutual benefit; a belief in the positive role that international treaties, conventions, and, more generally, international law can play in international relations; an aversion to war, except for wars to defend oneself and one's freedom of religion; and, finally, the adoption of a peaceful incremental approach to the pursuit of Islamic unity that does not necessitate the resurrection of the institution of the caliphate.

These same themes, brought to life by members of the first generation, also dominate the discourses of Bahi (Chapter 4) and of the scholar sheikhs of the third generation (Chapters 5–7). However, the discourses of the six scholar sheikhs that this work covers are not replicas of each other. There are important variations in the substance of their discourses and in their writing styles. Bahi, Qaradawi and Fadlallah tend to be more skeptical about the prospects of maintaining international peace over the long haul, in their view because of the policies of non-Muslim powers, who constantly encroach on the sovereignty and freedoms of Muslim states. Shaltut, Abu Zahra, and especially Zuhaili demonstrate greater faith in the ability of humanity, or the international community in modern parlance, to preserve international peace or at least to quickly restore peace after short and limited wars.

At the risk of oversimplification, there is a greater tendency on the part of Bahi, Qaradawi, and Fadlallah to view war as natural and inevitable. Shaltut, Abu Zahra, and especially Zuhaili, the legalist *par excellence*, are more likely to treat war as an aberration, or a deviation from the principal condition, which is peace. Zuhaili even goes to the extreme of viewing war as a learned behavior that can be unlearned (more on this in Chapter 6). Bahi stands out as the sharpest and most sophisticated critic of socialism and more generally of materialist ideologies, including unchecked capitalism. Stylistically, Bahi and Fadlallah tend to be polemical in their discourses on non-Muslim powers, depicting the policies of Western powers as colonial, or neocolonial, while dwelling on their adverse effects on the Muslim world and more generally the developing world. Chapter 4 turns to Bahi's contributions to the mainstream perspective.

Notes

1 Biographic information was obtained from the following sites: "Mahmoud Shaltut,"(n.d.), *Marefa* https://www.marefa.org/%D9%85%D8%AD%D9%85%D9%88%D8%AF_%D8%B4%D9%84%D8%AA%D9%88%D8%AA, accessed 11 July 2019; Shaymaa Abdel Hadi, "A'ima fi Sutur.. al-Sheikh Mahmoud Shultut", (Imams in brief. Sheikh Mahmoud Shaltout), *al-Ahram Gate* (2018), http://gate.ahram.org.eg/News/1932134.aspx, accessed 11 July 2019; Diana Ahmad, "al-Sheikh Shaltut.. Sheikh al-Taqribiyeen wa Fatwah al-Azima bi Jawaz al-Taabud bi Madhab al-Shia, Raddaan 'alaa man Yukafirun al-Muslimeen al-Shia," (Sheikh Shaltout ... the sheikh of rapprochement and his great fatwa permitting worship according to the Shiite sect, in response to those who disbelieve Shiite Muslims), *al-Hiwar al-Motamadden* (2012), http://www.ahewar.org/debat/show.art.asp?aid=298110#null, accessed 11 July 2019 and "Al-Sheikh Shaltut Mata Fawr Istiqalatah min al-Mashyakha," (Sheikh Shaltout died immediately after his resignation from the sheikhdom), (2007), Al-Ittihad, https://www.alittihad.ae/article/141158/2007/%d8%a7%d9%84%d8%b4%d9%8a%d8%ae-%d8%b4%d9%84%d8%aa%d9%88%d8%aa-%d9%85%d8%a7%d8%aa-%d9%81%d9%88%d8%b1-%d8%a7%d8%b3%d8%aa%d9%82%d8%a7%d9%84%d8%aa%d9%87-%d9%85%d9%86-%d8%a7%d9%84%d9%85%d8%b4%d9%8a%d8%ae%d8%a9, accessed 11 July 2019.

2 For information on Sheikh al-Maraghi, see: "Muhammad Mustafa Al-Maraghi," (n.d.), *Marefa*, https://www.marefa.org/%D9%85%D8%AD%D9%85%D8%AF_%D9%85%D8%B5%D8%B7%D9%81%D9%89_%D8%A7%D9%84%D9%85%D8%B1%D8%A7%D8%BA%D9%8A, accessed 11 July 2019.

Abdel Jawad Suleiman, "Al-Risala Magazine/Issue 888/Sheikh Muhammad Mustafa Al-Maraghi", *Wikisource* (1950), https://ar.wikisource.org/wiki/%D9%85%D8%AC%D9%84%D8%A9_%D8%A7%D9%84%D8%B1%D8%B3%D8%A7%D9%84%D8%A9/%D8%A7%D9%84%D8%B9%D8%AF%D8%AF_888/%D8%A7%D9%84%D8%B4%D9%8A%D8%AE_%D9%85%D8%AD%D9%85%D8%AF_%D9%85%D8%B5%D8%B7%D9%81%D9%89_%D8%A7%D9%84%D9%85%D8%B1%D8%A7%D8%BA%D9%8A, accessed 11 July 2019.
3 Shaltut played an active part in the *'ulama* "revolt" against al-Maraghi's removal.
4 'Abd al-Raziq, *al-Islam wa Usul al-Hukm* (Islam and the Principles of Governance) (Cairo: Dar al-Kitab al-Masri, 1925).
5 Further discussion of Law 103 is deferred to Chapter 4 on Bahi.
6 Yusuf Qaradawi, *Ibn al-Qarya wa al-Kuttab* (Son of the Village and the Kuttab), Vol. 2 (Cairo: Dar al-Shuruq, 2004), 280.
7 For references to this fatwa, see: Mohamad Sharqawi, "al-Sheikh Mahmoud Shaltut... Qada 'ala 'usturat: wa e'badu Allah 'ala al-Madahib al-Arbaa" (Sheikh Mahmoud Shaltut... annihilated the myth: "And worship God according to the four schools of thought"), *Sout al-Omma* (2019), http://www.soutalomma.com/Article/872463/, accessed 11 July 2019.
8 See Mohamad Al-Hasun (n.d.), "'inkar al-Sheikh al-Qaradawi li Fatwa Sheikh al-Azhar Mahmoud Shaltut (Jamada al-'ula 1430)," (Sheikh al-Qaradawi's denial of the fatwa of al-Azhar's Sheikh Mahmoud Shaltut (Jumada I 1430)), *Al-Hasun*, https://www.alhasun.com/activities-2815.html, accessed 11 July 2019; "(al-Sheikh al-Thalith wa al'arbaeun li al-jamae al-Azhar)... Mahmoud Shaltut" ((The forty-third Sheikh of Al-Azhar Mosque) Mahmoud Shaltut), (2019), *Islamist Movements*, https://www.islamist-movements.com/37836, accessed 11 July 2019.
9 See Diana Ahmad, 'al-Sheikh Shaltut.. Sheikh al-Taqribiyeen wa Fatwah al-Azima bi Jawaz al-Taabud bi Madhab al-Shia, Raddaan 'alaa man Yukafirun al-Muslimeen al-Shia' (Sheikh Shaltut ... the sheikh of rapprochement and his great fatwa permitting worship according to the Shiite sect, in response to those who disbelieve Shiite Muslims), *al-Hiwar al-Motamadden* (2012), http://www.ahewar.org/debat/show.art.asp?aid=298110#null, accessed 11 July 2019; and especially Hassan Salhab, *al-Sheikh Mahmoud Shaltut: Qira'a fi Tajribat al-islah wa al-Wihda al-Islamiya* (Sheikh Mahmoud Shaltut: a Reading of an Attempt at Reform and Islamic Unity) (Beirut: Markaz al-Hadara li-Tanmiyat al-Fikr al-Islam, 2008).
10 Yusuf Qaradawi, *Khitabuna al-Islami for 'Asr al-'Awlama* (Our Islamic Discourse in the Era of Globalization) (Cairo: Dar al-Shuruq, 2004), 48–49.
11 The biographic information is drawn from: Adil Salahi, "Scholar Of Renown: Muhammad Abu Zahrah," *Arab News* (2001), http://www.arabnews.com/node/216148, accessed 5 July 2016.

Ahmad Tamam, "Abu Zahra, 'alem You`raf Qadrahu" (Abu Zahra, a Scholar Known for His Worth), *al-Multaka al-Fuqhi* (2008), https://www.feqhweb.com/vb/threads/%D8%A3%D8%A8%D9%88-%D8%B2%D9%87%D8%B1%D8%A9-%D8%B9%D8%A7%D9%84%D9%85-%D9%8A%D8%B9%D8%B1%D9%81-%D9%82%D8%AF%D8%B1%D9%87.2047/, accessed 5 July 2016; http://www.worldlibrary.org/articles/muhammadsunnah.or/history;

Majd Makki, (n.d.). 'al- Allama al-Faqih al-Sheikh Muhammad Abu Zahra' (The Scholar Jurist Sheikh Muhammad Abu Zahra), *Syrian Scholars Association*, http://www.islamsyria.com/portal/cvs/show/496, accessed 5 July 2016; Ahmad Tamam, "Abu Zahra.. 'alem You`raf Qadrahu (fi Zikra Miladeh: 6 min zhi al-Qaada 1315 h)" (Abu Zahra ... a Scholar Known for His Worth (On the anniversary of his birth: 6 of Dhu al-Qi'dah 1315 AH), *Islam Online* (2021), https://islamonline.net/archive/%D8%A3%D8%A8%D9%88-%D8%B2%D9%87%D8%B1%D8%A9-%D8%B9%D8%A7%D9%84%D9%85-%D9%8A%D8%B9%D8%B1%D9%81-%D9%82%D8%AF%D8%B1%D9%87/, accessed 5 July 2016.

12 Adil Salahi, "Scholar of Renown: Muhammad Abu Zahrah," *Arab News* (2001), http://www.arabnews.com/node/216148, accessed 5 July 2016.
13 The fatwa was issued in 1963. For the fatwa and reactions to it, see
14 For the conflicting views of Abu Zahra and Shaltut on conventional banks, see: Bilal Ramadan, 'Hukum al-Ta'amulat al-Bankiya Lam Yaaref Kalima Niha'iya al-Imam Shaltut wa Tantawi wa Ali Jomaa Abahuha... wa Abu Zahra wa Jad al-Haq w Ibn Baz Harramouha' (The Judgment on Banking Transactions did not know the final word: Imam Shaltout and Tantawi, and Ali Jumah permitted it . . . and Abu Zahra, Jad Al-Haq and Ibn Baz prohibited it), *Youm 7* (2013), https://www.youm7.com/story/2013/2/24/, accessed 5 July 2016.
15 Muhammad Abu Zahra, *Tahrim al-Riba: Tandhim Iqtisadi* (Prohibiting Usury: An Economic System) (Jeddah: al-Dar al-Sa'udia lil-Nashr wa al-Tawzi', 1985).
16 Yusuf Qaradawi, *al-Sheikh al-Ghazali kama 'Areftuh: Rihlat Nisf Qarn* (Sheikh Ghazali as I Knew Him: The Journey of Half a Century) (Cairo: Dar al-Shuruq, 2000), 7.
17 "Muhammad Abu Zahra," (n.d.), *al-Maktaba al-Shamela*, http://shamela.ws/index.php/author/1153, accessed 5 July 2016.
18 Law 103 established the Islamic Research Academy to replace *Hay'at Kibar al-'Ulama'*, as al-Azhar's leading body.
19 A list of his publications is found at: "Maktabet Sheikh Muhammad Abu Zahra" (Sheikh Muhammad Abu Zahra Library), (n.d.), *Al Meshkat*, http://www.almeshkat.net/vb/showthread.php?t=125220, accessed 10 July 2016.

20 These four books were Abu Zahra's only works to be translated into English under the title: *The Four Imams: Their Lives, Works and their Schools of Thought*. (Translated by Aisha Bewley) (New Delhi: Millat Book Centre, N.A.).
21 Muhammad Abu Zahra, *Ibn Taymiyya: Hayatuh wa-'Asruh: Ara'uh wa Fiqhuh* (Ibn Taymiyya: His Life and Era: Opinions and Jurisprudence) (Cairo: Dar al-Fikr al-'Arabi, 2005).
22 Muhammad Abu Zahra, *Ibn Hazm: Hayatuh wa-'Asruh: Ara'uh wa Fiqhuh* (Ibn Hazm: His Life and Era: Opinions and Jurisprudence) (Cairo: Dar al-Fikr al-'Arabi, 2007).
23 Muhammad Abu Zahra, *Al-Imam Zaid, Hayatuh wa-'Asruh: Ara'uh wa Fiqhuh* (Al-Imam Zaid: His Life and Era: Opinions and Jurisprudence) (Cairo: Dar al-Fikr al-'Arabi, 2005).
24 Muhammad Abu Zahra, *Al-Imam al-Sadiq: Hayatuh wa-'Asruh: Ara'uh wa Fiqhuh* (Al-Imam al-Sadiq: His Life and Era: Opinions and Jurisprudence) (Cairo: Dar al-Fikr al-'Arabi, 2005).
25 For one of dozens of references to the Shias as a sect within Islam, see Abu Zahra, *al-Wihda al-Islamiya*, 246–49.
26 Mahmoud Shaltut, *al-Islam: 'Aqida wa Sharia* (Islam: a Creed and a *Sharia*) (Cairo: Dar al-Shuruq, 2001) (18th printing), 453–56. Shaltut and Abu Zahra use the Arabic terms *al-asl* (basic principle) and *al-hala al-asliya* (principal condition), interchangeably.
27 Abu Zahra, *al-'Alaqat al-Duwaliya fi al-Islam*, 50.
28 Abu Zahra, *al-'Alaqat al-Duwaliya fi al-Islam*, 50.
29 Abu Zahra, *al-'Alaqat al-Duwaliya fi al-Islam*, 50–56.
30 In the few pages devoted to international relations in his *al-Islam: 'Aqida and Shari'a*, Shaltut refers to peace as the original condition in international relations at least three times. Shaltut, *al-Islam: 'Aqida wa Sharia* (Islam: a Creed and a *Sharia*) (Cairo, Dar al-Shuruq, 2001) (18th printing).
31 Verse 49:9, "If two groups of believers fight each other make peace between them. If one group transgresses against the other fight the transgressing group until it returns to the judgment of God."
32 See, in particular, Mahmoud Shaltut, *Min Tawjihat al-Islam* (From the Guidance of Islam) (Cairo: Dar al-Shuruq, 2004), 74.
33 See, in particular, Mahmoud Shaltut, *al-Islam wa al-Wujud al-Duwali lil-Muslimin* (Islam and the International Presence of Muslims) (Cairo: Matba'at Dar al-Jihad, 1958), 46–55.
34 Shaltut, *al-Islam: 'Aqida wa Shari'a*, 132. See also Shaltut, *Min Tawjihat al-Islam*, 52–53, 194.
35 Abu Zahra, *al-'Alaqat al-Duwaliya fi al-Islam* (International Relations in Islam), 37.
36 Abu Zahra, *al-'Alaqat al-Duwaliya fi al-Islam*, 51.

37 The relevant verses are 2: 136–137, "Say: We believe in God and in what was revealed to us, In what was revealed to Abraham, to Ishmael, to Isaac and Jacob and the Tribes, In what was revealed to Moses and Jesus, In what was revealed to prophets by their Lord. We make no distinction between any of them, and to Him we surrender. If they then believe in what you believe, they are guided aright. If then they turn, it is they who are in discord. God will deal with them on your behalf..." 3: 64, "Say: People of the Book, let us rally around a discourse common to us and you: that we worship none by God, that we associate nothing with Him, that we do not take each other as lords apart from God. If they turn away, say: Bear witness that we are Muslims. " 4: 1: "O mankind fear your Lord Who created you from a single soul, and created from it its spouse and propagated from them many men and women." 5: 48, "Had God willed, he could have made you a single community – but in order to test you in what He revealed to you. So vie with one another in virtue. To God is your homecoming all of you, and he will then acquaint you with that over which you differed." 8: 61–62: "Should they incline to peace, incline to it too, and put your trust in God... But if they intend to deceive you, God is sufficient for you." 10: 99, "Had your lord willed it, all on earth, every single one, would have believed. Will you then compel people to become believers?" 11: 118–119; "Had your Lord willed, he would have created mankind a single nation. But they continue to differ, save for those to whom God has shown mercy. It is for this reason that he created them." 24: 54, "Say: Obey God and obey the Messenger. If they turn and go, upon him rests the burden, and upon you your own. If you obey Him, you will be guided aright. The Messenger is enjoined only to deliver the clear message." 29: 46, "Do not argue with the people of the Book, except in the best manner, save the wicked among them, and say: We believe in what has been sent down upon us, and sent down upon you. Our God and yours is One God, and to Him we submit." 42: 13, "He prescribed to you of religion what He once enjoined upon Noah, as also what We revealed to you and what we enjoined upon Abraham, Moses and Jesus: to follow the right religion and not be in dispute over it." 49, 13: "O mankind, we created you male and female, and made you into nations and tribes that you may come to know one another....".

38 Mahmoud Shaltut, *al-Quran wa al-Qital* (Fighting in the Light of the Quran) (Cairo: Dar al-Kitab al-'Arabi, 1951). The same work also appears under a more general title: *al-Islam wa al-'Alaqat Duwaliya fi al-Silm wa al-Harb* (Islam and International Relations in times of Peace and War) published by the office of Sheikh al-Azhar in 1951. An excellent translation into English is also available. *The Qur'an and Combat: Imam Mahmoud Muhammad Shaltut*, Translated by Lamia al-Khraisha. (Amman: The Royal Ahl Al-Bayt Institute for Islamic Thought, 2012).

39 Shaltut, *al-Quran wa al-Qital*, 12–23.

40 Shaltut, *al-Quran wa al-Qital*, 30–37, 41.

The Second Generation: Mahmoud Shaltut | 95

41 Mahmoud Shaltut, *al-Islam wa al-Wujud al-Dawli lil-Muslimin* (Islam and the International Presence of Muslims) (Cairo: Matbaʿat Dar al-Jihad, 1958), 32–33.
42 Shaltut, *al-Quran wa al-Qital*.
43 Abu Zahra makes the same point. Muhammad Abu Zahra, *al-Mujtamaʾ al-Insani fi dhil al-Islam* (Human Society in the Shade of Islam) (Jeddah: al-Dar al-Saʿudia lil-Nashr wa al-Tawziʿ, 1981), 14.
44 Shaltut is assuming here that Judaism and Christianity also respect religious freedom.
45 Shaltut, *al-Quran wa al-Qital*, 35.
46 Shaltut, *al-Islam wa al-Wujud al-Dawli lil-Muslimin*, 22.
47 Muhammad Abu Zahra, *Nazhariyat al-Harb fi al-Islam* (Theory of War in Islam) (Cairo: Wizarat al-Awqaf, al-Majlis al-Aʿla lil-Shuʾoun al-Islamiya, 2008). First published as an article in *al-Majala al-Masriya lil-Qanun al-Duwali*, 1958.
48 Abu Zahra, *al-ʾAlaqat al-Duwaliya fi al-Islam*, 29–30.
49 Abu Zahra, *Nazhariyat al-Harb fi al-Islam*, 28–30.
50 Abu Zahra, *al-ʾAlaqat al-Duwaliya fi al-Islam*, 46.
51 Abu Zahra, *al-Mujtamaʾ al-Insani fi dhil al-Islam*, 18.
52 For references to Islam as an imperial religion, see Shabbir Akhtar, *Islam as Political Religion: The Future of an Imperial Faith* (Oxfrdshire: Routledge, 2010).
53 Shaltut, *al-Islam: ʿAqida wa Shariʾa*, 451.
54 Abu Zahra, *al-ʾAlaqat al-Duwaliya fi al-Islam*, 50–51.
55 Abu Zahra, *al-ʾAlaqat al-Duwaliya fi al-Islam*, 51.
56 Abu Zahra, *al-ʾAlaqat al-Duwaliya fi al-Islam*, 25.
57 Abu Zahra, *al-ʾAlaqat al-Duwaliya fi al-Islam*, 25–26 and *al-Mujtamaʾ al-Insani fi Dhil al-Islam*, 56; Shaltut, *al-Quran wa al-Qital*, 63.
58 Shaltut, *al-Islam: ʿAqida wa Shariʾa*, 452.
59 Shaltut, *al-Islam wa al-Wujud al-Dawli lil-Muslimin*, 16.
60 Abu Zahra, *al-Mujtamaʿ al-Insani fi Dhil al-Islam*, 13.
61 Abu Zahra, *al-ʾAlaqat al-Duwaliya fi al-Islam*, 21–25.
62 Shaltut, *Min Tawjihat al-Islam*, 75.
63 Shaltut, *Min Tawjihat al-Quran*, 230.
64 Shaltut, *al-Quran wa al-Qital*, 46; *Min Tawjihat al-Islam*, 195.
65 Abu Zahra, *al-ʾAlaqat al-Duwaliya fi al-Islam*, esp. 28–38.
66 Abu Zahra, *al-Mujtamaʾ al-Insani fi dhil al-Islam*, 167.
67 Abu Zahra, *al-ʾAlaqat al-Duwaliya fi al-Islam*, esp. 36–44, *al-Mujtamaʾ al-Insani fi dhil al-Islam*, esp. 45–55.
68 Abu Zahra, *al-ʾAlaqat al-Duwaliya fi al-Islam*, esp. 28–38.
69 Shaltut, *al-Islam: ʿAqida wa Sharia*, 135.
70 Abu Zahra, *al-ʾAlaqat al-Duwaliya fi al-Islam*, 56.

71 Al-Shaybani is often depicted as the father of Islamic international law. For academic works on al-Shaybani, see Khaled Ramadan Bashir, *Islamic International law: Historical Foundations and al-Shaybani's Siyar* (North Hampton: MA, Edward Elgar Publishing, 2018).
72 Abu Zahra, *al-'Alaqat al-Duwaliya fi al-Islam*, 58–60.
73 Abu Zahra, *al-'Alaqat al-Duwaliya fi al-Islam*, 42.
74 Abu Zahra, *Nazhariyat al-Harb fi al-Islam*, 49.
75 Hannah Arendt, *The Human Condition* (Chicago: The University of Chicago Press, 1958).
76 Shaltut, *Min Tawjihat al-Quran*, 10.
77 Abu Zahra, *al-'Alaqat al-Duwaliya fi al-Islam*, 21–26.
78 Abu Zahra, *al-'Alaqat al-Duwaliya fi al-Islam*, 42.
79 See, in particular, the section entitled "treaties and peace" in Abu Zahra, *al-'Alaqat al-Duwaliya fi al-Islam*, 79–84, 79.
80 Shaltut, *al-Islam: 'Aqida wa Shari'a*, 456.
81 These six points are derived from a close reading of Shaltut's *al-Quran wa al-Qital, Min Tawjihat al-Islam* and *al-Islam: 'Aqida wa Sharia* and Abu Zahra's *al-'Alaqat al-Duwaliya fi al-Islam*.
82 Shaltut, *al-Islam: 'Aqida wa Shari'a*, 456.
83 Abu Zahra, *al-'Alaqat al-Duwaliya fi al-Islam*, 42–44.
84 Thomas Hobbes, *Leviathan* (London: Penguin Books, 1968), 231.
85 Abu Zahra, *al-'Alaqat al-Duwaliya fi al-Islam*, 21–26.
86 Shaltut, *al-Islam: 'Aqida wa Shari'a*, 454.
87 The principal verses on war that Shaltut, Abu Zahra, and subsequent mainstream Islamists build their arguments on are: 2: 193–194: "Fight them until there is no longer forced apostasy and the religion is God's. If they desist, no aggression is permitted except against the wicked. Whoever commits aggression against you, retaliate against him in the same measure as he committed against you. Fear god and know that God stands by the pious." 2: 251: "Had God not restrained mankind, some by means of others, the earth would have become chaotic. But God is gracious towards His creation." 4: 84: "So fight in the cause of God; you are answerable only to yourself. And encourage the believers—perhaps God will check the might of the unbelievers. For God is more mighty and more grievous in torment. 4: 90–91: "Therefore if they stand aside and do not fight you, and propose submission to you, God grants you no further sway over them... If they do not stand aside and propose submission to you, nor hold back their hands then seize them and kill them wherever you find them. Over these We have granted you explicit sway." 9: 36: "And fight the polytheists, all of them, as they fight you all." 22:39–40: "Leave is granted to those who are being attacked, for they were wronged, and God is assuredly capable of sending them victory. They are those who were driven out of their homes without just cause, only because they said: Our Lord is God.

Had God not caused people to restrain one another, destruction would have fallen upon monasteries, churches, oratories and place of prayer, where the name of God is often mentioned. God will assuredly uphold those who uphold Him. God is All-Powerful, Almighty."

88 Abu Zahra, *al-'Alaqat al-Duwaliya fi al-Islam*, 51. He makes the same assertion in *Nazhariyat al-Harb fi al-Islam*, 37, 44; and *al-Mujtama ' al-Insani fi Dhil al-Islam*, 202.
89 Abu Zahra, *al-'Alaqat al-Duwaliya fi al-Islam*, 52.
90 Abu Zahra, *al-'Alaqat al-Duwaliya fi al-Islam*, 53–54.
91 Shaltut, *al-Quran wa al-Qital*, 30.
92 Shaltut, *al-Quran wa al-Qital*, 36.
93 Sayyid Sabiq, *Fiqh al-Sunna* (Beirut: Dar al-Kitab al-'Arabi, 1973), Vol. 2, 613.
94 Sabiq, *Fiqh al-Sunna*, Vol. 2, 595.
95 Sabiq, *Fiqh al-Sunna*, Vol. 2, 598.
96 Sabiq, *Fiqh al-Sunna*, Vol. 2, 613–18.
97 Sabiq, *Fiqh al-Sunna*, Vol. 2, 617.
98 Abu Zahra, *Nazhariyat al-Harb fi a-Islam*, 37.
99 Shaltut, *al-Quran wa al-Qital*, 36.
100 Sabiq, *Fiqh al-Sunna*, Vol. 2, 612.
101 Verse 5:2, "Let not the hatred of some who barred your way to the sacred mosque lead you to aggression. Join hands in virtue and piety, but join not hands in sin and aggression. Fear God, for God is severe in punishment." Sabiq, *Fiqh al-Sunna*, Vol. 2, 612.
102 Verse 7:56, "Do not corrupt the land once it has been set right." Sabiq, *Fiqh al-Sunna*, Vol. 2, 612.
103 Abu Zahra, *al-'Alaqat al-Duwaliya fi al-Islam*, 109.
104 Abu Zahra, *al-'Alaqat al-Duwaliya fi al-Islam*, 44–45; *Nazhariyat al-Harb fi al-Islam*, 20–22, 94.
105 Abu Zahra, *Nazhariyat al-Harb fi al-Islam*, 61.
106 Hannah Arendt, *On Revolution* (New York: Viking 1970), 10.
107 Abu Zahra, *Nazhariyat al-Harb fi al-Islam*, 65–67.
108 Abu Zahra, *Nazhariyat al-Harb fi al-Islam*, 54–56.
109 Abu Zahra, *al-'Alaqat al-Duwaliya fi al-Islam*, 105–09; *Nazhariyat al-Harb fi al-Islam*, 21–22.
110 Abu Zahra, *al-'Alaqat al-Duwaliya fi al-Islam*, 105–09.
111 Abu Zahra, *Nazhariyat al-Harb fi al-Islam*, 35.
112 Shaltut, *al-Quran wa al-Qital*, 36.
113 Abu Zahra, *al-'Alaqat al-Duwaliya fi al-Islam*, 109–10; and *al-Mujtama' al-Insani fi Dil al-islam*, 202.
114 Abu Zahra, *al-'Alaqat al-Duwaliya fi al-Islam*, 112.
115 Shaltut, *al-Quran wa al-Qital*, 42–46, 52.

116 Shaltut, *al-Quran wa al-Qital*, 46.
117 Shaltut, *al-Quran wa al-Qital*, 47.
118 Shaltut, *al-Quran wa al-Qital*, 47–50.
119 Shaltut, *al-Quran wa al-Qital*, 51.
120 Shaltut, *al-Quran wa al-Qital*, 54–55.
121 Shaltut, *al-Quran wa al-Qital*, 53.
122 Shaltut, *al-Quran wa al-Qital*, 55.
123 Muhammad Abu Zahra, *al-Wihda al-Islamiya* (Cairo: Dar al-Fikr al-'Arabi, 2011). First published by Cairo: Dar al-Jihad in 1958, 7.
124 Shaltut, *al-Quran wa al-Qital*, 25, 26.
125 Shaltut, *al-Islam 'Aqida wa Sharia*, 433.
126 Shaltut, *al-Islam 'Aqida wa Sharia*, 433.
127 Shaltut, *al-Islam 'Aqida wa Sharia*, 434–35; *al-Wujud al-Dawli lil-Muslimin*, 52.
128 Kenneth Cragg, *the Qur'an and the West* (Washington, DC: Georgetown University Press, 2005), 156.
129 Shaltut, *al-Islam wa al-Wujud al-Dawli lil-Muslimin*, 52.
130 Shaltut, *al-Islam wa al-Wujud al-Dawli lil-Muslimin*, 21.
131 Rachid Al-Ghannouchi, *al-Hurriyyat al-'Amma fi al-Dawla al-Islamiya* (Public Freedoms in the Islamic State) (Beirut: Markaz Dirasat al-Wihda al-'Arabiya, 1993), 94.
132 Abu Zahra, *al-Wihda al-Islamiya*, 143.
133 Abu Zahra, *al-Wihda al-Islamiya*, 80–85.
134 Abu Zahra, *al-Wihda al-Islamiya*, 100. A few pages later (152), he names around fifteen of the Prophet's companions who, according to Shia tradition, thought that the first Caliph should have been Ali and not Abu Bakr. He neither accepts nor rejects this Shia narrative. See also *Tarikh al-Mazhaheb al-Islamiya*, 13, 23.
135 Abu Zahra, *al-Wihda al-Islamiya*, 99–123.
136 Abu Zahra, *al-Wihda al-Islamiya*, 172–207.
137 Abu Zahra, *al-Wihda al-Islamiya*, 200.
138 See, for example, Nasr, *Mawlana Mawdudi*, esp. Chapter 5 "The Islamic State," 80–106. Other academic works on Mawdudi include Roy Jackson, *Mawlana Mawdudi and Political Islam: Authority and the Islamic State* (London and New York: Routledge, 2011). Abu Zahra and Mawdudi coauthored a short pamphlet that was translated into English, which attests to their intellectual and probably personal affinity. Sayyid Abu al-A'la Mawdudi and Muhammad Abu Zahra, "The Role of Ijtihad and the Scope of legislation in Islam," *Muslim Digest* 9, no. 2 (January 1959): 15–20.
139 Abu Zahra, *al-Wihda al-Islamiya*, 220–21.
140 Abu Zahra, *al-Wihda al-Islamiya*, 220.
141 Abu Zahra, *al-Wihda al-Islamiya*, 201–16.
142 Abu Zahra, *al-Wihda al-Islamiya*, 218.

143 Abu Zahra, *al-Wihda al-Islamiya*, 208–09.
144 Abu Zahra, *al-Wihda al-Islamiya*, 208–09.
145 Abu Zahra, *al-Wihda al-Islamiya*, 279–81, 313.
146 Abu Zahra, *al-Wihda al-Islamiya*, 281–83.
147 Abu Zahra, *al-Wihda al-Islamiya*, 291.
148 See Michael Doyle, "Kant, Liberal Legacies and Foreign Affairs," *Philosophy and Public Affairs* 2, no. 3 (1983): 205–35; Michael Doyle, "Kant, Liberalism and World Politics," *American Political Science Review* 80, no. 4 (1986): 1151–69; and Kenneth Waltz, "Kant, Liberalism and War," *American Political Science Review* 56, no. 2 (1962): 331–40.
149 See Karl W. Deutsch, et al., *Political Community and the North Atlantic Area: International Organization in the Light of Historical Experience* (Princeton, N.J.: Princeton University Press, 1957).
150 Abu Zahra, *al-Wihda al-Islamiya*, 269–72.
151 Abu Zahra, *al-Wihda al-Islamiya*, 277–78.
152 Abu Zahra, *al-Wihda al-Islamiya*, 225–42.
153 Abu Zahra, *Tarikh al-Mazhaheb al-Islamiya*, 19; *al-Mujtamaʿ al-Insani fi Dhil al-Islam*, 224.
154 Abu Zahra, *al-Wihda al-Islamiya*, 220–68.
155 Abu Zahra, *al-Wihda al-Islamiya*, 217–19.
156 Jack Snyder, "Introduction," in *Religion and International Relations Theory*, ed. Jack Snyder (New York: Columbia University Press, 2011), 9.

4

The Second Generation: Sheikh Muhammad al-Bahi

Introduction

The second and final chapter on the contributions of the scholar sheikhs of the second generation, this chapter focuses on the international relations discourse of another leading Azharite figure, Sheikh Muhammad al-Bahi. A long-time member of al-Azhar, the founding director of al-Azhar University (1961–1962) and the minister of al-Awqaf (religious endowments) and the affairs of al-Azhar (September 1962–March 1964), Bahi had a multifaceted—intellectual, professional, and personal—relationship with the older Sheikh Shaltut and the younger Yusuf al-Qaradawi. In a sense, Bahi represented a bridge between the second and third generations of moderate-reformist scholar sheikhs. Bahi, in his capacity as general director of the Department of Culture at al-Azhar, commissioned the young Qaradawi and his friend Ahmad al-'Assal, to collect and edit the numerous lectures, Quranic exegeses and fatwas of Sheikh Shaltut into a publishable form.[1] As noted in Chapter 3, Shaltut was not a prolific writer, despite his extensive lectures, numerous fatwas, and short essays. Bahi, however, thought the Sheikh of al-Azhar should have a substantive published record. Had it not been for the initiative of Bahi and the efforts of Qaradawi and 'Assal, much of the discourse of Sheikh Shaltut would have been lost, and it would have been difficult for this author to reconstruct Shaltut's understanding of international relations.

In his memoirs, Qaradawi praises Bahi's books for "having left an echo in cultural and intellectual circles" since they confronted "Marxian thought which says religion is a myth and opium; and secular thought that says Islam is a religion and not a state." Qaradawi adds that Bahi, known for his harshness (*shidatuh*) and even roughness (*'unfuh*) in his relations with his staff, treated him with utmost kindness, which he interpreted as a "favor from God upon His servant."[2]

Bahi wrote more extensively on political and social issues, including international relations, than Shaltut or even Abu Zahra. He is credited with authoring over seventy manuscripts, published first in Cairo and later in Beirut between the 1950s and early 1970s. Bahi was more inclined than Abu Zahra and Shaltut to dwell on contemporary problems in international relations, such as the colonial legacy, especially in the Muslim world; the evolution of the Cold War and its implications for the developing world; and the then raging ideological, economic, and political struggle between Western capitalism and Eastern socialism.

Less preoccupied than members of the first generation in demonstrating Islam's compatibility with reason, science and technological and industrial progress, which he took for granted, Bahi devoted himself to the more ambitious goal of proving Islam's superiority to both capitalism and socialism as ideational systems. In Bahi's worldview, Islam's superiority over all other human designed systems emanates from its divine origin; its understanding of the conflicting tendencies within human nature (*al-fitra al-insaniya*); and its articulation of an all-encompassing system of religious ethics (*al-khuluqiya al-Diniya*) that is simultaneously moral and practical (i.e., does not impose serious hardships on the individual or community). Bahi effectively articulated the mainstream Islamist view that anchoring individual and group conduct in Islam's religious ethics is the surest path to achieving worldly satisfaction and material progress, while simultaneously elevating the individual's and the community's moral caliber.

Islam's centuries-old quest for a moral community is manifest in Bahi's writings. Anchored in religion, this moral community, often referred to as the Islamic society, ensures individual freedom and individual responsibility, social stability, and material and moral advancement. More importantly, though, it offers ample opportunities for individuals to act ethically and thus earn their reward in the afterlife. For Bahi, the believer's gaze should remain fixated on God and the afterlife, while concerned about, but not preoccupied with, the affairs of this world.[3] While definitely not a Sufi, Bahi maintains consistently that wealth and worldly success are not signs of God's favor. God bestows wealth on whoever He wants, irrespectively of whether they believe or disbelieve in Him, Bahi argues.[4] Bahi, thus, stands out among contemporary Islamists in depreciating the importance of wealth and worldly success at both the individual and group levels as measures of worthiness in the eyes of God. The rewards of this world and its tribulations pale in comparison to what awaits us in the afterlife in the form of eternal salvation or eternal damnation.[5] Humans should be fully engaged in the affairs of this world, but never lose sight of its transient nature.

Sacrificing for the sake of the other while placing others' wellbeing ahead of one's own wellbeing (*al-ithar*) are central to Islamic ethics.[6] A moral community is, thus, defined in terms of the moral conduct of its members and its own ethical conduct relative to other human communities and not in terms of its material advancement. In this respect, the initial Muslim community that the Prophet Muhammad founded in Medina was highly advanced in terms of its internal solidarity and the ethical conduct of its members, despite its poverty and reliance on primitive forms of production in comparison to subsequent human societies.[7] Shaltut, Abu Zahra, and Bahi paint the same picture of the nascent Muslim community in Medina, an "imagined" community that is the reference point for contemporary Islamists of all shades.

What binds a moral community is a communal spirit (*rouh Jami'iya*), whereby every member cares for the wellbeing and feels for the suffering of other members.[8] Bahi's ample references to a communal spirit, a notion rarely used by other contemporary Islamists, may indicate the influence of Hegel on his thought. A detailed treatment of Hegelian philosophy and its impact on the German-educated Bahi are beyond the scope of this book. Suffice it to say here that the notion of the "spirit" that plays a pivotal role in Hegel's explanation of progress in human history plays an equally important role in Bahi's political and social discourse.

Bahi constantly reminds the reader that while subsequent human societies achieved higher levels of material advancement and prosperity, none even came close to matching the moral fortitude and ethical standards of the initial Muslim community that the Prophet Muhammad founded at Medina. Subscribing to a circular rather than a linear view of human history, and here significantly departing from Hegel,[9] Bahi maintains that only by reinstating the moral code that bound this initial Muslim community can Muslim societies reverse their current decline.[10]

It is within this context of building, or resurrecting, a moral community that is anchored in Islam that we can comprehend Bahi's overlapping concerns with the following five themes, which inform Bahi's discourse on international relations: 1) safeguarding the political, economic, and cultural independence of Muslim societies; 2) freeing Muslim societies from the shackles of imported ideologies (*al-ideologiat al-mustawrada*) that emanate from European history and experiences; 3) reconfiguring domestic political and socioeconomic orders along Islamic axes; 4) promoting the political and economic integration of Muslims in the pursuit of an Islamic union; and 5) pursuing relations of peace, dialog, and collaboration with non-Muslims, as long as the latter do not aggress against Muslims or seek their domination and exploitation.

Following a biographic sketch, this chapter critically examines Bahi's perspectives on international relations, focusing on the following four axes: the underlying principles of international relations; Bahi's critique of capitalism and socialism and his call for an Islamic alternative; war and jihad; and the road to Islamic unity.

Bahi: A Biographical Sketch

Muhammad al-Bahi came from al-Buhayrah province in Northern Egypt.[11] He was born in 1905, the same year that 'Abduh died and Sayyid Sabiq (another Islamist thinker whose views were briefly examined) was also born. In his autobiography, Bahi describes himself as coming from a relatively comfortable rural background.[12] He credits his father's financial generosity for his inclination to refrain from a preoccupation with material pursuits.[13] At the age of 21, Bahi joined al-Azhar, but he canceled his registration during the first year, opting instead to attend selected lectures and to study for the 'alimiyya examinations, the license to teach religion, on his own. Of the 480 candidates, unenrolled at al-Azhar, who sat for the extended written and oral examinations, only four passed, with Bahi coming in first. Bahi then embarked on a degree in rhetoric and literature at al-Azhar. A few months shy of graduation, he was offered a scholarship, named after the late Muhammad 'Abduh, to pursue doctoral studies in Germany. The renowned Azharite thinker, Sheikh Mustafa Abdel Raziq, later Sheikh al-Azhar, was a member of the selection committee.[14] Abdel Raziq had two questions for Bahi. The first question was straightforward. Would Bahi choose to major in history or in philosophy? Bahi chose philosophy on the ground that the topic of his thesis was the influence of Greek philosophy on Arabic literature. The second question was trickier. As an Azharite, how would he cope with coed classes in Germany? Bahi's witty and satisfactory answer was that he would just focus on the lectures and not be distracted by other matters.[15]

On September 27, 1931, Bahi, along with another unnamed scholarship recipient, set sail for Trieste in Italy before journeying by train to Berlin, Germany.[16]

The Second Generation: Sheikh Muhammad al-Bahi | 105

Bahi recollects the fanfare that surrounded the departure of this small official delegation. There was a farewell ceremony attended by government officials that was preceded by a private audience with King Fouad. King Fouad left a positive impression on the young Bahi, who admired the "wisdom of his thought" and the "politeness of his speech."[17] Bahi recollects that the king praised Germany's industrial achievements among others, noting that these advancements reflected the knowledge disseminated by German universities.[18] Bahi's account suggests the presence of certain pro-German sympathies within Egyptian nationalistic circles at the time. Sending a small delegation to pursue advanced studies in Germany was possibly an attempt to break away from British and French hegemony over the dissemination of European knowledge. In support of this claim, Bahi notes, in passing, that Egyptian officials close to Britain tried to sabotage his scholarship, but to no avail.[19] Before embarking on his European journey, Bahi and his companion paid a courtesy visit to Sheikh al-Azhar, Muhammad al-Ahmadi al-Zawahiri. Suspecting that the two students would try to secure teaching posts at al-Azhar upon graduation, the Sheikh duly informed them that all that European universities taught was atheism and that al-Azhar had no need for their graduates.[20] This brief encounter with Sheikh al-Azhar then was indicative of a future stormy relationship that Bahi would have with its traditional *'ulama*. While more conservative in his outlook than 'Abduh, Bahi shared 'Abduh's disdain for the traditional *'ulama*.

Bahi spent his first year in Germany in Berlin, learning German and some English, becoming sufficiently proficient in German by the year's end to commence his doctoral studies at Hamburg University, where he also studied Greek and Latin. Bahi provides a highly sympathetic account of life in Germany in the 1930s, with no experience of any sort of discrimination on grounds of his different nationality and religion.[21] The only disturbing element in his experience is that Bahi seems to subscribe, wittingly or otherwise, to the Nazi narrative regarding the Jews. Bahi accepts the distinction between German and Jew; laments that many jobs were offered to recent Jewish migrants from Eastern Europe while thousands of Germans, especially those discharged from the army, could not find employment; chides German women for (allegedly) preferring the company of Jewish men over fellow German men; and commends German universities for swiftly substituting German faculty for the dismissed Jewish faculty.[22] Whether this anti-Jewish undertone was the result of Bahi's own experiences in the Germany of the 1930s, or emerged later in life as result of the escalating Arab-Israeli conflict, is rather unclear. In May 1936, Bahi successfully defended his dissertation on Muhammad 'Abduh's thought, his relationship to Afghani and his educational and social reforms. Written in German, the dissertation was not translated into Arabic or any other language. While there are hardly any references to the dissertation in Bahi's subsequent published work, written exclusively in Arabic, the influence of German philosophy, especially dialectic reasoning, on his argumentation style is evident.

After a short visit to Egypt where he was welcomed by several Azharite Sheikhs, including Sheikh Shaltut, Bahi returned to Germany for further studies, this time on a scholarship from al-Azhar. He stayed in Germany until the outbreak of World War II when he returned to Egypt for good.[23] Of the scholar sheikhs examined in this work, Bahi had the longest sojourn in Europe, and only he and 'Abduh mastered a European language, German and French, respectively. Bahi's positive experience in Germany was not replicated some twenty years later when he spent the 1955–1956 academic year at the Institute of Islamic Studies at McGill University, Canada, as a visiting faculty member. The mature Bahi was shocked at the way Islam was being taught at the Institute. He felt that the faculty pursued a colonial agenda, disguising their attacks on Islam under a veneer of scientific inquiry. Bahi was particularly critical of some of the faculty of Muslim backgrounds who, he believed, participated in this malicious colonial campaign to smear Islam. At the end of his stay at McGill, Bahi deposited a highly critical report of the work of the Institute, which he claimed contributed to the resignation of its then director.[24] Bahi's negative experiences at McGill provided the backdrop for his most celebrated work: *Modern Islamic Thought and its Relationship to Western Colonialism*, whose first edition was published in 1957, with subsequent editions appearing until 1970, referred to in detail in this chapter, as it provides us with major insights into Bahi's construct of international relations.[25]

Around 1939, Bahi was offered employment at al-Azhar to teach philosophy in the prestigious Faculty of Principles of Religion as well as psychology in the Education Department, then part of the Faculty of Arabic Language.[26] His appointment at a grade higher than Azharite teachers who only studied at al-Azhar triggered an immediate backlash from the traditional *'ulama*.[27] From the outset, Bahi saw himself as a force of change at al-Azhar, with several ideas for educational reform, which by and large reflected his European experience. Like Shaltut, he allied himself with Sheikh Mustafa al-Maraghi, Sheikh al-Azhar between 1935 and 1945, who sought educational reform over the opposition of the traditional *'ulama*.

A turning point in Bahi's career occurred in 1961 when an unprecedented plan for reforming al-Azhar was adopted, which came to be known as Law No.

103.[28] Bahi was one of two representatives of al-Azhar invited to attend the long parliamentary session at which the law was adopted and was able to introduce one minor change to the language of the law.[29] Clearly, though, the impetus behind this ambitious reform plan came from outside the walls of al-Azhar. Despite his very limited contribution to formulating law No. 103, Bahi became heavily involved in implementing one pivotal dimension of the reform, namely overseeing the operations of the newly founded al-Azhar University. At the initiative of President Nasser, Bahi was appointed interim director of the University; six months later on *al-Adha* feast, Nasser confirmed him in the new position.

Bahi used his new position to push for major curricular reforms as well as reorganize the teaching faculty at al-Azhar. A major and controversial element in the curriculum reform was adding a preparatory year with two aims: introducing students who came from al-Azhar secondary schools, like Bahi himself, to Mathematics and European languages, mainly English; and providing students who came from a non-Azharite background (e.g., public schools) with a stronger background in the Arabic language and religious sciences. While insisting on the preparatory year, Bahi diluted opposition from students by offering them subsidized meals and housing.[30] However, opposition from the traditional *'ulama* was stiffer and better organized. Bahi also sought to ensure that faculty taught in their areas of specialization. As in many universities, some faculty were not teaching in accordance with their specialties, but the problem seems to have been more widespread at al-Azhar.[31] He also insisted on research as a promotion criterion and not just seniority. Bahi offered to relieve established faculty of all teaching duties for one year with full pay in order for them to focus on their research. After that, they could apply for higher academic ranks, instead of maintaining their existing ranks, which paid slightly less money. Most traditional *'ulama* suspected that Bahi was plotting to phase them out and fought back. Bahi's tenure as director was too brief and too contentious for him to see these reforms through.

In September 1963, Bahi was moved from the directorship position to the Cabinet as Minister of Religious Endowments and Affairs of al-Azhar. Bahi notes in his autobiography that, a few years later, he found out that this apparent promotion was designed to remove him graciously from the directorship of al-Azhar University.[32] Bahi's term as minister was equally brief, ending in the next cabinet reshuffle in March 1964. It was characterized by frequent clashes first with Sheikh Shaltut, despite their former friendship, over the management of al-Azhar;[33] also with the aforementioned Sheikh Sayyid Sabiq (Chapter 3) who was serving then as the Director General of the Ministry of Religious Endowments, before being pushed out by Bahi; and with the Interim Director of al-Azhar

University, who replaced him when he became minister.[34] Most importantly, and most consequentially for his career, Bahi quarreled with what he refers to as hardcore Marxian elements within the regime. Qaradawi writes in his memoirs that Bahi departed from the Ministry "with just his salary and the enmities he brought upon himself."[35]

In his autobiography, Bahi blames his abrupt departure from the cabinet and from the public arena to the plotting of Marxian elements who, according to him, sought to terminate the financial autonomy of al-Azhar by confiscating the religious endowments and subverting the role of *'ulama* to that of spreading socialist teachings even when these contradicted the spirit of Islam.[36] The autobiography was obviously written a few years after all these elements were purged by President Anwar Sadat who, incidentally, is mentioned only once in the autobiography and in a positive way. Bahi seems to have read too much into his departure from the cabinet in 1964. Cabinet reshuffles were and still are quite common in Egypt.

After 1965, Bahi became increasingly pessimistic about his own prospects and those of Egypt. He felt that the Nasser regime was seeking to silence him by denying him public forums to speak and censoring his books.[37] Bahi refers to 1966 as being a particularly ominous year for two reasons. At the personal level, he had a confrontation with Field Marshal 'Abdel Hakim 'Amer, whose power at the time was second only to Nasser's. The story ran as such. A new owner acquired the small villa that Bahi had rented since 1963. The sale was negotiated by a certain real estate agent, Mustafa 'Amer, who turned out to be the brother of Field Marshal 'Amer. Mustafa 'Amer tried to get Bahi to evacuate the villa because the new owner wanted to live there.[38] Citing the new rental law that prohibited the removal of tenants even if the owner needed the residence for personal use, Bahi refused to evacuate and approached Marshal 'Amer, whom he obviously knew, in the hope that he would restrain his brother. The meeting with the Marshal did not go well. 'Amer wanted to know Bahi's opinion of the banned Muslim Brotherhood Movement and the writings of Sayyid Qutb, especially his controversial work *Ma'alem fi al-Tariq* (*Milestones*).[39] To 'Amer's chagrin, Bahi defended Qutb's writings, noting that they were in accordance with the Quran, irrespectively of what the politicized press wrote about them. According to Bahi, his defense of Qutb infuriated 'Amer, who rose to his feet ushering the meeting's end.[40] In brief, Bahi's defiance toward powerful regime elements contradicts Fawaz Gerges depiction of him as a "close functionary of the Nasser regime."[41]

Equally important, and as of 1966, Bahi's books were censored in Egypt. The latest (fifth) edition of his most celebrated work *al-Fikr al-Islami al-Hadith* was stopped at the press after Bahi refused to tone down his harsh criticisms of Marxism and socialism. The Egyptian authorities also banned his latest book *Tahafut al-Fikr al-Madi al-Tarikhi* (The Demise of Historic Materialist Thought) and unleashed an unprecedented attack in the national press against its contents and its author.[42] Bahi started to publish his works in Beirut with *Dar al-Fikr al-'Arabi*. An established scholar by then, his writings were welcomed by a growing segment of the Arab public that was increasingly turning to Islam for answers, especially after the defeat of Arab armies in the June 1967 war with Israel.

It was against this backdrop of withdrawal from public life, disillusionment with the direction that Egypt and al-Azhar were taking, and heightened anxiety about his own personal safety that Bahi, probably around 1970, wrote the very bleak conclusion to his autobiography. The conclusion lists a litany of complaints against political and social life in Egypt, and more generally the Arab and Muslims worlds. Underscoring the many hardships he encountered in life, Bahi ends his autobiography on a sour note: "This mortal life is not worth the wing of a mosquito."[43] The pessimism that pervades the autobiography reminds us of another Islamic thinker from the medieval period, Abu al-'Ala' al-Ma'arri (973–1057). While Bahi does not explicitly refer to the renowned poet and philosopher, it is highly unlikely that an Islamic thinker of his stature had not read al-Ma'arri.

The Underlying Principles of International Relations

Bahi's construct of international relations is grounded in a broader understanding of relations between human societies. For Bahi, human societies are characterized by profound differences, primarily in terms of the principles upon which they are founded. Western societies are founded on the capitalistic principle of private ownership of the means of production, while socialist societies are based on the contrary principle of collective ownership. Yet, the Islamic society aspired for cannot be established on any principle or creed except Islam itself.

A principal preoccupation of Bahi is to demonstrate that the Islamic society he calls for would be at peace with other societies, as long as they do not seek to dominate and exploit it or impose their ideologies upon it. "Peace with dignity" is what the Islamic society aspires for, he notes.[44] While broader, Bahi's notion of "peace with dignity" is comparable to Shaltut's "armed peace." In *al-Din wa al-Dawla* (Religion and the State), Bahi notes that Islam is a "call for peace as well as a system of government."[45] The preservation of peace between Muslim societies and non-Muslim ones hinges on three related components. First, Muslim societies should refrain altogether from aggressive or threatening actions against non-Muslim societies, as long as the latter do not demonstrate any hostile intensions toward them.[46] Bahi, thus, subscribes to a defensive view of jihad, as will be detailed in a subsequent section.

Second, Muslims should act in good faith and honor all the commitments that have been undertaken with non-Muslim societies, as long as the latter honor their commitments. For Bahi and Abu Zahra, reciprocity is the cardinal principle in dealings between different societies. In this regard, Bahi, just like Shaltut and Abu Zahra, unequivocally embraces international treaties, conventions, and institutions that are entered into freely and on the basis of reciprocity. Thus, despite his reservations from an Islamic point toward the operations of Western banks, Bahi vehemently defends the role of the International Bank of Settlements (IBS) in facilitating trade and financial and other economic ties between states. Bahi underscores that the fees the IBS charges its clients do not constitute usury but are payments for the technical advice and other services that it renders.[47]

Third, and most importantly, Islamic society prioritizes building its material and non-material bases of power, in the economic, political, and cultural realms, in order to ensure the resources and the will to ferociously fight back whenever it is attacked or its core interests are threatened. In line with other contemporary mainstream Islamists, especially Qaradawi and Fadlallah, Bahi associates peace with power, defined in terms of economic, military, and psychological preparedness. Before discussing Bahi's construct of power, addressed in the section on jihad, we need to turn to his extensive critique of both capitalism and socialism and his espousal of an Islamic alternative.

Bahi's Critique of Capitalism and Socialism and Call for an Islamic Alternative

Bahi's extensive discourse on international relations, written mainly between the mid-1950s and early 1970s, must be read against the backdrop of the raging Cold War and the accompanying struggle between capitalism and socialism. Bahi perceived the conflict between the US-led and the Soviet-led camps as primarily an ideological conflict, pitting capitalism against socialism, which he also calls communism, Marxism, Marxism-Leninism, and Marxian-materialism. Bahi maintains that the hold of each of these two ideologies, or philosophies, over the citizens of the respective camps as well as globally, did not emanate from its intrinsic worth (*qimatha al-zhatiya*), but rather from military power or, more precisely, the "power of [splitting] the atom and of the missile; a power the like of which humanity had not known."[48] Bahi warns repeatedly of the dangers associated with the possession of massive nuclear arsenals by the two superpowers. In one of his late, and possibly most theoretical, works *al-Islam fi al-Waqi' al-Ideologi al-Mu'asir* (Islam in the Contemporary Ideological Landscape), Bahi writes that "these two societies (capitalistic and socialist) are threatened with extinction; each threatens the other with extinction and they threaten the rest of the world with extinction."[49]

For Bahi, capitalism and socialism have achieved global hegemony by a blend of coercion and deceit. Both ideologies are morally defunct ones that play on individual frailties, fear in the case of socialism, and greed in the case of capitalism, in order to survive and thrive. While they contradict one another, the two ideologies are products of the same materialistic philosophy that emerged in Europe in the 19th century, as a reaction to both "idealist philosophy" and the teachings of the Catholic Church.[50] They deny the spiritual element of humanness, viewing humans as physiological beings who do not possess a soul.[51] They view progress exclusively as material advancement, neglecting the human need for spirituality and for a moral compass to guide individual and collective action. Both ideologies encourage atheism, by absenting God from the life of man.[52] But while capitalism conceals its opposition to religion, socialism celebrates this rejection.[53] The following two sections discuss Bahi's critique of each of capitalism and socialism, while the third section discusses his Islamic alternative.

Bahi's Critique of Capitalism and of the West

Bahi's critique of capitalism is embedded in a broader and far-reaching critique of the West, a critique revolving around two axes: life in Western societies, and the West's historic relationship with the developing World, particularly the Muslim world, which is defined by colonialism and neo-colonialism.

Life in Western Societies

For Bahi, capitalism enshrines the freedom to accumulate wealth and to dispose of it at the owner's discretion. Bahi subscribes to the Marxian critique that capitalism reduces freedom to economic freedom, but even that freedom is enjoyed only by the few, the capitalists. Anyone who has read Marx and Engels's *The Communist Manifesto* would find Bahi's critique of capitalism quite familiar. One should not exaggerate, though, the similarities between Marx and Bahi. Bahi was not impressed with Marx's philosophy, noting in passing that Marx was "more of a revolutionary than a philosopher."[54] Nevertheless, Bahi subscribes to the Marxian view that capitalism is inherently exploitative and unsustainable in the long run.

While capitalism is far more efficient than socialism as a system of production, it fails miserably when it comes to maintaining cohesion within society by cementing the social bond. Bahi depicts Western capitalistic society as a "fragmented society dominated by selfishness and egoism and characterized by psychological anxiety and feelings of insecurity."[55] Clearly, the problem with capitalism does not lie in its emphasis on private ownership of the means of production. Bahi and Islamists in general unequivocally embrace private ownership. Bahi seems to think that the problems of capitalism would be overcome if only capitalists had a social consciousness and acted justly toward workers and the less fortunate members of society. Bahi is adamant, though, that in the absence of a religiously anchored system of ethics, individuals are incapable of developing a social consciousness or a communal spirit (*rouh jama'iya*).[56] Social consciousness emanates from the conscience (*damir*) of the individual whose source is belief in God and fear of God.[57] Bahi and more generally mainstream Islamists are incapable of recognizing the validity of moral systems that, while detached from religion, emphasize human freedom and human dignity, embrace human diversity and human solidarity, value peace, and view wars as limited enterprises that are fought for defensive purposes.

What distinguishes Bahi's critique of capitalism from that of secular leftist critics' is its anchor in religion. In *al-Din wa al-Dawla*, Bahi compares contemporary capitalist society to the ancient society of Midian, as portrayed in Quranic verses 7:85–93, 11:84–95, and 29:36–37. In the Quranic narrative that Bahi interprets quite allegorically, the merchants of Midian constantly cheated or shortchanged buyers. They "did not give full share in the measure and balance, acting unjustly" (7.85).[58] Bahi's interpretation of these verses leads him to argue that exploitation did not start with capitalism but is as old as human civilization. Its principal source is greed, which is rooted in human nature, when not informed by religion. Bahi writes:

> The selfishness of the capitalists in the so called free world today manifests itself in their insistence on directing politics, the economy and society; just as the selfishness of the society of Midian manifested itself in its rejection and defiance in the face of the advice of Shu'ayb and its insistence on preserving the exploitative situation irrespective of the consequences.[59]

What sets capitalism apart is the unprecedented scale at which exploitation has taken place since the 19th century, due to the globalization of economic activities.[60] Equally important, Bahi views exploitation as a transgression against God and not just against fellow humans. In Bahi's religiously anchored worldview, capitalism is sinful on two counts. First, capitalists accumulate their wealth, i.e., their capital, at least in part by exploiting workers. Exploitation, by its very nature, is sinful. Second, and equally importantly, capitalists hoard their wealth; by refusing to share it with the less fortunate, viewing it as exclusively theirs.[61] Hoarding wealth, instead of using it for the public good, is also sinful. Only through following the Islamic alternative that he advocates can these twin sins of capitalism be rectified.

Later in his life, and largely due to his growing disillusionment with the socialist experiment in Egypt and the Arab world, Bahi considerably softened his views on capitalism. Thus, in a late work, *Tahafut al Fikr al-Madi al-Tarikhi* (The Demise of Historic Materialist Thought), Bahi acknowledges that capitalism underwent several reforms, especially in the second half of the 20th century. These state-introduced reforms improved wages, fringe benefits, and working conditions for laborers, while rendering the distribution of wealth more equitable.[62] But while, in its reformed version, capitalism is superior to socialism, it remains grossly inferior to the Islamic system of wealth creation and distribution which he advocates.

As indicated above, Bahi remains highly skeptical of the ability of Western societies to address capitalism's capital accumulation and distribution problems because, in his view, capitalists, and citizens of Western societies in general, lack a social consciousness (or a communal spirit) that only religion can provide.[63] The egoism, materialism, and secularism that are hallmarks of Western societies, thus, impair their ability to address major socioeconomic problems and to provide individuals with a sense of security and social belonging. Individualism, materialism, and secularism erode the social bond; they atomize individuals and render them incapable of a broader vision than their narrow selfish interests. They also put them in a constant state of anxiety.[64] While it is difficult to ascertain whether Bahi had read Freud or the psychoanalytic literature that emerged after Freud, his remarks on the psychological effects of Western civilization reflect a certain familiarity with the literature on the psychological implications of modernity.

The West's Historic Relationship with the Developing World, Especially its Muslim Component

The discourse of Bahi is characterized by a strong anticolonial tone that only Sayyid Fadlallah of the third generation matches. This anticolonial bent is evident in his first published and most quoted work: *al-Fikr al-Islami al-Hadith wa 'Alaqatuh bi al-Isti'mar al-Gharbi* (Modern Islamic Thought and its Relation to Western Colonialism). This massive work revolves around two connnected themes: the multiple goals that Western colonialism sought to achieve in the Muslim world since the second half of the 19th century and the Islamic responses to Western colonialism and neocolonialism.

To begin, Bahi contends that the Western colonizers were primarily interested in exploiting the natural resources and the riches of the Muslim world,[65] but colonialism had equally important political, cultural, and indeed religious goals. Politically, the colonial powers sought at first to colonize the Muslim world, turning it into part of their global empires, but as of the 1920s, colonialism started shifting toward indirect rule or domination by empowering local elites that were loyal to the colonial powers.[66] This shift toward domination and manipulation, rather than direct rule, of the Muslim world accelerated after World War II, because of the strengthening of anti-colonial movements.

While highly aware of the economic and political motives of colonialism and neocolonialism, Bahi is most concerned with their overlapping cultural and religious motives. Bahi argues that, from the early days of colonialism, Western powers recognized that the easiest way to rule Muslim societies was to infiltrate their cultures with Western ideas and values and to erode their attachment to Islam by fostering novel and distorted interpretations of Islam.[67] It is within this context of subjugating the Muslim world that the ideas of individualism, secularism, and state-centered nationalism and materialism were introduced by the Western powers and their local collaborators, who comprised politicians, state functionaries, and, above all, Westernized intellectuals, such as Sayyid Ahmad Khan (1817–1898) in India[68] and Taha Hussein (1889–1973) in Egypt.[69]

Limitations of scope preclude a detailed treatment of Bahi's principal accusations against the West in the cultural and religious realms. Suffice it to say here that Bahi views any attempt to separate religion from politics in Muslim societies as a Western ploy to undermine Islam in order to facilitate the domination of Muslims. Bahi goes a step further, accusing the West of seeking to undermine Islam not merely for instrumental reasons, i.e., to facilitate the subjugation of Muslim societies, but also because of its deep-seated hostility toward the Islamic religion that goes back to the crusaders' era, if not earlier.[70]

Bahi repeatedly alleges that the West has not forgiven the Muslims for defeating the crusaders and denying them control over the holy sites in Jerusalem, which the Christians coveted as much as the Muslims did.[71] Stated bluntly, Bahi contends that while secularism distanced itself from Christianity, from which it emerged through a dialectical process, it inherited its intense hostility toward, and indeed fear of, Islam. For Bahi, the secularists and the church, especially the Catholic Church, were more than willing to cast aside their profound differences and to work together to undermine Islam.[72] Clearly, Bahi was not the only Islamist thinker of his generation to draw a close association between the contemporary West and the historic crusades, and to argue that the colonial and postcolonial policies of the West were a continuation of the historic crusades, at least to a large extent. His countryman, the renowned Islamist thinker and preacher (*da'iya*) Sheikh Muhammad Ghazali (1917–1996), railed against the crusader West (*al-Gharb al-salibi*), claiming that its onslaught on the Muslim world, and more generally the developing world, drove Muslim and Third World leaders into the arms of communist Russia.[73] Sheikh Ghazali exerted major influence on the thought of many contemporary Islamists, including Qaradawi (Chapter 5).

To recapitulate, Bahi identifies at least four adverse consequences of colonialism and neo-colonialism: 1) fragmenting the hitherto united Muslim world into separate and often rival political entities; 2) creating and accentuating divisions within each Muslim society between a small minority that allied itself with the West, for various material and ideational reasons, and the rest of the population that sought, against great odds, to preserve the Islamic character (*al-shakhsiya al-Islamiya*) of society; 3) estranging Muslim societies from one another, for example, by promoting the ideology of pan-Arabism as an alternative to identifying with the one Muslim *umma*; and 4) rendering these societies dependent on either the capitalist West or the socialist East in both the economic and ideological realms.[74] With regard to this last point, Bahi consistently maintains that the governing elites in Muslim societies always acted as if they had to choose between one of two models of economic and social development: the capitalist model or the socialist model;[75] for a combination of material and ideational reasons, they never seriously contemplated following the Islamic model of governance.

Al-Fikr al-Islami al-Hadith is not just about the alleged Western campaign to divide, dominate, and manipulate the Muslim world. The work is equally concerned with the responses to this ongoing campaign from within the Muslim world. Broadly speaking, Bahi distinguishes between two contradictory responses. These responses represent contending schools of thought, i.e., theoretical approaches that were triggered by contact with the West. The first approach sought to accommodate or indeed appease the Western colonial powers through a variety of interrelated strategies, such as embracing the Western model that separated religion from politics and thus denying Islam's comprehensive system for the organization of the state and society (the case of Kemal

Ataturk in Turkey[76]); claiming to adhere to Islamic principles in order to gain legitimacy, while refusing to undertake any concrete steps to Islamize society and even blocking attempts to do so by societal groups; and advancing distorted interpretations of Islam that emphasized its mystical side (e.g., Sufism) instead of viewing it as the principal source of guidance for the believer on matters of creed and conduct.[77] Bahi categorically rejects this accommodational approach, accusing its advocates of colluding with the colonial West to undermine Islam and render it peripheral to the political, social and intellectual life in Muslim societies.

The second school of thought, Bahi contends, rose to defend Islam against the unjust attacks of Western and Westernized intellectuals. Bahi identifies Afghani and 'Abduh, along with figures like 'Abduh's disciple, Rashid Rida, and the Indian activist, poet, and philosopher Muhammad Iqbal (1877–1938), as representatives of this second approach.[78] Bahi presents a highly sympathetic, indeed romanticized, accounts of their views, emphasizing their contributions to reviving Islam (*tajdid al-Islam*) by cleansing it from unhealthy influences and returning it to its roots in the Quran and the Sunna; refuting the criticisms leveled against Islam, especially regarding its incompatibility with reason, the sciences and more generally modernity; and spreading its teachings among Muslims populations that had grown ignorant of the true message of Islam. Bahi clearly identifies himself as belonging to this second approach. In summary, while Bahi's views on the West softened over time, he retained a skeptical attitude toward Western powers and their intentions toward the Islamic world, a mistrust of the West that is a hallmark of his international relations discourse. Qaradawi and Fadlallah, in particular, of the third generation shared this skeptical-critical attitude toward the West.

Bahi's Critique of Socialism

Bahi is even harsher in his critique of socialism as an ideology, which he invariably refers to as Marxism, Marxism-Leninism, Bolshevism, and historic materialism. This ideology provided the foundation of a type of politico–socio–economic system that first appeared in Russia at the end of World War I before spreading to China, and Eastern and Central Europe in the wake of World War II. While acknowledging that socialist ideology represented a popular response to the exploitation and abuses of capitalism in 19th-century Europe, Bahi contends that it never represented a viable alternative to capitalism due to its utopianism and incompatibility with human nature (*al-fitra al-insaniyya*).[79]

As a system of ideas, or theory, socialism (or Marxism) was used by ideologues, such as Marx, Engels, and Lenin, to stimulate the hatred of the workers toward the capitalists in order to bring down capitalism and place power in the hands of a small group of revolutionaries who subscribed to radical agendas of violent change.[80] Bahi never considered Marx or Lenin to be serious theorists; he viewed them as master manipulators or demagogues who exploited the plight of agricultural and industrial workers in order to grab and hold on to power. While Bahi's first published work, *al-Fikr al-Islami al-Hadith*, devoted almost equal weight to refuting capitalist and socialist ideologies, his later and far more polemical work, *Tahafut al-Fikr al-Madi al-Tarikhi*, was preoccupied with demonstrating the multiple failures of socialist regimes in terms of competing with the quantity and quality of industrial output in the West, fulfilling their promises of equitable distribution of wealth, or providing their citizens with any measure of freedom, including freedom from want.[81]

What rankles Bahi about socialism is not its utopianism, but its sheer deceitfulness,[82] promising the population one thing, while delivering the exact opposite. For Bahi, the "dictatorship of the proletariat" is, thus, replaced by the "dictatorship of the individual [leader], the party, and the ideology."[83] More generally, the "better future" Marxian ideology promises, once capitalism is overthrown, turns out to only "bring greater poverty and greater deprivation, rendering Marxian society a society of the impoverished."[84]

Despite its heavy polemics, *Tahafut al Fikr al-Madi al-Tarakhi* is an insightful work. Bahi seems to have fully grasped the principal ailments that socialist systems suffered from, which included technological backwardness, insufficient incentives for workers, the appearance of a new class of party apparatchiks exploiting the system for its own advantage, the absence of individual freedoms, and the inability to deal with dissent except through repression. Writing in the late 1960s, Bahi recognized that the socialist regimes in Eastern and Central Europe lacked internal legitimacy and owed their existence to brute Soviet power. Writing in the same period, Sheikh Ghazali launched an even more polemical attack against the Soviet Union and communism.[85]

The Islamic Alternative

Bahi's detailed critiques of the capitalist West and the socialist East precede, and set the stage for, the Islamic alternative to both systems that he espouses. Bahi's Islamic alternative enshrines the principle of private ownership of wealth (*al-Mal*), while stressing that wealth must be accumulated through lawful means, i.e., without exploiting workers or shortchanging buyers, and spent, in part, for public benefit.[86] For Bahi, God is the source of all wealth as indicated by several of His Names, such as *al-Razeq* and *al-Wahhab*.[87]

According to Bahi, those who possess wealth are merely entrusted with it, for ultimate ownership of wealth as of all things belongs to God alone.[88] While the wealthy are entitled to spend part of their wealth on their own welfare, they must also share it with the less fortunate through *zakat* (alms giving) and *ihsan* (charity).[89] Bahi distinguishes between the ownership of wealth and its uses, for while wealth ought to remain in private hands, it must be used for the public benefit. Those who own wealth have the dual responsibility of accumulating their wealth lawfully, i.e., without exploitation, and to spend a significant part of it for the benefit of the public.[90] While Islamic thinkers over the ages have written extensively on the lawful versus unlawful means of wealth accumulation, the principal contribution of Bahi seems to lie in his equal emphasis on the obligation to spend a significant part of one's wealth on the public good.

To reiterate, in Bahi's envisioned Islamic society, most wealth is privately held. The accumulation and the distribution of private wealth are, nevertheless, regulated by the *sharia* and guided by the communal spirit that influences all members of society, both rich and poor.[91] This communal spirit mitigates income disparities, ensuring that those who own wealth do not hoard it or spend it frivolously, but share it with the less fortunate through both *zakat* and *ihsan*. In one of his more polemical utterances, Bahi states that Islamic society is the only human society that is not afflicted by class conflict and class struggle.[92] While Bahi is adamant about the universality of the Islamic message, he only proposes the Islamic alternative for Muslim or majority-Muslim societies. Thus, while non-Muslim societies are free to choose their political and socioeconomic systems, there is only one viable and authentic option for Muslim societies, Islam.

Much of Bahi's international relations discourse revolves around the need to protect the freedom of Muslim societies to choose Islam as the organizing principle of their polities, economies, and societies without interference from the capitalist West or the socialist East.[93] Thus, in *al-Islam fi al-Waqi' al-Ideologi al-Mu'asir*, Bahi refers to the Muslim world as *dar al-Islam* (the abode of Islam)[94], emphasizing that it should not be part of the capitalistic West or the socialist East, but should constitute a third block (*kutla thalitha*) on the world stage, with Islam as its governing system of ideas or ideology.

The Meaning and Purposes of Jihad

Bahi's critical view of the capitalist West and the socialist East does not translate into advocating armed confrontation with either camp. In line with the other contemporary Islamists examined in this work, Bahi subscribes to a defensive view of Jihad, but his treatment of the subject is far less detailed than that of the other scholar-sheikhs of the second and third generations discussed here. Bahi does not devote an entire work to jihad but addresses the subject in the context of his discourses on the relations between Muslim and non-Muslim societies and the organization of the envisioned Islamic society.

Bahi's succinct, yet informative, discourse on Jihad is guided by two preoccupations: 1) refuting certain notions about jihad that he claims are propagated by orientalists and Muslim thinkers who subscribe to an accommodational position vis-à-vis either the capitalist West or the socialist East, and 2) underscoring the defensive purposes of jihad.

For Bahi, the first "falsehood" is that Jihad was limited to the time of the Prophet and his companions, after which it was no longer incumbent on Muslims to engage in Jihad. Bahi categorically rejects this notion, accusing those propagating it of seeking to weaken and dominate Muslim societies by denying them the most potent tool to defend their independence and Islamic character.[95] Bahi does not mince words: the notion that the time of jihad has lapsed is a foreign idea implanted by colonial and neocolonial powers and propagated by their local cronies, such as the Qadiani and the Ahmadi movements in India and Pakistan.[96]

Bahi repeatedly asserts that jihad has a principal role to play in the life of contemporary Muslim societies, for as long as the world remains divided between believers and nonbelievers, and it will remain so until the end of time, those who believe will need to defend their existence, their beliefs and their way of life against those who disbelieve.[97] Bahi, thus, argues, "As long as life includes truth and falsehood, righteousness and deviance, justice and oppression, good and evil, the thing and its' opposite ... fighting is necessary to combat corruption, the dominance of evil ... and disbelief in God and in higher values."[98] He goes on to state, "Jihad is a permanent duty as long as there are humans on this earth and as long as they oscillate between belief and disbelief and between truth and falsehood... those who believe will never cease to exist and those who disbelieve will never cease to exist unless life on earth comes to an end and all existence moves to the otherworld."[99]

In brief, jihad cannot be restricted to a specific period in time or a specific place. It is a fixture of human life and every Muslim society must avail of it when the need arises. Bahi's perspective on fighting as a necessity, due to the presence of aggression in this world, (*min sunnan al-Hayat*) is echoed in the discourses of the scholar-sheikhs of the third generation, especially Qaradawi's and Fadlallah's.

A second "myth" propagated by the enemies of Islam, according to Bahi, is that jihad is a means to impose Islam on others and/or subjugate them to Muslim rule in order to dominate and exploit them. For Bahi and contemporary mainstream Islamists, those who equate jihad with aggression seek to discredit jihad and to discredit Muslims and Islam. It is in the context of refuting the claim that Islam spread through violence that Bahi underscores jihad's defensive nature. For Bahi, Jihad does not aim at conquest for material gain, but at defending the very existence of Muslim societies.[100] When Muslims are subject to attack, God commands them to fight back, enjoining them to overcome their reluctance to risk their lives, as in verse 2:216.[101] This divine command to repel attack in order to maintain one's independence and one's dignity stands irrespectively of time and space. God, however, forbids Muslims from initiating hostilities against those who have not attacked or threatened to attack them, as in Quranic verse 2:190.[102] "The believer does not resort to war and fighting against the enemy, unless forced to," he argues.[103] Bahi advances, though briefly, the mainstream thesis that Muslims prefer peace to war and resort to war, or jihad, only to defend themselves, writing that Muslims seek peace as long as "peace preserves their dignity and their honor (*al-'iza*)."[104]

Bahi's discourse on jihad is related to his discussion of the elements and the purposes of power. In *al-Din wa al-Dawla*, Bahi devotes a chapter, different from the one on jihad, to the topic of "ensuring the safety of the *umma*," in which he briefly discusses the tangible and the intangible elements of power, military preparedness, and internal cohesion and high morale, respectively.[105] Like Qaradawi and Fadlallah after him, Bahi places equal emphasis on both dimensions of power, the tangible and the intangible. He also underscores the defensive purposes of power, which is indispensable for preserving the security of the Muslim *umma*, but should not be used for conquest or for imposing one's creed on others.[106] Military preparedness does not preclude being ready for peace, if the enemy shows an inclination toward peace, Bahi maintains.[107]

In addition to emphasizing its defensive nature, Bahi, in line with mainstream Islamists, does not confine jihad to fighting. Other forms of jihad that he mentions include the jihad of the tongue or of speech, (*jihad al-lisan*) and the jihad of the heart (*jihad al-qalb*). The jihad of the tongue, or of the pen, is intellectual jihad. It revolves around refuting the arguments of the diverse critics of Islam, who comprise orientalists, Christian missionaries, secularists, and, above all, materialistic atheists, who represent the most vociferous enemies of Islam. While this form of jihad is incumbent upon all Muslims, Bahi calls on Muslim intellectuals in particular to rise to the defense of Islam by demonstrating the falsehood of the allegations against it, especially regarding Islam's aggressiveness and its incompatibility with the modern world, i.e., Islam's supposed backwardness. In Bahi's view, Afghani, 'Abduh, Rida, and Iqbal were among the pioneers of this intellectual jihad in the contemporary era.[108]

The jihad of the heart, on the other hand, revolves around unequivocally embracing Islam and enabling it to take hold of the life of the individual and of the group. Aware that the modern world presents Muslims, as individuals and as communities, with numerous temptations to abandon Islam and to follow one of the two hegemonic materialist ideologies, capitalism and socialism, Bahi appeals to fellow Muslims to strive, with their hearts and their minds, to steer clear of both ideologies and to adhere to Islam alone. He concludes his chapter on jihad in *al-Din wa al-Dawla* by stressing that "jihad in the path of God" should manifest itself today by "renouncing both sides: the radical Marxist and the capitalist."[109] While more detailed and clearer, Qaradawi's treatment of the different forms of jihad (Chapter 5) is similar to Bahi's treatment.

Bahi's discourse on jihad has all the ingredients of the mainstream outlook, namely that Jihad takes multiple forms but is mostly associated with fighting for a just cause using just means. Accordingly, Muslims fight to defend their persons, properties, and above all their beliefs.[110] Religious differences, or even disbelief, do not constitute, *per se*, legitimate grounds for fighting, unless those who disbelieve attack the Muslims first or seek by force to turn them away from Islam.[111] Last but not least, fighting for conquest or for material gain, even when done by Muslims against non-Muslims, is not a form of jihad. While the mainstream Islamists of the third generation (Chapters 5–7) provide more extensive treatments of jihad than Bahi's, they all subscribe to the same aforementioned tenets.

The Road to Islamic Unity

Bahi's discussion of Islamic unity is also brief, dispersed throughout his writings. While sharing Rida and Abu Zahra's nostalgia for the lost caliphate, Bahi, unlike Abu Zahra, does not present a roadmap for restoring the caliphate or for establishing a similar office with significant authority over the various Islamic states. Bahi, nevertheless, remains unequivocal in embracing the classic Islamic notion that the Muslims constitute one distinct *umma* whose unity was ordained by God and emphasized in the Quran and the Sunna of the Prophet.[112] His discourse on Islamic unity can be organized under two broad themes, the role of colonial powers in shattering Islamic unity, and the approach that Muslim societies need to follow to restore a semblance of unity in their relations and the form that this unity can take.

Colonialism and the Loss of Islamic Unity

Bahi blames the division of the Muslim world on European colonial powers, which, as of the second half of the 19th century and benefitting from their military and technological advancements, began their military encroachment on the Muslim world.[113] Bahi notes that, on the eve of World War I, the Ottoman Sultanate was the only remaining independent Islamic power of any consequence on the international stage. The rest of the Muslim world had been forcefully incorporated into the empires of the colonial powers, principally Britain and France, against the will of its people[114].

At the conclusion of the Great War (World War I), the Western powers and Bolshevik Russia together ensured the demise of the Ottoman Empire and imposed secularism on Turkey, Bahi argues. In this regard, Bahi presents a very insightful, though not necessarily historically accurate, analysis of the geostrategic goals that the Western powers and Bolshevik Russia sought to achieve by pressuring Turkey to abolish the caliphate, embrace secularism and turn westward.[115] Bahi argues that the Turks did not freely choose secularism or closer ties with the West; these were steps forced on Turkey by external players in order to shatter any lingering dreams of restoring Islamic unity.[116] Bahi contends that the nascent Soviet Union welcomed secularism in Turkey because it undermined the religious bond between its Muslim population and the rest of the Muslim world, thus facilitating the subjugation and indeed de-Islamization of this population.[117] Bahi's hostility toward the capitalist West and the socialist East emanates in part from his deep-seated belief that both camps conspired to destroy the unity of the Muslim *umma*.[118] While Abu Zahra seems to place equal weight on internal and external factors in the breakup of the Muslim world, Bahi places most of the blame on the outside world. Bahi, however, does criticize the rulers of the newly independent Islamic states for failing to make any concrete progress toward restoring a semblance of Islamic unity.

Restoring Islamic Unity

While the term "Islamic state" (used in the singular to connote the state representing the one Muslim *umma*) permeates the discourses of mainstream contemporary Islamists, including those of the third generation, it rarely appears in the writings of Bahi.[119] Bahi, thus, seems to have reconciled himself to the reality of the permanent division of the Muslim world into independent states to a greater extent than fellow contemporary Islamists. Bahi, however, refrains from using the term Islamic states (in the plural), using instead the more classical term *mamalek* (realms), which together constitute one realm, *dar al-Islam* (the abode of Islam).[120]

As an astute observer of the political, socioeconomic, and demographic challenges assailing Muslim societies, Bahi is convinced that these multiple challenges can only be addressed through concerted action on the part of the different states that govern the one Muslim *umma*. He envisions Islamic unity in terms of unity of action, rather than formal political unity, i.e., a singular government for the whole Muslim world. For Bahi, the unity of the Muslim *umma* in the contemporary era, characterized by the consolidation of power in the hands of multiple Muslim rulers (*wulat al-amr*), can only manifest itself in the form of close ties of cooperation between Muslim rulers and their peoples in the security, foreign policy, socioeconomic and cultural domains.

In the security domain, every Muslim ruler should consider an attack on any Muslim land as an attack on his own land and should thus call for jihad against the attacker.[121] In line with nearly all Islamic thinkers, Bahi conceives of jihad as directed primarily against non-Muslims powers. With regard to conflicts among Muslim societies, including military conflicts, Bahi underscores that all should be resolved through mediation based on the Quran and the Sunna.[122] That Muslim societies should solve their problems with each other without any external intervention, mainly through arbitration, is a common theme in the IR discourses of all contemporary mainstream Islamists.

Bahi further maintains that Muslim countries should coordinate their foreign policies, especially regarding the threats posed by global Zionism, capitalism, and socialism.[123] There are various references in Bahi's discourse to the close ties between these three ideologies, and the need for Muslim countries to steer clear of them and embrace an Islamic alternative. Bahi further warns Muslim leaders to avoid undermining each other's authority and to refrain from trying to export imported ideologies, particularly socialism, to other Muslim countries.[124] These references ought to be read as thinly disguised criticisms of the Nasserist regime, which Bahi believed was trying to export its brand of Arab socialism to the more conservative Arab countries.

Bahi has more to say on collaboration in the economic and social domains. He, for instance, proposes the establishment of an international organization that collects the *zakat* from oil and mineral producing countries and then invests this money in the development of the agricultural and industrial sectors in poorer Muslim countries.[125] Bahi argues that oil rich countries need to share their wealth with poorer Muslim countries for both religious and pragmatic reasons. Religiously speaking, all needy Muslims, irrespectively of nationality, are entitled to receive a share of the *zakat* and of *ihsan*. For Bahi, it is not in the spirit of Islam to confine *zakat* and *ihsan* to one's kin and one's ethnicity (or one's country); their benefits should extend to the entire Muslim *umma*, irrespective of geography, in order to maintain its social cohesiveness.[126] Bahi believes that disparities in wealth, within and between Muslim societies, were the second most important reason behind the erosion of social solidarity among Muslims,[127] with the most important reason being illiteracy (*al-ummiya*) about Islam's teachings.[128] From a practical, pragmatic, point of view, Bahi argues that by sharing part of their wealth with the poorer countries, rich Muslim countries will reduce the envy and possible resentment of the poorer countries.[129] He further argues that throughout Islamic history, the envy and resentment of some parts of the *umma* toward others contributed to the weakening of social solidarity and facilitated foreign intervention.[130]

Equally important, and as part of his discussion of the demographic challenges facing highly populated Muslim states such as Egypt, Bahi recommends that Muslim rulers cooperate to facilitate the migration of blue collar workers, especially skilled ones (*al-hruafiyyin*), from the highly populated poor countries to the more affluent ones that are facing labor shortages, like the Gulf states.[131] In other words, the economies of the Muslim countries should complement one another and Muslim countries should give priority to each other in their international economic relations.[132]

In brief, Bahi construes Islamic unity as an association of politically independent but economically and culturally interdependent states whereby Muslim rulers (*wulat al-amr*) 1) respect the authority of one another and do not interfere in each other's internal affairs; 2) cooperate to repel any external attack on any part of the Muslim world, relying on the religiously sanctioned institution of jihad[133]; 3) resolve conflicts among themselves through mediation based on the Quran and the Sunna[134]; and 4) pursue close economic and cultural ties; and facilitate the movement of people, including labor, from one Muslim realm to the other. In this last regard, Bahi subscribes to the classical Islamic notion that Muslims should be able to travel freely across Muslim realms and that Muslims should show hospitality to fellow Muslims, irrespective of ethnicity or region. Bahi thus writes, "Islam does not permit its adherents to treat one another inappropriately. It is not permissible, according to religion, for the Muslims of Africa to treat the Muslims of Asia any differently than they treat each other, on the pretext that Africa is not their homeland." He goes on to note, "The Muslim from any tribe or any continent is the brother of the [other] Muslim in religion." The source of this brotherhood among the believers is their common belief in Islam, Bahi argues.[135] Implementing these steps in pursuit of Islamic unity is left entirely, though, in the hands of the various *wulat al-amr*. The role of the *umma* seems to be confined to exerting pressure on *wulat al-amr* to move in that direction.

Conclusion

Of the six scholar sheikhs surveyed in this work, Bahi was arguably the best informed about the intellectual scene outside the Muslim world. Thus, his discourse on international relations does not only reflect his Islamic background but is equally informed by his comprehension of Western ideologies, including Marxism, and his keen interest in developments on the world stage, especially regarding the colonial legacy and the ideological and political confrontation between the capitalistic West and the socialist East. Bahi's style of argumentation is, however, quite similar to that of other contemporary Islamists. Rarely, if ever, does he present an argument or a critique without firmly anchoring it in the Quran. Bahi is, however, less inclined to quote extensively from the *hadith* of the Prophet than the other sheikhs are. More importantly, and despite his strong attacks against colonialism, neocolonialism, and especially socialism, Bahi subscribes to and has helped articulate the mainstream Islamist view on 1) the desirability of international peace, dialog and cooperation; 2) the impermissibility of coercing non-Muslims to embrace Islam; 3) the defensive purposes of jihad; and 4) the need for a gradual and a peaceful approach to restoring Islamic unity. Each of these themes receives a more detailed treatment in the discourses of the scholar sheikhs of the third generation. It is to these discourses that the subsequent Chapters 5–7) turn.

Notes

1. Yusuf Qaradawi, *Ibn al-Qarya wa al-Kuttab* (Son of the Village and the Kuttab), Vol. 2 (Cairo: Dar al-Shuruq, 2004), 281–84. Qaradawi provides interesting details on the process of editing and collecting the works of Shaltut. Shaltut's longest works—*al-Islam 'Aqida wa Shari'a* and *Min Tawjih al-islam*—were collected from various sources, edited and organized by Qaradawi and Assal under Bahi's supervision. The title of the latter book was chosen by Bahi.
2. Qaradawi, *Ibn al-Qarya wa al-Kuttab*, 281.
3. Muhammad al-Bahi, *al-Din wa al-Dawla min Tawjih Al-Quran Al-Karim* (Religion and the State in Light of the Noble Quran) (Cairo: Maktabat Wahba, 1980), 95, 98, 104–06; *al-Islam fi Hal Mashakil Al-Mujtama'at al-Islamiya Al-Mu'asira* (Islam and Solving the Problems of Contemporary Muslim Societies) (Cairo: Maktabat Wahba, 1981, 3rd ed.), 39–40, 56.
4. Bahi, *al-Din wa al-Dawla*, 109–10, 409–11.
5. Bahi notes that the Prophet Muhammad was often referred to as *"al-ithari"* because he put the welfare of others before his own welfare. Muhammad al-Bahi, *al-Islam fi al-Waqi' al-Ideologi Al-Mu'asir* (Islam in the Contemporary Ideological Landscape) (Beirut: Dar al-Fikr, 1970), 25.
6. Bahi, *al-Islam fi al-Waqi' al-Ideologi Al-Mu'asir*, 12–14.
7. Bahi, *al-Islam fi al-Waqi' al-Ideologi Al-Mu'asir*, 25.
8. Muhammad al-Bahi, *Tahafut Al-Fikr Al-Madi Al-Tarikhi bayna al-Nazariya wa Al-Tatbiq* (The demise of historical materialist thought between theory and practice) (Cairo: Maktabat Wahba, 1975) (3rd Printing), 61–63.
9. Bahi, *al-Din wa al-Dawla*, 9, 22.
10. Bahi, *al-Islam fi al-Waqi' al-Ideologi Al-Mu'asir*, esp. 9–27.
11. This biographic section is based on the following sources: "Muhammad al-Bahi ... al-Faylasuf wa al-Islami al-Aeid mina al-Ishtirakiya" (Muhammad al-Bahi, the philosopher and Islamist who returned from socialism) (2016), *Al Jazeera*, http://www.aljazeera.net/encyclopedia/icons/2016/6/19/bahi, accessed 26 July 2018.

    "Muhammad al-Bahi," (n.d.), *Wahat al-Kotob*, http://www.kotobdown.com/author/184271856762315, accessed 26 July 2018.

    Issam Tlaima, "Mufakkeron min Misr: Dr. Muhammad al-Bahi" (Thinkers from Egypt: Dr. Muhammad al-Bahi), *4Shbab* (2016), https://www.youtube.com/watch?v=uVpi3rSLRx0, accessed 26 July 2018. Muhammad al-Bayoumi, "Dr. Muhammad al-Bahi, rahimahu Allah taala, mufakkeran w mosle7an" (Dr. Muhammad al-Bahi, may God have mercy on him, a thinker and reformer), *Rabetat al-'Ulama al-Suriyeen* (2016), https://islamsyria.com/site/show_cvs/776, accessed 26 July 2018.

    Muhammad al-Bahi, *al-Ikhaa` al-Dini, wa Mujamma' al-Adyan wa Mawqef al-Islam* (Religious brotherhood, the complex of religions and the position of Islam) (Cairo: Dar al-Tadamon, 1981).

"Muhammad al-Bahi," (n.d.), *al-Maktaba al-Azhariya al-Alamiya*, http://azh riyapdf.blogspot.com/p/blog-page_3364.html, accessed 26 July 2018. http://raffy. ws/author/29038/bahi. Most importantly, though, it draws heavily on Bahi's autobiography: Muhammad al-Bahi, *Hayati fi Rihab al-Azhar: Talib wa Ustazh wa Wazir* (My Life at the Encompasses of al-Azhar: as a Student, a Teacher and a Minister) (Cairo: Maktabat Wahba, 1983).
12 Bahi, *Hayati*, 27.
13 Bahi, *Hayati*, 27–28.
14 For biographic information on Sheikh Abdel Raziq, see, inter alia, Houssam al-Haddad (2021), "Sheikh Mostafa Abdel Raziq wa Mawaqefeh min al-Fan wa al-Falsafa wa al-Wahabiya" (Sheikh Mustafa Abdel Razek and his stances on art, philosophy and Wahhabism), https://www.islamist-movements.com/26073, accessed 15 March 2021; "Sheikh Mustafa Abdel Razek... Imam al-Azhar wa Emir al-Hujjaj" (Sheikh Mustafa Abdel Razek.. Imam of Al-Azhar and Prince of Pilgrims), (2020), https://islamst ory.com/ar/artical/3409221/%D8%A7%D9%84%D8%B4%D9%8A%D8%AE-%D9%85%D8%B5%D8%B7%D9%81%D9%89-%D8%B9%D8%A8%D8%AF-%D8%A7%D9%84%D8%B1%D8%A7%D8%B2%D9%82, accessed 15 March 2021.
15 Bahi, *Hayati*, 36.
16 Bahi, *Hayati*, 38.
17 Bahi, *Hayati*, 37.
18 Bahi, *Hayati*, 37.
19 Bahi, *Hayati*, 37.
20 Bahi, *Hayati*, 37.
21 Bahi, *Hayati*, 44.
22 Bahi, *Hayati*, 42.
23 Bahi, *Hayati*, 45.
24 Bahi, *Hayati*, 63–64, 130.
25 Bahi, *Hayati*, 130.
26 Bahi, *Hayati*, 46.
27 Bahi, *Hayati*, 46.
28 There is much literature on this important reform initiative. See Hamid Enayat, "Islam and Socialism in Egypt," *Middle Eastern Studies* 4, no. 2 (1968): 141–72, 155–56; and Brown, *Post-Revolutionary Azhar*, 4–9.
29 Bahi, *Hayati*, 67.
30 Bahi, *Hayati*, 7–71.
31 Bahi, *Hayati*, 74.
32 Bahi, *Hayati*, 124–25.
33 The friction with Shaltut apparently started when Bahi was appointed interim-director of al-Azhar University. When Bahi inquired why he was appointed (at first) interim director, he learned that this was at Shaltut's behest, who did not want Bahi to become director until he, Shaltut, received a salary increase. Shaltut also probably

did not support Bahi's reforms at al-Azhar University. As Minister in charge of the Affairs of al-Azhar, Bahi often bypassed Shaltut, making surprise visits to inspect mosques in the provinces without informing the Grand Imam. Bahi makes it abundantly clear that, while he continued to respect Sheikh Shaltut, he thought that, in his last years, the Grand Imam has succumbed to the influence of his in-laws and his favored students, who were using his high office for personal gain. Bahi, *Hayati*, 87–114.

34 In his memoirs, Qaradawi gently rebukes Bahi for his frequent clashes with other prominent scholar sheikhs (mainly Shaltut, Ghazali and Sabiq) over personal matters, despite their ideological affinity. Qaradawi, *Ibn al-Qarya*, Vol. 2, 314–16.
35 Qaradawi, *Ibn al-Qarya*, Vol. 2, 316.
36 Bahi, *Hayati*, 119–20.
37 Bahi, *Hayati*, 137–38.
38 Bahi, *Hayati*, 132.
39 Bahi, *Hayati*, 133.
40 Bahi, *Hayati*, 133.
41 Fawaz Gerges, *Making the Arab World: Nasser, Qutb and the Clash that Shaped the Middle East* (Princeton and Oxford: Princeton University Press, 2018), 196.
42 Bahi, *Tahafut al-Fikr al-Madi*, Introduction to 3rd Printing, 4–5.
43 Bahi, *Hayati*, 144.
44 Bahi, *al-Islam fi al-Waqi' al-Ideologi al-Mu'asir*, 26.
45 Muhammad al-Bahi, *al-Din wa al-Dawla min Tawjih al-Quran al-Karim* (Religion and the State in Light of the Noble Quran) (Cairo: Maktabat Wahba, 1980), 7.
46 Bahi, *al-Islam fi al-Waqi' al-Ideologi al-Mu'asir*, 26, 252–53.
47 Muhammad al-Bahi, *al-Islam fi Hal Mashakil al-Mujtama'at al-Islamiya al-Mu'asira* (Islam and Solving the Problems of Contemporary Muslim Societies) (Beirut: Dar al-Fikr, 1970), 202–03.
48 Bahi, *Tahafut al-Fikr al-Madi*, 62.
49 Bahi, *al-Islam fi al-Waqi' al-Ideologi al-Mu'asir*, 35.
50 Bahi, *al-Islam fi al-Waqi' al-Ideologi al-Mu'asir*, esp. 17–27.
51 Bahi, *al-Islam fi Hal Maskakil al-Mujtama'at al-Islamiya al-Mu'asira*, 236.
52 Bahi, *al-Islam fi Hal Mashakil al-Mujtama'at al-Islamiya al-Mu'asira*, 229.
53 Bahi, *al-Islam fi Hal Mashakil al-Mujtama'at al-Islamiya al-Mu'asira*, 244–45.
54 Bahi, *al-Islam fi Hal Maskakil al-Mujtama'at al-Islamiya al-Mu'asira*, 28.
55 Bahi, *al-Islam fi al-waqi' al-Ideologi al-Mu'asir*, 25.
56 Bahi, *Tahafut al-Fikr al-Madi*, esp. 61–63.
57 Bahi, *al-Islam fi Hal Mashakil al-Mujtama'at al-Islamiya al-Mu'asira*, 162–73.
58 Shaltut quotes the same verse and makes a similar argument to Bahi's regarding Islam's rejection of exploitation. Shaltut, *Min Tawjijat al-Islam*, 155–57.
59 Bahi, *al-Din wa al-Dawla*, 15–16.
60 Bahi, *al-Islam fi al-Waqi' al-Ideologi al-Mu'asir*, 68–77.

61 Bahi *al-Din wa al-Dawla*, 15–19; *Tahafut al-Fikr al-Madi al-Tarikhi*, 59–62; *al-Islam fi Hal Mashakil al-Mujtama'at al-Islamiya al-Mu'asira*, 42.
62 Bahi, *Tahafut al-Fikr al-Madi*, esp. 30–32.
63 Bahi, *Tahafut al-Fikr al-Madi*, 61.
64 Bahi, *al-Islam fi al-Waqi' al-Ideologi al-Mu'asir*, 25.
65 Bahi, *al-Fikr al-Islami al-Hadith wa 'Alaqatuh bi al-Isti'mar al-Gharbi* (Modern Islamic Thought and its Relation to Western Colonialism) (Beirut: Dar al-Fikr, 1970), Fifth edition (First edition published in 1957), esp. 20–21.
66 Bahi, *al-Fikr al-islami al-Hadith*.
67 Bahi, *al-Fikr al-Islami al-Hadith*, esp. 52–68.
68 Bahi, *al-Fikr al-Islami al-Hadith*, 40–45.
69 Bahi engages in a detailed critique of Taha Hussein's seminal work on Jahili poetry, *al-Shi'r al-Jahili*, alleging that Hussein merely mimicked the orientalist view of Islam. Interestingly, Bahi never mentions Hussein by name. Bahi, *al-Fikr al-Islami al-Hadith*, 234–48.
70 Bahi, *al-Fikr al-Islami al-Hadith*, esp. 66–68, 499.
71 Bahi, *al-Fikr al-Islami al-Hadith*, esp. 66–68, 423.
72 Bahi, *al-Fikr al-Islami al-Hadith*, esp. 6–68. In another work, Bahi refers to this bond as "secular-crusader thought." Bahi, *al-Fikr al-Islami fi Tatawuruh* (Islamic Thought and its Development) (Beirut: Dar al-Fikr, 1971), 4.
73 See Mohamed al-Ghazali, *al-Islam fi Wajh al-Zahf al-Ahmar* (Islam Facing the Red March) (Cairo: Nahdat Masr lil-Nashr wa al-Tawzi', 2005) (the work was dated 1966).
74 Bahi *al-Fikr al-Islami al-Hadith*, 29–36.
75 Bahi, *al-Islam fi al-Waqi' al-Ideologi al-Mu'asir*, 132–35.
76 For Bahi's critique of the Kemalist experiment in Turkey, see Bahi, *al-Islam fi Hal Mashakil al-Mujtama'at al-Islamiyya al-Mu 'asira*, 49–55; and *al-Fikr al-Islami al-Hadith*, 500.
77 Bahi argues that westerners favored Sufism because they thought it brought Islam closer to Christianity. Bahi, *al-Fikr al-Islami fi Tatawuruh*, 24.
78 Bahi, *al-Fikr al-Islami al-Hadith*, esp. 122–202, 423–96.
79 Bahi, *Tahafut al-Fikr al-Madi*, esp. 17–45.
80 Bahi, *Tahafut al-Fikr al-Madi*, esp. 22–23.
81 Bahi, *Tahafut al-Fikr al-Madi*, esp. 62–72.
82 Bahi, *Tahafut al-Fikr al-Madi*, esp. 8–15; *al-Fikr al-Islami al-Hadith*, 353–417.
83 Bahi, *Tahafut al-Fikr al-Madi*, 8.
84 Bahi, *Tahafut al-Fikr al-Madi*, 9.
85 Ghazali, *al-Islam fi Wajh al-Zahf al-Ahmar*.
86 See, especially, Bahi, *al-Din wa al-Dawla*, 121–58; *Tahafut al-Fikr al-Madi*, esp. 56–63.

87 Bahi, *Tahafut al-Fikr al-Madi*, 60; *al-Islam fi al-Waqi' al-Ideologi al-Mu'asir*, 134–39.
88 Bahi, *Tahafut al-Fikr al-Madi*, 56–57; *al-Islam fi Hal Mashakil al-Mujtama'at al-Islamiya al-Mu'asira*, 134–47.
89 Bahi, *al-Din wa al-Dawla*, 122–29; *al-Islam fi Hal Mashakil al-Mujtama'at al-Islamiya al-Mu'asira*, 134–47.
90 Bahi, *al-Din wa al-Dawla*, 126–42; *Tahafut al-Fikr al-Madi*, 59–61.
91 Bahi, *Tahafut al-Fikr al-Madi*, 61–63.
92 Bahi, *Tahafut al-Fikr al-Madi*, 61; *al-Islam fi al-Waqi' al-Ideologi al-Mu'asir*, 61.
93 Bahi, *al-Islam fi al-Waqi' al-Ideologi al-Mu'asir*, 131–34.
94 The term *dar al-Islam*, however, rarely appears in Bahi's writings.
95 Bahi, *al-Fikr al-Islami al-Hadith*, 62.
96 Bahi, *al-Fikr al-Islami al-Hadith*, 39–51.
97 Bahi, *al-Din wa al-Dawla*, 211.
98 Bahi, *al-Din wa al-Dawla*, 121.
99 Bahi, *al-Din wa al-Dawla*, 212.
100 Bahi, *al-Din wa al-Dawla*, 247, 284, 384, 462.
101 Bahi, *al-Din wa al-Dawla*, 212.
102 Bahi, *al-Din wa al-Dawla*, 214, 284. For the same idea, see *al-Islam fi Hal Mashakil al-Mujtama'at al-Islamiya al-Mu'asira*, 114.
103 Bahi, *al-Din wa al-Dawla*, 284.
104 Bahi, *al-Din wa al-Dawla*, 288.
105 Bahi, *al-Din wa al-Dawla*, 361–79.
106 Bahi, *al-Din wa al-Dawla*, 346–91.
107 Bahi, *al-Din wa al-Dawla*, 422.
108 Bahi's *al-Fikr al-Islami al-Hadith* recounts the intellectual contributions of these figures to the defense of Islam.
109 Bahi, *al-Din wa al-Dawla*, 222.
110 Bahi, *al-Din wa al-Dawla*, 211–14.
111 Bahi, *al-Din wa al-Dawla*, 303–404.
112 See Bahi, *al-Islam fi al-Waqi' al-ideologi al-Mu'asir*, 131–32.
113 Bahi, *al-Fikr al-Islami al-Hadith*; *al-Islam fi al-Waqi' al-Ideologi al-Mu'asir*, 134.
114 Bahi, *al-Islam fi al-Waqi' al-Ideologi al-Mu'asir*, 88–90.
115 Bahi, *al-Islam fi Hal Mashakil al-Mujtama'at al-Islamiya al-Mu'asira*, 50–51, 148.
116 Bahi, *al-Islam fi Hal Mashakil al-Mujtama'at al-Islamiya al-Mu'asira*, 148–49.
117 Bahi, *al-Islam fi Hal Mashakil al-Mujtama'at al-Islamiya al-Mu'asira*, 51–53.
118 Bahi, *al-Islam fi Hal Mashakil al-Mujtama'at al-Islamiya al-Mu'asira*, 149.
119 Bahi, however, uses the term at least three times in *al-Din wa al-Dawla*, 397, 401, 402.
120 Bahi, *al-Islam fi al-Waqi' al-Ideologi al-Mu'asir*, 131–32. Bahi also uses the term *al-Bilad al-Islamiya* (country of Islam) quite frequently.

121 Bahi, *al-Islam fi Hal Mashakil al-Mujtamaʿat al-Islamiya al-Muʿasira*, 120.
122 Bahi, *al-Islam fi Hal Mashakil al-Mujtamaʿat al-Islamiya al-Muʿasira*, 214–15, 238; *al-Din wa al-Dawla*, 332–33.
123 In *Tahafut al-Fikr al-Madi*, Bahi emphasizes that all three ideologies are directed against Islam. See, esp., 55.
124 Bahi, *al-Islam fi Hal Mashakil al-Mujtamaʿat al-Islamiya al-Muʿasira*, 154.
125 Bahi, *al-Islam for Hal Mashakil al-Mujtamaʿat al-Islamiya al-Muʿasira*, 153–54.
126 Bahi, *al-Islam fi Hal Mashakil al-Mujtamaʿat al-Islamiya al-Muʿasira*, 150–54.
127 Bahi, *al-Islam fi Hal Mashakil al-Mujtamaʿat al-Islamiya al-Muʿasira*, 150–51, 227–28.
128 Bahi, *al-Islam fi Hal maskakil al-Mujtamaʿat al-Islamiya al-Muʿasira*, 150–51.
129 Bahi, *al-Islam fi Hal maskakil al-Mujtamaʿat al-Islamiya al-Muʿasira*, 154.
130 Bahi, *al-Din wa al-Dawla*, 339–42.
131 Bahi, *al-Islam fi Hal Mashakil al-Mujtamaʿat al-Islamiya al-Muʿasira*, 152–53.
132 Bahi, *al-Islam fi al-Waqiʿ al-Ideologi al-Muʿasir*, 131–35.
133 Bahi, *al-Islam fi al-Waqiʿ al-Ideologi al-Muʿasir*, 121.
134 Bahi, *al-Islam for Hal Mashakil al-Mujtamaʿat al-Islamiya al-Muʿasira*, 151–52.
135 Bahi, *al-Islam fi al-Waqiʿ al-Ideologi al-Muʿasir*, 132.

5

The Third Generation: Sheikh Yusuf al-Qaradawi

Introduction

This is the first of three chapters on the scholar sheikhs of the third generation, examining the international relations discourse of the most regionally and internationally renowned of the six turbaned scholars in this work, namely Sheikh Yusuf al-Qaradawi (hereafter referred to as Qaradawi). Qaradawi has attracted considerably more attention from the scholarly community, the media, and the lay public, than the other five scholar sheikhs have.[1] Various academics have referred to Qaradawi as "the immensely influential and respected theologian,"[2] "one of the most respected Sunni scholars,"[3] "arguably the most influential contemporary Islamic scholar,"[4] and "Global Mufti," as underscored in the title of a comprehensive work on the life and the thought of Qaradawi[5].

Noting that Qaradawi is "frequently identified as perhaps the most influential Islamic scholar in the Islamic World today," Raymond William Baker situates him as an element in the "core group of new Islamists" that included, besides Qaradawi, prominent Egyptian figures, such as the "journalist Fahmy Huwaidy, the lawyer and specialist on *sharia* Muhammad Selim al Awa, and the judge and historian Tareq al Bishri, in addition to [Sheikh Muhammad] al Ghazaly[6] and [Kamal] Abul Majd."[7] Baker argues that these "new Islamists" not only renounced violence but also gave priority to educational reform and raising awareness of Islamic values over political action. Equally important, he contends that they did not claim to possess a monopoly over interpreting Islam, while advocating a mainstream, or centrist (*wasati*), interpretation of Islam.

Qaradawi's fame and the keen interest in his writings, fatwas and opinions on a wide range of issues emanate from at least five related factors. To start with, Qaradawi has been far more politically active than the other Sunni scholar sheikhs were; his political activism was only matched by that of the Shiite cleric Sayyid Fadlallah (Chapter 7). Qaradawi is indeed the embodiment of the scholar activist, adopting and propagating strong and often controversial views on a wide variety of issues pertaining to his native Egypt, the broader Middle East, the Arab-Israeli conflict, and Western relations with the Arab and Muslim worlds. Qaradawi's political activism will be addressed in the subsequent biographical section.

Second, Qaradawi has made extensive use of the broadcast media and the internet to propagate his fatwas and opinions on a plethora of topics, including issues of international relations, to regional and international audiences. His regular appearances on the popular *Sharia and Life* program on Al-Jazeera television since its first episode was aired on November 3, 1996, have allowed him access to a wide regional and indeed global audience.[8] As Lynch notes, Al-Jazeera played a "crucial role in amplifying his [Qaradawi's] influence."[9] Qaradawi has also established a footprint on the Internet. He has been the principal inspiration behind the *IslamOnline*[10] and *IslamWeb* portals, while maintaining his own website (*Qaradawi.net*) and Twitter account.[11] Qaradawi's extensive use of the media earned him the title of "media Shaykh."[12] Jacqueline Brinton refers to Qaradawi as the "prototype of Muslim religious authority on satellite television, blending interactive legal advice with popular public presentation."[13]

Third, Qaradawi has traveled extensively throughout the Arab and Islamic worlds, while also visiting several West European countries and the United States of America. His many trips outside his adopted home, Qatar, have enabled him to interact with scores of Muslim scholars, activists, and audiences from literally the whole world. Qaradawi's good rapport with numerous *'ulama* of diverse nationalities, as well as his remarkable organizational and fundraising skills, have been his pathway to important leadership positions within the global community of Sunni *'ulama*, such as the presidency of the Islamic Union of Muslim Scholars (IUMS)[14] and the European Council on Fatwa and Research (ECFR).[15]

Fourth, with his many books, such as the immensely popular *al-Halal wa al-Haram fi al-Islam* (The Lawful and the prohibited in Islam), as well as with his many sermons, numerous fatwas, opinions, television appearances, and tweets, Qaradawi has cultivated a large and transnational readership and following among lay Muslims in the Arab world and beyond. His highly accessible, indeed modern, style of writing in his theoretical works, such as his two-volume *Jurisprudence of Jihad*, has undoubtedly enhanced his appeal. More importantly, his allure has been increased by his almost exclusive focus on contemporary issues impacting the lives of Muslim individuals and communities, such as the struggle against authoritarian and secular rule in much of the Arab world, the cause of Palestine and the challenges facing diasporic Muslim communities living in largely secular, or even Christian influenced, polities and societies. Of the five Sunni scholar sheikhs considered here, Qaradawi has been the most vocal in his criticisms of authoritarian rule in the Arab world and in his insistence that the rulers are the servants of the people to be freely chosen by them.[16]

Finally, Qaradawi's mainstream, i.e., moderate and balanced, approach to the Quran and the Sunna; his unequivocal opposition to the radical *takfiri* groups[17]; and his emphasis on the defensive purposes of jihad, the centrality of peaceful relations and dialog and cooperation with non-Muslims, has enhanced his appeal to moderate Muslims, respected academics such as Marc Lynch, and non-Muslim audiences. Although the term moderate is open to various interpretations, and there is little moderation in Qaradawi's views on such diverse issues as Palestine, apostasy (*al-ridda*), extramarital relations, and homosexuality, Qaradawi's discourse is clearly at odds with that of radical groups such as al-Qaeda and its successor, the Islamic State in Iraq and Syria (ISIS). Qaradawi's unequivocal condemnation of targeting civilians in Iraq after 2003 outraged Abu Mosab al-Zarqawi, the leader of the Islamic State in Iraq (ISIS's predecessor), who released a statement condemning the "sultans of the airwaves." The statement addressed Qaradawi as such, "You had abandoned the mujahedeen in their confrontation with the biggest enemy."[18] The biographic section below will shed further light on Qaradawi's life-long opposition to radical *takfiri* groups.

While drawing on the available academic literature, this chapter relies primarily on a close reading of that section of Qaradawi's voluminous oeuvre that concerns international relations. Rather surprisingly, this pivotal component of Qaradawi's discourse has thus far received scant attention from academics.[19] Following a brief biographic section, the chapter discusses Qaradawi's understanding of the principles that underpin international relations. It then turns to Qaradawi's extensive discourse on war and jihad before addressing his views on Islamic unity.

Qaradawi: A Biographic Sketch

In terms of familial and educational backgrounds, there are major similarities between Qaradawi and the previously discussed Egyptian scholar sheikhs. Qaradawi was born in 1926 in the village of Safat Turab in the Gharbieh province in Egypt to a poor and rural family.[20] He had a rough childhood, losing his father at the age of 2 and his mother at around 14. His family circumstances, however, did not prevent him from pursuing a classic education at the *kuttab* in his home village before joining the al-Azhar Institute in Tanta. While still in Tanta, Qaradawi was influenced by the Muslim Brotherhood (MB), particularly after he heard the founder of the Brotherhood, Hassan al-Banna, preach, and after he witnessed the well-organized Brotherhood marches in that town. According to most accounts, Qaradawi joined the movement in 1943.[21] Qaradawi was first arrested in 1949, during the first major crackdown on the Muslim Brotherhood in monarchical Egypt. It was during his brief imprisonment in 1949 that Qaradawi met the prominent Brotherhood intellectual and preacher, Sheikh Muhammad al-Ghazali, who, after al-Banna, became a major influence on his thought.

Qaradawi's association with the Muslim Brotherhood proved to be lifelong, although he never held an official position within the movement. Husam Tammam, a member of the Brotherhood and a long-term acquaintance, describes Qaradawi as "the legitimate child of the Muslim Brothers Movement and Organization, and a protagonist of the broader Islamist movement that has emerged since the 1960s."[22] According to Tammam, Qaradawi was offered the position of the General Guide (*al-Murshid al-'Am*) of the Muslim Brotherhood twice, in 1976 and then in 2002; he declined the offer on both occasions.[23] A great deal has been written on Qaradawi's relationship with the Muslim Brotherhood, including by Qaradawi himself, but this is not the place to review this material.[24] What is worth emphasizing, though, is that Qaradawi always maintained that his writings and his fatwas reflected his personal interpretations of the Quran, the Sunna, and the Islamic tradition, and not those of the Muslim Brotherhood or of any political group. Equally important, Qaradawi was always ready to openly criticize the leadership of the Brotherhood, when he believed it was adopting radical positions.[25]

Qaradawi was personally impacted by the deteriorating relationship between the free officers who carried out the 1952 Egyptian coup and the Muslim Brotherhood, which initially supported the overthrow of the monarchy.[26] He received a short prison sentence between January and March 1954, and then a longer sentence between December 1954 and June 1956.[27] His second stay in prison was longer and harsher. In his memoirs, Qaradawi provides a vivid, though nonsensational, account of the conditions under which he and several Brotherhood members were imprisoned: crowded cells, rotten food, twice a day access to toilets and the confiscation of personal copies of the Quran and of religious books. Beatings and humiliations of the inmates were also common.[28] Qaradawi suffered a minor but permanent injury to his right foot when he received fifty lashes on the soles of his feet.[29] Qaradawi boasts that since he was still in his late twenties, in good health, and fit, he endured prison conditions far better than the older and less fit inmates did. Qaradawi was detained and interrogated one last time, for about 50 days, in the summer of 1962, when he was spending his summer vacation in Egypt.[30] Qaradawi then suspended his visits to his native Egypt until after the end of the Nasser era.

Shortly after his release from prison in the second half of June 1956, Qaradawi started his search for gainful employment. He also tried to resume his studies at Faculty of Theology at al-Azhar but had to wait until the summer of 1957 to re-enroll. Qaradawi had to settle for a teaching position at a private nonreligious school in Zamalek in Cairo because the authorities barred him from teaching or preaching at al-Azhar. He also agreed to tutor the daughter of the school owner in order to increase his income. Conditions for Qaradawi, and more generally for the Muslim Brotherhood, improved temporarily in the wake of the tripartite aggression on Egypt in autumn 1956, which the Brotherhood denounced. Brotherhood members, including former inmates, were encouraged to preach at mosques in order to raise the population morale and were compensated for that. Qaradawi was commissioned to preach at a popular mosque in Zamalek and later in Sinai and the city of 'Arish.[31] However, the honeymoon between the authorities and the Muslim Brotherhood was short-lived and ended around June 1957, when news spread that the guards at the notorious Tora prison had massacred dozens of Muslim Brotherhood inmates.[32] Qaradawi was recalled from preaching, but thanks to the personal intervention of the Minister of Religious Endowments, Sheikh Muhammad Baqouri,[33] he was employed at the ministry on condition that he did not preach. About a year later, Qaradawi and his friend, fellow Muslim Brotherhood member Ahmad 'Assal whom Baqouri also employed at the Ministry, requested to be transferred to al-Azhar, arguing that it was their home. They personally presented their transfer request to Sheikh al-Azhar, Sheikh Shaltut, whom they regarded as a mentor. Shaltut granted their request on the spot, instructing the director of his office, his son-in-law, to find them suitable posts within the institution.[34]

Qaradawi and Assal began work at the department of Islamic culture, which was headed by none other the aforementioned Muhammad al-Bahi. The first task that Bahi assigned to the young sheikhs was to collect, edit, and organize the scattered articles, lectures, speeches, Quranic commentaries, and fatwas of Sheikh al-Azhar Shaltut. Qaradawi embraced this task with enthusiasm, viewing it as a service to God and to the *umma*. Bahi had the immediate concern of ensuring that the educated public recognized the scholarly accomplishments of Sheikh al-Azhar. Besides spearheding the process, Bahi's involvement seems to have confined to penning the preface to the collected works and providing the title of one volume. Shaltut relied heavily on Qaradawi. When the latter alerted him that his commentaries on certain Quranic verses were too brief, Shaltut invited Qaradawi to write himself the necessary elaborations.[35] Shaltut also turned to Qaradawi to summarize for him important books of jurisprudence and to supply the answers to questions that Shaltut received, such as whether or not it was permissible for soldiers not to fast during Ramadan.

A highlight of Qaradawi's term at al-Azhar was his encounter with the renowned Indo-Pakistani Islamic thinker and activist, Mawlana Abu al-A'la al-Mawdudi (1903–1979).[36] Qaradawi was familiar with Mawdudi's writings that were earlier translated into Arabic by a group within the Muslim Brotherhood.[37] When Mawdudi visited Egypt to see for himself the sites in Egypt that the Quran mentioned and to meet with Sheikh al-Azhar and prominent Islamic thinkers, Bahi assigned Qaradawi to accompany him throughout his stay and to introduce him to the departments of al-Azhar. Qaradawi also attended Mawdudi's meeting with Sheikh Shaltut. Qaradawi was to maintain a lifelong interest in political and intellectual developments in the Indian subcontinent, visiting both India and Pakistan on a number of occasions and meeting with Muslim scholars and giving lectures; his interest also extended from India to East Asia and Southeast Asia, as far as the Philippines. Qaradawi was to develop a strong intellectual bonding with the Indian scholar and activist, Sheikh Abu al-Hasan 'Ali Nadwi (1913–1999).

According to the prominent Tunisian thinker and leader of the Nahda Party, Rashid Ghannushi, Qaradawi's construct of the Islamic state was heavily influenced by the ideas of Nadwi, and by extension those of Mawdudi.[38] When Mawdudi passed away in September 1979, Qaradawi with a group of sheikhs from the Arab world attended the massive funeral in Lahore, Pakistan, where Qaradawi gave a sermon.[39] Like Qaradawi and Bahi, Mawdudi and Nadwi were strong critics of the European-secular project, contending that the exclusion of religion from politics and the public life would revert Muslims to a state of jahiliya.[40] In brief, Qaradawi's political discourse, especially regarding the Islamic state, reflects the cross-fertilization of ideas from the Arab world and the Indian subcontinent, making it more interesting to study. On the other hand, as Roy Jackson writes, Mawdudi himself was quite influenced by the views of Afghani, 'Abduh, and Rida[41]; the same applies to Nadwi.[42]

Qaradawi was handed one final important task at al-Azhar. In his memoirs, Qaradawi recollects that the Egyptian Ministry of Foreign Affairs asked the Ministry of Religious Endowments and al-Azhar to produce a number of "contemporary, accessible and scientific books" on specific topics to guide Muslims living in Western Europe and the United States on matters of worship (*'ibadat*) and on conducting their affairs (*mu'amalat*) in predominantly non-Muslim societies.[43] When the request reached al-Azhar, Sheikh Shaltut promptly forwarded it to Bahi. Bahi then directed Qaradawi to produce a comprehensive but accessible manuscript to explain what was allowed and what was prohibited in Islam.

The original intent was to translate the work into English and other languages, but Qaradawi was displeased with the original English translation and decided instead to publish the work in Arabic. This is the story behind Qaradawi's first and possibly most influential book, *al-Halal wa al-Haram fi al-Islam*. Rather unwittingly, Shaltut and Bahi, thus, contributed to launching Qaradawi's career as a prolific and serious author, arguably contributing to preserving the continuity of thought between members of the second generation (Shaltut and Bahi) and the third generation (Qaradawi) of reformist scholar sheikhs. To quote Graff and Skovgaard-Petersen, the book "can be read as part of the programme of the so-called Reformist school of thought of Muhammad 'Abduh and Rashid Rida from the beginning of the 20th century, which Qaradawi professes to belong to."[44] While it is incontestable that Qaradawi and Zuhaili were directly influenced by the ideas of Afghani, 'Abduh, and Rida, what also must be emphasized is the pivotal role played by the scholar sheikhs of the second generation (Shaltut, Abu Zahra, and Bahi) in the advancement of this influence.

The 1950s were trying but fruitful years for Qaradawi. Up until his brief imprisonment in December 1954, he was actively engaged as a preacher (*da'iya*) in Muslim Brotherhood circles, despite his concerns about the growing fissures within the movement. Qaradawi seems to have aligned with that faction of the Brothehood that sought an accommodation with the Nasser regime, one which failed to win the support of the majority of the Brotherhood.[45] He particularly steered cleared from any association with the "Secret Apparatus" (*al-Jihaz al-Khas* or *al-Tanzim al-khas*) of the Brotherhood for both ideological and pragmatic reasons;[46] his political activism was to clearly wane after his release from prison in June 1956.

While still in Egypt, and despite maintaining close personal ties with several Brotherhod members, including former inmates, and sympathizing with persecuted Brotherhood members, Qaradawi was to refrain by choice and by necessity from political speech and to focus on his studies and his work at al-Azhar. In addition to returning to the Faculty of Theology in order to pursue a doctorate in Islamic jurisprudence, Qaradawi studied law at the newly founded Arab University in Cairo and even enrolled in English language classes. Qaradawi was to obtain a license in law but opted not to pursue a higher degree in law in order to focus on his doctorate at al-Azhar. His many engagements, however, prohibited him from gaining proficiency in English, something he openly regretted.[47]

By 1960, Qaradawi was eligible for transfer outside Egypt, where he could earn a higher salary and escape state surveillance and the constant threat of arrest. Since 1957, Qaradawi had been in contact with a Qatari official, Sheikh Abdullah bin Turki al-Subaie, in charge of hiring Azharites to teach in Qatar.[48] He had earlier turned down an offer from Bahi to head the Azharite mission in the Libyan city of Misrata in order to be able to travel to Qatar, where he would earn a better salary. Qaradawi had to wait one more year until he was cleared to travel to his destination of choice. He arrived in Qatar in September 1961 to head the Azhar affiliated Religious Institute in Doha.

From his new headquarters in the oil-rich, small Sheikdom, Qaradawi embarked on a multidimensional career that involved preaching,[49] university teaching, and academic administration at the *Sharia* College at Doha University, as well as consulting to multiple Islamic financial houses. The globalization of the media as of the early 1990s greatly enhanced Qaradawi's reach to the Muslim public internationally. The name Qaradawi became closely associated with Al-Jazeera, due to the immense popularity of the network's *al-Shari'a wa al-Hayat* (Islamic Law and Life) program, on which he was the main interlocutor.[50] In addition to lending his name and providing moral support and guidance to the popular Islamic portals *Islamonline* and *IslamWeb*, Qaradawi established his own website, *Qaradawi.net*, which provides detailed information about his life and activities and offers visitors free access to his recent fatwas, speeches, electronic versions of several of his books, and transcripts of his past appearances on *al-Shari'a wa al-Hayat*.

Having spent almost his entire adult life in the public arena, Qaradawi, in his nineties at the time of writing, is the embodiment of the Islamist public intellectual and scholar-activist. As a young man, he lobbied for reforming the curriculum at al-Azhar, a preoccupation he shared with Bahi, participated in the popular struggle against British military presence in Egypt and was imprisoned and tortured by the Egyptian authorities under both the monarchy and the revolutionary regime. Thanks mainly to satellite television and the Internet, not to underestimate the considerable freedom of speech and of movement that he enjoyed in Qatar, the mature Qaradawi has been able to address audiences regionally and worldwide. Utilizing multiple traditional and novel venues, Qaradawi called for protests against the Danish cartoons of the prophet Muhammad[51] and the views expressed by Pope Benedict XVI, which were considered offensive to Islam, in his September 12, 2006, lecture at University of Regensburg in Germany.[52]

Closer to home, Qaradawi has been a vociferous critic of the state of Israel, denouncing all overtures toward it by any Arab or Muslim government, while warning the Palestinians against offering Israel any concessions, especially as far as Jerusalem.[53] Qaradawi also vehemently denounced the air campaigns that were often waged against Iraq during the 1990s, as in 1998.[54] His denunciations of US and Western policies toward Iraq reached a crescendo during the US-led invasion of Iraq in 2003.[55] In the first days of the 2003 US invasion of Iraq, Qaradawi participated in a large demonstration that marched toward the US embassy in Doha, Qatar.[56] But as Mark Lynch observes, Qaradawi's opposition to US policy in Iraq did not lead him to side with the Saddam Hussein's Baathist regime, toward which he was equally hostile.[57]

Qaradawi's position on the dictatorial regime of Saddam Hussein and its foreign policy blunders mirrored that of the "New Islamists," to borrow an expression from Baker's aforementioned book.[58] The "New Islamists," of whom Qaradawi was a leading figure, "recognized the immediate cause of the [1990 Gulf] crisis to be the criminal act of a dictatorial Arab regime that the Arab Islamic system proved unable to contain." Nevertheless, the "New Islamists," Baker adds, "Pointed out that the Arab weakness and disarray revealed by the crisis was particularly dangerous because of the larger threat of unconstrained Western power in the so-called New International Order."[59] Qaradawi was, at the same time, a critic of dictatorial Arab regimes, especially the secular Arab nationalist regimes, and of Western foreign policies toward the Arab and Islamic worlds. When these two forces clashed, as they did in the case of Iraq, Qaradawi and the "New Islamists" found it impossible to unconditionally back either side. Qaradawi's unequivocal endorsement of the Arab uprisings of 2011, however, led him to soften of his stance on Western intervention in the Arab world. Qaradawi's unmasked hostility toward the Muammar al-Qaddafi and Bashar al-Assad regimes after 2011 led him to endorse Western efforts to bring about regime change in both Libya and Syria.

In his mature years, Qaradawi devoted considerable attention—especially through his Presidency of the Islamic Union of Muslim Scholars (IUMS)[60] and the European Council on Fatwa and Research (ECFR)—to help ensure that European Muslims integrate themselves into their societies while maintaining their Islamic identity,[61] and he campaigned tirelessly on behalf of Islamic causes from Bosnia-Herzegovina and Chechnya, to Afghanistan, Iraq and especially Palestine.[62] Drawing on his credentials as a reputable Islamic scholar (*'alem*), preacher (*da'iya*), and as head of the IUMS, Qaradawi engaged in a number of sensitive initiatives, such as heading a delegation of prominent *'ulama* to Khartoum, Sudan, to protest the arrest of the prominent Sudanese Islamic thinker and activist Sheikh Hassan al-Turabi in 2001 and to plead for his release.[63] In summary, one cannot but agree with Graf and Skovgaard-Peterson's depiction of Qaradawi as a global phenomenon, for his influence transcends national borders, as does his conceptualization of Muslims as a single "transnational community" or *umma*, irrespective of differences of geography, history, ethnicity, and culture.[64]

The Underpinning Principles of International Relations

Qaradawi's construct of international relations is predicated on three interconnected notions. The first and second notions concern the comprehensiveness of Islam and the centrality of a *wasati* approach to comprehending Islam and to acting in accordance with its precepts, respectively. The third notion pertains to the presence of universal God-made laws (*sunnan kawniya*) that govern political and social reality, including international relations. Qaradawi is unequivocal that these *sunnan* apply to all humans, Muslims and non-Muslims. Qaradawi, thus, writes, "The *sunnan* of God do not favor a Muslim or a non-Muslim, whoever observes them prevails, and whoever fails to do so fails."[65]

The Comprehensiveness of Islam

Qaradawi, in line with nearly all Islamists, including the mainstream, believes in the comprehensive nature of Islam (*Shumul* or *Shumuliyyat al-Islam*). He quotes Sheikh Shaltut approvingly that "Islam is a creed and a *sharia*."[66] Building on the ideas of Shaltut, Hassan al-Banna, and other Islamists, Qaradawi maintains that

Islam simultaneously encompasses matters of belief, or creed (*'aqeeda*) and worship (*'ibadat*), as well as all aspects of human relations at both the individual and group levels (*mu'amalat*).[67] In Qaradawi's worldview, Islam has both private and public dimensions. At one level, it forms an intimate relationship between the created human being and his Creator. At another level, it provides an elaborate set of moral rules, and the mechanisms to enforce them, that govern relationships within society, as well as between different societies. These rules of conduct constitute the *sharia*, an integral and inseparable part of Islam. International relations definitely fall within this comprehensive Islamic purview on the individual, the community, and indeed the world.

Qaradawi turns to the Quran, the Sunna of the Prophet, and Islamic history to anchor his assertion that politics falls under Islam's comprehensive purview. Among the verses he quotes is verse 4:59, "O believers obey God and obey the Prophet and those set in authority over you. If you dispute among yourselves over any matter, refer it to God and the Messenger."[68] Qaradawi then turns to the Sunna of the Prophet, quoting the famous hadith, "whoever has died without having given an oath of fealty (*bay'a*), has died a *jahili* death (i.e. without knowledge of Islam)."[69] Most importantly, Qaradawi contends that, throughout their history and until the advent of colonialism, Muslims were ruled by fellow Muslims, who governed them based on the *sharia*.

Acknowledging that the Quran does not speak of an Islamic state or an Islamic government, Qaradawi insists that the Prophet Muhammad founded an Islamic state in Medina, a state that persisted throughout Muslim history until colonial times. Probably influenced by Abu Zahra's views on the matter, Qaradawi writes, "The history of Islam informs us that the Messenger of Allah (PBUH) strove to the utmost of his power and intellect – and aided by divine revelation – to found a state for Islam and a homeland for its call that would be exclusively for Muslims, with no authority over them, expect for the authority of the *sharia*." Qaradawi continues to note that, "Medina was the abode of Islam and the base of the new Islamic state that was headed by the Messenger of Allah (PBUH), who is the leader of the Muslims and their Imam, as he is their Prophet and the Messenger of Allah to them."[70] There is little in Qaradawi's discourse on the Islamic state that is not found in the writings of Abu Zahra, especially his *al-Wihda al-Islamiya*. Similarly, Qaradawi's discourse on the Islamic state suffers from the same tensions and ambiguities that characterize Abu Zahra's discourse.[71]

Qaradawi's extensive discourse on the comprehensiveness of Islam is based on the core Islamist thesis that there can be no separation between religion and politics in Islam. In several popular tracks, such as *Min Fiqh al-Dawla fi al-Islam, Ummatna Bayn Qarnayn*, and *Shumul al-Islam*, Qaradawi reiterates Bahi's claim that the separation between religion and politics is a malicious Western concept that infiltrated the Muslim world during the colonial era.[72] Echoing Bahi, Qaradawi writes:

> Crusader colonialism (*al-isti'imar al-salibi*), that came to govern the lands of Islam, succeeded in implanting in the minds of many Muslims an alien and malicious idea whose thrust is that Islam is a religion and not a state but a religion in the Western sense of the word religion. As for matters of state, they have nothing to do with religion. They are to be organized according to human reason as it addresses changed circumstances.[73]

Qaradawi repeatedly emphasizes that in lieu of the Christian credo "Render to God what is God's and to Cesar what is Cesar's," Islam proclaims, "Cesar and what belongs to Cesar belong to God."[74] Based on a close reading of *Min Fiqh al-Dawla fi al-Islam* (The Jurisprudence of the State in Islam), Shavit emphasizes that, for Qaradawi, "the separation of church and state is a western exception... and as such is irrelevant to Muslims."[75] According to Qaradawi, attempts to confine Islam to the realms of creed, worship, ethics, and moral conduct represent gross distortions of its comprehensive nature as an all-encompassing religion and a way of life that is valid across time and space.[76] These distortions resulted from the influence of imported ideologies, such as liberalism and socialism.[77] They ran against the grain of the Quran, the Sunna, and the Islamic tradition. Qaradawi quotes three renowned medieval Islamic scholars—Ibn Taymiyya, al-Imam al-Ghazali, and Ibn Khaldoun—arguing that each of them held firm to the idea that the establishment of Islamic rule, based on the *sharia*, was a pillar of religion.[78]

For Qaradawi, one cannot take certain parts of Islam, such as prayer and fasting, while disregarding others, such as prescribed punishments and jihad; thus, an eclectic perspective on Islam is simply impermissible. Turning to an example from daily life, Qaradawi compares Islam to a "medical prescription" that includes a specific diet, a battery of drugs, abstention from certain foods, and physical exercise. The patient must diligently follow the entire regimen to recover.[79] Stated more eloquently, Islam, for Qaradawi, is simultaneously a creed that addresses all matters of belief and a *sharia* that governs individual and group conduct, including relations between Muslim and non-Muslim societies, i.e., international relations. In *From the Jurisprudence of the State in Islam*, Qaradawi proclaims openly and loudly, "If you remove politics from Islam, Islam becomes another religion. It becomes Buddhism, Christianity or some other religion, but it cannot be Islam."[80] According to Qaradawi, "some people, with Western inclinations (*al-mutagharibun*), deny that political Islam is true Islam (*al-Islam al-sahih*) that God legislated in His Book (the Quran) and in the Sunna and that the noble Prophet, and his rightly guided successors, applied."[81] Elsewhere, he notes, "the Islam that the Quran and the Sunna brought, and which the *umma* practiced from the predecessors (*al-salaf*) to the successors (*al-khalaf*), is a comprehensive Islam that does not recognize compartmentalization."[82]

Qaradawi's unshakeable belief in the comprehensive nature of Islam ought to be traced, primarily, to his embrace at a very young age, around 14, of the ideas of Sheikh Hassan al-Banna, the founder of the Muslim Brotherhood. Qaradawi's popular track *Shumul al-Islam* (the Comprehensive Nature of Islam) was primarily an elaboration on al-Banna's famous twenty principles for guiding the life of the Muslim. The title of Qaradawi's book is inspired by al-Banna's first principle, which underlines the comprehensive nature of Islam. According to this first principle, Islam is "a state and a homeland, a government and an *umma*, a [source of] ethics and power and of compassion and justice. It is culture, law, science and justice. . ... It is a jihad and a peaceful call for Islam. It is an army and an idea. It is a sincere creed and a correct way of worship."[83] What is worth noting is that Qaradawi places al-Banna firmly within the tradition of reformist Islam, while viewing the Muslim Brotherhood as the legitimate child of the awakening current (*tayyar al-sahwa*) within Islam.[84] Rather perceptively, though, Qaradawi notes that al-Banna took more from Rida than he did take from 'Abduh.[85]

Other early prominent members of the Muslim Brotherhood, such as Sheikh Muhammad al-Ghazali (1917–1996), fully subscribed to al-Banna's emphasis on the comprehensiveness of Islam, rendering this notion central to the ideology of the Muslim Brotherhood. In *al-Sheikh al-Ghazali Kama 'Araftuh*, Qaradawi acknowledges the influence of al-Banna and al-Ghazali, along with other sheikhs such as Mahmoud Shaltut,[86] on the formulation of his understanding of the comprehensiveness of Islam.[87] As noted by Qaradawi, al-Ghazali supplanted al-Banna's twenty principles with ten principles of his own, which addressed, inter alia, 1) the rights of women in Islam[88], 2) popular rule, 3) the defensive purposes of jihad, 4) the impermissibility of imposing religion by coercion, 5) the importance of abiding by international laws and conventions as long as they do not violate the *sharia*, and 6) the necessity of peaceful relations, dialog, and collaboration with non-Muslim societies.[89] While Qaradawi's treatment of al-Ghazali's ten supplementary principles is rather brief, it is evident that he fully subscribed to them; as these themes came to permeate his discourse. While Qaradawi maintained his intellectual independence from the Muslim Brotherhood, his political thought, including his perspective on international relations, provides us with major insights into the ideology of the Muslim Brotherhood, fluid as that ideology may be.

Throughout, Qaradawi denounces those voices that challenge the comprehensive nature of Islam, maintaining that they "go against (*yakhrujun 'an*) the established consensus of the *umma*, which, throughout its history, believed that Islam encompasses creed and *sharia*, religion and state, worship and leadership, prayer and jihad."[90] An important feature of Qaradawi's discourse is the close association that he draws between the comprehensiveness of Islam (*shumul al-Islam*), on the one hand, and the middle path, centrist and moderate, approach of Islam to matters of religion and matters of personal and group conduct (*wasatiyyat al-Islam*), on the other. While embraced by other mainstream Islamists, these two notions became largely associated with the discourse of Qaradawi. Al-Khateeb writes, "If Qaradawi is not the creator of the idea of *shumuliyya*, at the very least he is the one who was capable of transforming it into a popular awareness by making Islam understandable as a way of life for a large number of Muslims."[91]

The Wasati Approach to Islam and to International Relations

Several mainstream Islamist scholars, such as Zuhaili, as will be discussed in Chapter 6, have elaborated on *al-wasatiyya* (also written *al-wasatiyyah*)[92] applying it to their constructs of international relations. Qaradawi identifies 'Abduh and Rida, as well as Shaltut and Abu Zahra, along with Banna and other 20th-century sheikhs, as advocates of the *wasati* approach to Islam, who influenced his own embrace of *wasatiyya*.[93] The notion of *wasatiyya*, nonetheless, became so heavily associated with the discourse of Qaradawi that Rashid al-Ghannushi penned a short treatise on Qaradawi's understanding of *wasatiyya* and its centrality to his political discourse.[94] Qaradawi has written extensively on *al-wasatiyya*, explaining its multiple meanings, its origins in the Quran and the Sunna, and its implications for politics, society, and international relations. As Qaradawi notes, his embrace of the *wasati* approach started during his adolescence[95] and was evident from his first published work, *The Lawful and the Prohibited in Islam*. Emphasizing his lifelong commitment to *wasatiyya*, Qaradawi points out that he consciously used the word *bayn* (between or in-between) in several of his book titles, since the positions he adopted in these works represented middle grounds between extremes.

Qaradawi's book on the jurisprudence of Islamic *wasatiyya* (*Fiqh al-Wasatiyya al-Islamiyya*) is undoubtedly one of the most comprehensive and theoretical works on the subject to have been written in Arabic. In this book, one of the last he wrote, Qaradawi quotes all the Quranic verses that include the word *wasat* or a derivative of it to show the centrality of this notion to Islam. He then quotes other verses that refer to similar terms, particularly *wazn/mizan* (scale, balance) and *qadr/miqdar* (measure, measurement).[96] Qaradawi makes frequent references to verse 2:143, "Thus, We have appointed you as a median nation, To be witnesses for mankind, And the Prophet to be a witness for you."[97] Guided by this verse, Qaradawi writes:

> As for the *wasatiyya* of the Muslim *umma*, it derives from the *wasatiyya* of its religion and its message, the *wasatiyya* of its approach and its system. This approach is a *wasati* approach [that is fit] for a *wasati umma*. It is the approach of temperateness and balance that is free of excess and of negligence: in its creeds and its rules, in its rites and its codes, in its values and its ethics, in its understandings and its standards, in its morals and its traditions, in its feelings and its emotions, and in its internal ties and external relations.[98]

The *wasatiyya* of Islam, according to Qaradawi, is discernible in its creed that combines reason and faith,[99] its rites (not cumbersome for its followers), and its legal system or *sharia* that balances justice and mercy. The *wasatiyya* of Islam further reflects itself in the *wasati* character and *wasati* dispositions of the Muslim *umma*, as clarified by verse 2:143. Qaradawi reads in the above verse a divine injunction to the Muslim *umma* to adopt a wasati stance between "otherworldliness and worldliness, idealism and realism, rationality and emotion ... and between constancy and evolution."[100]

Qaradawi, thus, contends that the Muslim *umma* occupies a *wasati* position among other nations and in the world,[101] its role being to mediate conflicts and facilitate dialog among different nations and to lead the world by word and by example. Bearing in mind that Qaradawi is first and foremost a jurisprudent, the thrust of his thesis is that the *wasatiyya* of Islam warrants a *wasati* interpretation of its *sharia*, a thesis he strives to demonstrate. Since the *sharia* applies to the political and social realms, including international relations, a *wasati* approach is consequently the most suitable path to pursue in the conduct of international relations. The remainder of this section elaborates further on Qaradawi's *wasati* approach to international relations.

In line with other Islamists, Qaradawi's construct of international relations focuses on relations between Muslim and non-Muslim societies. Relations amongst Muslim societies are internal matters that pertain to the one Muslim *umma* and, thus, lie outside the purview of international relations. For Qaradawi, Islam is a *wasati* religion that represents the golden mean between the excessive pacificity of the teachings of Christianity and what he considers the extreme aggressiveness against others that the Torah sanctions and indeed enjoins the Jewish people to engage in toward other people and nations.[102] Borrowing from the discourse of Sheikh Shaltut, whom he quotes extensively, Qaradawi notes that this middle ground manifests itself in Islam's invocation to Muslims to seek peace with other nations, while keeping their vigilance and continuous military preparedness, therefore not allowing others to gain military advantage over them, as in Quranic verse 8:60 "Prepare against them whatever force and war cavalry you can gather to frighten therewith the enemy of God and your enemy."[103]

In international relations, Qaradawi's *wasatiyya* entails communicating with non-Muslim societies on the bases of parity, reciprocity, mutual benefit, and mutual respect. Qaradawi frequently quotes the Quranic verses that emphasize the permissibility, indeed desirability, of collaborating with non-Muslims who have not aggressed against Muslims, particularly verses 60:8, "As for those who have not fought against you over religion nor expelled you from your homes, God does not forbid you to treat them honorably and act with fairness toward them, for God loves those who act with fairness"; and 49:13, "O mankind, We created you male and female, and made you into nations and tribes that you may come to know one another."[104] Elaborating on the meaning of the term "*lita'arafu*" (to know one another) in the above verse, Qaradawi notes that "ignorance of the other" constitutes a principal source of harm in "human relations," as it creates unnecessary distance between humans.[105] In the same vein, Qaradawi quotes and elaborates on the Quranic verses emphasizing that Muslims must call for Islam using logical argument and gentle exhortation as in verses 16:125, "Call to the way of your Lord with wisdom and fair counsel, and debate with them in the fairest manner" and 29:46, "Do not argue with the People of the Book, except in the nest of manner."[106] In line with the scholar sheikhs of the second generation, Qaradawi further argues that Quranic verses 2:256, "There is no compulsion in religion. Right guidance has been distinguished from error" and 10:99, "Had your Lord willed it, all on earth, every single one, would have believed. Will you then compel people to become believers?" instruct Muslims to refrain altogether from seeking to coerce others to embrace Islam.[107]

Still, Qaradawi's *wasati* approach equally emphasizes safeguarding the independence and sovereignty of the Muslim *umma* against foreign encroachment. In line with the mainstream Islamists of the second generation, especially Bahi,

Qaradawi is particularly weary of the negative influence of foreign ideologies on the Muslim world, be they capitalism, liberalism, materialism, secularism, or Marxism. Qaradawi embraces Bahi's core claim that both capitalism and socialism constitute foreign ideologies that are not suitable for the Muslim world. For both scholar sheikhs, Muslim societies must build their political and socioeconomic orders on Islamic foundations, and not on the basis of any external system of ideas. While embracing the substance of Bahi's critique of colonial and neocolonial policies of Western powers and the former Soviet Union, Qaradawi's style is less polemical than Bahi's.

It is significant that Qaradawi does not question the democratic character of Western political systems or their legitimacy in the eyes of their own people, critiquing them primarily on what he considers the exploitative and unjust policies of these powers toward the Muslim world and their incessant attempts to impose their cultural values and norms on Muslim societies. Generally, Qaradawi's critique of Western policies toward the Muslim world revolves around three core themes. The first is Western complicity in the creation of the state of Israel on Arab and Muslim lands, and subsequent Western backing for Israeli expansion and displacement and oppression of the Palestinian people; the second is Western support for dictatorships all over the Arab and Muslim worlds, despite Western rhetoric about democracy and human rights; and the third is Western efforts to export their cultural values and lifestyle to the Muslim world. This last point deserves further clarification because of Qaradawi's highly nuanced image of the West. Qaradawi distinguishes between political culture in the West and other less desirable aspects of Western culture.

Qaradawi has nothing but admiration for a democratic political culture that protects individual rights, free enterprise, free speech and media, transparent and competitive elections, and holding government officers accountable before the public. Equally important, Qaradawi acknowledges the hegemony of this democratic political culture in most Western societies. The one nonpolitical aspect of Western culture that he strongly objects to is the extreme, non-*wasati*, approach to individual freedom, which equates freedom with license, i.e., everything goes. Qaradawi is adamant that freedom must be bound by reason and should not contradict God's commandments, thus categorically rejecting the legalization of two types of social relations that he believes to be unnatural and to run contrary to God's commandments, homosexuality, and out- of-wedlock heterosexual sexual relationships, common in the West.

In line with other Islamists, both mainstream and radical, Qaradawi considers homosexual relations to be unnatural, sinful, and criminal relations, which endanger public morality and the moral and social fabric of society.[108] Legalizing homosexuality, including legalizing same sex marriage, manifests the decadence of Western societies, as it represents an extreme and unbalanced view of individual freedom. However, Qaradawi's critique of out-of- wedlock heterosexual relations is far more nuanced. Qaradawi focuses not on the relationship itself, but on its "unintended consequences" in the form of children born outside the protective nexus of the nuclear family and, even worse, abortion. An ardent critic of abortion, Qaradawi argues that the fight against abortion represents a common ground between Christians, Muslims, and all believers.[109] To recapitulate, in line with his *wasati* approach, Qaradawi embraces opening up to the West and selectively borrowing from it, including learning from its democratic practices and culture. Qaradawi's *wasatiyya*, however, simultaneously entails outright rejection of uncritically imitating the West and embracing certain Western values that emphasize separation of religion and politics, including acceptance of atheism, excessive materialism, unbounded individual freedoms that degenerate into decadent acts rejected by all three Abrahamic religions and not just Islam.

In comparison to the scholar sheikhs of the second generation, Qaradawi devotes more attention to contemporary problems in international relations, such as terrorism (and the distinction between terrorism and legitimate resistance or jihad), US military intervention in the Arab and broader Islamic worlds, the plight of Muslim communities worldwide who are facing oppression and/or discrimination, and, above all, the Arab-Israeli conflict. But what sets Qaradawi apart from the mainstream Islamists of the second generation is mainly his greater emphasis on power as a principal ingredient of international relations. This "preoccupation" with power, which he shares with Fadlallah, leads Qaradawi to write extensively on the empowerment of Muslim societies in the political, economic, military, and cultural domains. While Qaradawi's extensive discussion of power is covered in the subsequent section on war and jihad, it is worth emphasizing here that Qaradawi views Muslim power as a deterrent against aggression, in line with verse 8:60, "Prepare against them whatever force and war cavalry you can gather to frighten therewith the enemy of God and your enemy," and not as a means of dominating and exploiting others or coercing them to adopt Islam. Qaradawi's construct of power as primarily a deterrent against aggression and as a means to repel aggression when it takes place rather than as an instrument to dominate others is in line with his *wasatiyya*.

The Laws that Govern International Relations

A prominent feature of Qaradawi's discourse on international relations lies in his emphasis on the universal God-made laws (*al-sunnan al-kawniyya*) that govern international relations. For Qaradawi, the physical universe (cosmos) and the political and social realms, including international relations, are governed by universal laws that humans cannot change. These universal laws apply to all humans, Muslims and non-Muslims alike. A close reading of his discourse reveals that he believes in the presence of at least three such universal laws (or *sunnan*): causality, change, and mutual restraining.

Causality

Causality operates in both the natural world and the political and social realms, including the realm of international relations. Wars, a constant feature of international relations, result from a blend of the absence of international authority, international anarchy in realist parlance; the domestic structure of certain states that encourages aggressive colonial and neocolonial policies; and human nature.[110] Victory in war results primarily from three factors. The first factor is military preparedness. The second factor pertains to military planning and the adoption of the right military strategy and tactics, while the third factor relates to the maintenance of discipline and high morale during combat. Discipline and high morale, in turn, derive from faith in God and belief in the justice of one's cause; as well as from the troops' confidence in and respect toward their leadership. The military successes of the Prophet Muhammad, and the rightly guided caliphs who succeeded him, did not result from divine providence alone. For Qaradawi and the other mainstream Islamists, these victories would not have been possible without the operation of all of the above three factors.

Thus, in Qaradawi's perspective, the Muslim defeat in the battle of Uhud in 625 should be attributed to the breakdown of discipline in the ranks of the Muslims toward the end of the battle. The causes of the defeat, or setback, at Uhud are to be located in the observable realm of human conduct, and not in the realm of metaphysics. It is this belief in causality that enables Qaradawi to theorize about international relations, his theoretical insights revolving around two principal themes: change is the norm in international relations as far as the rise and fall of major powers or civilizations; and international relations are governed by the universal law of mutual restraining (*sunnat al-tadafu'*).

Change in International Relations

Qaradawi addresses at some length the question of change in international relations. As for the Muslim *umma*, Qaradawi's principal unit of analysis, international relations dates back to the founding of the first "state of Islam" (*dawlat al-Islam*), to use his terminology, in Medina under the leadership of the Prophet Muhammad. In line with other mainstream Islamists, Qaradawi locates the origins of the engagement by the Islamic state in international relations to the correspondence between the Prophet Muhammad and the Byzantium and Persian sovereigns in the Levant and Persia, respectively, in which the Prophet called them to Islam.[111] In the mainstream Islamist narrative that Qaradawi among others adopts, these early encounters with foreign, non-Arab entities were characterized by conflict and confrontation because of the stiff resistance to the peaceful expansion of the message of Islam by foreign rulers and their plots against the nascent Islamic state and the Prophet himself.[112]

Qaradawi, like the other mainstream Islamists, does not attribute early Islamic military successes to divine providence alone. Mainstream Islamists emphasize the role of the "human element" in achieving these military victories, particularly the wisdom and foresight of the early Muslim caliphs; the zeal and high discipline of the numerically inferior Muslim armies; the military ingenuity of Muslim commanders, such as Khaled ibn al-Walid and Amr ibn al-'As; and the just and humane treatment extended to the inhabitants of conquered territory, including respecting their freedom of religion and lifting the prior oppression by their Byzantium and Persian overlords. According to the same narrative, Islam as both a state and a civilization reached its apex in the early Abbasid period, around the reign of the Caliph Haroun al-Rashid and his two sons, al-Amin and al-Ma'moun, just two centuries after its inception.

At this apex, the Islamic state embodied a civilization that blended faith with reason, promoted scientific discovery, and dispensed justice to all its subjects irrespectively of race, clan, socioeconomic standing, or religion, while developing a comprehensive legal system, the *sharia* that derived from the Quran and the Sunna of the Prophet Muhammad.[113] Significantly, Qaradawi, and especially Zuhaili, emphasize the contributions of the Islamic civilization to the development of the emerging body of international law. A recurrent theme to be found in their discourses is on the Islamic rules of warfare, especially regarding the humane treatment of the prisoners of war (POW), predating by centuries the 1949 Geneva Convention on their treatment.[114]

Qaradawi's analysis of the causes of the decline of the Islamic state bears major resemblance to Abu Zahra's, with both scholar sheikhs attributing its decline, as of the middle Abbasid period, to a combination of internal and external factors. Qaradawi, though, places less emphasis on the topic than Abu Zahra does, especially in his *al-Wihda al-Islamiyya*. On the internal level, Qaradawi, in line with Abu Zahra, outlines several factors. The first factor was the transition to hereditary dynastic rule, under the Umayyads, instead of selecting the Caliph through the *bay'a* (oath of fealty or allegiance) of those who connect and separate, or bind and loosen (*ahl al'-aqd wa al-hal*). The second factor revolved around the concomitant emergence of autocratic rule, according to Qaradawi the result of copying the practices of the defeated Persian and Byzantium rulers that negated the Islamic principle of *shura* (consultation). Other factors included the decline in the role of the Arab element within the growing Islamic state, the rise of the influence of the Turkish and Persian elements, and the growing sectarian divisions in the single *umma*, especially between the Sunnis and the Shias. On the external level, Qaradawi points to the negative effects of the crusades and more seriously of Mogul invasions that impacted most of the Islamic world.[115]

The decline of the Islamic state was to rapidly accelerate in the 19th century as a result of the incessant European and Russian wars against the Ottoman empire, which stood for the Islamic state, and the concomitant military incursions into the Arab and Muslim worlds, starting with the Napoleonic invasion of Egypt in 1798 and followed by the French onslaught into Muslim North Africa in the mid-19th century and the British occupation of Egypt in 1882. For Qaradawi and other Islamists, this process of decline culminated in the official dissolution of the caliphate in 1924.[116]

A hallmark of Qaradawi's discourse is his major optimism regarding the prospects of reversing this decline through the awakening of the Muslim *umma* and of Islamic civilization. Qaradawi devotes far greater attention to the idea of Islamic awakening (*al-sahwa al-Islamiyya*) than other mainstream Islamists do. He has written a series of books on the Islamic awakening, such as *The Islamic Awakening from Adolescence to Maturity*[117] and *The Islamic Awakening and the Concerns of the Arab and Muslim World*,[118] while devoting much attention to this topic in other writings.

Qaradawi's perspective on change in international relations bears major resemblance to that of Bahi. Broadly speaking, the two scholar sheikhs subscribe to a circular rather than a linear view of human history: one that focuses on the rise and fall and then reemergence of civilizations. The rapid rise of the Muslim *umma* and of Islamic civilization in the first two centuries after the *hijra* was followed by a long period of decline, indeed disintegration, prompted by both internal and external factors, yet a decline that was only temporary in nature. Both Bahi and Qaradawi argue that the onslaught of European colonialism as of the 19th century prompted an immediate response from various parts of the conquered Islamic world. While identifying the principal figures and movements which militarily and politically resisted Western colonialism, Bahi and Qaradawi write at length about the intellectual resistance to colonialism, especially by religious figures, such as the scholar sheikhs of the first generation and several others from the Islamic world.[119]

The Islamic awakening that Qaradawi elaborates on in most of his writings must be read in the context of this intellectual and cultural resistance to perceived Western colonialism and neo-colonialism.[120] Bahi and Qaradawi argue that this intellectual resistance must also target local advocates of full scale borrowing from the West at the expense of Islamic culture and values. Bahi and especially Qaradawi are vociferous critics of what they refer to as the Westernization current (*tayyar al-taghrib*) within the Islamic world. For Bahi, Qaradawi and the other mainstream Islamists, the Islamic awakening aims primarily to reverse the decline of the Muslim *umma* in the political, economic, military and particularly cultural domains. A key dimension of this Islamic awakening is the pursuit in earnest of Islamic unity. While a subsequent section of the chapter addresses Qaradawi's discourse on Islamic unity, suffice it to say here that restoring the unity of the Islamic *umma* is a pivotal step for it to play a leading role on the world stage, as a *wasati* (moderate and balanced) *umma* that is entrusted with conveying the universal message of Islam to humanity.[121]

Qaradawi's appeal to the broad public in the Arab and Muslim worlds emanates in part from the optimism he conveys regarding the prospects of an imminent reversal in the decline of the Muslim *umma*. In the opening pages of the popular *Our Umma between two Centuries*, Qaradawi envisages that just as the 20th century was the century of the Western powers, especially the United States, the 21st century is bound to be the century of the Muslim *umma*.[122] Although we are still in the first quarter of this century, there is little evidence that Qaradawi's prediction is coming true.

The Law of Mutual Restraining

In *The General Characteristics of Islam*, Qaradawi identifies realism (*al-waqi'iyya*) as one of Islam's characteristics.[123] Qaradawi explains that realism entails a realistic outlook on this world that recognizes both the good and the bad elements in it and a realistic outlook on human nature. For Qaradawi, humans are driven by, indeed torn between, conflicting tendencies due to their dual nature as earthly beings and spiritual beings. Adam, the father of humanity, was molded from clay into which God breathed a spirit; human nature is prone toward both good and evil, perversion and piety, as in verses 91:7–8, "By the soul and He who gave it symmetry, inspiring it with its perversion and its piety."[124] Qaradawi represents a hegemonic view within Islam on human nature. As Ron Geaves notes: "Thus Islam does not posit the idea of a corrupted being fallen from grace through original sin but rather a person prone to forgetfulness and weakness, but whose innermost being is altruistic and drawn toward goodness, epitomized by the possibility of complete submission and obedience."[125]

The two notions of *waqiʿiyya* and *wasatiyya* (two general characteristics of Islam) are closely intertwined in Qaradawi's discourse, including his thoughts on international relations. Qaradawi argues that the realism of Islam represents a *wasati* stance between excessive idealism and base materialism. That means that the realist dimension of Islam recognizes that there is evil in this world, which needs to be punished in domestic society and defended against in international relations, and that people are capable of great deeds as well as of bad ones. Islam's equally important idealist dimension emphasizes the need to encourage the good and fight against the bad or evil. Qaradawi concludes that Islam purports an idealist form of realism (*al-waqiʿiyya al-mithaliyya*).[126]

This section argues, though, that Qaradawi's perspective on international relations bears greater resemblance to the "Western" realist school than it does to the "Western" idealist, liberal-internationalist, one. Qaradawi's realism manifests itself in the emphasis he places on a number of Quranic verses that refer to the "law of mutual restraining" (*sunnat al-tadafuʿ*), especially verses 2:251, "Had God not restrained mankind, some by means of others, the earth would have become chaotic," and 22:40, "Had God not caused people to restrain one another, destruction would have fallen upon monasteries, churches, oratories and other places of prayer, where the name of God is often mentioned." Guided by the above verses, Qaradawi notes, "It is through this mutual restraining—whereby groups restrain one another—that God saves the earth and those who dwell on it from tyranny. Otherwise, the oppression and injustice of tyrants would spread to the entire earth and the World would turn to a jungle in which the strong devour the weak."[127]

Although it is a law from God for the benefit of mankind, the law of mutual restraining works through the conscious actions of groups. Qaradawi argues that, "Muslims [consciously] resort to war and fighting when they are compelled to do so by *sunnat al-tadafu'*, which is one of the *sunnan* upon which God established this world."[128] The law of mutual restraining is not a mechanical law that operates without human agency in the same way that structural realists, such as Kenneth Waltz and John Mearsheimer, view the balance of power.[129] The law of mutual restraining has both realist and idealist dimensions. From a realist point of view, groups must actively resist the aggression of other groups to ensure their self-preservation, broadly construed to include independence and freedom of religion. From an idealist viewpoint, though, if aggression is not opposed, the world will become corrupt due to the absence of justice. For Qaradawi and mainstream Islamists, the preservation of justice at both the domestic and international levels is a principal aim of the *sharia*.

Accordingly, Qaradawi sees in the active resistance of aggression through the waging of jihad a prime example of Islam's idealist realism. In line with Western realists, Qaradawi emphasizes the centrality of power to international relations and, more generally, human relations. Qaradawi thus notes, "In reality, life cannot be set right without power, [power that] protects what is right and resists what is invalid, enforces justice and fights evil, Prevents Cain from transgressing against Abel." He goes on to stress, "This is the idealist realism of the ethics of Islam, the legislations of Islam and the guidance of the Quran."[130] To support this view, he quotes verse 16:126, "And if you punish, you are to punish with the like of what you were punished; but if you bear with patience, then best it is for the patient."[131]

The idealist realism of Qaradawi manifests itself in utterances such as, "Islam aspires for a world in which peace and security prevail and in which people come to know one another and have cordial relations; but Man does not attain all his heart's desires."[132] Elsewhere, he writes, "Islam calls for peace, is keen on preserving peace and legitimates different means to spread and consolidate it," but he immediately cautions, "Islam cannot prevent war in the entire world, that is why it prepares for war and prepares whatever power it can to meet the enemy." He then quotes verse: 2:216, "Fighting has been prescribed for you, although it is a matter hateful to you."[133] Qaradawi's emphasis on Islam's realism finds its echoes in Reinhold Niebuhr's, the renowned 20th century American theologian and advocate of Christian realism, understanding of Christianity. As noted by Eric Patterson, for Niebuhr, "Christianity is the most realistic and meaningful perspective for apprehending world affairs at the individual and corporate levels."[134] In the conclusion, I return to the realist elements in Qaradawi's perspective on international relations.

To recapitulate, Qaradawi's (and Fadlallah's) stress on the law of mutual restraining bears major resemblance to the realists' emphasis on the balance of power, but whereas Western realists derive the balance of power theory from their reading of Western history, Qaradawi and Fadlallah derive it primarily from their interpretation of Islam's sacred text and only secondarily from their reading of the conflictual and often bloody interactions of Islam with Western civilization. Grounded in the Quran and Islamic tradition, Qaradawi and Fadlallah present a variant of soft, or better righteous, realism that one may refer to as Islamic realism.[135] It is a realism tempered by an emphasis on justice, reciprocity in treatment, honoring of international agreements, mercy where feasible, and virtue. While centered on the law of mutual restraining, Qaradawi's realism emanates from 1) a nuanced reading of human nature that recognizes that aggression is innate to humans, but does not define the totality of human nature; and 2) a belief in the absence of an international authority that can protect the weak from the aggression of the powerful. Qaradawi and Fadlallah's view of the international system as anarchic in nature is in line with the realist reading. As noted, Qaradawi's realism is nevertheless tempered by his emphasis that Muslims must conduct both their internal and external affairs in line with the *sharia*, which commands justice, and mercy when possible, and prohibits aggression. Qaradawi's extensive discourse on jihad, discussed below, reflects his idealist–realist understanding of Islam, especially the *sharia*.

On Jihad and Fighting

The comprehensiveness of Islam, its *waqi'iyya* and its *wasatiyya*, as argued by Qaradawi, definitely apply to one of the most important collective activities of the Muslim *umma*, the waging of war or jihad. Clearly, the scholar sheikhs of the second generation addressed the topic of jihad. Shaltut (as discussed in Chapter 3) wrote a short track on fighting in Islam, and the topic appears frequently in the discourses of Abu Zahra and Bahi. In his *Fiqh al-Jihad*, Qaradawi quotes approvingly entire passages from Shaltut's *al-Quran wa al-Qital*. Nevertheless, the topic of jihad is more extensively addressed by the scholar sheikhs of the third generation. Zuhaili's first and arguably most important work was on war, *The Effects of War* (treated in Chapter 6), while each of Fadlallah and Qaradawi devoted a long manuscript to the subject of jihad. Qaradawi's two-volume work on the jurisprudence of jihad (*fiqh al-jihad*) constitutes one of the most comprehensive treatments of the subject by a contemporary Islamist. As Zaman notes, "Qaradawi's jurisprudence of jihad is a self-conscious and confident work of ijtihad."[136] Zaman further describes the work as, "The most extensive Muslim discussion produced in the aftermath of 9/11 to grapple with issues of war, violence, and terrorism."[137] The following section first throws light on the influence of al-Banna and the thought of the Muslim Brotherhood on Qaradawi's construct of jihad. It then systematically discusses Qaradawi's extensive discourse on the forms (or meanings) of jihad, the purposes of jihad as *qital* (fighting), the rules that govern the conduct of fighting, and the ending of fighting (or of war).

The Influence of al-Banna on Qaradawi's Construct of Jihad

The aforementioned *Shumul al-Islam* by Qaradawi emphasizes the centrality of jihad to the thought of al-Banna and of the Muslim Brotherhood, explaining how jihad relates to the other aspects of Islam in the thought of al-Banna and in the program of the Brotherhood. As previously noted, while maintaining his intellectual independence and refusing any official position within the Muslim Brotherhood, Qaradawi openly identified with the movement, which, ever since its inception, has been the most popular and most influential Islamist group in the Arab world.[138]

Qaradawi recollects that in 1945 he attended a Muslim Brotherhood rally in Tanta, which featured an address by al-Banna.[139] According to Qaradawi, al-Banna's impromptu speech focused on the issues of Palestine and the British occupation of Egypt and the Sudan, which for the Brotherhood constituted one indivisible country.[140] Al-Banna, Qaradawi notes, proposed an incremental approach to dealing with the British occupation. The first step was to negotiate with the British occupier, without infringing on the right to complete independence. If negotiations failed, the Egyptians and the Sudanese, as one people, would then resort to the second step, which was to boycott all British products. Only if the first two steps failed would jihad against the British be declared.[141] Thus, for al-Banna, at least as understood by Qaradawi, jihad was a means to a just end but not an end in itself and a last resort if other, more peaceful, means failed to bring about the desired just outcome.[142]

Qaradawi notes that al-Banna identified two purposes for jihad. The first was to ensure that Muslims had the freedom to call for Islam by peaceful means. In this case, it was sufficient for a number of Muslims to engage in jihad, but jihad was not incumbent on all Muslims (*jihad kifaya*). The second was to repel aggression against Muslims lands. In this case, jihad was incumbent on those

Muslims directly impacted by aggression (*jihad 'ayn*).[143] The thrust of Qaradawi's argument is that al-Banna never advocated jihad for offensive purposes, or as a means to coerce others to embrace Islam. While Qaradawi offers a far more detailed reading of the purposes of jihad, there is no incongruity (at least according to Qaradawi) between his own reading of jihad and that of al-Banna; and, by extension, of that of the Muslim Brotherhood.

Qaradawi does not diminish the centrality of jihad to the thought of al-Banna and to the ideology of the Movement that al-Banna founded. Furthermore, Qaradawi does not conceal his admiration for the symbol, or logo, of the Muslim Brotherhood, a Quran flanked by two swords, with the Arabic word *"wa-a'ido"* (and prepare) appearing beneath.[144] He also repeats approvingly Brotherhood slogans, such as "Jihad is our path and dying in the path of God is our highest wish"; and "Islam is a religion and a state, worship and leadership, prayer and jihad, Quran and Sword."[145] What Qaradawi rejects, though, is the identification of jihad with Islam. For Qaradawi and mainstream Islamists, Jihad is one dimension of Islam, but it does not define the totality of Islam. Moreover, jihad has several meanings and dimensions, with fighting (*qital*) as only one of these dimensions. Qaradawi thus writes, "The term jihad is significantly broader than fighting, every Muslim has to be a *mujahid*, but not necessarily a fighter (*muqatil*). For fighting is due to certain causes."[146]

The Forms of Jihad

While there is general agreement among mainstream Islamists that jihad takes multiple forms, with *qital* (fighting) being just one of them, Qaradawi clearly identifies and discusses these different forms, i.e., dimensions, of jihad while relating them to one another. In line with traditional and more recent treatments of the subject, including Abu Zahra's, Qaradawi derives the term jihad from its related Arabic roots, juhd (exerting effort) and *jahd* (enduring hardship). Jihad is, thus, defined as exerting effort and enduring hardship in the path of God since jihad stands for striving in the path of God. Other contemporary mainstream Islamists construed jihad in a similar fashion. According to a summary of the views of the renowned Islamic scholar Abdul Hamid Abu Sulayman, "Jihad represents the all-out effort of Muslims to do good and avoid evil in all aspects of their lives. It may involve fighting but it is not necessarily confined to it. It is, in brief, the striving to fulfill one's duties and obligations to God, community and country."[147] For Qaradawi there are five forms of jihad: jihad of the soul, jihad against Satan, jihad to reform society, jihad of speech, and jihad as fighting. The following section briefly addresses these different yet connected forms of jihad, relying primarily on Qaradawi's two-volume *The Jurisprudence of Jihad*.

Jihad *al-nafs* (the struggle to elevate the soul) is the most basic form of jihad. It is the struggle of human beings to elevate themselves beyond just heeding the demands of the flesh. Since God created Adam, the father of humanity, from clay, humans by their very nature must satisfy the demands of the body to survive as individuals and as a species. This "handful of clay" from which God molded Man "made him fit to develop the earth (*'amarat al-ard*) and to deal with it," Qaradawi writes.[148] There is, thus, nothing wrong with the human quest for food, shelter, clothing, mating, and reproduction. But God endowed every human being with an immortal soul (*nafs*), thus distinguishing humanity from every other created species, and humans must listen equally to the demands of the soul. Otherwise, they will be like beasts. Jihad of the soul revolves around tempering, though not altogether extinguishing, the desires of the flesh, with Islam being a *wasati* religion, enjoining believers to balance between the worldly and the otherworldly, or spiritual, in their lives.[149]

Humans should live in this world, partake of its pleasures in moderation, and accept its hardships, but their gaze should also be fixed on God, their Creator. The jihad of the soul, thus, requires obeying God's commandments of one's own volition, even when these conflict with one's desires and selfish interests. Individuals must take the time to perform daily prayers, fast the holy month, abstain from alcohol and unlawful foods, pay the *zakat* (alms), and act justly toward others, even when this is not to their advantage. They must also risk their lives and endure the hardships of fighting when fighting is necessary to protect their lives and freedom of belief, as prescribed in verse 2:216, "Fighting has been prescribed for you, although it is a matter hateful to you."[150]

Closely related to jihad *al-nafs* lies the fight against the temptations of Satan (al-*Shaytan*), constantly whispering to humans and encouraging them to disobey God, to indulge in the pleasures of the flesh without restraint and to act unjustly toward others. Armed by faith and by reason, humans will, of their own accord, fight against the temptations of Satan and stay on the straight path (*al-surat al-mustaqim*).[151] Jihad against Satan requires channeling the "hatred and aggression instincts that are intrinsic to human nature toward Satan."[152] Some humans, however, lack the faith and the wisdom to do so and will succumb to the temptations of Satan and to their own base desires, bringing harm on themselves and on others. For Qaradawi and mainstream Islamists, the state and society play a key role in protecting humans against the temptations of Satan and their own base inclinations. Qaradawi refers to these two forms of jihad as spiritual jihad (*al-jihad al-rouhi*).[153]

This brings us to the third type of jihad, the jihad to remove injustice, fight vice, and corruption and, more broadly, reform society. In Qaradawi's worldview, a symbiotic relationship exists between the individual and society.[154] The individual must strive to promote justice, social solidarity, and virtue in society, while society must cultivate in the individual love of virtue and justice and the embrace of social solidarity through, for example, *zakat*. As a *wasati* religion, Islam is as much about the community, or better the *umma*, as it is about the individual. Individuals bear responsibility for the moral character of their society, in proportion to how much power they hold in it, but even the weak must strive to elevate the moral caliber of society, even if only with their hearts or with their speech.

Speaking truth to power is a form of jihad, Qaradawi argues.[155] Qaradawi's vision of societal reform is similar to the reformist scholar sheikhs of the first and second generations' vision. It represents a return to the initial Islam of the Quran, the Sunna, and the first generation of Muslims, with selective borrowing from the West, especially in the scientific fields. For mainstream Islamists, the closer that society is to living in accordance to the principles of the *sharia*, the fewer the temptations for people to go astray. Qaradawi elevates the duty of the individual to work for reforming society to the status of jihad, citing a number of prophetic hadiths that exalt this form of jihad, while referring to it as civilian jihad (*al-jihad al-madani*), primarily to distinguish it from military jihad.

Calling for Islam with logical arguments, persuasion, gentle exhortation, and exemplary conduct constitutes the fourth form of jihad. Since this jihad through speech (*jihad al-lisan* or *al-jihad al-da'awi*) involves multiple venues of communication, Qaradawi highlights the key role that broadcast media (mentioning his own television program on Al-Jazeera) and the Internet (giving the example of Islamonline) should play in raising awareness about the tenets of Islam and disseminating its teachings. This form of jihad has two dimensions. It involves calling on Muslims to return to the original purity of Islam as conveyed by the Quran and the Sunna, to appreciate the comprehensive nature of Islam, and to avoid both extremism and laxity in religion. It also involves spreading the message of Islam, a universal message, among non-Muslims by peaceful means, as noted in verses 16:123 and 29:46, referred to above. In line with the other mainstream Islamists, Qaradawi maintains that peacefully calling for Islam is categorically different from coercing non-Muslims to embrace Islam, for there can be no coercion in religion.[156]

Jihad has an equally important military dimension, which Qaradawi often refers to as *al-jihad al-'askari* (military jihad). This final form of jihad, military jihad, centers on fighting the enemy (*qital al-a'da'* or simply *qital*). Qital, Qaradawi writes, is the "final branch of the branches of jihad, it is fighting by the sword, namely using arms in the face of enemies."[157] Qaradawi makes important distinctions that must be borne in mind with regard to military jihad. To start with, he clarifies that not all fighting is jihad, but it is jihad only when fighting is for a just cause, or more precisely when it is fighting in the path of God. Qaradawi then defines war as "the use of arms and material power by one group against another, this group can be a tribe against one or more tribes, or several tribes against other tribes, or a state against one or more states, or a group of states against another group of states."[158]

Qaradawi maintains that there is a fundamental difference between jihad as a religious notion (*mafhoum dini*) and war as a worldly notion (*mafhoum dunyawi*),[159] but this is not a totally convincing argument, especially since he always maintains that Islam is a comprehensive religion that covers both the worldly and the other-worldly. War is too important a human affair to fall out of the purview of religion, when one construes religion the way Qaradawi and Islamists do. What Qaradawi actually means is that jihad is a war that is fought for just causes, namely to defend Muslims against aggression and to ensure their religious freedom, their freedom from oppression, and their freedom to peacefully call for Islam.[160] In line with Abu Zahra, Qaradawi argues that most of the wars that Muslims fought throughout history were just wars. Fadlallah (Chapter 7) makes the same argument. However, Qaradawi and mainstream Islamists are not content to equate jihad with just war in the Western tradition, although Zuhaili comes close to doing that. They are emphatic that jihad is unique to Islam as a religion and a civilization. Accordingly, even when non-Muslim powers, such as the United States or NATO, fight for a just cause, such as the US-led NATO campaign to free the Kosovars from the occupation and oppression of the Serbs, their war cannot be construed as jihad.

Last but not least, Qaradawi distinguishes between jihad as *qital*, on the one hand, and violence (*al-'unf*) and terrorism (*al-irhab*), on the other. Qaradawi refutes the Western critiques that jihad emanates from Islam's violent tendencies, emphasizing that Islam is a religion of peace and mercy, and that the Prophet Muhammad was sent to humanity as a messenger of mercy as in Quranic verse 21:107, "We sent you not but as a mercy to mankind."[161] Qaradawi is equally emphatic that jihad is categorically different from terrorism. He interprets the word *turhibun* in Quranic verse 8:60 to mean frighten the enemy in order to deter it from attacking Muslims.[162]

Qaradawi devotes a section of *Fiqh al-Jihad* to elucidate the difference between jihad and terrorism. Qaradawi is emphatic that in terms of the aims and rules that govern its conduct, jihad should not be equated with terrorism. For Qaradawi and mainstream Islamists, conflating these two phenomena represents a deliberate attempt to discredit Islam. Similarly, Zuhaili added a chapter to the last edition of his *Athar al-Harb* on the distinction between jihad and terrorism. Both Qaradawi and Zuhaili denounced the September 11, 2001, attacks on the United States, depicting them as terrorist acts.[163] While Fadlallah sought to cast some doubts on the identity of the perpetuators of the September 11 attacks, he denounced them on both juristic and practical grounds. From a juristic perspective, the attacks targeted civilians who cannot be held accountable for the actions of their government. The 9/11 attacks were suicidal attacks (*hajamat intihariyya*) and not acts of martyrdom, unlike the operations carried out against the Israeli occupation of Palestine and before that of South Lebanon.[164] In a work written prior to the 9/11 attacks, prominent Lebanese Shia cleric and author, sheikh Muhammad Mahdi Shams al-Din, emphasized that attacks on "foreigners (*al-ajaneb*) in their own countries, whether these take the form of bombing commercial establishments and public installations, or hijacking planes and ships" do not fall under the "title of jihad and are thus not legitimate under that title."[165]

The Causes of Military Jihad

Qaradawi's analysis of the causes of jihad, or the just causes for fighting, is very much in line with the analyses of Shaltut and Abu Zahra, although Qaradawi writes in more detail on the subject. Qaradawi appears to have spent more time researching this topic, with a thorough and close examination of the views of dozens of early, medieval, and contemporary Islamic scholars, than did Abu Zahra and Shaltut, who primarily relied on interpreting the pertinent verses in the Quran and giving examples from the conduct of the Prophet. Qaradawi notes that it took him around six years to write his two-volume manuscript on jihad. Qaradawi's succinct definition of military jihad sums up its causes. "Military jihad," Qaradawi writes, "is jihad as *qital*, it is jihad that is directed at the enemies of the *umma*, who attack its religion, its land and its people." He goes on to note, "this *jihad* commits the *umma* to repel the attack, in defense of its sanctuaries and what it holds sacred. Evil is to be stopped by evil and the initiator is the aggressor."[166]

A legitimate question arises regarding the prioritization of the purposes of jihad as *qital*. Why does Qaradawi start by identifying the defense of religion? The answer can be found in Qaradawi's and other mainstream Islamists' narratives on the origins of *qital*. Qaradawi maintains that Muslims had to endure the oppression of the Quraysh polytheists for 13 years without fighting back. Their endurance of the hardships inflicted on them because of their belief was clearly a form of jihad.[167] It was only with verse 22:39, "leave is granted to those who are being attacked, for they were wronged, and God is assuredly capable of sending them victory" that God granted Muslims permission to fight back their oppressors, who were harming and persecuting them in order to turn them back from Islam.[168]

After the establishment of the first Islamic state in Medina, the purposes of jihad expanded to include defending the city and its inhabitants, Muslims and Jews alike, against aggression. Qaradawi expands on the mainstream Islamist argument that jihad was not intended as a means to coerce non-Muslims to embrace Islam. He challenges the argument that the purposes of *qital* changed over the Prophetic mission of Muhammad, and that the aforementioned verse 22:39—that authorized fighting only for defensive purposes—was abrogated (or superseded) by verse 9:5, "Once the sacred months are shorn, kill the polytheists wherever you find them, arrest them, imprison them, besiege them, and lie in wait for them at every side of ambush. If they repent, perform the prayer and pay the alms, let them go on their way: God All-Forgiving, Compassionate to each."

It is in this context that Qaradawi provides an exhaustive treatment of the principal verses that govern the purposes of fighting, namely verses 2:190–194, "Fight in the name of God those who fight you, but do not commit aggression... Slay them wherever you fall upon them, and expel them from where they had expelled you; apostasy by force is indeed more serious than slaying... Whoever commits aggression against you, retaliate against him in the same measure as committed against you."[169] Qaradawi maintains that these verses among others commanded Muslims to repel the aggression of the polytheists who harmed, tortured, and persecuted them because of their religion and sought to turn them away from Islam, unjustly drove them from their homes in Mecca, and initiated fighting against Muslims at the Sacred Mosque (*al-Masjid al-Haram*) and during the Sacred Month (*al-Shahr al-Haram*).[170]

Qaradawi goes into great detail to rebuke the claim that the verse of the sword, often identified verse 9:5, abrogated all earlier verses that authorized jihad only for the defensive reasons noted above.[171] It is important to set this debate regarding the verse of the sword in the context of the broader controversy over the purposes of *qital* between the advocates of defensive jihad and the advocates of offensive jihad, to use Qaradawi's typology.[172] The first camp, to which Qaradawi and the mainstream Islamists belong, views *qital* as a means to defend the Muslims' freedom of belief and their right to preserve their lives, property, and independence, as well as to call others to Islam. Those who belong to the offensive camp, on the other hand, insist that, ever since the revelation of the verse of the sword, Muslims have been commanded to fight all non-Muslims until they embrace Islam or pay the *jizya* as a sign of submission.

Qaradawi launches a three-pronged critique of the argument of the offensive camp regarding the verse of the sword. To start with, Qaradawi contends that there is no consensus among Muslim scholars regarding the abrogation principle, namely that later Quranic verses abrogate earlier ones.[173] Qaradawi himself accepts abrogation but in the narrowest sense, while categorically rejecting the opinion that verse 9:5 abrogated earlier verses about the purposes of fighting.[174] Equally important, Qaradawi challenges the offensive camp to identify which among a number of verses is the verse of the sword. While verse 9:5 is the one most commonly identified, there is no consensus on that. Verse 9:36, "And fight the polytheists, all of them, as they fight you all," and verse 9:41, "March forth, then, whether light or heavy in armor. Labor hard in the cause of God, with your property and persons" are sometimes identified as the verses of the sword.[175]

Qaradawi more significantly emphasizes that when read holistically, as it should be, the Quran preaches peace, dialog, justice, nonaggression, and freedom of belief. Examining the Quran on any topic, such as fighting, requires a careful examination of all the pertinent verses, while relating them to each other and to the contexts in which they were revealed.[176] Qaradawi poses and answers an important rhetorical question. How can one verse, or a few verses, abrogate between 114 and 140 verses (or 200 verses by one count) that preach peace and dialog, and restrict the purposes of fighting to defense against aggression, while instructing Muslims to accept peace when the other side is inclined toward it?[177] In the same vein, Qaradawi emphasizes the centrality of justice to the Quran and the message of Islam. He sees no justice whatsoever in fighting others who do not threaten Muslims, simply because they are not Muslims.

In the process of critiquing the views of the offensive camp (*al-hujumiyyoun*), Qaradawi draws on the opinions of renowned early and medieval Islamic scholars, such as Abu Bakr Ahmad bin-Ali al-Razi al-Jassas (d 981), Fakhr al-din al-Razi (d 1210), and especially Ibn Taymiyya (d 1328). Qaradawi offers excellent summaries of the proofs presented by these scholars to dispel the notion that verse 9:5 abrogated the earlier verses concerning fighting.[178] In this context, he rejects the opinion of a number of Wahhabi *'ulama* who questioned the authenticity of a famous fatwa by Ibn Taymiyya in which he forbade fighting unbelievers simply because of their unbelief. Qaradawi draws on Abu Zahra's famous book on Ibn Taymiyya to validate the fatwa's authenticity. Moving to the contemporary period, Qaradawi summarily presents the opinions of prominent thinkers such as the Syrian scholar Jamal al-Din al-Qasimi (1866–1914), and sheikhs 'Abduh, Rida, Muhammad al-Ghazali and Shaltut, all of whom rejected the notion that Muslims were commanded to fight all unbelievers until they embraced Islam or paid the *jizya*.[179]

The possibility of the presence of certain ambiguities in the Quran regarding the purposes of fighting is anathema for a devout Muslim and a serious Islamic scholar such as Qaradawi. Reuven Firestone, however, contends that such ambiguities do exist, because a few Quranic verses, the verses of the sword, point in a different direction than the majority of verses regarding the legitimate purposes of fighting.[180] Arguably, mainstream Islamists, such as Qaradawi, hold the higher ground due to the preponderance of verses that embrace peace and restrict the purposes of *qital*. Nonetheless, radical Islamists, such as Sayyid Qutb, can draw on a few Quranic verses to legitimize their call for open-ended jihad against unbelievers. Sayyid Qutb is specifically referred to here not only because of the central place he occupies within the radical/offensive camp, but also because Qaradawi devotes a short section of his *Fiqh al-Jihad* to refute Qutb's ideas on jihad, despite his admiration of Qutb.[181]

To sum up, in line with the scholar sheikhs of the second generation, Qaradawi views peace as the norm in international relations, with war as the exception. War is a necessity that results from the aggression of others. Qaradawi thus writes, "Islam only authorizes war to repel aggression and to fight those who fight Muslims, or who seek to turn them away (by force) from their religion, or who hurt and torment the weak amongst them."[182] He goes on to identify the rules that govern fighting once war erupts, covered in the next section.

The Conduct of Fighting

As with the purposes of jihad, Qaradawi's treatment of the rules that govern the conduct of *qital* is in line with that of the scholar sheikhs of the second generation, particularly Shaltut and Abu Zahra. Accordingly, this section will cover these rules in some brevity to avoid repetition and what will be further discussed in Chapters 6 and 7 on Zuhaili and Fadlallah. Prior to combat, the enemy should be given the choice of embracing Islam or paying the *jizya*. Fighting ensues only after both options are rejected. If at any point during the battle, the enemy accepts either of the above two options, fighting ceases.[183] Accordingly, once the enemy demonstrates an inclination toward peace, Muslims are enjoined to accept peace in line with verse 8:61, "Should they incline to peace, incline to it also and put your trust in God."[184] In such circumstances, however, the *imam*, or the *wulat al-amr*, would have considerable leeway to ascertain the sincerity of the enemy and to act.

Discipline, high morale, and faith in God are essential ingredients for prevailing in war. Defeat in a battle results from a combination of poor military preparedness, breakdown of discipline, as what occurred in the battle of Uhud, or low morale.[185] Both Qaradawi and Fadlallah elaborate extensively on the centrality of faith in God for the maintenance of discipline and high morale among both combatants and civilian populations during war. In passing, one may note that Qaradawi attributes the defeat of the Arab states, Egypt in particular, in the 1967 War against Israel to the interplay of all the above factors.[186] In line with Shaltut and Abu Zahra, Qaradawi prohibits any destruction of civilian property that is not necessary for military purposes.[187] The killing of women, children, the elderly, the infirm, monks, and hermits is prohibited, on the ground that they do not normally take part in fighting,[188] but if any member of these protected groups participates in combat, even by advising or raising the morale of the enemy, he/she loses their noncombatant status and their slaying becomes lawful.[189]

In the contemporary era, Qaradawi considers all the Jewish citizens of the state of Israel to be combatants due to his view of the militarized nature of the state. Stated more plainly, Qaradawi considers every Jewish citizen of Israel, male or female, to be a soldier or a potential soldier in light of the universal draft laws in Israel.[190] Since Arabs and Muslims are in a state of war with Israel, due to its occupation of a core part of *dar al-Islam*, targeting Israeli civilians is lawful.[191] With great passion he writes, "Those they call civilians are in reality soldiers in the army of the children of Zion (*Bani Sahyoun*)."[192] If some Arab Israelis are killed, Qaradawi treats them as collateral damage. In this context, Qaradawi and Zuhaili resurrect the traditional notion of *tatarus* (literally the enemy use of Muslims as human shields), arguing that the killing of Muslims becomes lawful when the enemy uses them as human shields.[193] Qaradawi is a vociferous critic of the state of Israel, or the "Zionist entity," as he prefers to call it.[194] While, arguably, the other mainstream scholar sheikhs share his views on Israel, only Qaradawi and Fadlallah addressed this matter at length and in such a polemical manner. In a sweeping statement, Qaradawi writes that, "We consider the entire [non-Muslim world] to be an abode of treaty (*dar 'ahd*), except for the Zionist entity: Israel."[195]

Qaradawi's vehement opposition to the 1979 Egyptian-Israeli Peace Treaty and the 1993 Oslo Accords between the Palestinian liberation Organization and Israel[196] as well as his open support for suicide attacks against Israel all contributed to his image in the West as a radical Islamist. In Qaradawi's defense, one may note that he only legitimized suicide attacks as a last resort, since the Palestinians, in his view, were denied conventional weapons (such as tanks and missiles) to defend themselves.[197] Qaradawi cautions Palestinians to weigh the potential costs, in terms of Israeli retaliation, versus the potential benefits, in terms of weakening Israeli confidence and morale, of suicide operations. A careful reading of his discourse indicates that he does not favor these operations, especially if there are other, including peaceful, means of resistance, but he leaves the ultimate decision to the leaders of the Palestinians.[198] Equally important, he leaves the door ajar for a peaceful settlement between Israel and the Palestinians. The terms he set for such a settlement, including the absolute right of return for the Palestinians to any part of Israel they were expelled from, complete Arab/Muslim sovereignty over East Jerusalem and the Aqsa Mosque and a sovereign and well-armed Palestinian state, are unlikely to be taken seriously by any Israeli official.

Prisoners of war may not be killed or tortured, and are to be treated humanely, in accordance with verses 76:8–9, "They had dispensed food, though held dear, to the poor, the orphan and the prisoner, Saying: We are feeding you only for the sake of God. From you we seek neither reward nor thanks." Elaborating on the above verses, Qaradawi writes, "Islam demands that prisoners of war be treated in a humane manner that ensures their dignity, protects their rights and safeguards their humanity."[199] At the end of war, prisoners of war are to be released, either in exchange for Muslim prisoners (*fida'*) or as an act of mercy (*minna*), in line with verse 47:4, "When you encounter the unbelievers, blows to necks it shall be until, once you have routed them, you are to tighten their fetters. Thereafter it is either gracious bestowal of freedom or holding them to ransom, until war has laid down its burdens."[200] Based on the centuries old Islamic tradition, Qaradawi, however, recognizes that during his life, the Prophet also authorized the slaying of some prisoners and the enslaving of others.[201]

Both Qaradawi and Zuhaili write extensively in an attempt to reconcile between 1) the Quranic injunction to release prisoners, upon the cessation of hostilities and 2) the multiple references in the Islamic tradition to the Prophet's practice of slaying some prisoners and enslaving others. The two scholar sheikhs make essentially the same argument, namely that in ordering the killing of a few "dangerous" prisoners and the enslaving of others, the Prophet was acting in his capacity as the wise leader of the nascent Muslim community and not on the basis of a revelation from God. The Prophet's decisions in this matter were, thus, context bound and absolutely correct judgments, but they did not constitute a Sunna to be emulated by subsequent Muslim leaders.[202] Most importantly, Qaradawi and Zuhaili are unequivocal that prevalent international norms and conventions that prohibit the killing or the enslavement of prisoners of war are to be followed to the letter by Muslims states. These norms and conventions, Qaradawi and Zuhaili argue, are in line with the intents of religion (*maqasid al-din*) and with the pertinent Quranic verses regarding the treatment of prisoners, particularly verse 49:4.[203] We shall return to this important argument in the following chapter on Zuhaili. While Fadlallah's discussion on the fate of prisoners of war is shorter, his views on the matter are nearly identical to those of his Sunni counterparts (see Chapter 7).

The Ending of War

In line with traditional views, Qaradawi identifies four principal ways for ending war. To start with, war ends anytime that the enemy surrenders either by embracing Islam or by agreeing to pay the *jizya*. As previously argued by Abu Zahra, the mere act of pronouncing the two testimonies, namely that there is no god but Allah and that Muhammad is the Prophet of Allah, is sufficient proof of the acceptance of Islam.[204] Conquered populations that refuse to embrace Islam of their own volition acquire the status of *dhimmis* (protected people) and are required to pay the *jizya*.[205] Qaradawi argues repeatedly that the payment of the *jizya* is not intended to humiliate non-Muslim populations but to ensure that they are contributing their fair share to the wellbeing of the community.[206] *Dhimmis* would have all the rights and duties of the Muslim population, including representation in parliament and the government and service in the army. *Dhimmis* are, however, to be excluded from top command positions in the army and from the judiciary body, which should be based on the *sharia*.

Aware of the negative connotations of the term *dhimmis*, especially among Christian citizens of majority Muslim Arab states such as his native Egypt, Qaradawi sees no problem in dropping its use. That applies to the *jizya* tax that need not be applied, since Christians pay other taxes and serve in the armies of most majority-Muslim states.[207] While Qaradawi and Zuhaili's stances on the *jizya* tax are almost identical, Zuhaili is more explicit in stating that it has lost its meaning in most majority-Muslim countries.

War also ends if the two sides agree to a cessation of hostilities. This cessation can be either a temporary or a permanent one. In the first case, it would take the form of a truce (*hudna*), while in the latter case, it would the form of a peace treaty (*sulh*).[208] Qaradawi addresses at some length the difference between a truce and a peace treaty and the opinions of traditional scholars on whether it is permissible for the *imam*, or the *wulat al-amr*, to conclude open-ended peace treaties, i.e., ones that do not expire after specified period.[209] The conclusion he reaches is identical to that of Abu Zahra and Zuhaili, namely that there is nothing in the Quran or the Sunna of the Prophet that prohibits entering into open-ended peace treaties when that is in the interest of the Muslims.[210] Qaradawi, Zuhaili, and Fadlallah all leave considerable leeway to *wulat al-amr* and sometimes to military commanders to negotiate truces and peace treaties on condition that their terms do not violate the *sharia*.

The third option for ending a war is for the Muslim side to withdraw from battle without any agreement.[211] Qaradawi gives here the example of the renowned Muslim commander Khalid ibn al-Walid. Fearing the annihilation of the Muslim army at the battle of Mu'tah (September 629), Khalid ibn-al-Walid, who assumed command after the slaying of the three previous commanders, withdrew from battle against the more numerous Roum (Byzantines). For Qaradawi, there was nothing wrong or shameful in Khalid's decision to withdraw, which was the right decision to make under the circumstances.[212]

The last, and least favored, scenario entails losing the war. Unlike other mainstream Islamists, Qaradawi does not shy away from discussing at some length the possibility of the war ending with the defeat of the Muslim side. In this case, the Muslims must do all they can to protect themselves and to prepare in earnest to reverse their fortunes. Turning to the Islamic tradition, Qaradawi identifies a few instances when Muslim rulers agreed to pay tribute to non-Muslim powers when they judged that they stood little chance of prevailing in war.[213] In the context of elaborating on the consequences of defeat in war, Qaradawi addresses the issue of Muslim populations in occupied territories (territories that are lost to *dar al-harb*), particularly the Palestinian population in what became the state of Israel.[214] Qaradawi is determined that the Arab Muslims and Christians in the state of Israel should stay and not migrate to a neighboring Muslim state, as called for in verse 4:97, "Was not the land of God wide enough for you to emigrate into?"[215] Emigrating from "occupied Palestine" would be tantamount to abandoning it to the abode of war.[216]

To sum up, while Qaradawi's claim to offer a fresh perspective on jihad is exaggerated, his extensive treatment of the subject throws light on a pivotal dimension of the mainstream Islamist perspective on international relations. Qaradawi views jihad within the context of the law of mutual restraining, one of the *sunnan* upon which God established this world. While jihad is an exclusively Islamic notion, it is prompted by conditions that impact all human societies. Aggression is intrinsic to human nature, though it does not define its totality, and the aggression instinct is amplified in polities and societies that are not based on Islam. Since the anarchic nature of the international system permits some nations to aggress against others, Muslims are compelled to resist aggression in order to defend their independence and their freedoms. Qaradawi embodies the mainstream Islamist view that Jihad (as *qital*) is a means to defend the independence and freedoms of the Muslim *umma* but is not an end in itself. While jihad is primarily defined by its just purpose, it also entails waging war in accordance with ethical principles that, while derived from the *sharia*, are also in line with contemporary international norms and conventions. It is the legally minded Zuhaili, though, who best develops this argument on the compatibility of the *sharia* with international law, especially international humanitarian law.

The Road to Islamic Unity

In line with the other mainstream scholar sheikhs, Qaradawi devotes considerable attention to the topic of Islamic unity, his views on the subject bearing major resemblance to those of Abu Zahra, especially as conveyed in Abu Zahra's *al-Wihda al-Islamiyya*. Abu Zahra's treatment of the subject is, however, more systematic than that of Qaradawi, who wrote a short treatise on the subject, entitled *The Muslim Umma: A Reality and not an Illusion*.[217] The subject of Islamic unity also appears in most of Qaradawi's other manuscripts. For Qaradawi, the realization of Islamic unity represents the major, indeed the ultimate, goal of the Islamic awakening that he tirelessly calls for. All the principal elements of the mainstream Islamist view on Islamic unity find echoes in Qaradawi's discourse.

To begin, Qaradawi's principal unit of analysis is the Muslim *umma*, which comprises all believers, whether in domestic politics or international relations. Thus, whoever pronounces the two testimonies, that there is no god but Allah and that Muhammad is the Prophet of Allah, is an integral part of the Muslim *umma*, whether or not Islam has entered their heart. The rights and duties of the Muslim, as codified in the *sharia*, apply to all Muslims irrespectively of where they live. The one Muslim *umma* is founded on the brotherhood of all believers in Islam, as found in several Quranic verses, particularly, 49:10, "The believers are indeed brothers" and 3:103, "He brought harmony to your hearts so that, by His blessing, you became brothers."[218]

Qaradawi raises the religious bond *(al-rabita al-diniyya)* over all other social bonds as do the other mainstream Islamists. While aware that most Muslims have multiple loyalties to the Muslim *umma* as well as to their respective ethnic, linguistic, or national groups, Qaradawi insists that the Islamic identity must eclipse all other identities, but without obliterating them. With considerable passion, Qaradawi writes, "the truth, about which there can be no doubt, is that Islam elevates the religious bond over any other bond, whether it is the bond of kinship, region, race or class; the Muslim is the brother of the Muslim, the believers are brothers and the Muslims are one *umma*."[219]

Nonetheless, attachment to a particular clan, ethnic, or linguistic group, or a geographic locale, is a natural attachment that Islam acknowledges. Qaradawi notes that the Prophet Muhammad remained attached to his birthplace Mecca, even after his migration to Medina, and despite the persecution that he and his Companions suffered at the hands of the polytheists of Mecca.[220] From the outset, the Muslim *umma* was characterized by tribal and even ethnic diversity, bringing together migrants from Mecca and the original residents of Medina and its environs, and it also included non-Arabs, such as Bilal from the Habasha (Ethiopia) and Salman al-Farsi (from Persia), who were leading members of the nascent Muslim community.[221]

The rapid expansion of Islam outside the Arabian Peninsula significantly added to the ethnic and linguistic diversity of the *umma*, with another element of diversity that ingrained itself in the body of the one *umma*, namely the emergence of different schools of jurisprudence (*Mazhaheb*, singular *Mazhhab*), according to Qaradawi. In line with Shaltut and Abu Zahra, Qaradawi adopts an ecumenical approach not just toward the four recognized Sunni Mazhaheb but also toward the Shias (Twelvers, Zaydis, and Ismailis). Despite his apprehensions later in life over alleged Iranian attempts to promote the Twelver Shia *mazhhab* among the Sunnis,[222] Qaradawi consistently recognizes the Shias as an integral part of the Muslim *umma*.

Qaradawi also celebrated the Iranian revolution of 1979, praising Iran for establishing an Islamic system of government that was compliant with the *sharia*, and he blamed Saddam Hussein for launching the Iran–Iraq war that raged in the 1980s.[223] This did not stop him, though, from gently rebuking the Iranian regime for allegedly underrepresenting Iran's Sunni population in its parliament and the cabinet and for denying Tehran's Sunni population, that he estimated at two million, the right to establish a mosque.[224] Qaradawi's criticisms of the Shias increased following the 2003 occupation of Iraq and the uprooting of the Saddam Hussein Baathist regime, although he had no sympathy whatsoever toward Saddam Hussein or the Baath. Qaradawi accused the Iraqi Shias of discriminating against and targeting their Sunni Brethren with assassinations and even "ethnic cleansing" in places such as Basra. These sporadic attacks against the Shias, however, were interpreted to pertain exclusively to their political behavior in specific contexts and not to their creed. In his memoirs, Qaradawi attributes heightened tensions between the Sunnis and Shias, wherever they occur, to foreign intervention or to grave injustices inflicted by one side on the other.[225] In sum, Qaradawi's fluid vision of Islamic unity includes the Islamic Republic of Iran and the Shias.

Qaradawi acknowledges further than other mainstream Islamists the division of the Islamic world into independent, and often, rival territorial nation states (*duwal Islamiyya iqlimiyya*).[226] His discourse includes far more references to Islamic states (in the plural) than the discourses of the scholar sheikhs of the second generation who minimize using this term in the plural and refer to the singular-universal Islamic state. Qaradawi is also aware of the multiple challenges that stand in the way of realizing the political, military, and socioeconomic unity of the entire Muslim *umma*.

Unlike Abu Zahra who presents a roadmap for restoring Islamic unity, Qaradawi's vision on how to restore this unity is highly fluid. Thus, while his discourse abounds with lamentations over the loss of the caliphate, the "historic fortress" that protected the *umma*,[227] he does not insist on resurrecting this institution. In a relatively early work, *The Jurisprudence of the State in Islam*, Qaradawi insists that Muslims are required to work for restoring the caliphate, enthusiastically embracing the call for establishing a universal Islamic state that would be headed by the Caliph, but without providing much detail on the shape that it would take.[228] Qaradawi wavers between two forms, a confederation of provinces or provincial states and a federation.[229]

Qaradawi's views on Islamic unity, however, seem to have evolved over time. In his later works, particularly his *Jurisprudence of Jihad*, Qaradawi construes Islamic unity largely in the form of closer cooperation and coordination between the existing Muslim or majority-Muslim states in the economic, military, foreign policy, and especially cultural domains.[230] Qaradawi advances many proposals for achieving far greater cooperation among the Islamic states, but these are not neatly related and do not constitute a blueprint for realizing this desired unity. One of his proposals is to establish an "Islamic Court of justice" that would act in a similar fashion to the International Court of Justice (ICJ), adjudicating territorial disputes between provincial Islamic states (*duwal Islamiyya qitriyya*).[231]

Qaradawi provides specific examples of disputes (e.g., the conflicts between Morocco and the Polisario Front over the fate of Western Sahara, and between Sudan and Egypt over the Hala'ib triangle) that would fall under the jurisprudence of this International Islamic Court. Unlike the ICJ, which lacks enforcement powers, its hypothetical Islamic counterpart would possess such powers. Qaradawi, thus, envisions an Islamic armed force that encompasses soldiers from all or most Islamic states, which would forcefully implement the rulings of the Islamic Court.[232] Qaradawi invokes another comparison, in this case to the United Nations Security Council (UNSC).[233] The envisioned Islamic Court would look more like the UNSC, acting under Chapter 7 and not hindered by veto power, than the ICJ. The utopian element in this loosely articulated vision cannot be missed on any serious scholar of international relations.

More realistically, Qaradawi calls for far closer economic cooperation between the Islamic states, especially in the areas of freeing the movement of goods, capital and people between the various Islamic provinces (*aqalim*).[234] Qaradawi is struck at the ability of the European countries to overcome their historic differences and bloody wars and move swiftly toward economic integration, while the Islamic provincial states, despite ruling over parts of a single *umma* whose members are divinely enjoined to act as one body, have been unable to do the same.[235]

For Qaradawi, the most important manifestation of Islamic unity, however, lies in coordinating Islamic efforts to confront existential threats to the Muslim *umma*, particularly the Israeli threat, by pooling all available military, financial, and diplomatic resources. Qaradawi repeatedly argues that if there is a single issue over which the Muslim *umma* must act in concert as one body then it is the issue of Palestine and more specifically resisting Israeli efforts to exert sovereignty over Jerusalem, the cite of al-Aqsa Mosque. In *Fatwas for the Sake of Palestine*, Qaradawi maintains that, "Palestine in its entirety does not belong exclusively to the Palestinians, for them to dispose of as they deem fit; it belongs to the *umma*, the *umma* in its entirety."[236] As its title indicates, Qaradawi's other short polemical track on the subject, *Jerusalem the Cause of Every Muslim*, makes the same argument.[237]

Conclusion

Building on the thought of the scholar sheikhs of the first and second generations, while also drawing heavily on centuries old Islamic tradition, Qaradawi provides a detailed treatment of several interrelated issues that are at the core of contemporary international relations. As a jurisprudent, he seeks authoritative answers to pivotal questions, such as: What are the universal laws (*al-sunnan al-kawniyya*) that govern international relations? Is peace, or war, the principle (*al-asl*) in relations between Muslims and non-Muslims? How can international peace be preserved given the conflicting tendencies within human nature, the expansionist tendencies of non-Muslim states and the absence of an international authority? What are the just causes for fighting? What are the rules that govern the conduct of fighting and how does fighting (or war) end? How can the Islamic states overcome their current division and move toward Islamic unity?

Although other Islamists have grappled with these questions, Qaradawi's answers are thorough, informed by the opinions of scores of Islamic scholars from different eras, and above all properly anchored in the Quran and the Sunna. Also, Qaradawi's answers to these questions have a sense of definitiveness or finality. Qaradawi is not merely interested in contributing to ongoing debates but aims at concluding these debates by formulating properly researched, balanced, and well-reasoned answers that provide guidance to the Muslim *umma* on pivotal matters. Qaradawi approaches these questions not as a detached scholar but as a jurisprudent, or indeed as an authoritative reference (*marja'iyya*)[238] who can now put matters to rest, having consulted all available opinions and having gone back to the roots as embodied in the Sunna and the Quran. While Qaradawi maintains that his approach to political and social issues, including issues of international relations, is informed by Islam's idealist-realist outlook on life, this chapter has argued that Qaradawi's perspective is closer to realism than it is to idealism. Chapter 6 turns to the discourse of a friend of Qaradawi, the Syrian scholar sheikh Wahbah al-Zuhaili, for whom the mix between realism and idealism, or liberal internationalism, tilts toward the latter pole.

Notes

1   There is sizeable academic literature on Qaradawi. This literature, however, hardly addresses Qaradawi's international relations discourse. Arguably, the most comprehensive work on Qaradawi is Bettina Graf and Jakob Skovgaard-Peterson, eds., *Global Mufti: The Phenomenon of Yusuf Qaradawi* (New York: Columbia University Press, 2009). Studies devoted to specific aspects of Qaradawi's thought include: Aaaron Rock-Singer, "Scholarly Authority and Lay Mobilization: Yusuf al-Qaradawi's Vision of Da'wa, 1976–1984," *The Muslim World* 106 (2016): 588–604; Scott Kugle and Stephen Hunt, "Masculinity, Homosexuality and the Defense of Islam: A case Study

of Yusuf al-Qaradawi's Media Fatwa," *Religion & Gender* 2, no. 2 (2012): 254–79; Shaul Bartal and Nesya Rubinstein-Shemer, *Hamas and Ideology: Sheikh Yusuf al-Qaradawi on Jews, Zionism and Israel* (Oxford and New York: Routledge, 2018). Also, a number of books on contemporary Islamic thought make significant references to Qaradawi's thought. See, especially, Zaman, *Modern Islamic Thought*, 18–24, 65–74, 114–18, 131–2, 150–7; and Asma Afsaruddin, *Striving in the Path of God: Jihad and Martyrdom in Islamic Thought* (Oxford: Oxford University Press, 2013), 224–31.

2 Alain Gabon, "Can Mainstream Sunni Islam Counter the Islamic State? A Critique of Adis Duderija's The Salafi Worldview and the Hermeneutical Limits of Mainstream Sunni Critique of Salafi Jihadism," *Studies in Conflict & Terrorism* (2019). Doi: https://doi.org/10.1080/10576X.2019.1657296.

3 Kugle and Hunt, "Masculinity, Homosexuality and the Defense of Islam," 258.

4 Alexandre Caeiro, "The Shifting Moral Universes of the Islamic Tradition of Ifta': A Diachronic Analysis of Four Adab al-fatwa Manuals," *The Muslim World* 96 (2006), 661–85, 669.

5 Graf and Skovgaard-Peterson eds. *Global Mufti*.

6 Ghazaly [more commonly written Ghazali] was a major intellectual influence on the young Qaradawi. Qaradawi wrote a popular work on Sheikh Ghazaly. Qaradawi, *al-Sheikh al-Ghazaly Kama 'Areftuh*.

7 Raymond William Baker, *Islam without Fear: Egypt and the New Islamists* (Cambridge: Oxford University Press, 2003), 4, 10. To my knowledge, Baker was the one who coined the term "New Islamists." Baker's notion of "New Islamists" corresponds well with my notion of mainstream, or moderate-reformist, Islamists. According to Baker, the distinguishing feature of the "New Islamists" is their embrace of a centrist, mainstream (i.e., *wasati*) approach to Islam.

8 Concurrently with his regular appearances on *al-Sharia and Life*, Qaradawi had another religious program on Qatar national television titled *Hadi al-Islam* (the Guidance of Islam). Ehab Galal, "Yusuf al-Qaradawi and the New Islamic TV," in *Global Mufti*, eds. Graf and Skovgaard-Petersen, 149–80. See also Marc Lynch, *Voices of the New Arab Public: Iraq: Al-Jazeera and Middle East Politics Today* (New York: Cambridge University Press, 2006), esp. 7, 26–28, 48, 79, 86–87, 125–26, 230, 234–35.

9 Lynch, *Voices of the New Arab Public*, 235. Lynch reiterates this point on page 235.

10 In launching this project, Qaradawi acknowledges the support he received from Sheikha Moza bint Nasser, the wife of the former Qatari Emir Sheikh Hamad bin Thani. Qaradawi, *Fiqh al-Wasatiyya al-Islamiyya wa al-Tajdid: Ma 'alem wa Manarat* (The Jurisprudence of Islamic Wasatiyya and Renewal: Landmarks and Signposts) (Cairo: Dar al-Shuruq, 2010), 23.

11 For Qaradawi's presence on the Web, see, especially, Bettina Graf, "Sheikh Yusuf al-Qaradawi in Cyberspace," *Die Welt des Islams*, New Series 47, Issue 3–4, Islam and Social Norms: Approaches to Modern Muslim Intellectual History (2007): 403–21.

The Third Generation: Sheikh Yusuf al-Qaradawi | 177

12 Caeiro, "The Shifting Moral Universes of the Islamic Tradition of Ifta," 669.
13 Jacquelene Brinton, *Preaching Islamic Renewal: Religious Authority and Media in Contemporary Egypt* (Oakland, CA: California University Press, 2016), 68.
14 For information about the IUMS, see http://islamopediaonline.org/websites-institutions/international-union-muslim-scholars-dublin-ireland (Accessed on April 12, 2012). The active Twitter account of the IUMS (@iumsonline) still features pictures of Qaradawi and short quotes by him.
15 For Qaradawi's influence in Europe, see, especially Alexandre Caeiro and Mahmoud al-Saify, "Qaradawi in Europe, Europe in Qaradawi?" in *Global Mufti*, eds. Graf and Skovgaard-Petersen, 109–48. See also Zaman, *Modern Islamic Thought*, 95–96.
16 For Qaradawi's defense of popular rule, as long as it does not contradict the Sharia, see, in particular, Yusuf Qaradawi, *Min Fiqh al-Dawla fi al-Islam* (The Jurisprudence of the State in Islam) (Cairo: Dar al-Shuruq, 2011), esp. 43–59.
17 For Qaradawi's criticisms of the thought and practices of *takfiri* groups, see Qaradawi, *Ummatna Bayn Qarnayn*, 74–77; Yusuf Qaradawi, *al-Islam wa al-'Unf: Nazharat Ta'siliyya* (Islam and Violence: Foundational Views) (Cairo: Dar al-Shuruq, 2005), 44–58. Equally important, Qaradawi provides a thorough critique of the *takfiri* elements in the thought of Sayyid Qutb. See Qaradawi, *Ibn al-Qarya wa al-Kuttab*, Vol. 3, esp. 68–72.
18 Lynch, *Voices of the New Arab Public*, 234.
19 See, however, Baroudi, "Sheikh Yusuf Qaradawi on International Relations," 2–36; and Baroudi, "The Islamic Realism of Sheikh Yusuf Qaradawi (1926–) and Sayyid Mohammad Hussein Fadlullah (1935–2010)," 94–114.
20 This biographic section is based primarily on Qaradawi's three-volume autobiography. Yusuf Qaradawi, *Ibn al-Qarya wa al-kuttab* (Son of the Village and the Kuttab), Vols. 1–3 (Cairo: Dar al-Shuruq, 2002, 2004, and 2006). Al-Khatib also offers a detailed intellectual biography of Qaradawi. Mutaz al-Khatib, *Yusuf al-Qaradawi: Faqih al-Sahwa al-Islamiya Sira Fikriya Tahliliya* (Yusuf Qaradawi: The Jurisprudent of the Islamic Awakening: An Analytical Intellectual Biography) (Beirut: Center for Civilization for the Development of Islamic Thought, 2009). Based largely on the above two sources, the introductory chapter of the edited volume on Qaradawi, *Global Mufti*, provides a succinct biography. Graf and Skovgaard-Peterson, Introduction, in Graf and Skovgaard-Peterson eds. *Global Mufti*, 1–17.
21 Qaradawi, *Ibn al-Qarya wa al-kuttab*, Vol. 2, 124. Skovgaard-Peterson notes, however, that Qaradawi joined the Movement in 1941. Skovgaard-Petersen, "Yusuf al-Qaradawi and al-Azhar," in *Global Mufti*, eds. Graf and Skovgaard-Petersen, 32.
22 Husam Tammam, "Yusuf al-Qaradawi and the Muslim Brothers: The Nature of a Special Relationship" in Graf and Skovgaard-Petersen, *Global Mufti*, 55.
23 Tammam, "Yusuf al-Qaradawi and the Muslim Brothers," 72.
24 See especially Tammam, "Yusuf Qaradawi and the Muslim Brothers," 58–83. Even authors who make marginal references to Qaradawi in their works invariably associate him with the Muslim Brotherhood. See Aaaron Rock-Singer, *Practicing Islam*

in Egypt: Print Media and Islamic Revival (Cambridge: Cambridge University Press, 2019). For Qaradawi's account of his relationship with the Muslim Brotherhood, see especially volumes 1 and 2 of his memoirs *Ibn al-Qarya wa al-Kuttab* and his *Shumul al-Islam* (The Comprehensiveness of Islam) (Cairo: Maktabat Wahba, 2011); and *al-Sheikh al-Ghazali kama 'Areftahu*.

25 Gerges, *Making the Arab World*, esp. 366–67.
26 Several works address this important chapter in Egypt's modern history. See Carrie Rosefsky Wickham, *The Muslim Brotherhood: Evolution of an Islamist Movement* (Princeton: Princeton University Press, 2013), 27–29; Fawaz Gerges, *The Making of the Arab World*; Robert S. Leiken and Steven Brooke, "The Moderate Muslim Brotherhood," *Foreign Affairs* 86, no. 2 (2007): 107–21, 109–100.
27 Qaradawi, *Ibn al-Qarya wa al-Kuttab*, Vol. 2, 109–202.
28 In addition to the "falaka" or beating the soles of the feet of the inmates, Qaradawi describes two popular methods utilized by the prison guards. The first method is to force the inmates to stand still in the heat of the sun for hours or until they faint and collapse. The second method (intended mainly as a form of humiliation) is to line up the inmates in two columns facing one another. One inmate would then slap the inmate facing him, after which the slapped inmate slaps back.
29 Qaradawi explains that the injury was caused by the limited medical attention he received afterwards, which caused his wounds to fester.
30 Qaradawi, *Ibn al-Qarya wa al-Kuttab*, Vol. 2, 411–27.
31 Qaradawi, *Ibn al-Qarya wa al-Kutab*, Vol. 2, 234–59.
32 For Qaradawi's recollections of this episode, see, *Ibn al-Qarya wa al-Kuttab*, Vol. 2, 239–48.
33 Qaradawi writes that Baqouri was part of the first generation of MB members and that he swore allegiance to the MB founder Sheikh Hassan al-Banna. According to Qaradawi, Baqouri defected from the MB shortly after the 1952 Revolution and gained the confidence of Nasser, who relied on him to propagate pro-regime views. Qaradawi's account leaves little doubt that, despite his official break with the MB, Baqouri did go out of his way to provide jobs to several MB members, despite the MB's troubled relationship with the regime. As noted in Chapter 3, Baqouri succeeded Bahi as the director of al-Azhar University in 1963, retaining that post until 1985. Although Bahi's biography includes many negative references to Baqouri, Qaradawi has nothing but praise for both Baqouri and Bahi.
34 Qaradawi, *Ibn al-Qarya wa al-Kuttab*, Vol. 2, 280.
35 Qaradawi, however, makes it clear that Shaltut did read and personally approve of all the additions he made. *Ibn al-Qarya wa al-Kuttab*, Vol. 2, 281–84.
36 For works on Mawdudi, see Roy Jackson, *Mawlana Mawdudi and Political Islam: Authority and the Islamic State* (London and New York, Routledge, 2011). For Qaradawi's own references to the thought of Mawdudi and the influence it had in the Arab world, see, and inter alia, Qaradawi, *Ummatna Bayn Qarnayn*, 67–68.

37 Qaradawi, *ibn al-Qarya wa al-Kuttab*, Vol. 2, 285–86.
38 Rachid al-Ghannouchi, *al-Wasatiya al-Islamiya 'ind al-Imam Yusuf al-Qaradawi* (Political *Wasatiya* according to Imam Yusuf al-Qaradawi) (Jeddah: Mu'asasat Ru'a Thaqafiyya, 2009), 89–100.
39 Mutaz al-Khatib, *Yusuf al-Qaradawi: Faqih al-Sahwa al-Islamiya Sira Fikriya Tahliliya* (Yusuf Qaradawi: The Jurisprudent of the Islamic Awakening: An Analytical Intellectual Biography) (Beirut: Center for Civilization for the Development of Islamic Thought, 2009).
40 See, inter alia, Toth, *Sayyid Qutb*, 269–71.
41 Jackson, *Mawlana Mawdudi and Political Islam*, 103–06.
42 See, inter alia, Toth, *Sayyid Qutb*, 269–71.
43 Qaradawi, *Ibn al-Qarya wa al-Kuttab*, Vol. 2, 289–90.
44 Graff and Skovgaard-Petersen, "Introduction," in *Global Mufti*, eds. Graff and Skovgaard-Petersen, 4.
45 Qaradawi, *Ibn al-Qarya wa al-Kuttab*, Vol. 2, 70–74.
46 In his memoirs, Qaradawi emphasizes that he always believed that action should be made public and not done in secret. Covert activities are only legitimate when dealing with a foreign occupier (such as the British in Egypt or the Israelis in Palestine). They are not to be resorted to in dealing with one's own government, even when it is despotic and deviates from the *sharia*. Qaradawi's rejection of any covert action against the government of a majority-Muslim state became a hallmark of his philosophy, setting him apart from *takfiri* groups and indeed at loggerheads with them. For the Secret Apparatus, see Richard P. Mitchell, *The Society of the Muslim Brothers* (Oxford: Oxford University Press, 1993; first published 1969), esp. 30 and 205; Fawaz Gerges, *Making the Arab World*, (Princeton: Princeton University Press, 2018), 72–3, 91, 172.
47 Qaradawi, *Ibn al-Qarya wa al-Kuttab*, 218.
48 Qaradawi provides ample information about his relationship with al-Subaie in his autobiography as well an in an editorial published in the Qatari newspaper al-Sharq. Yusuf Qaradawi, "al-Subaie Raed Nahdat al-taaleem al-deeni fi Qatar" (Al-Subai'i pioneered the renaissance of religious education in Qatar), *al-Sharq* (2015), https://al-sharq.com/article/25/06/2015/%D8%A7%D9%84%D9%82%D8%B1 %D8%B6%D8%A7%D9%88%D9%8A-%D8%A7%D9%84%D8%B3%D8 %A8%D9%8A%D8%B9%D9%89-%D8%B1%D8%A7%D8%A6%D8%AF- %D9%86%D9%87%D8%B6%D8%A9-%D8%A7%D9%84%D8%AA%D8 %B9%D9%84%D9%8A%D9%85-%D8%A7%D9%84%D8%AF%D9%8A %D9%86%D9%8A-%D9%81%D9%8A-%D9%82%D8%B7%D8%B1, accessed 5 March, 2020.
49 When in Qatar, Qaradawi preached at the Umar bin al-Khattab mosque.
50 Ehab Galal, "Yusuf al-Qaradawi and the New Islamic TV," in *Global Mufti*, Graf and Skovgaard-Petersen, 149–80.

51 See inter alia Qaradawi's interview with *al-Shari'a wa al-Hayat*, February 24, 2008. http://qaradawi.net/2010-02-23-09-38-15/4/843.html?tmpl=component&print= 1&layout=default&page= (Accessed on April 12, 2012).
52 Yusuf Qaradawi, *al-Baba wa al-Islam* (The Pope and Islam), https://www.al-qaradawi.net/node/1766, accessed 23 April, 2012.
53 See, in particular, Yusuf Qaradawi, *al-Quds Qadiyat Kul Muslim* (Jerusalem the Cause of Every Muslim) (Cairo: Maktabat Wahba, 1998).
54 Qaradawi, *Fiqh al-Jihad*, 734–35.
55 John Esposito, *The Future of Islam* (Oxford: Oxford University Press, 2010), 105.
56 Olivier da lage, "The Politics of Al Jazeera or the Diplomacy of Doha," in *The Al Jazeera Phenomenon: Critical Perspectives on New Arab Media*, ed. Mohamed Zayani (London: Pluto Press, 2005), 49–65; 60–61.
57 Qaradawi, *Fiqh al Jihad*, 735–36.
58 Baker, *Islam without Fear*. For Baker's definition of the "New Islamists" see, esp. 1–2.
59 Baker, *Islam without Fear*, 216–17.
60 For information about the IUMS, see http://islamopediaonline.org/websites-institutions/international-union-muslim-scholars-dublin-ireland. (Accessed on April 12, 2012).
61 Qaradawi was the first Islamic scholar to address at length the issues facing Muslim communities in the West. See, in particular, Yusuf Qaradawi, *Fi Fiqh al-Aqaliyyat al-Muslima: Hayat al-Muslimin Wasat al-Mujtama'at al-Ukhra* (Regarding the Jurisprudence of Muslim Minorities: The lives of Muslims in non-Muslim societies) (Cairo: Dar al-Shuruq, 2001).
62 Graf and Skovgaard-Petersen, "Introduction," 8.
63 W. J. Berridge, *Hasan al-Turabi, Islamist Politics and Democracy in Sudan* (Cambridge: Cambridge University Press, 2017), 299–306.
64 Graf and Skovgaard-Petersen, "Introduction," 12.
65 Qaradawi, *Fiqh al-Jihad*, 852.
66 Yusuf Qaradawi, *al-Tataruf al-'Ilmani fi Muwajahat al-Islam: Namuzhaj Turkiya wa Tunis* (Secular Extremism confronting Islam: the Models of Turkey and Tunisia) (Cairo: Dar al-Shuruq, 2001), 35.
67 Qaradawi, *Al-Tataruf al-'Ilmani fi Muwajahat al-Islam*, esp. 27–46.
68 Yusuf Qaradawi, *Shumul al-Islam* (The Comprehensive Nature of Islam), (Cairo: Maktabat Wahba, 2011), 55.
69 Qaradawi, *Shumul al-Islam*, 56.
70 Qaradawi, *Shumul al-Islam*, 57.
71 For the tensions and ambiguities in Abu Zahra's discourse on the Islamic state, see Sami E. Baroudi, "The Problematic Notion of the Islamic State in the Discourses of Contemporary Islamists: The Case of Sheikh Muhammad Abu Zahra (1898–1974)," *Middle Eastern Studies* 56, Issue 3 (2020).
72 Qaradawi, *Shumul al-Islam, Min Fiqh al-Dawla fi al-Islam*, 8–30.

73 Qaradawi, *Shumul al-Islam*, 51–52.
74 Qaradawi, *Min Fiqh al-Dawla fi al-Islam*, 114; *Khitabuna al-Islami for 'Asr al-'Awlama*, 55; *al-Khasa'es al-'Amma lil-Islam* (The General Characteristics of Islam) (Cairo: Maktabat Wahba, 1977), 101; *Al-Tataruf al-'Ilmani fi Muwajahat al-Islam*, 27; *Shumul al-Islam*, 101.
75 Shavit, *Scientific and Political Freedom in Islam*, 138.
76 Qaradawi, *Min Fiqh al-Dawla fi al-Islam*, esp. 112–28.
77 Qaradawi, *Ummatna Bayn Qarnayn*, 90–95.
78 Qaradawi, *Min Fiqh al-Dawla fi al-Islam*, esp. 260–73.
79 Qaradawi, *Shumul al-Islam*, 46.
80 Qaradawi, *Min Fiqh al-Dawla fi al-Islam*, 112.
81 Qaradawi, *Min Fiqh al-Dawla fi al-Islam*, 128.
82 Qaradawi, *Shumul al-Islam*, 67.
83 Qaradawi, *Shumul al-Islam*, 15.
84 Qaradawi, *Shumul al-Islam*, 9.
85 Qaradawi, *Shumul al-Islam*, 9.
86 In this work, Qaradawi refers to Shaltut as a "prominent international figure with many followers." Qaradawi, *al-Sheikh al-Ghazali kama 'Araftuh*, 32.
87 Qaradawi, *al-Sheikh al-Ghazali kama 'Araftuh*, esp. 13–32.
88 Both Qaradawi and al-Ghazali thought that al-Banna's stance on women's rights was unnecessarily restrictive. Accordingly, al-Ghazali's first supplementary principle (to al-Banna's twenty principles) addresses the rights of women to education and participation in the public affairs of the community on an equal footing with men, while observing Islamic ethics and etiquette. Qaradawi, *Al-Sheikh al-Ghazali kama 'Araftuh*, 34.
89 Qaradawi, *al-Sheikh al-Ghazali kama 'Araftuh*, 34–35; *Khitabuna al-Islami for 'Asr al-'Awlama*, 66.
90 Qaradawi, *Min Fiqh al-Dawla fi al-Islam* (From the Jurisprudence of the State in Islam), 4.
91 Mutaz al-Khatib, "Yusuf al-Qaradawi as an authoritative reference (Marja'iyya)" in Graf and Skovgaard-Petersen, *Global Mufti*, 85–108, 94.
92 In the academic literature, *wasati* is variously translated as middle path, centrist, mainstream, and moderate, while *wasatiya* is commonly translated as moderation, mainstream, and centrism. See, in particular, Mohammad Hashim Kamali, *The Middle Path of Moderation in Islam: The Quranic Principle of Wasatiyyah* (Oxford: Oxford University Press, 2015); and Sagi Polka, "Taqrib al-Madhahib – Qaradawi's Declaration of Principles Regarding Sunni–Shi'i Ecumenism," *Middle Eastern Studies* 49, no. 3 (2013): 414–29. Polka offers a more detailed treatment of Qaradawi's *wasatiyya* in *Shaykh Yusuf al-Qaradawi: Spiritual Mentor of Wasati Salafism* (Syracuse: Syracuse University Press, 2019).
93 Qaradawi, *Fiqh al-Wasatiyya al-Islamiyya*, 106–24; *Shumul al-Islam*, 87.

182 | *Contemporary Islamist Perspectives on International Relations*

94 Rachid al-Ghannouchi, *al-Wasatiyya al-Siyasiyya 'ind al-Imam Yusuf al-Qaradawi* (Politcal *Wasatiyya* in the view of Imam Yusuf Qaradawi) (Jeddah: Mu'assat Ru'a Thaqafiyya, 2009).
95 Qaradawi, *Ibn al-Qarya wa al-Kuttab*, Vol. 1, 14.
96 Qaradawi, *Fiqh al-Wasatiyya al-Islamiyya*, 37–39.
97 Qaradawi, *Fiqh al-Wasatiyya al-Islamiyya*, 15, 21, 33, 34, 36, 37, 40, 62, 83–85.
98 Qaradawi, *Fiqh al-Wasatiyya al-Islamiyya*, 40.
99 Qaradawi's discourse is replete with reference to the compatibility of reason and faith in Islam. See, inter alia, Qaradawi, *Al-Khasa'es al-'Amma lil-Islam* (The General Characteristics of Islam) (Cairo: Maktabat Wahba, 1977), 53–66.
100 Yusuf Qaradawi, *Kayf Nata'amal Ma' al-Qur'an al-'Azim* (Approaching the Magnificent Quran) (Cairo: Dar al-Shuruq, 1999), 100.
101 Qaradawi, *Fiqh al-Wasatiyya al-Islamiyya*.
102 Qaradawi, *al-Islam wa al-'Unf*, 20–24.
103 For references to this verse, see Qaradawi, *Fiqh al-Jihad*, 93, 107, 554, 556, 561, 625.
104 For references to the verse, see, inter alia, Qaradawi, *Khitabuna al-Islami for 'Asr al-'Awlama*, 51, 66, 126.
105 Qaradawi, *Khitabuna al-Islami for 'Asr al-'Awlama*, 66.
106 See, *inter alia*, Qaradawi, *Khitabuna al-Islami fi 'Asr al-'Awlama*, 32–35; *al-Islam wa al-'Unf*, 9.
107 See, inter alia, Qaradawi, Fiqh al-Jihad, 322–23, 469–72, 499.
108 For a critical analysis of Qaradawi's views on homosexuality, see Scott Kuhle and Stephen Hunt, "Masculinity, Homosexuality and the Defence of Islam: A Case Study of Yusuf al-Qaradawi's Media Fatwa," *Religion and Gender* 2, no. 2 (2012): 254–79.
109 Qaradawi, *Ummatna Bayn Qarnayn*, 233.
110 Baroudi, "The Islamic Realism of Sheikh Yusuf Qaradawi (1926) and Sayyid Muhammad Hussein Fadlallah," 103–06.
111 Yusuf Qaradawi, *Nahnu wa al-Gharb* (Us and the West), (2005), https://www.al-qaradawi.net/node/5041, accessed 12 April 2012.
112 Qaradawi, *Fiqh al-Jihad*, 259, 1219–20.
113 Qaradawi, *Nahnu wa al-Gharb*, 2–3.
114 Qaradawi, *Fiqh al-Jihad*, 955–78.
115 Yusuf Qaradawi, *Tarikhuna al-Muftara 'Alayh* (Our Slandered History) (Cairo, Dar al-Shuruq, 2005). Most Shia scholars reject this view of Islamic history. See, in particular, Ahmad Rasem al-Nafis, *Al-Qaradawi: Wakil Allah Am Wakil Bani Ummayya?* (Al-Qaradawi: The Deputy of God; or that of the Umayyads?? (Beirut: Dar al-Mizan, 2006).
116 Qaradawi, *Fiqh al-Jihad*, 1075, 1077.
117 Yusuf Qaradawi, *al-Sahwa al-Islamiyya Min al-Murahaqa ila al-Rushd* (Cairo: Dar al-Shuruq, 2002).

118 Yusuf Qaradawi, *al-Sahwa al-Islamiyya wa Humum al-Watan al-'Arabi wa al-Islami* (Beirut: Mu'asasat al-Risalah, 1993).
119 See, inter alia, Qaradawi, *al-Sahwa al-Islamiyya wa Humum al-Watan al-'Arabi wa al-Islami*, 79–88.
120 Qaradawi, *al-Sahwa al-Islamiyya wa Humum al-Watan al-'Arabi wa al-Islami*, 138–45.
121 See Yusuf Qaradawi, *al-Hulul al-Mustawrada wa kayfa janat 'ala Ummatna* (Imported Solutions and the injustice they did to our Umma) (Cairo: Maktabat Wahba, 1993) (written in 1971), esp. 4–7.
122 Qaradawi, *Ummatna Bayn Qarnayn*.
123 Qaradawi, *Al-Khasa'es al-'Amma lil-Islam*, 144–72.
124 Qaradawi, *al-Tataruf al-'Ilmani fi Muwajahat al-Islam*, 70; *Khitabuna al-Islam fi 'Asr al-'Awlama*, 109.
125 Ron Geaves, *Aspects of Islam* (Washington, D.C., Georgetown University Press, 2005), 36.
126 Qaradawi, *al-Khasa'es al-'Amma lil Islam*, 144–45.
127 Qaradawi, *Fiqh al-Jihad*, 442. This argument is reiterated several times in *Fiqh al-Jihad*. See 548.
128 Qaradawi, *Fiqh al-Jihad*, 442.
129 Kenneth N. Waltz, *Theory of international Politics* (Reading, MA: Addison-Wesley, 1979); John H. Mearsheimer, *The Tragedy of Great Power Politics* (New York and London: W. W. Norton & Company, 2001).
130 Qaradawi, *Fiqh al-Jihad*, 447.
131 Qaradawi, *Fiqh al-Jihad*, 447.
132 Qaradawi, *Khitabuna al-Islami fi 'Asr al-'Awlama*, 117.
133 Qaradawi, *Fiqh al-Jihad*, 81, 84, 435, 443.
134 Eric Peterson, "Christianity and Power Politics Themes and Issues," in *Christianity and Power Politics Today: Christian Realism and Contemporary Political Dilemmas*, ed. Eric Peterson (New York: Palgrave Macmillan, 2008), 7.
135 For righteous realism, see Anatol Lieven and John Hulsman, *Ethical Realism: A Vision for America's Role in the World* (New York: Pantheon Books, 2006), Richard Crouter, *Reinhold Niebuhr: On Politics, Religion and Christian Faith* (Oxford and New York: Oxford University Press, 2010); and Joel Rosenthal, *Righteous Realists: Political Realism, Responsible Power, and American Culture in the Nuclear Age* (Baton Rouge and London: Louisiana State University Press, 1991).
136 Zaman, *Modern Islamic Thought in a Radical Age*, 304.
137 Zaman, *Modern Islamic Thought in a Radical Age*, 261.
138 Works on the Muslim Brotherhood abound. See, in particular, Carrie Rosefsky Wickham, *The Muslim Brotherhood: Evolution of an Islamist Movement* (Princeton and Oxford: Princeton University Press, 2013) and Fawaz Gerges, *Making the Arab World: Nasser, Qutb and the Clash that Shaped the Middle East* (Princeton and Oxford: Princeton University Press, 2018).

139 Qaradawi, *Ibn al-Qarya wa al-Kuttab*, Vol. 1, 149, 229–35.
140 Qaradawi, *Shumul al-Islam*, 5; *Ibn al-Qarya wa al-Kuttab*, 231–32.
141 Qaradawi, *Shumul al-Islam*, 81–82.
142 Qaradawi, *Ibn al-Qarya wa al-Kuttab*, 233–35.
143 Qaradawi, *Shumul al-Islam*, esp. 97.
144 *Waa'ido* is the first word in the often Quranic verse 8:60, "Prepare against them whatever force and war cavalry you can gather to frighten therewith the enemy of God and your enemy."
145 Qaradawi, *Shumul al-Islam*, 96.
146 Qaradawi, *Khitabuna al-Islami fi 'Asr al-'Awlama*, 167.
147 Ralph H. Salmi, Cesar Abdul Majid, and George K. Tanham, *Islam and Conflict Resolution: Theories and Practices* (Lanham, Maryland: University Press of America, 1998), 105.
148 Qaradawi, *Khitabuna al-Islami fi 'Asr al-Awlama*, 83.
149 Qaradawi, *Khitabuna al-Islami fi 'Asr al-'Awlama*, 86–94.
150 The discourse of Qaradawi is full of references to, and extrapolations from, this verse. See *Khitabuna al-Islami fi 'Asr al-'Awlama*, 17; *Fiqh al-Jihad*, 58, 80, 81, 84; *al-Islam wa al-'Unf*, 10.
151 Qaradawi, *Fiqh al-Jihad*, 171–86.
152 Qaradawi, *Khitabuna al-Islam fi 'Asr al-'Awlama*, 110.
153 Qaradawi, *Fiqh al-Jihad*, 225.
154 Qaradawi, *al-Sahwa al-Islamiyya wa Humum al-Watan al-'Arabi wa al-Islami*, 96–97.
155 Qaradawi, *Min Fiqh al-Dawla fi al-Islam*, 115.
156 Qaradawi, *al-Sahwa al-Islamiyya min al-Murahaqa ila al-Rushd*, 301; *Min Fiqh al-Dawla fi al-Islam*, 60–63.
157 Qaradawi, *Fiqh al-jihad*, 55.
158 Qaradawi, *Fiqh al-Jihad*, 56.
159 Qaradawi, *Fiqh al-Jihad*, 57.
160 Qaradawi, *Fiqh al-Jihad*, 60.
161 Qaradawi, *Fiqh al-Jihad*, 60; *al-Islam wa al-'Unf*, 16; *al-Sahwa al-Islamiyya min al-Murahaqa ila al-Rushd*, 281.
162 Qaradawi, *Khitabuna al-Islami fi 'Asr al-'Awlama*, 174.
163 See Qaradawi, *Khitabuna al-Islami fi 'Asr al-'Awlama*, 164.
164 Mohammad Fadlallah, *al-Mudanas wa al-Muqadas: Amerka wa Rayat al-Irhab al-Duwali* (The Unsacred and the Sacred: America and the Banner of International Terrorism) (Beirut: Riad el-Rayyes Books, 2003), 19–21.
165 Muhammad Shams al-Din, *Fiqh al-'Unf al-Muslah fi al-Islam* (Jurisprudence of Armed Violence in Islam), (Beirut: al-Mo'asasa al-Dawliya Lil Derasat wa al-Nashr, 1998), 59.
166 Qaradawi, *Fiqh al-Jihad*, 241.
167 Qaradawi, *Fiqh al-jihad*, 243–46.

168 Qaradawi, *Fiqh al-Jihad*, 247, 443.
169 Qaradawi, *Fiqh al-Jihad*.
170 Qaradawi, *Fiqh al-Jihad*, esp. 442–67.
171 For a succinct statement of this critique, see Qaradawi, *al-Sahwa al-Islamiya min al-Murahaqa ila al-Rushd*, 302–04.
172 For Qaradawi's discussion of the views of each camp, see *Fiqh al-jihad*, 255–427.
173 For a clear treatment of abrogation theory with a focus on the fighting verses in the Quran, see Reuven Firestone, *Jihad: The Origins of Holy War in Islam* (New York and Oxford: Oxford University Press, 1999), 45, 48–51, 64, 68.
174 Qaradawi, *Fiqh al-Jihad*, 278–303.
175 Qaradawi, *Fiqh al-Jihad*, 310–14.
176 Qaradawi, *al-Sahwa al-Islamiyya min al-Murahaqa ila al-Rushd*, 308.
177 Qaradawi, *Fiqh al-Jihad*, 303–33.
178 Qaradawi, Fiqh al-Jihad, esp. 277–346.
179 Qaradawi, *Fiqh al-Jihad*, 396–403.
180 Firestone, *Jihad*, 48–51.
181 Qaradawi, *Fiqh al-Jihad*, 421–24. In his memoirs, Qaradawi provides a more detailed critique of the ideas of Sayyid Qutb. Qaradawi, *Ibn al-Qarya wa al-Kuttab*, Vol. 3, 50–72.
182 Qaradawi, *Fiqh al-Jihad*, 274.
183 Qaradawi, *Fiqh al-Jihad*, 827.
184 For references to this verse, see Qaradawi, *Fiqh al-Jihad*, 262, 268, 319, 323, 819, 821; *Khitabuna al-Islami fi 'Asr al-'Awlama*, 175.
185 In the same vein, Fadlallah provides a detailed treatment of the battle of Uhud in his Friday Sermon of May 19, 1989, reprinted in Mohammad Fadlallah, *Salat al-Jum 'a, al-Kalima wa al-Mawqif: Tawthiq li-Khutub al-Jum'a 1989* (Friday Prayer, Discourse and Stance: Documentation of Friday Sermons 1989), 179–88.
186 Qaradawi, *Ibn al-Qarya wa al-Kuttab*,90–106, 239–43.
187 Qaradawi, *Fiqh al-Jihad*, 768–69.
188 Qaradawi, *Fiqh al-Jihad*, 748–52; *al-Umma al-Islamiyya Haqiqa la Wahm*, esp. 9, 16, 30; *Fiqh al-Dawla fi al-Islam*, 65–66.
189 Qaradawi, *Fiqh al-Jihad*, 753–56.
190 Qaradawi, *Fiqh al-Jihad*, 1186, 1192–93. See also Esposito, *The Future of Islam*, 102–04.
191 Qaradawi, *Fiqh al-Jihad*, 1192–93.
192 Qaradawi, *Fiqh al-Jihad*, 1192, 1325–26.
193 Qaradawi, *Min Fiqh al-Dawla fi al-Islam*, 262. Fadlallah makes the same argument. Mohammad Fadlallah, *al-Haraka al-Islamiyya Ma Laha wa Ma 'Alayha* (The Islamic [Activist] Movement: What Stands for It, and What Stands Against It) (Beirut: Dar al-Malak, 2004), 119.
194 Qaradawi, *Fiqh al-Jihad*, 1201–08.
195 Qaradawi, *Fiqh al-Jihad*.

196 Yusuf Qaradawi, *Fatawa min Ajl Filastin* (Fatwas for the Sake of Palestine) (Cairo: Maktabat Wahba, 2003), esp. 21; and *al-Quds Qadiyat kul Muslim*, esp. 19–20, 145–58.
197 Qaradawi, Fiqh al-Jihad, 1192–99.
198 Qaradawi, *Fiqh al-Jihad*, 1198–99.
199 Qaradawi, *Fiqh al-Jihad*, 955.
200 Qaradawi, *Fiqh al-Jihad*, 955–79.
201 Qaradawi, *Fiqh al-Jihad*, 962–66.
202 Qaradawi, *Fiqh al-Jihad*, 968–78.
203 Qaradawi, *Fiqh al-Jihad*, 978–79.
204 Qaradawi, *Fiqh al-Jihad*, 828.
205 Qaradawi, *Fiqh al-Jihad*, 831.
206 Qaradawi, *Fiqh al-Jihad*, 1038–44.
207 Qaradawi, *Fiqh al-Jihad*, 851, 1046–47.
208 Qaradawi, *Fiqh al-Jihad*, 819.
209 Qaradawi, *Fiqh al-Jihad*, 819–26.
210 Qaradawi, *Fiqh al-Jihad*, 824.
211 Qaradawi, *Fiqh al-Jihad*, 815–16.
212 Qaradawi, *Fiqh al-Jihad*, 1219.
213 Qaradawi, *Fiqh al-Jihad*, 858–60.
214 Qaradawi, *Fiqh al-Jihad*, 887.
215 Qaradawi, *Fiqh al-Jihad*, 883–88.
216 Qaradawi, *Fiqh al-Jihad*, 887–88.
217 Yusuf Qaradawi, *al-Umma al-Islamiyya Haqiqa la Wahm* (Cairo: Maktabat Wahba, 1994).
218 Qaradawi, *Fiqh al-Jihad*, 1067; *al-Umma al-Islamiyya Haqiqa la Wahm*, 8, 9, 25, 27.
219 Qaradawi, *Min Fiqh al-Dawla fi al-Islam*, 273.
220 Qaradawi, *al-Umma al-Islamiyya Haqiqa la Wahm*, 20.
221 Qaradawi, *al-Umma al-Islamiyya Haqiqa la Wahm*, 17.
222 Qaradawi, *Fiqh al-Jihad*, 1088–89.
223 Qaradawi, *Fiqh al-Jihad*, 1079.
224 Qaradawi, *Fiqh al-Jihad*, 1089.
225 Qaradawi, *Ibn al-Qarya wa al-Kuttab*, Vol. 3, 36.
226 Qaradawi, *al-Umma al-Islamiyya Haqiqa la Wahm*, esp. 7, 11, 33.
227 See Qaradawi, *al-Umma al-Islamiyya Haqiqa la Wahm*, esp. 9, 16, 30.
228 Qaradawi, *Min Fiqh al-Dawla fi al-Islam*, 82–88.
229 Qaraadwi, *al-Umma al-Islamiyya Haqiqa la Wahm*, 29–30.
230 See, inter alia, Qaradawi, *al-Sahwa al-Islamiyya wa Humum al-Watan al-'Arabi wa al-Islami*, 153–57.
231 Qaradawi. *Fiqh al-Jihad*, 1082–83.
232 Qaradawi, *Fiqh al-Jihad*, 1082–83; *al-Umma al-Islamiyya Haqiqa la Wahm*, 30.

233 Qaradawi, *Fiqh al-Jihad*, 1082–83.
234 Qaradawi, *al-Umma al-Islamiyya Haqiqa la Wahm*, 37.
235 Qaradawi, *Fiqh al-Jihad*, 1092.
236 Qaradawi, *Fatawa min Ajl Filastin*, 13.
237 Qaradawi, *al-Quds Qadiyat kul Muslim* (Cairo: Maktabat Wahba, 2000).
238 For this depiction of Qaradawi as a marja'iyya within the Islamic world, al-Khateeb, "Yusuf al-Qaradawi as an authoritative reference (Marja'iyya)" in Graf and Skovgaard-Petersen, *Global Mufti*, 85–108.

6

The Third Generation: Sheikh Wahbah al-Zuhaili

Introduction

The second of three chapters on the scholar sheikhs of the third generation, this chapter focuses on the discourse of Sheikh Wahbah al-Zuhaili. Zuhaili did not achieve the same regional and international renown as his friend Qaradawi, or even the Lebanese Shiite cleric Sayyid Fadlallah (Chapter 7), and his writings on international relations, despite their major insights into how contemporary Islamists conceptualize the matter, have also received scant attention from academics in the Arab world and beyond. Because the views that Zuhaili advances are key to this book's central argument regarding the presence of a strong mainstream Islamist perspective on international relations, one quite distinct from the radical perspective, his views receive detailed treatment in this chapter, using the same axis points adopted in analyzing the discourses of the previous scholar sheikhs.

It is worth noting at the outset that the discourse of Zuhaili is, by and large, a continuation of that of his two teachers at al-Azhar and Cairo University, Sheikh Shaltut and Sheikh Abu Zahra (Chapter 3). It also shares a great deal with the discourse of Qaradawi, despite Zuhaili's more legalist-idealist tone. Zuhaili expands in detail on the arguments of the scholar sheikhs of the second generation, while consciously using a comparative approach to the analysis of international relations that draws on both the *sharia* and public international law.

Lebanese academic and moderate Islamist Radwan El-Sayyed emphasizes Zuhaili's role within the moderate-reformist strand of political Islam, writing, "Zuhaili ... is one of the jurisprudents of the reformist Islamic current (*al-taqlid al-Islami al-islahi*) that established itself at al-Azhar during the era of Sheikh Mohammad Mustafa al-Maraghi and Sheikh Mustafa 'Abd al-Raziq, pupils of Mohammad 'Abduh who preserved his legacy at al-Azhar."[1] Like Qaradawi, Zuhaili embraced the *wasati* (moderate or middle path) approach to Islam. In an important academic work on the *wasati* approach, Mohammad Hashim Kamali highlights the contributions of both Qaradawi and Zuhaili to its development and mainstreaming. Kamali adopts Zuhaili's definition of *wasatiya*, namely that "In the common parlance of the people of our time, wasatiyyah means moderation and balance (*i'tidal*) in belief, morality and character, in the manner of treating others and in the applied systems of socio-political order and governance."[2]

Yet, what sets Zuhaili apart from the other scholar sheikhs examined in this work is his detailed knowledge of Western-inspired public international law, and his insistence that the *sharia* and public international law are compatible. Zuhaili, thus, writes that the "Islamic system [the *sharia*] and international humanitarian law are in agreement in terms of their means and their principal objectives." Both legal systems aim to ensure that "every human being is granted a humane and a dignified treatment in times of peace and in times of war," Zuhaili argues.[3] Following a short biographical section, this chapter examines Zuhaili's views on the principles underlying international relations, war and fighting in Islam, and the road to Islamic unity.

Biographical Sketch

A few years younger than Qaradawi, Wahbah Mustafa al-Zuhaili (also written al-Zuhayli) was born in 1932 in the town of Dayr Atiyah, not far from Damascus. *Dayr* is the Arabic word for monastery, which indicates that the town has an established Christian presence. At the time of Zuhaili's birth, the town had, and still has, a mixed Christian–Muslim population who, at least until the eruption of the Syrian war, lived together in peace.[4] While not much weight need be assigned to this geographic fact, it is worth emphasizing that Zuhaili always shows respect, and not just tolerance, toward Christianity and Christians. He is one of few contemporary Islamists to acknowledge openly that the *jizya* tax has lost its meaning in the contemporary era since Christians now serve in the armies of majority Muslim states and pay their taxes just as Muslims do.[5]

As with most of the scholar sheikhs examined in this work, Zuhaili came from a conservative background; his father was a merchant and a farmer of some means, while his illiterate mother is simply referred to as a woman who lived her entire life according to the *sharia*.[6] In a televised interview, Zuhaili reminisced that, according to a family story, the family's name derived from the name of the city of "Zahlé" in the Beqa valley in Lebanon because his great grandfather emigrated from there decades earlier.[7] Zuhaili received his primary schooling in Dayr Atiyah and his secondary schooling in Damascus, graduating at the top of his class in 1952. He then traveled to Cairo, the center of religious learning in the Arab world, for his university studies, where he attended al-Azhar and obtained his 'alimiyya degree in 1956; 'Ain Shams University, earning a license in jurisprudence in 1957; and the Faculty of law at Cairo University, from which he earned his masters' degree in 1959 and his doctoral degree in jurisprudence in 1963.

In total, Zuhaili spent ten years in Cairo from 1953 until 1963, pursuing advanced studies in jurisprudence, with an emphasis on Islamic jurisprudence. Zuhaili was fond of his Cairo years, noting that he devoted himself entirely to his studies, never missing a lecture and always dealing with the utmost respect with his teachers and taking their advice to heart.[8] Zuhaili does not seem to have been affected by the ups and downs in Egyptian-Syrian relations of the time, mainly the formation of the United Arab Republic (UAR) between Egypt and Syria in 1958 and the subsequent Syrian cessation in 1961. Unlike the young Qaradawi who fell under the sway of the thought of the Muslim Brotherhood, there is no evidence that Zuhaili was attracted to the movement, or to any other political movement.

Zuhaili's choice of universities is rather revealing, reflecting his interest in learning about the Western, mainly Roman, legal system in addition to mastering Islamic *sharia* law. Thus, at al-Azhar, he studied the four principal schools of Sunni Islamic jurisprudence with some of the most prominent sheikhs of the time, including two future sheikhs of al-Azhar, Sheikh 'Abd al-Rahman Taj (1986–1975), who was Sheikh al-Azhar between 1954 and 1958, and Sheikh Shaltut. But at the more secular 'Ain Shams and Cairo Universities, he also learned about the Western legal tradition, especially public international law, from famous Egyptian legal scholars, such as Hamed Sultan and Muhammad Hafedh Ghanem, on whose works he leaned in his doctoral dissertation. It is worth noting that at Cairo University, Zuhaili also studied with Sheikh Abu Zahra, who was to influence his outlook on war, and more generally on international relations. Several references will be made in this chapter to the continuity of thought between Abu Zahra and Zuhaili.

Zuhaili's belief in the merits of the comparative analysis of legal systems culminated in his embrace of a comparative approach to the analysis of war in his doctoral dissertation, defended in February 1963 before a jury that included specialists in both public international law and *sharia* law. In the dissertation's introduction, Zuhaili enumerated the merits of a comparative approach to the study of the multiple dimensions of war that brought together the insights of the Islamic *sharia* and those of the Western-inspired public international law. The lengthy dissertation, about 800 pages, was published in early 1963 under the revealing title, *Effects of War: A Comparative Jurisprudential Study*.[9] It quickly won praise from many quarters in the Arab and Muslim worlds, becoming Zuhaili's most influential and most recognized political work. While Zuhaili continued to publish sporadically on international relations and more generally on political and social issues until the 21st century, none of his subsequent political works had the same depth and rigor as the *Effects of War*. Ample references will be made in this chapter to this seminal work on international relations that draws on both the Islamic *sharia* and public international law.

It is worth emphasizing at this point that while scores of Islamic scholars before Zuhaili compared the positions of the four principal schools of Islamic jurisprudence—with a few extending the comparison to include the Shiite Ja'fari *mazhhab*—on various concrete issues, including that of war, Zuhaili pushed the comparison a step further. He consciously sought to compare the view of war in the Islamic *sharia* and in public international law, with the aim of demonstrating that there are no major incompatible differences between these two legal traditions. Zuhaili's core thesis, advanced in all of his international relations works, is that the *sharia* and public international law are highly compatible. Although Zuhaili does not make this point specifically, his thesis on the compatibility of the *sharia* and public international law is part of the broader mainstream Islamist perspective that maintains that Islam is compatible with modernity and that Muslims can engage with the modern world and be part of it without compromising their religion.

Upon graduation, Zuhaili returned to his native Syria to pursue a classic career of teaching and scholarship at Damascus University. He rose through the academic ranks, achieving full professorship in 1975. Between 1967 and 1969, he served as interim head of the Department of "Islamic Jurisprudence and its Madhhabs" at Damascus University. Zuhaili also regularly delivered the Friday sermon at *al-'Uthman* Mosque in Damascus and at *al-Iman* Mosque in Dayr

Atiyah during the summer months. He also made frequent radio and television appearances in Syria and the Gulf, delivering a full commentary on the Quran over the span of several years on Syrian radio.

In his long life and equally long academic career, retiring from Damascus University in 1997 but contracted to continue teaching for an additional five years, Zuhaili was the embodiment of the quietist *'alim*, detesting political agitation and generally refraining from any direct criticisms of the powers that be. Zuhaili summed up his approach to public discourse in a succinct statement: "I always said what I wanted to say, but I said it in a wise way."[10] Radwan El-Sayyed notes that Zuhaili "observed strict neutrality (*hiyadan sariman*) when it came to daily politics, despite his academic writings that dealt with public affairs from an Islamic standpoint."[11]

Zuhaili was equally at home in the left leaning, authoritarian, and relatively secular Syria and Libya, and in Saudi Arabia and the conservative Arab sheikdoms, where he spent considerable time in the 1980s and 1990s as a visiting faculty member and guest speaker. Zuhaili also traveled widely throughout the Arab and Muslim worlds, but never spent considerable time in a non-Muslim country. Zuhaili's growing professional ties to the Gulf monarchies were largely prompted by financial and practical considerations as universities in the Gulf, such as Kuwait University and *al-'Ayn* University in the United Arab Emirates, where he was a visiting faculty member between 1984 and 1989, paid significantly higher salaries than Damascus University. There were also monetary compensations for serving on state-sponsored boards and committees. Zuhaili was, moreover, concerned about losing his job at Damascus University, as there was official talk in the 1980s about closing down the Department of Islamic Jurisprudence of which he was a member, following the clashes with the Muslim Brotherhood earlier in the decade.[12] These Gulf ties also reflected Zuhaili's social conservatism, never a fan of socialism and preferring pan-Islamism over pan-Arabism, and relatively close to Wahhabism on matters of doctrine.[13]

Zuhaili's relationship with the Syrian authorities was correct but far from cordial. Zuhaili consciously avoided treading in the path of his colleague and friend Sheikh Mohammad Said Ramadan al-Bouti (1929–2013) who was very close to the Assad regime and defended it even at the height of the Syrian revolution. Despite his general quietism, Zuhaili maintained his intellectual and indeed political independence and did not toe the official regime line. In one sermon, Zuhaili, for example, denounced all political parties as having no basis in Islam. The sermon was not well received by the authorities, given the role of the Baath party in Syrian politics, and Zuhaili felt it would be best if he took off to Egypt for some time.[14]

Zuhaili also clashed with a small Lebanese Sunni Islamist movement, *al-Ahbash*, that was closely allied with the Assad regime. On a trip to Indonesia, Zuhaili made a side remark that the rather mystical and anti-Wahhabi *al-Ahbash* was a misguided group that was also spreading misguidance (*fi'a dalla wa-mudilla*).[15] *Al-Ahbash* retaliated by launching a vicious personal attack on Zuhaili, accusing him of being a puppet of the Saudi royal family and of receiving ten-thousand US Dollars of Saudi money in exchange for attacking them and for exalting the virtues of the founder of Wahhabism, Sheikh Muhammad Ibn 'Abd al-Wahab. They even twisted his last name to "Zubaili" (from *zebala*; the Arabic word for garbage). Given their very close ties to the Syrian authorities, it is highly unlikely that the *Ahbash* would have so vehemently attacked a prominent Syrian religious and pubic figure without having received a green light from Damascus.[16]

More seriously, Zuhaili rose to the defense of his friend Sheikh Yusuf Qaradawi when Iran's representative to the January 2007 "Doha Conference for Dialogue of Islamic Schools of Thought," Ayatollah Mohammad-Ali Taskhiri, criticized Qaradawi's remarks at the Conference's opening session.[17] Known for his harsh polemics, Qaradawi had accused Tehran of spreading Shiism in predominantly Sunni countries and regions. Zuhaili staunchly defended Qaradawi, referring to him as "our teacher, our sheikh, and our imam."[18] Moreover, he reiterated Qaradawi's accusation that Iran was resorting to various methods to spread its Shiite *mazhhab* in predominantly Sunni countries, including his native Syria. He then mentioned an incident in the Syrian village of Tal Abiad between the local Sunni population and "recent converts to Shiism who (according to Zuhaili) called on the Secretary General of Hezbollah to intervene on their behalf."[19] While Zuhaili's criticisms were directed at a specific aspect of Iranian policy, namely its alleged attempts to spread Shiism amongst Sunnis, they can be also read as a gentle rebuke of the Syrian government for not doing enough to stop such attempts, despite their destabilizing effects on Sunni-Shia relations.

Zuhaili's relations with the Assad regime soured following the eruption of the Syrian revolt in March 2011. In his last published work, *al-Qanun al-Duwali al-Insani*, Zuhaili had the chance to address, even if briefly, the Arab uprisings that were in full swing in the spring of 2011, when he was completing the work. Zuhaili unequivocally took the side of the protesting Arab public from Tunisia to Egypt, Libya, and his native Syria. He voiced strong criticisms of Arab regimes for their violent suppression of the peaceful protesters and, above all, for their neglect, for decades, of the political and socioeconomic demands of their people. While the Syrian uprising was only named in a footnote, the brief discussion about the causes of the uprisings and the inappropriateness of the violent responses to them, definitely applied to Syria.[20]

Despite these critical remarks, Zuhaili's book was published in 2012 by a Damascene press house, but his criticisms of the Assad regime were dispassionately stated and confined to a couple of pages in his latest book and to remarks made in private to close friends.[21] Refusing to take sides in the escalating Syrian conflict, Zuhaili continued to live quietly in regime-controlled Damascus, making very few public statements.[22] The Syrian conflict took a heavy toll on Zuhaili, who was in his eighties when the conflict erupted. A close friend, Radwan El-Sayyed, who used to visit him in Damascus before and after the eruption of the Syrian conflict, wrote that Zuhaili was heartbroken by the turn of events, and frequently said that he wished he died before witnessing all the carnage. In an editorial eulogizing the scholar sheikh, El-Sayyed wrote that Zuhaili, while opposed to the repression of the Assad regime and sympathetic to the demands for regime change, was also stunned by Qaradawi's open call for the violent overthrow of the Assad regime, on the ground of its apostasy, just a few years after Qaradawi had showered praise on Bashar al-Assad.[23] His health failing, Zuhaili died of natural causes in early August 2015.

The Underpinning Principles of International Relations

As previously noted, Zuhaili's discourse on international relations is a continuation of that of Shaltut and Abu Zahra. Zuhaili even adopts much of the terminology of Shaltut and Abu Zahra, using, for example, the term "armed peace" (*al-salam al-musalah*) that was probably coined by Shaltut, in exactly the same way Shaltut had understood and used it. All three scholar sheikhs emphasize the centrality of justice, virtue, reciprocity, and honoring one's covenants in international relations, and they reject the binary division of the world into *dar al-silm* and *dar al-harb*. While Zuhaili's outlook on international relations is closer to the liberal-internationalist school of international relations than that of the realist Qaradawi, the two scholar sheikhs have the same outlook on the defensive purposes of jihad and definitely view peace as the general principle (*al-asl*) in relations between Muslims and non-Muslims.

Relations among Muslim Societies

It must be noted at the outset, that Zuhaili, in line with all the other scholar sheikhs examined in this work, sharply distinguishes between relations among Muslim societies on the one hand, and relations between Muslim and non-Muslim societies on the other. Only the latter type of relations falls within the purview of international relations, while the former constitutes matters that are internal to the one Muslim *umma*. Based on four Quranic verses and one prophetic hadith[24], Zuhaili writes, "There is supposed to be permanent peace amongst Muslims... but if fighting erupts amongst them it is then an internal matter to the *umma*; and the *umma*, represented by its government, is to resolve the conflict through peaceful means... but if peaceful means fail force ought to be used against the aggressing group."[25]

The idealist, sometimes utopian, streak that characterizes Zuhaili's international relations discourse manifests itself mostly in his vision of almost entirely peaceful relations among Muslim societies. Zuhaili even claims that according to these Quranic verses, wars among Muslims would be very rare occurrences, since their recurrence "would lead to the political demise [of the *umma*] and would set the stage for the domination of foreigners (*tasalut al-ajaneb*) over the land of Islam."[26] Unwittingly, Zuhaili faces a contradiction here, for he is aware that relations among Muslims have not been as harmonious, or "brotherly," as the Quran envisioned, which may (just may) imply that the Quran did not accurately foresee the future of the *umma* whose creation it established.

Relations between Muslim and Non-Muslim Societies

Similarly to Abu Zahra and Shaltut, Zuhaili's starting position is that peace is the basic principle (*al-asl*) in relations between Muslims and non-Muslims, while war is the exception. Zuhaili, however, develops this view to a far greater extent than his predecessors do, firmly anchoring it in Quranic verses and *hadiths*. Zuhaili also maintains that this view represents an important point of intersection between the *sharia* and public international law.[27] In one of several instances of this assertion, Zuhaili writes, "In reality, the basic principle in the relations between Muslims and non-Muslims is peace; war is forced on humanity and on Muslims as a means to ward off evil and aggression and to protect the right to peacefully call for Islam." Zuhaili goes on to note, "Islam always inclines towards peace and not war." This predisposition toward peace is "in accordance with the view of the jurists of international law who maintain that the natural state (*al-hala al-tabi'iya*) [in international relations] is peace, while war is a temporary and transient state whatever its reason is," Zuhaili argues.[28]

In *Athar al-Harb*, Zuhaili identifies nine related Islamic principles that govern human relations in general, and international relations in particular.[29] These principles are briefly discussed below in the order Zuhaili presents them.

The first principle is to respect and honor all humans, and to deal with them as equals, irrespective of differences of gender, ethnicity, nationality, or religion. For Zuhaili, humanity is one, despite its division into distinct tribes and nations, as in Quranic verse 49:12, "O Mankind, we created you male and female, and made you into nations and tribes that you may come to know one another." The divine intent behind the division of humanity is for people to get to know each other (*al-taʿaruf al-Insani*) and to collaborate with each other (*al-taʿawun al-Insani*) for the joint exploitation of the earth for mutual benefit.[30] In this regard, Zuhaili places major emphasis on human dignity (*al-karama al-insaniya*), which ought to be respected at all times. "Anything that represents an affront to the dignity of the human being—irrespectively of religion, sect, or ethnic origin—is prohibited" in Islam, he argues.[31]

Principles two to four emphasize that relations with other nations ought to be based on compassion and benevolence (principle two), justice (principle three), and virtue and morals (principle four).[32] The fifth principle is to honor all covenants and agreements that Muslims voluntarily enter into with other nations. Zuhaili thus writes, "The organization of relations between Muslims and non-Muslims is based primarily on signed treaties and charters (*mawatheeq*) that provide the bases for settling any dispute."[33]

The sixth principle emphasizes reciprocal treatment in dealing with others (*al-muʿamala bil-mithl*), as long as reciprocity does not involve engaging in unethical acts, such as killing prisoners or mutilating the bodies of fallen enemy combatants, even when the enemy engages in such practices. Zuhaili's understanding of reciprocity is very much in line with the stipulations of public international law; for him, reciprocity entails mutual respect for the sovereignty and independence of each state, equal diplomatic representation and diplomatic immunity, relatively unimpeded international trade, and full protection of the persons and properties of citizens of the other state.[34]

The seventh principle regulates fighting. It stipulates that wars should be fought without engaging in excesses and without causing unnecessary destruction (*la takhreeb wala tadmeer li-ghayr daroura*); wars should end when the enemy ceases its aggression; and once a war is over, every effort should be made to eradicate its adverse consequences and to return the parties to the original condition (*al-hala al-asliya*) of peace. As will be discussed in the section on war and fighting, the regulation of fighting is a preoccupation of Zuhaili, on which he writes extensively.

The eighth principle concerns the manner of calling to Islam (*al-daʿwa ila al-Islam*), which should be pursued exclusively through persuasion and logical proof (*al-burhan*) and without any coercion, while respecting the right of the individual to freely choose what to believe in. While Zuhaili, in line with the other scholar sheikhs examined here, firmly anchors this position in the Quran and the Sunna, he also frames it within the "modern" lexicon of human rights, emphasizing the right of every individual to "freedom, justice, equality, learning about other civilizations and advancement."[35] As Chapter 7 will demonstrate, the Lebanese Shia Scholar Sheikh Sayyid Muhammad Hussein Fadlallah subscribes to the same view. Finally, the ninth, and arguably most important, principle returns us to the mainstream Islamists' pivotal notion that peace is the basic principle in relations with non-Muslims, while war is a means to "repel aggression, aid the oppressed, and protect freedom of belief."[36]

Throughout his discourse, Zuhaili maintains that Muslims prefer peace to war since Islam is a religion of peace. Relative to the centrality of peace, Zuhaili writes, "peace is the path to preserve human life and human dignity and to enable humans to live a free and a decent life." He then adds, "This is Islam's clear path, and the path for humanity's advancement and the preservation of civilizations." Thus, for Zuhaili, "What prompts fighting (*al-baʻith ʻala al-qital*), or jihad in Islam, is repelling aggression."[37] In *Athar al-Harb*, and elsewhere, Zuhaili spells out the legitimate reasons for fighting. "There is no resort to jihad, or war, except when necessary to repel aggression, support the oppressed whose freedoms are denied and protect those who peacefully call for Islam," he maintains.[38]

Zuhaili is unequivocal that disbelief in Islam, or mere difference in religion, does not constitute valid grounds for fighting, while aggression, broadly construed, does.[39] Of the six scholar sheikhs examined in this work, Zuhaili provides the most detailed and internally consistent account of the relationship between peace and war. In this account, peace is the original condition, or basic principle, in relations between individuals, groups, and states (this is in line with a Lockean state of nature), until this peace is broken by specific acts of aggression that cannot be tolerated, such as the persecution of the early Muslims by Quraysh. War then becomes a necessity to repel aggression, as in several Quranic verses, including, 2:251, "Had God not restrained mankind, some by means of others, the earth would have become chaotic," and 22:40: "Had God not caused people to restrain one another, destruction would have fallen upon monasteries, churches, oratories and other places of prayer."

But every war must come to end when the conditions that precipitated it are removed, namely when aggression has been repelled, oppression has been lifted and freedom of belief has been ensured.[40] In Zuhaili's normative-legalist view, war is always a means to an end, while peace is an end in itself. As a means to an end, war requires justification (in terms of locating its causes within the *sharia* and/or public international law); but as an end in itself, peace does not require justification. When war ends, the hitherto warring factions immediately revert to the original condition of peace and must work together to eliminate the adverse consequences of the prior war and to strive to maintain peace. In brief, reflecting the influence of moderate-reformist scholar-sheikhs (particularly, Shaltut, Abu Zahra, and even 'Abduh), as well as the influence of public international law, Zuhaili's perspective on war is closer to the liberal-internationalist one than it is to the realist perspective.

In the appendix of *Athar al-Harb*, Zuhaili expands on the nine principles discussed above to identify 54 articles, which govern international relations in times of peace and times of war, noting that these articles constitute a "law for peace and war in Islam."[41] These articles (*mawaad*) can be divided to two categories: 1) general principles that govern the conduct of international relations (these are largely more precise statements of the nine principles), and 2) more specific rules that govern specific cases in international relations (e.g., diplomatic representation and treatment or prisoners of war). Articles 1–3 articulate the general principles, while the subsequent articles address specific situations. Despite the fact that they overlap with the nine principles discussed above, the following section briefly discusses articles 1–3, and then throws light on some of the most important remaining 51 articles.

The first article sums up Zuhaili's vision of international relations, stipulating that, "The basic principle (*al-asl al-'am*) in the relations between Muslims and non-Muslims is peace and not war. The world is one abode, in which war is a necessity. War entails the emergence of a zone of peace and a zone of war, which are different in certain juridical rules."[42] This article has three parts, and we have already addressed the first part, namely that peace is the basic principle or norm in the relations between Muslims and non-Muslims. The equally important second part centers on the notion that the world has become one abode, which contradicts the classic Islamic distinction between the abode of peace (*dar al-silm*) and the abode of war (*dar al-harb*).

Unfortunately, Zuhaili is not entirely consistent on this point, because elsewhere, he also adopts the view that the world is divided into three abodes, the abode of peace, the abode of war and the abode of the covenant, also the view of Abu Zahra as discussed in Chapter 3. Adding to the confusion, Zuhaili attributes both views to the same renowned medieval jurist al-Shafi'i.[43] Zuhaili, however, suggests a path to reconcile these two apparently contradictory views of the world, by noting that war is the cause of the division of the world into more than one abode. This means that the basic principle (*al-asl*) is the unity of the world as one abode, while its division into several abodes is a consequence of war.[44]

While fraught with some ambiguities, the notion that the world has become one abode, due to globalization, i.e., the growing economic, political, and cultural ties between the different groups and nations, is of major significance, and warrants singling out as a distinguishing feature of Zuhaili's perspective on international relations. The third part of article one, addressing the legal consequences of the eruption of war, will be treated in the section on war and jihad.

The second article clearly states a recurrent theme in the discourse of Zuhaili and that of the mainstream Islamists, namely that there can be no coercion in religion.[45] Zuhaili writes, "Coercion in religion is prohibited in Islam, and religious freedom is guaranteed as long as it does not threaten public order." Zuhaili repeatedly emphasizes that the call for Islam should be pursued by persuasion, logical proof, and the ethical conduct of Muslims, and not by intimidation or threats of violence.[46]

The caveat regarding "threats to public order" is very important and warrants a brief discussion. Zuhaili articulates the mainstream Islamist view that religious freedom should not be used as a pretext to defame Islam and to seek turning Muslims away from their religion by spreading false information about Islam, such as by depicting it as a violent religion that rejects the other. Equally important, religious freedom does not protect Muslim apostates who publicize their turning away from Islam. While adhering to the classic view that the punishment for apostasy is death, but only after the apostate rejects the appeals to renounce apostasy and return to Islam, Zuhaili argues that this punishment is not because of the act itself but because of its political repercussions on the unity and the morale of the Muslim community. Apostasy is punishable only because it threatens public order, and not for religious reasons. Muslims who become atheists or embrace another religion, while keeping this matter private, cannot be punished in this life for God will decide their fate.[47]

The third article summarizes the lawful purposes of jihad. Zuhaili writes, "Jihad is lawful where there is aggression. It is the *wulat al-amr* who decide on whether to call for jihad. What prompts jihad is aggression and not difference in belief. The purposes of jihad are to protect freedom of belief, the freedom to call for Islam, aiding the oppressed, and protecting oneself and one's homeland."[48] A further discussion of jihad is covered in the subsequent section on war and jihad.

The remaining 51 articles address specific situations that arise in times of peace and war. Article 4, for example, stipulates that wars should be fought according to established rules that limit destruction to civilian property, while emphasizing reciprocal treatment, for example, mutual agreement not to use chemical or biological weapons and to treat war prisoners in accordance with international humanitarian law. Arguably, the most important part of article 4 prohibits the use of nuclear weapons because "they cause mass destruction and indiscriminately kill those whose killing is not lawful, namely innocent civilians, women and the elderly."[49]

Articles 7–15 outline the "Islamic system for ensuring the safety" (*nidham al-aman*) of non-Muslims, including citizens of other states, who reside temporarily or permanently in Islamic lands. Under this system, the persons and properties of non-Muslims would be protected, and non-Muslims would have the right to own property and to engage in lawful economic activities. Non-Muslims are subject to *sharia* law just as Muslims are, except in matters of their religious beliefs, such as marriage and divorce.[50] The rather interesting article 8 allows residents of an enemy state during peace and wartime to enter Muslim lands for peaceful purposes, such as to engage in commerce, to explore ways of ending the war, or to learn about Islam.

Articles 21 and 26 stipulate that wars should not necessarily lead to the termination of all economic activities between the states at war.[51] *Wulat al-amr* should decide whether to terminate or to maintain economic relationships with an enemy state, with the broad guidelines that trade should not be in armaments or material that supports the enemy's war effort.[52] Zuhaili here fully subscribes to Abu Zahra's view that wars are fought between states and not their citizens.

Articles 16–28 cover diplomatic representation, the conclusion of treaties, and the conduct of economic relations with non-Muslim states. Zuhaili acknowledges the necessity of mutual diplomatic representation between Muslim and non-Mulim states for facilitating political and economic dealings.[53] He is also a strong advocate of the need to base international relations on binding international treaties and conventions that organize and codify the multiple relationships between different states with both similar and divergent interests.[54]

Articles 29–40 spell out the rules of warfare. Article 29 prohibits the killing of women, children, priests, and more generally noncombatants, except when they are providing material aid or counsel to the enemy combatants. Article 30 clarifies that in the case of war with another state, the latter's citizens residing in Islamic lands may not be killed or harmed, but may be expelled if their betrayal is feared. In that case, their properties may not be confiscated, unless it becomes manifest that they are fighting with the enemy, but are to be safeguarded until the war ends; then said properties are to be restored to them.[55]

Articles 31–36 concern the humane treatment of prisoners of war and their eventual release after the war ends, either in exchange for one's own prisoners (*fida'*), or for a monetary ransom, or as an act of mercy (*al-mann*). Article 37 prohibits the mutilation of the bodies of fallen enemy combatants, while article 38, very similar to article 2, proclaims the impermissibility of acts of destruction to civilian property when these are not warranted by military necessity.[56] Articles 41–54 pertain to the ending of wars, a topic that will be discussed in the section on war and jihad.

To sum up, Zuhaili construes international relations as pertaining to relations between Muslims and non-Muslims. Peace is the basic principle (*al-asl*) in relations with non-Muslims, while war is a necessity brought about by the need to repel aggression and protect religious freedom and the freedom to call peacefully for Islam. The preservation of peace, which is broadly construed to include collaboration for mutual benefit and reciporcal international trade, hinges on dialog, getting to know the other; diplomacy, hence the importance of mutual diplomatic representation; and respect for international treaties and conventions and, more generally, for public international law that is highly compatible with the *sharia*. Elaborating by and large on the ideas of Shaltut and Abu Zahra, and totally in line with the views of Qaradawi and even the more polemical Bahi, Zuhaili's detailed construct of the underpinning principles of international relations is at the core of the moderate-reformist, i.e., mainstream, perspective.

War and Jihad

The notions of fighting (*qital*), jihad, and war are at the core of Zuhaili's construct of international relations. While regarding war as the exception rather than the norm in international relations, Zuhaili is aware of its importance because of its recurrence and its adverse consequences on humanity. This section is divided into three parts that address sequentially Zuhaili's views on the causes of war, the rules that govern the conduct of war, and the ending of war.

The Causes of War

Zuhaili's extensive discourse on war, as alluded to earlier, is normative and legalistic. Zuhaili is primarily preoccupied with distinguishing between just versus unjust causes for fighting. Unjust wars are prompted by greed, material considerations, and the drive to dominate and exploit others, found in many though not all humans and human collectives. Just wars, on the other hand, are prompted by the legitimate need to defend one's life, property, and homeland, as well as to defend one's freedom to practice one's religion and peacefully call for it. In his rather dense discourse on the causes of war, Zuhaili rejects the notion of human nature as the reason behind war. Zuhaili is adamant that war is not intrinsic to human nature, but is a learned behavior. In one well-crafted statement on war and human nature, Zuhaili writes:

> It is true that war has been with humanity since its beginning, and [it is true that] war may be necessary to defend the rights of the *umma*, to aid an ally or a neighbor, or to solve a social problem that could not be resolved by peaceful means. . . . But it is not true that it is in the nature of humans to seek war, for war is a social phenomenon that can be eradicated.[57]

Zuhaili does not read in the many references to war in the Quran any validation of the claim that wars are inevitable because they stem from human nature. Zuhaili argues that "no religion could have succeeded in sawing the seeds of goodness and eliminating the seeds of evil in humans had the drive to war been intrinsic to human nature."[58] Zuhaili then addresses psychologists who stress the role of instincts, particularly the aggression instinct, in motivating human behavior. Zuhaili argues that even if such instincts do exist, they can still be "modified and reformed, since instinctive behavior is determined by external circumstances and by the social milieu."[59] In summary, the claim that wars arise from human nature cannot be properly anchored in either religion or psychology.

However, to note that war is not intrinsic to human nature is not to deny that aggression often pays off, whether in terms of expanding the territory of a state or dominating other states. Zuhaili firmly believes that aggression will eventually trigger armed resistance, as in Quranic verses 2:251, "Had God not restrained mankind, some by means of others, the earth would have become chaotic," and 22:40, "Had God not caused people to restrain one another, destruction would have fallen upon monasteries, churches, oratories and other places of prayer, where the name of God is often mentioned."

For mainstream Islamists such as Zuhaili, Jihad is the Islamic way of restraining aggressors. Accordingly, the primary purpose of jihad is to defend Muslims against aggression that is directed at their lives, properties, lands, or freedom of belief. Wars arise from the aggressive practices of states that seek to expand their territory and/or to dominate and exploit other states. Downplaying but not altogether ignoring the role of psychological factors in triggering war, Zuhaili locates its sources in the political, socioeconomic, and ideational structures of un-Islamic states, in line with Qaradawi and Bahi. Using the terminology of Kenneth Waltz, Zuhaili largely subscribes to a second image explanation of the causes of war that emphasizes state structure and state attributes.[60]

Two broad related themes dominate Zuhaili's discourse on the causes of war: identifying the just causes for fighting and demonstrating that most of the wars that Muslims fought throughout history were just wars. To begin, Zuhaili's primary distinction is between just wars and unjust wars. For Zuhaili and other mainstream Islamists, the just causes for fighting are those that are in line with the Islamic *sharia*, namely defending Muslims against aggression and against any attempts to force them to renounce their religious beliefs.[61] Lifting oppression, even when the oppressed are not Muslims, also constitutes a valid cause for fighting. Zuhaili maintains, though, that decisions about war are left entirely to the judgment of *wulat al-amr*, beyond self-defense in the case of actual or imminent attack.

Wulat al-amr must weigh all relevant factors, including safety of the state, obligations under international law and available resources, before embarking on any military engagement beyond the state's borders, even when for a just cause such as removing oppression. For Zuhaili, engaging in any military conflict, except in clear cases of self-defense, is a very serious matter that must be decided by level-headed leaders who are lawfully in charge of the affairs of the Muslim community, preferably after consulting persons of influence and power (*ahl al-'aqd wa al-hal*). Zuhaili, thus, writes, "*Wali al-amr* is the one who is responsible for declaring war, accordingly no individual Muslim, or a group of Muslims, may declare war according to his/their own opinion and inclination."[62]

After establishing the just causes for fighting, Zuhaili strives to demonstrate that most of the wars that Muslims fought were just wars. For Zuhaili and mainstream Islamists, all the wars that the Prophet and the first four rightly guided caliphs fought were just wars. Zuhaili and other mainstream Islamists specifically address the wars with each of the Byzantine and the Persian Empires. They argue that these wars were defensive in nature, for they aimed at defending the nascent Muslim community from the aggressive plots of these larger empires and at ensuring the right of their oppressed populations to embrace Islam of their own free volition.[63]

Zuhaili does acknowledge, though, that following the establishment of dynastic rule, first under the Umayyads, Muslim rulers did not always fight for just causes. Zuhaili specifically notes the wars of the Ottoman Empire emphasizing, in passing, that not all of them met the criteria of just wars.[64] Zuhaili, nevertheless, articulates the mainstream Islamist thesis that, throughout their history, Muslims were far more just in their wars than non-Muslims were. This applies to both the causes for which they fought and the manner in which they fought.

The Conduct of War

For wars to be just, they must first be fought for just causes, but they must also be fought in accordance with certain rules of warfare, whose origins lie in the *sharia*. Zuhaili's presentation of the rules of warfare is very similar to that of Qaradawi, while building on the thought of Shaltut and Abu Zahra. What distinguishes Zuhaili's discourse, though, is his emphasis on the compatibility of these Islamic rules with prevalent international laws, norms, and conventions, especially as conveyed in international humanitarian law.[65] Zuhaili emphasizes that "international law in its formative stages was influenced by Islamic civilization, especially as a result of the crusader wars."[66] Zuhaili promotes the thesis that Muslims impacted the development of Western rules with regard to war during these wars, especially as far as the humane treatment of prisoners of war, the prohibition of the mutilation of the bodies of fallen combatants, the avoidance of undue harm to civilians, and forbidding certain types of weapons.[67]

In line with the other mainstream Islamists, Zuhaili maintains that, unless in extreme cases of an imminent enemy attack, Muslims should announce to their enemy their intent to go to war and the grounds for their action. The enemy should also be given the chance to acquiesce to their demands in order to avoid war.[68] Once hostilities start, Muslims should do their utmost to avoid destroying the property and infrastructure of the enemy, except when this is an absolute military necessity.[69] Even more, Muslims should distinguish between combatants and noncombatants and should not target the latter.[70] Noncombatants, however, become legitimate targets of attack when they support the war effort, such as by motivating enemy fighters to keep on fighting.[71]

Zuhaili writes extensively on the subject of the treatment of prisoners of war, according to the opinions of Islamic jurists as well as under international law. The gist of his argument is that the overwhelming majority of Islamic jurists emphasize the humane treatment of prisoners of war and forbid their killing or enslavement.[72] Zuhaili struggles to demonstrate that although the Prophet Muhammad executed a few prisoners, these were very rare cases prompted by the viciousness and dangers posed by these prisoners.[73] Zuhaili underscores the Prophet's exhortation to the Muslims to treat their prisoners humanely, as called for in verse

76:8, "They had dispensed food, though held dear, to the poor, the orphan and the prisoner."[74] Zuhaili emphasizes that once hostilities are over, prisoners of war should be released either in exchange for Muslim prisoners, or money (*fida'*), or unconditionally (*minna*).[75]

Zuhaili is equally adamant that there is no Quranic injunction that justifies enslavement of prisoners of war. While acknowledging that Muslims did enslave some prisoners of war, Zuhaili argues that this was done in line with the practices of the time and had no basis in the Quran. Zuhaili is unequivocal that the prohibition of all forms of slavery under contemporary international law, definitely including enslavement resulting from war, is in line with the intents of Islam and that Muslim states should wholeheartedly embrace this prohibition.[76]

In summary, wars are fought between states or political units and not between their people.[77] The conduct of wars is governed by firm rules that regulate how they are initiated, and prohibit the targeting of civilians, the unnecessary destruction of civilian property, the use of weapons of mass destruction, and the killing, torture, or enslavement of prisoners of war. Furthermore, Zuhaili rejects the notion of total wars, or wars that are fought until the annihilation of the enemy or one's own annihilation, for just wars are limited wars that are fought for specific reasons and must end when their causes are removed.

The Ending of Wars

Zuhaili's extensive treatment of war covers in detail how wars end. In *International Relations in Islam*, Zuhaili states five alternative ways for ending a war,[78] a detailed discussion of which is found in his earlier work, *The Effects of War*. First, war ends when the enemy accepts Islam.[79] Declaring one's Islam is done by pronouncing the two testimonies. Zuhaili insists that upon uttering these two pronouncements, an enemy combatant or noncombatant cannot be killed, enslaved, harmed, or deprived of their property.[80] The dual act of surrendering to God and acknowledging that Muhammad is His Prophet (the two testimonies) ends all prior enmity with the Muslims. If war were to continue, it becomes strife within the Muslim community itself (*fitna*). Based on Quranic verse 49:14, "The Bedouins say: We believe. Say: You do not believe. Instead you may say: We surrender, but faith has not entered your hearts," Zuhaili distinguishes between publicly declaring One's Islam and believing in Islam and categorically rejects testing the beliefs of any recent convert to Islam, or any Muslim, in order to ascertain their motives for embracing Islam.[81] In brief, if the enemy, whether as individuals or collectively, declares its Islam, irrespective of the sincerity of this declaration, war ends.

The second way by which war ends is by signing a truce that ends hostilities for a specific duration (*hudna*) or a peace treaty that ends war permanently (*sulh*).[82] Similar to Qaradawi, Zuhaili provides an exhaustive review of the opinions of Muslim jurisprudents on whether truces should be for a specific duration or indefinite. Zuhaili literally quotes all the Quranic verses that prohibit aggression and that exhort Muslims to honor to the letter the terms of the truces and treaties they enter into, thus refraining from any deception (*ghadr*), duplicity (*khida'*), or coercion (*qahr*).[83] In line with Qaradawi, he concludes that both open-ended truces and permanent peace treaties are not only lawful but are also desirable in Islam. Zuhaili, thus, writes, "Treaties are lawful in Islam, for they provide the effective means for guaranteeing peace, reinforcing security and protecting human rights."[84] The conclusion of a permanent peace treaty or a truce renders future jihad against that entity unlawful. In a similar vein, the Lebanese Shiite scholar, Sheikh Muhammad Mahdi Shams al-Din, writes, "There is agreement among Muslim jurists that jihad, as a juristic concept, is only valid against those unbelievers (*kufar*) with whom Muslims do not have relations based on treaties or truces; and who do not live, or reside, amongst Muslims based on *dhimmi* relations, or similar arrangements."[85] We shall return briefly to Shams al-Din's views on international relations and jihad in Chapter 7 on Fadlallah.

War can also end with the total defeat of the enemy and the conquest of its land. In that case, the conquered land becomes part of the abode of Islam. Its residents would have the choice between embracing Islam and thus immediately acquiring the rights and assuming the duties of Muslims or accepting the status of dhimmis in return for paying the *jizya*, which would ensure their legal and economic rights, but not provide them with the political rights of full citizens.[86] Zuhaili is not entirely consistent in his discourse on dhimmis and *jizya*. In line with traditional views, he frequently recognizes the legality of treating non-Muslims as dhimmis and imposing a *jizya* on them.[87] In other references, though, he questions the continued relevance of the dhimmi status and the appropriateness of the *jizya*.[88]

One way of reconciling the issue is to argue that granting non-Muslims the status of dhimmis represents the minimum, the floor beneath which no Muslim government should descend. The *sharia*, however, does not prohibit governments from granting further rights to their non-Muslim citizens, such as dropping the *jizya* tax in return for their paying all the taxes that Muslims pay and serving in the army.[89] Zuhaili, thus, does not object to granting non-Muslims full citizenship rights, except for the right to serve as head of state or as chief commander of the army. This is almost identical to Qaradawi's stance on the matter.

A fourth way in which war ends is by simply withdrawing from the battlefield without any agreement when the *wali al-amr* and the military commanders reach the conclusion that victory is not within reach or that it would require unacceptable sacrifices. Zuhaili remains quite vague relative to this scenario and does not seem to reflect much on its impracticality in the modern era. It is hard to consider that a legal scholar of Zuhaili's caliber was not aware of the logistical difficulties of withdrawing an army from battle without any explicit or tacit agreement with the enemy.

The final scenario for ending war revolves around accepting arbitration by a third party that need not be a Muslim state or entity.[90] Zuhaili writes in detail on the history of arbitration in Islam, starting with the arbitration of the conflict between the fourth caliph, Ali, and his foe, the Wali of Damascus, Muawiya. Arguing for the legitimacy of arbitration in that case, Zuhaili, in line with the mainstream Sunni view, denounces the stance of the khawarej who refused arbitration.[91] For Zuhaili, the submission of military disputes to arbitration represents yet another point of intersection between public international law and the *sharia*. In summary, there are multiple ways for ending a war. A Muslim victory in the form of the surrender of the enemy is the most favored, albeit not the only, way for ending a war.

The Road to Islamic Unity

While a firm believer in Islamic unity, Zuhaili's discourse on the subject is not as extensive as that of Abu Zahra and Bahi (Chapters 3 and 4), or even Qaradawi's (Chapter 5). His views on Islamic unity can, therefore, be discerned from a careful reading of the limited, but insightful, references to the subject that he makes. To start with, Zuhaili subscribes fully to the mainstream Islamist view that the unity of the Muslim *umma*, as stated in the Quran[92] and the Sunna, must manifest itself on the material plane in the form of political and economic unity and a common defense posture that guarantees the security of all Muslim lands. Zuhaili commences by summarizing the view of the majority of Muslim scholars (*jamaheer 'ulama al-Islam*) on the subject of political authority in Islam. He writes, "The established general principle among the majority of Muslim scholars is that there can only be a single political authority in all the Islamic lands in the Mashriq and the Maghreb, because Islam is the religion of unity and the

Muslims constitute one umma whose beacon is cooperation and solidarity and whose enemy is division and discord."[93] While subscribing to the majority view, Zuhaili also refers to the minority opinion that legitimates the presence of several Islamic states due to geographic distance between one Islamic province and another with no common borders, attributing this minority view to the Twelver Shias, the Zaydis, and even a few Sunni scholars such as al-Jahez.[94]

While anchored in the Islamic tradition, Zuhaili's brief discourse on Islamic unity introduces some novel ideas, especially regarding the federal nature of the Islamic state. Zuhaili, thus, believes that the "Islamic state is a federal state that is founded on the principle of religious and Islamic brotherhood."[95] Zuhaili even boasts that the Islamic state was the first manifestation of a federal state, predating the American federal state by many centuries,[96] while providing a highly sympathetic reading of the US federal model, contending that it would be quite suitable for the Muslim world.[97] Zuhaili seems convinced that the major global powers, since the 20th century—the United States, the former Soviet Union, and the emergent European Union—are multinational entities bound together by the common ideas and principles of individual freedom and capitalism in the United States versus socioeconomic equality and social justice in the former Soviet Union.

Thus, while grounding his call for Islamic unity in the Quran and the Sunna, Zuhaili underscores the pragmatic reasons behind seeking this unity, namely to bolster the presence of the Muslims on the world stage by uniting them in a political entity that can deal effectively with the major powers, the United States, the former Soviet Union/Present Russia, and the emergent European Union. However, Zuhaili remains quite vague on the internal organization of the federal Islamic state he proposes. He simply states that the Islamic state would be based on the principles of justice, equality, *shura*, and reciprocity in dealing with others. In line with other mainstream Islamists, Zuhaili maintains that the *sharia* would be the source of all laws in the Islamic state, thus limiting the need for a strong legislative body, since legislation would rely primarily on extrapolating from the *sharia*.[98]

The Islamic state would thus be run by a caliph or imam who is selected by those who loosen and bind and who would delegate extensive powers to *wulat al-amr* of the various provinces. The main check on the powers of the caliph and the *wulat al-amr* would come from the judges, who would rule on the compatibility of the actions of the rulers with the *sharia*. For Zuhaili and other mainstream Islamists, those in power are primarily bound by the *sharia* and only secondarily by public opinion through the vague process of *shura*, or consultation. Broadly speaking, the Islamic state that the mainstream Islamists envision is neither a dictatorship nor a Western style democracy that is based on notions of separation of powers, strong legislatures, and popular sovereignty. Painting with broad strokes, it is characterized by a strong executive, a relatively weak legislature and an independent judiciary that is guided by the *sharia*.

Conclusion

There are major similarities, but also some subtle differences, between Qaradawi and Zuhaili with regard to their views on international relations. Both scholar sheikhs take as their point of departure the pivotal notion that peace—rather than war—is the general principle (*al-asl al-'am*) in international relations. They both adopt broad construals of peace that go beyond nonaggression to include dialog for the purpose of better understanding the other and bridging differences, and cooperation for mutual benefit on the basis of reciprocity. Their perspectives on war and jihad are quite similar too. Influenced by the views of the scholar sheikhs of the second generation, especially Shaltut and Abu Zahra, Qaradawi and Zuhaili view jihad as primarily defensive in nature, aiming at protecting Muslims lands from an actual or imminent attack and not at territorial aggrandizement or material gain. Equally important, and again expanding on the views of the scholar sheikhs of the second generation, Zuhaili and Qaradawi maintain that Muslims do not fight in order to coerce others to embrace Islam. "No coercion in religion" is arguably one of their most quoted Quranic verses. Finally, both turbaned scholars embrace a peaceful and incremental approach to Islamic unity. Qaradawi, however, writes more extenively on the subject than Zuhaili.

These similarities notwithstanding, there are subtle differences in the views of the two scholar sheikhs. Qaradawi (as well as Bahi and Fadlallah) places greater importance on the centrality of power to international relations than Zuhaili does. It is true that Zuhaili's discourse abounds with references to the need for Muslim societies to strengthen their power base and to be always ready for war, but Zuhaili's principal preoccupation is not with power but with international law. His extensive international relations discourse is centered on demonstrating the compatibility of *sharia* with international law, especially international humanitarian law. Generally, Zuhaili writes in more detail than the other mainstream scholar sheikhs do about the requisites of a just war, in terms of both causes and conduct of war, and about demonstrating that most, albeit not all, of the wars that Muslims fought met the criteria of a just war. While there is a discernable normative-legalist streak in the discourses of all mainstream Islamists, this streak is most visible, in fact dominant, in the discourse of Zuhaili. Chapter 7 turns to the discourse of the only Shia scholar that this work examines, Sayyid Muhammad Hussein Fadlallah.

Notes

1 Radwan El-Sayyed, "al-Sheikh Wahbah al-Zuhaili wa al-Taqlid al-Fiqhi wa al-Thawra al-Souriya" (Sheikh Wahbah al-Zuhaili, the jurisprudential tradition and the Syrian Revolution), *al-Sharq al-Awsat* (2015), http://aawsat.com/node/429266, accessed 29 August 2019.
2 Kamali, *The Middle Path of Moderation in Islam: The Quranic Principle of Wasatiyyah* (Oxford: Oxford University Press, 2015), 11.
3 Zuhaili, *Al-Qanun al-Duwali al-Insani wa Huquq al-Insan: Dirasa Muqarina* (International Humanitarian Law and Human Rights: A Comparative Study) (Damascus: Dar al-Fikr, 2012), 155.
4 See "Deir Atiyeh," (n.d.), *Wikipedia*, https://ar.wikipedia.org/wiki/%D8%AF%D9%8A%D8%B1_%D8%B9%D8%B7%D9%8A%D8%A9, accessed 7 July 2019.
5 Wahbah Zuhaili, *Haq al-Huriya fi al-'Alam* (The Right to freedom in the World) (Damascus: Dar al-Fikr, 2000), 96.
6 Biographical information derived mainly from the websites below: "Wafat al-Allama Wahbah al-Zuhaili al-Mofassir al-Fakih al-Usuli al-Suri" (The death of the scholar "Wahba Al-Zuhaili" the Syrian fundamentalist jurist interpreter), (2015), *Sabq Online Newspaper*, https://sabq.org/KNDgde, accessed 7 July 2019.
"Wahbah al-Zuhaili," (n.d.), *al-Maktaba al-Shamela*, http://shamela.ws/index.php/author/1052, accessed 7 July 2019. "Wahbah al-Zuhaili fi Zimmat Allah" (Wahbah al-Zuhaili Passed Away), (2015), *Islam Web*, http://articles.islamweb.net/Media/index.php?page=article&lang=A&id=206125, accessed 7 July 2019. https://www.islamweb.net/ramadan/index.php?page=article&lang=&id=20484
"Al-Zuhaili ... Ahad Monahedy al-Tamaddod al-Irani fi Surya" (Al-Zuhaili ... One of the Opponents of Iranian Expansion in Syria), (2015), *Bawabat al-Harakat al-Islamiya*, http://www.islamist-movements.com/30764, accessed 7 July 2019.
"Dr. Wahbah al-Zuhaili – Rahamahu Allah" (Dr. Wahbah al-Zuhaili – May God have mercy on him), (2015), *Syria Noor*, https://syrianoor.net/article/214, accessed 7 July 2019.
"Al-Ustaz al-Dr. Wahbah al-Zuhaili" (Mr. Dr. Wahbah al-Zuhaili), (2016), *Naseem al Sham*, https://www.naseemalsham.com/persons/dr_badi/subjects/view/54251, accessed 7 July 2019.

"Lakatat Modee'a min Hayat al-Dr. Wahbah al-Zuhaili" (Bright Clips from the Life of Dr. Wahbah Al-Zuhaili), (2015), *Dar Al-Fikr*, https://www.youtube.com/watch?v=OyRylAX1QJA, accessed 7 July 2019."Hadith al-Zekrayat Maa Dr. Wahbah al-Zuhaili" (Talking memories with Dr. Wahbah al-Zuhaili), (2011), *Dr. Jasem Tv*, https://www.youtube.com/watch?v=JiypwMdXEuY, accessed 7 July 2019.

7 "Hadith al-Zekrayat Maa Dr. Wahbah al-Zuhaili" (Talking memories with Dr. Wahbah al-Zuhaili), (2011), *Dr. Jasem Tv*, https://www.youtube.com/watch?v=JiypwMdXEuY, accessed 7 July 2019.

8 "Hadith al-Zekrayat Maa Dr. Wahbah al-Zuhaili" (Talking memories with Dr. Wahbah al-Zuhaili), (2011), *Dr. Jasem Tv*, https://www.youtube.com/watch?v=JiypwMdXEuY, accessed 7 July 2019.

9 Zuhaili, *Athar al-Harb: Dirasa Fiqhiya Muqarina* (Effects of War: A Comparative Jurisprudential Study), 4th ed. (Damascus: Dar al-Fikr, 2009). This chapter relies on the fourth edition of *Athar Al-Harb*, which includes some new material, especially on the distinction between jihad and terrorism. The work's core argument has not changed at all since the first edition appeared in early 1963.

10 "Hadith al-Zekrayat Maa Dr. Wahbah al-Zuhaili" (Talking memories with Dr. Wahbah al-Zuhaili), (2011), *Dr. Jasem Tv*, https://www.youtube.com/watch?v=JiypwMdXEuY, accessed 7 July 2019.

11 Radwan El-Sayyed, "Al-Sheikh Wahbah al-Zuhaili wa al-Taqlid al-Fiqhi wa al-Thawra al-Souriya" (Sheikh Wahbah Zuhaili, the Jurisprudential Tradition and the Syrian Revolution), *al-Sharq al-Awsat*, 13 August 2015. http://aawsat.com/node/429266, accessed 27 August 2019.

12 "Hadith al-Zekrayat Maa Dr. Wahbah al-Zuhaili" (Talking memories with Dr. Wahbah al-Zuhaili), (2011), *Dr. Jasem Tv*, https://www.youtube.com/watch?v=JiypwMdXEuY, accessed 7 July 2019.

13 Zuhaili notes that he was accused of being a Wahhabi because in his sermons he would call on worshipers to plead directly to God and not to seek the intercession (*shafa'a*) of holy men, or even of the Prophet. YouTube Interview.

14 "Hadith al-Zekrayat Maa Dr. Wahbah al-Zuhaili" (Talking memories with Dr. Wahbah al-Zuhaili), (2011), *Dr. Jasem Tv*, https://www.youtube.com/watch?v=JiypwMdXEuY, accessed 7 July 2019.

15 Zuhaili's remarks can be found at "Pandangan Dr Wahbah Az Zuhaili berkenaan dengan Ahbash" (Dr. Wahbah Az Zuhaili's views on Ahbash), (2009), *Hakim Hulaimi*, https://www.youtube.com/watch?v=BR_TuQ1IbxQ, accessed 1 September 2015.

16 For *al-Ahbash* attack on Zuhaili, see "Shata'em al-Sufiya al-Ashaera lel Sheikh al-Zuhaili wa Ettehamahu bil Tejseem" (Ash'ari Sufi insults of Sheikh al-Zuhaili and Accusing him of Anthropomorphism), (2010), https://www.youtube.com/watch?v=WW7s2WI4cgM, accessed 1 September 2015. See also Baroudi and Behmardi, "Sheikh Wahbah al-Zuhaili on International Relations," 365.

The Third Generation: Sheikh Wahbah al-Zuhaili | 213

17 Taskhiri is a prominent Iranian cleric and diplomat and trusted aide to Iran's supreme leader, Ayatollah Ali Khamenei. Having served for a while as Iran's ambassador to Syria, he had close ties to the Assad family. For information about Taskhiri, see "Mohammad Ali Taskhiri," (n.d.), *Marefa.org*, https://www.marefa.org/%D9%85%D8%AD%D9%85%D8%AF_%D8%B9%D9%84%D9%8A_%D8%AA%D8%B3%D8%AE%D9%8A%D8%B1%D9%8A, accessed 1 September 2015.
18 Baroudi and Behmardi, "Sheikh Wahba al-Zuhaili on International Relations," 364.
19 Baroudi and Behmardi, "Sheikh Wahba al-Zuhaili on International Relations," 364.
20 Zuhaili, *Al-Qanun al-Duwali al-Insani wa Huquq al-Insan: Dirasa Muqarina* (International Humanitarian Law and Human Rights: A Comparative Study) (Damascus: Dar al-Fikr, 2012), esp. 46–47.
21 El-Sayyed, "Al-Sheikh Wahbah al-Zuhaili wa al-Taqlid al-Fiqhi wa al-Thawra al-Souriya."
22 After Sheikh al-Bouti was killed, along with 40 worshippers, in a massive explosion that rocked the mosque where he was preaching, Zuhaili publicly eulogized him, but without addressing the circumstances of his death. al-Zuhaili's eulogy can be found at "Kalimat Dr. Wahbah al-Zuhaili Fi Ta`been al-Dr. al-Bouti Rahamahu Allah" (Dr. Wahba Al-Zuhaili's speech at the memorial of Dr. Al-Bouti, may God have mercy on him), https://www.youtube.com/watch?v=PAKB9OztE0g, accessed 10 August 2015.
23 El-Sayyed, "Al-Sheikh Wahbah al-Zuhaili." For further laudatory references to al-Zuhaili's contributions as a jurisprudent, see El-Sayyed's lecture at the "international conference on issuing fatwas" that was held in Cairo on 17–18 August 2015. Lecture reprinted at Radwan El-Sayyed (2015), "al-Islam fi Zaman al-Inshikakat" (Islam in the time of divisions), *Beirut News Arabia*, http://www.beirutme.com/?p=14371, accessed 27 August 2019.
24 The verses are 49: 10, "The believers are indeed brothers, so make peace among your brothers"; 3: 103, "And hold fast, all of you, to the rope of God and do not fall into dissention" and 8: 46, "Obey God and His Messenger, and do not quarrel, or else you will falter and your spirit will flag," and 9: 49, "The pertinent hadith is "You should kill anyone who comes to you ... wanting to bring discord to your unity or disperse your gathering"".
25 Zuhaili, *Athar al-Harb*, 68.
26 Zuhaili, *Athar al-Harb*, 69.
27 Zuhaili, *Athar al-Harb*, esp. 127, 145–46.
28 Zuhaili, *al-'Alaqat al-Duwaliya fi al-Islam*, 106.
29 Zuhaili, *Athar al-Harb*, 500–17.
30 Zuhaili, *Athar al-Harb*, 500.
31 Zuhaili, *Athar al-Harb*, 500.
32 Zuhaili, *Athar al-Harb*, 501–04.

33 Zuhaili, *Athar al-Harb*, 504.
34 Zuhaili, *Athar al-Harb*, 505.
35 Zuhaili, *Athar al-Harb*, 506.
36 Zuhaili, *Athar al-Harb*, 507–08.
37 Zuhaili, *Athar al-Harb*, 507.
38 Zuhaili, *Athar al-Harb*, 507.
39 Zuhaili, *Athar al-Harb*, 507.
40 Zuhaili, *Athar al-Harb*, esp. 642–43.
41 Zuhaili, *Athar al-Harb*, 837–44.
42 Zuhaili, *Athar al-Harb*, 837.
43 Zuhaili, *al-'Alaqat al-Duwaliya fi al-Islam*, 116–30; *al-Qanun al-Duwali al-Insani was Huquq al-Insan*, 85.
44 Zuhaili, *al-'Alaqat al-Duwaliya fi al-Islam*, 116–30.
45 See, inter alia, Zuhaili, *al-Qanun al-Duwali al-Insani*, 19–25.
46 Zuhaili, *al-'Alaqat al-Duwaliya fi al-Islam*, 114–15.
47 Zuhaili, *Haq al-Huriya fi al-'Alam*, 151–54.
48 Zuhaili, *Athar al-Harb*, 837. See also *al-'Alaqat al-Duwaliya fi al-Islam*, 29–33.
49 Zuhaili, *Athar al-Harb*, 837.
50 Zuhaili, *Athar al-Harb*, 838–39, *Haq al-Huriya fi al-'Alam*, 147.
51 Zuhaili, *Athar al-Harb*, 839–40.
52 Zuhaili, *Athar al-Harb*, 839.
53 Zuhaili, *Athar al-Harb*, 839.
54 Zuhaili, *Athar al-Harb*, 839–40.
55 Zuhaili, *Athar al-Harb*, 841.
56 Zuhaili, *Athar al-Harb*, 842.
57 Zuhaili, *Athar al-Harb*, 66.
58 Zuhaili, *Athar al-Harb*, 66.
59 Zuhaili, *Athar al-Harb*, 66.
60 Kenneth Waltz, *Man, the State and War: A Theoretical Analysis* (New York: Columbia University Press, 2001).
61 Zuhaili, *al-'Alaqat al-Duwaliya fi al-Islam*, 35–38, 110–13, *al-Qanun al-Duwali al-Insani*, 95–97, 142–43.
62 Zuhaili, *Athar al-Harb*, 167.
63 Zuhaili, *al-'Alaqat al-Duwaliya fi al-Islam*, 29–33, 142, *Athar al-Harb*.
64 Zuhaili, *al-'Alaqat al-Duwaliya fi al-Islam*, 141–42.
65 This is Zuhaili's core argument in his late work *al-Qanun al-Duwali al-Insani*.
66 Zuhaili, *Athar al-Harb*, 236, 498–518.
67 Zuhaili, *al-'Alaqat al-Duwaliya fi al-Islam*, 22; *al-Qanun al-Duwali al-Insani*, 85–86.
68 Zuhaili, *al-'Alaqat al-Duwaliya fi al-Islam*, 45–48.
69 Zuhaili, *al-Qanun al-Duwali al-Insani*, 83, 88–89. *Athar al-Harb*, 132–33.

70 Zuhaili, *al-'Alaqat al-Duwaliya fi al-Islam*, 52; *Athar al-Harb*, 168, 510, 533; *al-Qanun al-Duwali al-Insani*, esp. 69–82.
71 Zuhaili, *Athar al-Harb*, 534–35.
72 Zuhaili, *Athar al-Harb*, 515–16; *al-Qanun al-Duwali al-Insani*, 107–24.
73 Zuhaili, *Athar al-Harb*, 402, 407, *al-'Alaqat al-Duwaliya fi al-Islam*, 90.
74 Zuhaili, Athar al-Harb, 515; *al-Qanun al-Duwali al-Insani*, 116.
75 Zuhaili, *Athar al-Harb*, 424–25.
76 Zuhaili, *Athar al-Harb*, 424, *al-'Alaqat al-Duwaliya fi al-Islam*, 92.
77 Zuhaili, *Athar al-Harb*, 510, 533.
78 Zuhaili, *al-'Alaqat al-Duwaliya fi al-Islam*, 84–87.
79 Zuhaili, *Athar al-Harb*, 642–48.
80 Zuhaili, *Athar al-Harb*, 644–45.
81 Zuhaili, *Athar al-Harb*, 647.
82 Zuhaili, *Athar al-Harb*, 655–63.
83 Zuhaili, *al-'Alaqat al-Duwaliya fi al-Islam*, 146–55; *al-Qanun al-Duwali al-Insani*, 93–94.
84 Zuhaili, *al-'Alaqat al-Duwaliya fi al-Islam*, 148.
85 Shams al-Din, *Fiqh al-'Unf al-Muslah fi al-Islam*, 43.
86 Zuhaili, *Athar al-Harb*, 695–96, *al-'Alaqat al-Duwaliya fi al-Islam*, 84–85.
87 Zuhaili, *Athar al-Harb*, 682–93.
88 Zuhaili, *Haq al-Huriya fi al-'Alam*, 94.
89 Zuhaili, *Haq al-Huriya fi al-'Alam*, 96.
90 Zuhaili, *Athar al-Harb*, 811–18.
91 Zuhaili, *Athar al-Harb*, 812–13.
92 Zuhaili quotes verses 21: 92, "This then is your community, a single community" and 49: 10, "The believers are indeed brothers." Zuhaili, *al-'Alaqat al-Duwaliya fi al-Islam*, 136.
93 Zuhaili, *al-'Alaqat al-Duwaliya fi al-Islam*, 136.
94 Zuhaili, *al-'Alaqat al-Duwaliya fi al-Islam*, 136.
95 Zuhaili, *al-'Alaqat al-Duwaliya fi al-Islam*, 139.
96 Zuhaili, *al-'Alaqat al-Duwaliya fi al-Islam*, 139.
97 Zuhaili, *al-'Alaqat al-Duwaliya fi al-Islam*, 139.
98 Zuhaili, *al-'Alaqat al-Duwaliya fi al-Islam*, 138–9.

7

The Third Generation: Sayyid Muhammad Hussein Fadlallah

Introduction

There are multiple reasons for including Sayyid Muhammad Hussein Fadlallah (also written Fadlullah), a Shia scholar sheikh, in this book. To start with, the Shias (Twelvers, Zaydis, Alawites) constitute anywhere between 10 and 15 % of the Muslim population in the Arab world, with significant demographic presence in Iraq, Lebanon, Bahrain, and Yemen.[1] Important Shia minorities also live in Saudi Arabia and Kuwait. It is, thus, imperative to include at least one representative of this increasingly vocal and politicized community in the present study. Equally important, Fadlallah has a great deal in common with his Sunni counterparts who have been included in this work, whether in terms of religious background, regional and international renown, argumentation style, or outlook on international relations. A careful examination of his discourse on international relations reveals that the mainstream Islamist outlook discussed in this work has adherents from both the Sunni and Shia denominations of Islam.

Fadlallah's discourse also sheds light on the diversity of opinions within the mainstream Islamist camp, the moderate-reformist strand of political Islam, regarding the underpinning principles of international relations. All mainstream Islamists view peace, rather than war, as the norm in international relations.

Bahi, Qaradawi, and Fadlallah, however, emphasize the centrality of the balance of power, or the "law of mutual restraining," in the preservation of international peace. The outlook of these three scholar sheikhs on international relations is close to Western realism, while the more legalist-oriented Shaltut, Abu Zahra, and especially Zuhaili come close to the Western liberal view of international relations. Fadlallah's international relations discourse intersects markedly with the discourses of Bahi and, especially, Qaradawi, rendering it intriguing to shed light on the common "realist" elements in their discourses. Nonetheless, what joins mainstream Islamists is more significant than what separates them in terms of their perspectives on international relations.

Following a short biographic sketch, this chapter examines Fadlallah's views on the principles that underlie international relations, the purposes of fighting (or jihad) in Islam, the rules that govern the conduct of war, the ending of wars, and the road to restoring Islamic unity. With regard to this last point, Fadlallah shares his Sunni counterparts' view that the Shias form an integral part of the Muslim *umma*, and that all schemes for restoring Islamic unity must include the Shias. From the start of his long career as a *da'iya* (preacher) and a religious scholar, Fadlallah chose to address himself to a broad Islamic audience and not just to the Shias. His unit of analysis is the Muslim *umma*, and his discourse focuses on the principal challenges that the *umma* faces in the contemporary world.

However, before moving to these substantive issues, it is essential that we address one important preliminary question. What is the justification for treating Fadlallah as a moderate-reformist, i.e., mainstream, Islamist, rather than as a radical Islamist, as he has been largely portrayed in the West? Answering this question warrants a return to Chapter 1, which makes and defends the distinction between mainstream and radical Islamists. This distinction did not aim at denying the presence of shared elements between these two variants of political Islam. Mainstream and radical Islamists subscribe, in varying degrees, to the same negative view of the West, especially regarding Western intentions toward the Islamic world. Nevertheless, this negative image is more pronounced among radical Islamists, and radical Islamists are more likely to condone attacks on the West. Moreover, achieving, or restoring, Islamic unity is a common goal of all Islamists. Radical and mainstream Islamists only differ over the means for restoring this unity, with mainstream Islamists emphasizing a peaceful and incremental approach. The one *umma*, rather than a territorial nation-state, is the primary unit of analysis for mainstream and radical Islamists. Mainstream and radical Islamists also equally emphasize the comprehensive nature of Islam, rejecting any separation between politics and religion. The notion of a purely spiritual, apolitical Islam is anathema to all Islamists.

By Western standards, including the standards of Arab secularists and feminists, mainstream Islamists have adopted "radical," uncompromising positions on diverse social issues, from apostasy to abortion, extramarital affairs, and homosexuality. Most importantly, the position adopted by mainstream Islamists regarding Israel and the Arab-Israeli peace process, especially by Qaradawi and Fadlallah, who wrote extensively on the subject, cannot be considered moderate by any stretch of the imagination.

The terms moderate-reformist and mainstream are used throughout this book in a specific way, namely to connote an attitude toward international relations that 1) views peace, rather than war, as the norm, or fundamental principle; 2) emphasizes the need for dialog and collaboration with non-Muslim states on the basis of reciprocity and mutual benefit; 3) underscores the defensive purposes of jihad, the need to conduct war in accordance to certain rules, and the impermissibility of coercing others to embrace Islam; and 4) embraces a peaceful and incremental approach to achieving Islamic unity, while eschewing violent means. Fadlallah is explicit that the norm in international relations is peace, while war is the exception.[2] Fadlallah, however, construes both peace and war in relative rather than absolute terms, as will be noted here. His discourse includes many references to Islam as a "religion of love, loving and peace"[3] and a "religion of mercy" (*Din al-rahma*).[4] He has also written extensively on the centrality of openness (*al-infitah*) to and dialog (*al-hiwar*) with the other relative to the message of Islam.[5] Fadlallah also emphasizes the defensive purposes of jihad, categorically rejecting the argument that the reason to fight non-Muslims is their unbelief (*al-kufr*). Accordingly, he reads in verses 60:8–9[6] a divine injunction to Muslims to distinguish between two categories of unbelievers. The first group, Fadlallah argues, are those unbelievers who fought the Muslims because of their embrace of Islam, unjustly drove them from their homes, and aided those who persecuted them. God commands Muslims to fight those unbelievers because of their aggression. The second category connotes those unbelievers who did not act with enmity toward the Muslims. Fadlallah emphasizes that it is lawful to treat those unbelievers justly and honorably and to conclude agreements with them to preserve peace and lay the basis for cooperation for mutual benefit.[7] Fadlallah's treatment of how fighting is to be conducted, the rules of war, is also in line with that of his Sunni counterparts.

Finally, Fadlallah's approach to Islamic unity is quite similar to that of his Sunni counterparts. Fadlallah's treatment of the centuries' old Islamic rule, primarily by Sunni dynasties, is one of the gentlest to be encountered by a renowned Shia scholar. Fadlallah refrains altogether from engaging in anti-Sunni polemics or raising divisive points in the history of Sunni-Shia relations. His ecumenical approach to Islam is clearly intended to foster Islamic unity, a goal he shares with his Sunni counterparts.

In brief, Fadlallah meets all the elements of the definition of a mainstream Islamist, and it is only appropriate to consider his international relations' discourse in a book of this nature. This is not to deny, though, that there are radical elements in the discourses of Qaradawi and Fadlallah with regard to Israel and the Palestinian question, given their endorsement of suicide attacks, even when these target civilians, and their extreme reluctance to recognize the existence of the state of Israel, even if *de facto* and not *de jure*.[8] But if one were to rely on attitudes toward Israel as a litmus test of moderation, then hardly any mainstream Islamist would pass the test. In a brief reference, Bahi, for example, writes that "Western imperialism ... established (Israel)[9] as a Jewish state to prevent the Arab people from amalgamating (*al-takatul*) on the basis of a common Arabic language and a common Arab history."[10]

Sayyid Fadlallah: A Biographical Sketch

Sayyid Fadlallah was born in 1935 in the city of Najaf, one of Iraq's four cities that are revered by the Shias worldwide and that form a major center of religious learning. Both his parents were Lebanese, from the South of Lebanon, who moved to Najaf. His father, Sayyid 'Abdul Ra'ouf Fadlallah, was a renowned religious scholar (*mujtahid*) at the religious seminary (al-Hawza) of the city. His mother came from the Bazzi family, a prominent Shiite family from South Lebanon, which produced both religious and political leaders.[11] Comparatively speaking, Fadlallah came from a slightly more privileged background than his five Sunni counterparts did. One should not exaggerate, though, the level of material comfort that a religious scholar like Fadlallah's father could provide a family of ten children. In a comprehensive work on Fadlallah's life and thought, Jamal Sankari writes, "Sayyid Muhammad Hussein Fadlallah's childhood was conditioned by a climate of religious asceticism and erudition, a background of financial hardship, and by the harshness of the physical environment."[12] Equally important, Fadlallah, as a Sayyid, could trace his lineage to the prophet Muhammad through the latter's daughter, Fatima, and through Ali, the fourth caliph and the first Imam in Shia doctrine. That, by itself, earned him a level of respect and admiration among the Shia faithful and arguably among most devout Sunnis. Unlike his Sunni counterparts, Fadlallah came from a family of religious scholars as both his father and paternal grandfather were renowned *mujtahids*. But as this section will demonstrate, Fadlallah had many other fortes, besides his lineage. He was a skilled orator, a poet, an erudite scholar, an effective organizer, and a tireless advocate of the causes of the poor and the wretched.

While Fadlallah studied with different religious sources than those used in Sunni al-Azhar affiliated institutes, the basis of his studies—the Quran—was the same. As with the Sunni scholar sheikhs, Fadlallah internalized the Quran at an early age. His works are as anchored in the Quran as are the works of his Sunni counterparts. In his international relations' discourse, he quotes essentially the same verses that his Sunni counterparts quote, and he interprets these verses in a similar fashion. With his many endeavors, Fadlallah managed to complete a 24-volume exegesis of the Quran. His knowledge of the Quran is as deep and as detailed as that of his Sunni counterparts. Moreover, while his discourse, especially in his Friday sermons, abounds with references to the Shia heritage, the principal source he leans on throughout his discourse is the Quran, with ample references to the *hadith* too. A section of one of Fadlallah's many books is aptly titled: "The discourse of Islam is a Quranic discourse."[13] In summary, there are no marked differences between Fadlallah's argumentation style and the argumentation style of his Sunni counterparts, although Fadlallah tends to be more philosophical and reflective.

In line with the Sunni scholar sheikhs, Fadlallah underwent a similar rigorous religious education process at *al-Hawza*, whose instruction system was different from that followed at al-Azhar. There were no admission exams, or exams to determine promotion to the next year of study. The program of study comprised three consecutive levels: introduction (*muqadimaat*), intermediate (*sutuh*), and advanced (*bahth khariji*).[14] Fadlallah, like his father, successfully completed all three levels, achieving the status of a *mujtahid*, the Shia term for a religious scholar, around 1965. At Najaf, Fadlallah studied with some of the most renowned Shia scholars of the time. His mentors included three Grand Ayatollahs (*Ayatollah al-'Uzma*): the Iranian Mahmoud Shahroudi (1882–1974), the Iraqi Sayyid Muhsin al-Hakim (1889–1970), and Sayyid Abu al-Qasim al-Khoei (1899–1992).[15]

His *ijaza* (license) as a *mujtahid* was issued by Imam al-Khoei, his principal mentor in the advanced stage of his studies. Recognizing Fadlallah's talents and energy, al-Khoei designated him as his exclusive representative (*wakil*) in Lebanon, authorizing Fadlallah to collect the tithe (*al-khums*) from pious Shias in Lebanon and worldwide.[16] The Shia practice of paying one-fifth of their income on a voluntary basis to a religious scholar as well as the improved economic fortunes of many Lebanese Shias, especially those who migrated to Africa, provided Fadlallah with a significant source of income that, over the years, he judiciously used to build a dense nexus of schools, orphanages, other charities, and even income-generating activities. Fadlallah also established a radio station, (*izha'at al-Bachaer*), which regularly broadcast his Friday Sermons, and aired quotes of his pronouncements.[17] The financial resources at Fadlallah's disposal provided him with a level of financial independence from political authorities that none of his Sunni counterparts could dream of having. They also enabled him to exert patronage over a large segment of the Shia population, although his followers were mainly moved by his charisma and oratorical skills as a *Khatib*. The financial support that Qaradawi, the wealthiest of the Sunni scholar sheikhs, received from the state of Qatar and other benefactors pales in comparison.

Despite the rigors of his religious education, the young Fadlallah made time to read literature and poetry. The Iraq of the 1950s boasted a relatively sizable educated community that avidly consumed literary works that were emanating from Cairo, Beirut, Baghdad, and other parts of the Arab World. Taha Hussein, Badr Shaker al-Sayyab, Ahmad Shawqi, and Ilyas Abu Shabaka were among the literary figures whose works Fadlallah read.[18] Fadlallah also began to write poetry and participate in poetic competitions, to the chagrin of the more conservative elements of the religious establishment.[19] It is worth noting here that Qaradawi too composed poetry in his youth. His long poem, composed during his second imprisonment, was widely circulated among jailed Muslim Brotherhood members, earning him the scorn of the authorities and the admiration of Islamists.[20] In their mature years, both Qaradawi and Fadlallah repressed their penchant to compose poetry and focused on their sermons, fatwas, and religiously anchored scholarly works.

Fadlallah also began contributing editorials to the Iraqi periodical *al-Adwa' al-Islamiyya*, writing on Islamic subjects.[21] Fadlallah's first major work, entitled *Uslub al-Da'wa fi al-Qur'an*, (The Manner of calling for Islam in the Quran)[22] was written around 1960, when Fadlallah was only 25 years old. It was later followed by *al-Hiwar fi al-Qur'an* (Dialog in the Quran). These two early works are indicative of the direction that Fadlallah would take in his rich and prolific career as a preacher, *mujtahid*, and activist. They were written in a simple, straightforward style that appealed to lay readers, rather than to a narrow circle of jurists and religious scholars, and more significantly, they addressed issues of concern to the entire Muslim *umma*, veering clear of sectarian language in order to avoid rekindling old wounds between Sunnis and Shias. Most importantly, though, these works ought to be read against the backdrop of the political turbulence that Iraq witnessed in the aftermath of the 1958 Revolution that toppled the Hashemite monarchy. Under its first post-Revolution leader, Abd al-Karim Qasim (1958–1963), Iraq quickly became polarized between Prime Minister Qasim, who was backed by Iraq's Communist party (ICP),[23] on the one hand, and a loose coalition of Arab nationalists and religious figures from both the Sunni and Shia religious establishments, on the other.

The Shiite religious establishment at Najaf was alarmed at the growing influence of the ICP over Iraqi politics.[24] It also joined the Sunni religious establishment in opposing the recently promulgated Personal Status Law of 1959, which went beyond a strict interpretation of the *sharia* in expanding the rights of women.[25] The senior clerics at *al-Hawza* issued fatwas that prohibited belonging to the ICP and pressured the regime to disband the ICP and rescind the 1959 Personal Status Law.[26] A younger generation of rising Shiite scholars that included Fadlallah, the Lebanese Muhammad Mahdi Shams El-Din[27] and the Iraqi Sayyid Muhammad Baqir al-Sadr (1935–1980)[28] opted for a different approach. They resorted to a blend of political and social activism and public discourse that aimed to mobilize the Iraqi population behind an Islamist agenda that transcended sectarian divisions. In response to the multiple challenges posed by Western imperialism, communism, and an authoritarian left-leaning regime, these rising scholar sheikhs emphasized turning to Islam, especially to the Quran.

Underscoring the comprehensive nature of Islam (just as Qaradawi did), Fadlallah rejected borrowing alien concepts and notions to address the myriad political and socioeconomic challenges that faced Iraq, Lebanon, to which he relocated in 1965, and the broader Muslim *umma*. In line with his Sunni counterparts, Fadlallah became preoccupied, from a young age, with demonstrating that only by turning to Islam, especially the Quran, can the Muslim *umma* find answers to the perplexing questions it was facing. The Quran, read holistically and not selectively, and interpreted succinctly provides the linchpin of the discourses of mainstream Islamists.

It is now time to turn briefly to the substance of Fadlallah's first two works, noted above, which encapsulate his views on Islam and its relation to the political and social realms, including international relations. In both works, Fadlallah argues the centrality of dialog (*hiwar*), appeals to logic (*manṭiq*),[29] and appeals to innate human nature (*al-fiṭra al-insānīyya*)[30] to the peaceful spread of the Islamic message. Fadlallah here reiterates a core theme that also permeates the discourses of mainstream Sunni Islamists, namely that the message of Islam, as conveyed in the Quran, is so compatible with human reason and with human nature that no force is needed to spread it. Islam did not spread by the sword, as Orientalists claim, but by the sheer power of its values and its teachings that emphasize openness to the other (*infitah*), tolerance (*tasamuh*), and justice (*'adl*).[31] The role of force is to protect those peacefully calling for Islam from being killed or persecuted, and not to impose Islam on others, since "there can be no coercion in religion," as in verse 2:256. This verse, which is quoted extensively by all mainstream Islamists, also appears in all of Fadlallah's discourse. There is hardly a lengthy work by Fadlallah that does not refer to and elaborate on this verse.[32]

Both early works are also replete with reminders to those who seek to call for Islam, especially among the People of the Book, Christians and Jews, to pay heed to Quranic verses, such as 16:125, "Call to the way of your Lord with wisdom and fair counsel, and debate with them in the fairest manner," and 29:46, "Do not argue with the People of the Book except in the best manner."[33] Those who call for Islam (*du'at*) ought to resort to gentle exhortation and dialog with their non-Muslim interlocutors by highlighting the areas of agreement before debating divisive matters of religious belief or dogma.[34] Also, those who call others to Islam must do so in a wise manner that takes into account the social conditions and cultural traits of the people who are being entreated to embrace Islam.[35] The *du'at* ought to be in a state of "continuous movement, constantly searching for the best methods, best means, and shortest roads to guide the people and to win over their sentiments and minds to the side of the call to Islam, in accordance with Islam's principle of following the best direction in every matter and under all conditions and circumstances," Fadlallah argues.[36]

The centrality of dialog to the message of Islam is a recurrent theme in the discourse of another prominent Lebanese Shia cleric, Sheikh Muhammad Mahdi Shams al-Din. For Shams al-Din, "Islam, as a thought and as a *sharia*, emphasizes peace, reconciliation, and dialog in the case of difference."[37] While Shams al-Din did not write extensively on international relations, his views on the centrality of peace and dialog to international relations, the defensive purposes of jihad, and the impermissibility of coercing others to embrace Islam all place him firmly within the moderate-reformist mainstream camp of contemporary Islamists.[38]

In 1965, when he was around thirty years of age, Fadlallah completed his religious education at Najaf. He was issued his license to exercise ijtihad by his principal mentor, Grand Ayatollah al-Khoei.[39] The second and more active stage in Fadlallah's career, as a mujtahid, preacher, political activist, and overseer of multiple charitable organizations, was about to begin. The move to Lebanon, his ancestral land, was a landmark event for Fadlallah and for the Shia community in Lebanon.

Fadlallah was one of three Najaf trained scholars who not only dominated the Lebanese Shia religious establishment between the mid-1960s and the early 21st century, but who also came to play a leading role in articulating the voices of Lebanon's Shia community. The other two figures are Imam Musa al-Sadr[40] (the cousin of Imam Baqir al-Sadr) and Sheikh Muhammad Mahdi Shams al-Din (1936–2001).[41] Imam Musa al-Sadr disappeared under mysterious circumstances while on a visit to Libya in 1978. Shams al-Din, who succeeded al-Sadr as the President of Lebanon's Shiite Supreme Council (SSC), and Fadlallah remained active as religious and political leaders until their deaths in 2001 and 2010, respectively.

Fadlallah's immersion in Lebanese politics and in the politics of the region, especially since the onset of the Lebanese War in 1975, rendered him a controversial, and indeed divisive, figure in Lebanon and the Arab region. In the West and within conservative Arab circles, he was commonly identified as Hezbollah's spiritual guide. In 1985, he narrowly survived an assassination attack that claimed the lives of 80 bystanders, while injuring 200 others. Referring to a controversial book by Bob Woodward[42], Fadlallah accused the CIA and Saudi intelligence of being behind the attack.[43] Shortly before the attempt on his life was made, Fouad Ajami depicted Fadlallah as "Shia Beirut's most compelling preacher."[44]

While endorsing Hezbollah's rhetoric and positions, especially its resistance to Israel and coordination with revolutionary Iran, Fadlallah did not hold a formal position within Hezbollah, although he supplied it with rhetorical support, inspiration, and strategic guidance during its formative years.[45] Hezbollah itself always emphasized that its *marja'iyya* was the Supreme Leader in Iran, namely Ayatollah Khomeini until his death in June 1989 and then Ayatollah Khamenei. This did not change with Fadlallah's announcement of his own *marja'iyya* in 1995, a few years after the death of his mentor, Grand Ayatollah al-Khoei in 1992.[46]

The summer 2006 War between Israel and Hezbollah healed any rift between the two sides, as Fadlallah, who stayed in the southern suburbs despite incessant Israeli bombardment that demolished his residence, praised the party's steadfastness and resistance in the face of "Israeli aggression" and celebrated its "divine victory."[47] A final testament to Fadlallah's prominence was his large funeral procession on July 6, 2010, which was declared a day of national mourning in Lebanon. Hezbollah took the lead in organizing the funeral, with many of its cadres and thousands of its members participating in the funeral procession.[48] This partly reflected the party's ideological indebtedness to Fadlallah, and also its political acumen in recognizing the immensely popular cleric, even if posthumously, as one of its own.[49]

The Underpinning Principles of International Relations

Fadlallah's construct of international relations exists within the context of his understanding of Islam as a religion and a divinely ordained system that governs all aspects of individual and communal life. This construct also embodies Fadlallah's view of Islam as a dynamic religion that not only rejects tyranny, injustice, and oppression but also provides guidance on how to resist these evils. Fadlallah's notion of dynamic Islam (*al-Islam al-haraki*) translates into a vision of international relations that emphasizes active resistance to "oppressive" global and regional powers, particularly the United States and Israel, as well as Iraq under Saddam Hussein. This section first presents Fadlallah's views on the comprehensiveness of Islam, its dynamic nature, and its opposition to oppression. It then examines his construct of power and its centrality to resisting oppression and aggression and to advancing international justice. While the relationship between justice and international peace permeates the discourses of the other mainstream Sunni Islamists, Fadlallah fully develops the argument that there can be no international peace without international justice.

The Comprehensiveness of Islam

Fadlallah's discourse on the comprehensive nature of Islam is very much in line with the discourses of Qaradawi and the Sunni Islamists. The emphasis on the impossibility of separating political and social activism from a dynamic understanding of religion permeates Fadlallah's sermons and writings; thus, on the comprehensiveness of Islam, Fadlallah argues, "There is no separation between prayer and jihad, or between worship and politics... even prayer has a political meaning as a stance against the arrogant, the tyrants and all the oppressors"[50]; and "we reject separating religion from politics just like we reject separating man from his soul."[51] In Fadlallah's worldview, "religion's active role in human society encompasses all aspects of life: the political, the economical and the social."[52] In line with his Sunni counterparts, Fadlallah argues that Islam is different from Christianity and all other religions because it embodies a holistic system of ideas that guides all aspects of individual and group life. For Fadlallah, Islam "cannot be confined to the corner of the mosque," the mosque itself being not only a place of worship but also a political and a cultural arena. Mosques, Fadlallah writes, should be "restored to what they used to be: arenas for political, jihadist, and cultural work, as well as places of worship."[53] In brief, Islam is a dynamic system of thought that "molds a holistic [Islamic] persona, that is rooted in the creed, and covers all aspects of life offering rulings on all matters in such a manner that it does not leave any vacuum that others may fill."[54]

For Fadlallah, spirituality and faith, at the core of religion, should translate into active engagement in the political and social life of the *umma*.[55] Faith summons Muslims to strive to overcome sectarian and other divisions within the one *umma*, and it also empowers them to resist tyranny, oppression, and injustice, irrespective of whether these emanate from within the *umma* or from outside sources. Fadlallah and the other Sunni scholar sheikhs are united in their rejection of Sufism, and more generally of apolitical interpretations of Islam.

Echoing Qaradawi, Fadlallah writes, "Islam is a creed and a system (*nizham*), which meet at the beginning of the road and do not ever get separated afterwards."[56] This Islamic system (*nizham Islami*) revolves around the establishment of the Islamic state. In line with his Sunni counterparts, Fadlallah argues that Islam started as a peaceful call to Islam directed at the polytheists of Mecca and Arabia, but faced with oppression and persecution, the preservation and propagation of this call to Islam required the establishment of the Islamic state.[57] Similarly, Fadlallah's image of the first Islamic society and state mirrors that of his Sunni counterparts. Fadlallah notes, "Medina witnessed the emergence of the first well-knit (*mutamasik*) Islamic society within the framework of a state that met all the conditions and requirements of statehood."[58] The state came after the call for Islam and in support of that call. "The Islamic state represented God's sovereignty on earth," Fadlallah argues.[59] In Fadlallah's construct, the Islamic State is not an end in itself, but a means which preserves the message of Islam and conveys it to humanity in its entirety, employing all available peaceful means. The Islamic State, which first emerged in Medina, is the "politico-social body," whose principal purpose is to protect the call to Islam.[60] Fadlallah's instrumental view of the Islamic state allows him to adopt a far more critical stance toward existing majority-Muslim states than what his Sunni counterparts are willing to entertain. Fadlallah is, thus, far more critical of majority-Muslim states than his Sunni counterparts are, including Bahi and Qaradawi.

Nevertheless, Fadlallah's ontology of the state in Islam is identical to that of his Sunni counterparts. For all mainstream Islamists, the Islamic State, founded by the Prophet Muhammad, represented the indispensable and actually divinely ordained means to defend Islam and to provide it with the cradling environment to flourish and spread. The association between the Islamic state and the Prophetic mission that all Islamists, both mainstream and radical, emphasize helps explain the strong appeal of the notion of the Islamic state to the broad Arab and Muslim public, including in our contemporary era.[61]

The Dynamic Nature of Islam

While Qaradawi emphasizes the *wasatiyya* of Islam, Fadlallah underscores a dimension of Islam that is not often highlighted in the discourses of his Sunni counterparts, namely Islam's dynamic nature. For Fadlallah, Islam is a dynamic religion that embraces change, while holding tight to the constants of the Quran and the *sharia*. Fadlallah was not alone in detecting the dynamic element that runs through multiple verses of the Quran. Bernard Weiss had the following to say about the Quran's repeated invocations to humans to reflect on the "signs of God" that one observes in the natural world. Weiss writes:

> This theological reflection was inspired by the Qur'an itself, which alludes repeatedly to the "signs of God" (*ayaat Allah*) in the natural world and calls upon humans to ponder them. These signs consist, not of static objects, but of processes" the falling of the rain, the growth of plants, the development of complex forms of animal life, the movements of the celestial bodies, and so on.[62]

Moreover, Fadlallah's political and social theory, which encompasses his construct of international relations, exudes a revolutionary fervor that is not highly pronounced in the discourses of the previously discussed Sunni scholar sheikhs. Fadlallah's embrace of radical, indeed revolutionary, change within majority-Muslim states, and his adoption of much of the rhetoric of the Islamic Republic of Iran toward Western powers, especially the United States, and toward Israel, emanate from at least five overlapping factors, namely: 1) his Shii background that emphasizes the historic oppression of the Shias at the hands of the powers that be; 2) the influence of the 1979 Iranian Revolution which he wholeheartedly embraced;[63] 3) the perceived failure of Arab states to confront Israel and to defend the historic rights of the Palestinians and the rights of Muslims over Jerusalem; 4) his active resistance to Israel's occupation of South Lebanon, which lasted between 1978 and 2000; and 5) his own defiant and fiery, actually revolutionary, character.

The difference between Fadlallah and his Sunni counterparts is only a difference in degree, for we cannot dismiss the revolutionary element in the discourses of mainstream Islamists, such as Bahi and Qaradawi. Like Fadlallah, Bahi and Qaradawi condemned the governments of majority-Muslim countries for turning to the capitalistic West or to the socialist East for guidance in the organization of their polities, economies, and societies. They unabashedly advocated a return to the *sharia*, and the embrace of the Islamic solution (*al-hal al-Islami*) to all contemporary political and socioeconomic problems. They were also vociferous critics of Western colonialism, the former Soviet Union, the United States, and, above all, of Zionism. In terms of their perspectives on international relations, especially their embrace of realism and of power politics, Bahi and Qaradawi are closer to Fadlallah than they are to Shaltut, Abu Zahra, and the legally minded Zuhaili.

Stated briefly, at the core of Fadlallah's construct of international relations is his notion of motion or movement (*haraka*). Fadlallah views the universe to be in a continuous state of motion in accordance with the laws upon which God established it. Movement in the cosmos is not chaotic, for it is governed by universal laws (*sunnan kawniya*),[64] which can be gradually discovered by human reason and by science. Outside the realm of politics, Fadlallah's belief in the presence of these universal laws led him to declare that, since the beginning and the end of the lunar months can be scientifically determined, there is no point in waiting to see the new moon of Shawwal in order to end the fasting of Ramadan.

Thus, For Fadlallah, Islam teaches activism and not passivity. While Muslims should always think before they act, they must also translate their thoughts into action (praxis). A stoic attitude in the face of oppression and injustice is not in line with Islam's teachings.[65] Fadlallah interprets the often-quoted verse 22:40, "Had God not caused people to restrain one another, destruction would have fallen upon monasteries, churches, oratories, and other places of prayer, where the name of God is often mentioned" to mean that if righteous people do not actively resist oppression and corruption (*fasad*), great harm would befall them and would befall humanity.[66] Right must be backed by might, if it is to prevail. Power, the principal ingredient of international relations, is not a constant entity, so materially weak groups or states can empower themselves and can eventually prevail over stronger ones. In Fadlallah's religiously informed worldview, they are divinely commanded to do so. As Fadlallah and his Sunni counterparts never fail to remind us, the Muslim community started as a materially weak one, but through faith in God, trust in the Prophet, and internal solidarity, it quickly overcame its weakness and transformed itself to a formidable force on the international stage.

Generally, Fadlallah sees international relations primarily as an incessant struggle between the strong and the weak. While the strong will constantly seek to manipulate and dominate the weak, the latter must constantly strive to empower themselves by building their economies and militaries and by establishing stable and legitimate political systems that rest on popular support and popular trust in the leadership. The subsequent section will focus on Fadlallah's extensive discourse on power and empowerment.

Islam's Opposition to Oppression

For Fadlallah, the political and social realms are also governed by universal laws, which, nevertheless, provide individuals and groups with ample room to set their own destinies. When faced with tyranny, oppression, and injustice, people have to make a choice. They can acquiesce to these conditions, or they can rebel against them. At certain junctions, there is wisdom in acquiescing to injustice through the practice of *taqiyya* (dissimulation), such as when the power discrepancy is huge or when there is danger that resistance would lead to major strife within the *umma*.[67] Most of the time, though, a strategy of resistance to oppression and injustice is the right strategy, indeed the divinely ordained one.[68] Fadlallah's discourse makes repeated references to the oppression of Muslims at the hands of fellow Muslims, not only the historic oppression of the Shias but also the contemporary oppression of Sunni Islamists at the hands of secularists and Arab nationalists. In line with his Sunni counterparts, Fadlallah sees this type of oppression as an internal matter to the Muslim *umma* that the Muslim *umma* must rectify itself, without external intervention. The other type of oppression, the oppression of Muslims at the hands of non-Muslim powers, particularly the United States, the former Soviet Union, and Israel, falls duly within the remit of international relations. Here, Fadlallah categorically rejects a strategy of acquiescence, calling instead for resisting this oppression steadfastly and intelligently, using all available means, including the use of force or violence. In his principal work on jihad, *The Book of Jihad*, Fadlallah warns that tyrants (*al-tughat*) will misinterpret gestures of "love, mercy, and leniency" as manifestations of weakness and will respond by intensifying their oppression.[69] Oppression must be resisted, but resisting it requires the empowerment of the oppressed, so accordingly, the most fundamental principle of international relations is that force must be countered by equal or superior force. Fadlallah argues that as a dynamic religion, "Islam confronts oppression and deviance and destroys atheism and chaos." With fiery language, he goes on to note that "the legitimacy of terminating deviance (*al-inhiraf*) paves the way for terminating deviant people, when their termination is necessary for the termination of deviance."[70]

In the realm of international relations, Muslims are, thus, called upon to rectify the injustice that characterizes the relations between powerful and weak states. For Fadlallah, except in a few places such as the Islamic Republic of Iran, Muslims are dually oppressed by their governments and by the powerful states in the international system. In the Arab and Muslim worlds, widespread government suppression of Islamist movements and Islamist currents should be read against the backdrop of the prevailing unjust international order that seeks to keep Muslims, and more generally the oppressed, under the domination of oppressive non-Muslim powers. Fadlallah is highly skeptical of the motives of the powerful states in the international system.

This skepticism (or realism) has its sources in three planes, or images in the language of Kenneth Waltz[71]. First, it reflects Fadlallah's complex view of human nature that sees humans as capable of committing great evil when they possess excessive power and when they are not constrained by reason or religion. In *Kitab al-Jihad*, Fadlallah writes that, "Man is, in the first place, an animal. He possesses all that the animal possesses in terms of ferocious instinct and beastly desires." Fadlallah then cautions that man's "animal nature differs from the animal nature of other animals, since it is accompanied by reason that dilutes its excessiveness thus leashing instincts and calming the frenzy of desire."[72] The animal instincts in the human being and in the collective can be definitely reigned in through reason, religion, and authority, but can never be fully extinguished. Fadlallah's discourse includes many references to the mutually reinforcing roles of reason and religion in restraining the "natural" human inclination to follow base desires (*ahwa'*) and instincts. In a Friday Sermon, Fadlallah urged worshipers to "examine their desires in the light of reason and to examine their cravings (*shahwat*) in the light of the *sharia* of God and His Revelation to decide what to do and what not to do ... in order to delineate the road to paradise from the road to hell."[73]

Fadlallah's international relations discourse refers repeatedly to individual leaders who, driven by deep-seated hatreds, insecurities, and fanciful or unrealistic ideas, engaged in hurtful foreign policies. In a Friday Sermon, Fadlallah depicted former Iraqi dictator Saddam Hussein as a "mad tyrant, who acts militarily based on the madness that is rooted in his character."[74] For Fadlallah, Saddam Hussein's personality played a key role in triggering Iraq's "aggression" first against Iran in the Iran-Iraq war and later against Kuwait. In Fadlallah's view, Saddam's "aggressive" and "reckless" character inflicted great harm not only on Iran and Kuwait but also on Iraq itself.[75] Saddam's conduct also provided the

United States with the pretext to intensify its interventions in the region for its own benefit.[76] Fadlallah believes that the same applies to the United States.[77] George W. Bush's animosity toward Arabs and Muslims, and his identification with Israel and Zionism, influenced the US decisions to invade Afghanistan and later Iraq, and to back Israel unconditionally in its conflicts with the Palestinians and with neighboring Arab states.[78] Fadlallah vilifies at length another US statesman, whose personality and penchant to cause mischief, of course according to Fadlallah, played a major role in triggering the Lebanese civil war (1975–1989) and sawing division within the Arab world, namely the US former Secretary of State, Henry Kissinger (1973–1977).[79] Finally, Fadlallah argues that Israel's aggressive policies toward the Palestinians, the Lebanese, and the Arabs reflected both Israeli leaders' hatred of and contempt toward the Arabs, feelings shared by most of the Jewish population in Israel, as well as their fanciful belief that applying pressure on the Palestinians would lead them to compromise their historic right to the whole of Palestine.[80]

Second, and equally importantly, Fadlallah's skepticism regarding the intents of the major powers is predicated on his belief that their ruling elites are intent on exploiting and dominating other states for their self-interest. Fadlallah is highly critical of the democratic credentials of Western states, especially the United States. Influenced by the rhetoric of the Iranian Revolution, he sees democracy in the West as a façade that conceals deep political, racial, and socioeconomic inequalities, with the elites in all the major powers as focused on preserving their power and their privileges, rather than on advancing the interests of their people. Fadlallah, thus, argues that US policy toward the Arab and Muslim worlds largely reflects the interests of "monopolistic oil companies, the defense industry and US manufactring."[81] But unlike Qaradawi and Bahi, who emphasize the crusading/Christian proselytizing element in Western, including US, policy toward the Muslim world, Fadlallah contends that the modern West has, by and large, severed its ties with Christianity. In an important work on Christian-Muslim dialog, Fadlallah writes, "The struggle between dynamic Islam and imperialism does not take the form of a Christian-Muslim struggle. For the West is not Christian in its political system, its politics and its values, it is secular and moves within the sphere of domination, repression, and violence."[82] Thus, for Fadlallah, the arrogance (*al-istikbar*) that characterizes the relations of the Western powers with the Muslim, and broader, third world is a reflection of its secularist/atheist and materialist present and not its forgotten Christian past.

It must be noted here that Fadlallah constantly reminds his audience to distinguish between the people of Western Europe and America and their governments, and not to blame the people or harm them because of the misdeeds of their rulers.[83] In a statement from the early 1990s, Fadlllah notes, "We are not against the American people, but we are against the American administration in its management and its leadership of the World."[84] The only country where Fadlallah does not distinguish between the people and the government is Israel. In Fadlallah's view, the overwhelming majority of the Jewish people in Israel and worldwide share the Israeli leaders' hatred of and contempt toward the Palestinians.[85] Of the six scholar sheikhs discussed in this work, Fadlallah exhibits the greatest level of animosity not just toward Israel, but also toward the Jewish people as a whole. Fadlallah, thus, dwells on the history of alleged Jewish hostility toward and plotting against the Prophet Muhammad more than his Sunni counterparts do.[86]

Third and last, Fadlallah shares Bahi and Qaradawi's doubts about the effectiveness and the fairness of international institutions, including the United Nations. Unlike the legalist-minded Zuhaili, these three scholar sheikhs tend to view these international institutions as dominated by the powerful states and working to serve their interests. Fadlallah, thus, views the UN Security Council as a body that merely rubber stamps the decisions of the US National Security Council, conferring on it international legitimacy.[87] One should not confuse the skepticism of these three "realist" scholar sheikhs regarding the efficacy of international institutions and their deep-seated suspicions about the intents of the major powers, with an advocacy of a confrontational stance relative to these states. All three scholar-sheikhs understand that an open-ended confrontation with these powers would have disastrous consequences for the Muslim *umma*. What they advocate instead is a nuanced strategy that allows for significant cooperation with the major, non-Muslim powers for mutual benefit, but that also leaves ample room for the Muslim powers to act independently in pursuit of their common interests and to collectively challenge these powers when need be. For Fadlallah, while peace is desirable, it remains precarious, its preservation dependent on the ability of the weak powers in the international system to build their power bases in order to narrow the power differential between them and the powerful states. The road toward a more peaceful and a more just international order starts with the empowerment of the weak.

The Centrality of Power to International Relations

Fadlallah's discourse refers in detail to power and its centrality to human relations, especially international relations. Fadlallah, thus, writes, "It is a well-known fact that power today is the principal entry point to the realm of international relations that are based on parity and mutual respect."[88] Fadlallah's treatment of power is simultaneously philosophical and practical. He is one of a few contemporary Islamists to openly state that God is the creator of power (*khaleq al-quwa*), and to emphasize that since "power is a gift from God, the human being ought to use it in the path of God,"[89] underscoring the divine origin of power. As noted, power, for Fadlallah, is a dynamic entity which grows or diminishes based on multiple factors that have to do with population dynamics, geography, the economy, the legitimacy of the political system, the quality of the political and military leadership, and the morale of the population. In a Friday Sermon, Fadlallah urged worshippers to think of their current weakness vis-a-vis powerful states as only temporary in nature, reminiding them that "all the powerful in the world were once weak but then they grabbed power." He continued to note, "Great Britain used to rule the seas, but it is now a fourth, or fifth, rank power in the political, economical, and military realms, whaeras America used to be a colony of Britain and it is now the premier country in the world (*awal dawla fi al 'alam*)."[90]

Fadlallah assigns equal emphasis to the tangible and the intangible dimensions of power, with belief in the justice of one's cause and faith in God as important determinants of power.[91] Victory in battle does not only require proper military preparedness and the presence of an intelligent and dedicated political and military leadership but also depends on the high discipline and the high morale of the combatants. Faith in God instills in the believers discipline, perseverance, and generates high morale.[92]

Fadlallah discusses in detail the centrality of faith to the empowerment of the weak, emphasizing that God's message to the weak is to empower themselves, utilizing all available lawful means for that purpose; thus, his discourse is a discourse of empowerment, with power starting in the mind. Fadlallah writes, "We need to imbue the logic of power into our own logic as God intended us to do." He then quotes three Quranic verses that emphasize the centrality of power to the life of the believer.[93]

The quest for international justice, a preoccupation of all mainstream Islamists, depends on the ability and the willingness of the righteous to confront the wicked. When the balance of power is heavily tilted in favor of the latter, as is often the case, the righteous must invest in their own empowerment. Quoting verse 4:97, "Those whom the angels cause to die while wronging themselves—to them the angels shall say: What was your former condition? They shall respond: We were considered weaklings on earth. The angels shall say: was not the land of God wide enough for you to emigrate into," Fadlallah emphasizes that the oppressed weak (*al-mustad'afeen*) are divinely commanded to empower themselves in order to resist their oppressors. God will not forgive them if they fail to do so, Fadlallah argues.[94] Resigning to weakness when there are ways to overcome it is tantamount to sinning, for "God loathes the weak worshipper who, while possessing power, does not use it."[95] In summary, a hallmark of Fadlallah's discourse is the notion that humans can overcome their weaknesses by turning to God and by believing in their own worth and their own latent capacities.[96]

Despite its centrality to all human relations, power is not an end in itself but is a means to ensure survival, at a minimum; beyond that, it is the indispensable instrument for rectifying injustices at the local and the international levels. In Fadlallah's dynamic view of the universe and of the role of religion in it, the quest for power is universal. Different individuals and different entities, including states, however, deploy power for different purposes. Power can be used in a good way, namely to resist oppression and remove injustices, which is the positive dimension of power. But power can also be used in a bad way. It clearly can be employed to oppress and to dominate others, which represents the negative dimension of power. Fadlallah anchors this pivotal distinction between the two faces of power in Quranic verse 4:76, "Those who believe fight in the cause of God, and those who disbelieve fight in the cause of idolatry. So fight the followers of Satan, for Satan's cunning is feeble indeed."[97] While other mainstream Islamists address the issue of the proper legitimate uses of power, Fadlallah stands out for advancing the notion of the "ethics of power" (*akhlaqiyat al-quwa*).[98] Although this pivotal notion remains underdeveloped in his discourse, it is clear that he uses it to describe the circumstances under which it is lawful to use force and, more broadly, to define the legitimate purposes of power.

In Fadlallah's view, shared by the mainstream Sunni Islamists, Muslims, i.e., those who believe, seek power not to oppress and dominate others but to avoid the oppression and the domination of others.[99] Beyond self-defense, Muslims have the duty to employ their power in the aid of those who are oppressed worldwide, especially when they are Muslims. There are, however, nuanced differences among the mainstream Islamists regarding what forms of power are to be used beyond self-preservation. Compared to his mainstream Sunni counterparts, Fadlallah has a more ambitious, in fact revolutionary, international agenda that revolves around aiding the oppressed, including non-Muslims, and fighting the forces of arrogance, oppression and domination worldwide.

Mainstream Sunni Islamists, on the other hand, are extremely reluctant to advocate any agenda that commits Muslim governments to the use of force, except for self-defense. As long as the *wulat al-amr* exercise their prime duty to protect the homeland, they are to exercise judgment when it comes to the use of force outside their borders. They must engage in a careful analysis of the costs and benefits of such interventions, while taking into account the prior commitments of their nations under international law. Despite these important differences, there is a consensus amongst mainstream Islamists that power should be used in the service of justice since power is a means, and justice is an end. When power fails to serve justice, it becomes oppressive power that ought to be resisted.

At the risk of oversimplifying, it should be noted here that there is one basic, albeit profound, idea that all mainstream Islamists agree on, namely that Muslim states should not use their power to oppress other states nor should they aid oppressors. Fadlallah's vision of international relations emphasizes mutual respect for the freedom, security, and legitimate interests of all states. In one of multiple references to this theme, and addressing himself primarily to the major powers, Fadlallah notes:

> As Muslims, we have said, from the outset, that all that we want from [the rest of] the world is for it to respect our freedom if it wants us to respect its freedom, to respect our security if it wants us to respect its security and to interact positively with our interests if it wants us to interact positively with its interests. We understand that [the rest of] the world has interests in our [part of the] world and we have interests in [the rest of] the world. [The rest of] the world needs some of what we have; and we need some of what [the rest of] the world has. Let the relationship be based on mutual respect for rights, obligations and wealth.[100]

On Jihad and War

Whether in sermons, interviews with the media or book length studies, Fadlallah addressed the connected notions of jihad and resistance (*muqawama*) at length. This section relies primarily on Fadlallah's principal work on jihad, *The Book of Jihad*. Just as Qaradawi does, Fadlallah begins his discussion of jihad by deriving the term from its two Arabic roots *jahd* and *juhd*.[101] Fadlallah acknowledges that fighting is not the only form of jihad, noting that the jihad of speech (jihad *al-kalima*) that aims at winning over the minds and hearts of people with persuasion and the use of logical proofs is the primary form of jihad. The persecution that the first Muslims in Mecca endured, because of their embrace of the new religion, was clearly a form of jihad.[102] In line with the mainstream Sunni

Islamists, Fadlallah maintains that jihad as fighting emerged shortly after the *hijra* to Mecca, around the time of the battle of Badr.[103]

While his view of the purposes of jihad as *qital* is in line with that of his Sunni counterparts, especially Qaradawi, Fadlallah places major emphasis on resistance as a principal purpose of jihad. Fadlallah conflates the notions of jihad and *muqawama* (resistance), as is seen in the title of one of his works,[104] whereas his Sunni counterparts do not use the term *muqawama* that much. This could be a purely semantic difference, for no mainstream Sunni Islamist would deny that the resistance by Palestinians, by the Lebanese against Israel, or by the Iraqis against the post-2003 US occupation of Iraq, represent forms of jihad. For Fadlallah, the "Islamic resistance" to Israel in South Lebanon is a response to God's invocation to Muslims to resist aggression as in verse 8:60, "Prepare for them whatever force and war cavalry you can gather to frighten therewith the enemy of God and your enemy."[105]

Fadlallah's identification of jihad with resistance arguably reflects his unequivocal embrace of Hezbollah's "Islamic resistance" to the Israeli occupation of parts of South Lebanon (1978–2000). Fadlallah's colleague, Sheikh Muhammad Mahdi Shams El-Din, also identifies the close association between resistance and jihad, noting that resistance to occupation, whether by regular armies or by armed groups and "whether carried out in the open or in secret in the form of guerilla warfare," is a legitimate form of defensive jihad that is "required, without any doubt, by the Quran and the Sunna as well as by reason and the consensus of Muslims."[106] According to Shams al-Din, resistance Jihad is "incumbent on the whole *umma*, and on every group and every individual within it, until sufficient force has been marshalled to repel the aggression."[107]

The Purposes of Jihad

In *Kitab al Jihad*, Fadlallah identifies at least five purposes of jihad as *qital* (fighting).[108] The first purpose has more to do with building the power base, especially the military capabilities, of the Muslim community or Islamic state than with fighting *per se*. Fadlallah here argues that building the military and other capabilities of the Muslim community provides the believers with an extra layer of assurance that their lives and properties will be safe, and, above all, they will be free to practice Islam and to call for it, with the first and most fundamental level of assurance coming from faith itself. This first purpose of jihad can be understood as defending the Muslim community not just against actual aggression but also against potential aggression. One purpose of jihad is, thus, to "establish sufficient deterrent power that frightens the enemy of Islam and of the Muslims; and stop him from even thinking of aggressing against them." For further clarity, Fadlallah adds that this "purpose of jihad is a precautionary one (*wiqa'i*) to the core."[109] Fadlallah here is primarily addressing the role of power as a deterrent against aggression, bringing to sharp relief a principal argument that mainstream Islamists advance, namely that jihad ought to be construed broadly to include not just fighting but also preparing for fighting. Military preparedness reduces the risk of being defeated in war and also deters potential aggressors when the enemy realizes that the military and economic situation of the Muslims is superior to theirs.[110] Fadlallah's view of power as a deterrent against aggression is very much in line with the mainstream Sunni Islamists treatment of deterrence. The basis of what one may refer to as a mainstream Islamist perspective on deterrence can be found in Quranic verse: 8:60, "Prepare for them whatever force and war cavalry you can gather to frighten therewith the enemy of God and your enemy," that Fadlallah and the mainstream Islamists regularly quote.

The second purpose of jihad is to defend Muslims' freedom of belief against the oppression of unbelievers who seek to turn Muslims away from their religion or to restrict their freedom to call for Islam by peaceful means.[111] Underscoring the dynamic nature of Islam, Fadlallah does not waiver in his belief that Islam cannot be confined to a specific people or a specific geographic area, for the message of Islam is a universal message intended for the entire humanity.[112] Muslims are divinely commanded to spread the message of Islam by logical proofs, gentle exhortation and good example, but without resorting to any coercion or threats. Others, however, will place material obstacles to try and stop the peaceful spread of Islam, and in this case, it becomes lawful to fight them.[113] While there is full agreement among mainstream Islamists that it is lawful to fight those who place material obstacles in the face of the peaceful call for Islam, Fadlallah is far more forceful in making this point than his Sunni counterparts are. Fadlallah, nevertheless, fully subscribes to the mainstream Islamist thesis that force cannot be used to coerce others to adopt Islam.

Fadlallah clarifies the relationship between jihad and the call for Islam, noting, "Jihad provides the material power that protects the message of Islam and paves the way for its [peaceful] spread."[114] Fadlallah, however, insists that the line between ensuring others' freedom to choose Islam and coercing them ito embrace Islam should never be crossed. Fadlallah joins his Sunni counterparts in refuting the argument that Islam was spread by force, i.e., by the sword, noting that it was at times of peace that Islam spread the furthest, and that large populations in Africa, Asia, and other parts of the world embraced Islam without the faintest threat of the use of force.[115]

In line with the mainstream Sunni Islamists discussed here, Fadlallah maintains that the wars that the Prophet fought were defensive ones that aimed at protecting the nascent Muslim community from the aggression of the polytheists and at preserving the freedom to call for Islam.[116] Based on a review of the pertinent Quranic verses and prophetic *hadiths*, Fadlallah comes to the conclusion that "had the Prophet been allowed to carry out his mission [of peacefully calling for Islam] and had the Polytheists not stood in his way, persecute his supporters, prevent them from practicing Islam, and expel them from their homes, there would not have been war, nor would have there been fighting [with the polytheists.]"[117] Accordingly, the only legitimate purpose of force is to assure those who wish to embrace Islam of their own volition that no harm will befall them or befall their families, and that their properties, trade, and freedom will not be impacted. For Fadlallah, when moral power that emanates from faith is supplemented by material power, nothing will be able to stand in the way of the peaceful spread of Islam.

The third, and arguably most ambitious, purpose of jihad is to aid oppressed people everywhere against the powers that oppress them. In the contemporary era, these oppressive powers are either referred to collectively as the colonial and imperial powers, or the forces of international insolence, or are specifically named with the United States topping the list, but closely followed by Europe and Israel. But the term "oppressive powers" is broad enough to encompass the Iraqi regime under Saddam Hussein and the Arab regimes that pursued separate peace deals with Israel, particularly Egypt, Jordan, and the Palestinian National Authority. In Fadlallah's worldview, the conservative Gulf monarchies that have allied themselves with the United Sates against revolutionary Iran also clearly fall within the category of oppressive powers. Despite his fiery polemics against these oppressive international and regional powers, Fadlallah falls short of calling for jihad against them. As noted, Fadlallah criticized the September 11, 2011, attacks on the United States on both moral and practical grounds.[118]

He, however, legitimated armed resistance against the US occupation of Iraq by both Sunni and Shia groups, despite his deep-seated hatred of the Saddam Hussein regime.[119] Most importantly, Fadlallah was unequivocal in embracing the resistance against Israel in South Lebanon and in Palestine, viewing it as the most exalted form of Jihad in the contemporary period, given Israel's "aggression" against Arabs and Muslims and its occupation of Jerusalem and the Aqsa Mosque. Fadlallah's open call for jihad was, thus, restricted to specific theaters

(Post-2001 Afghanistan, post-2003 Iraq, South Lebanon, and the Palestinian territories) that, in the view of all mainstream Islamists and indeed of Arab nationalists, were parts of the Arab world that were invaded by external non-Muslim powers.[120] Despite his fiery anticolonial and anti-Zionist polemics, Fadlallah did not call for carrying the fight with the oppressors beyond these locales.

Jihad also aimed at undermining the power of polytheists and smashing their might in order to minimize the harm they could inflict on Muslims and to erode their ability to stop the peaceful spread of the message of Islam.[121] Fadlallah here invokes the psychological and politico-social environment in pre-Islamic Arabia, noting that the Arabs appreciated material power and would not have easily sided with the weak nascent Islamic state against the mighty Quraysh and its allies. Breaking the military might of Quraysh, as the Prophet did at the battle of Badr, was necessary to assure the Muslims of the justice of their cause and to enhance the prestige of the nascent Islamic state in the eyes of the Arabs.[122] In line with his Sunni counterparts, Fadlallah maintains that the polytheists were the party that initiated aggression against the Muslims by persecuting them and driving them from Mecca.

The battle of Badr was, in the first place, just retaliation against the aggression of the polytheists who persecuted the first Muslims, but it also served to demonstrate the growing military prowess of the nascent Muslim community.[123] Fadlallah is aware that material power has not lost its luster in the contemporary era. In facing the polytheists of the contemporary period, namely, the Marxists, the materialists, the atheists, the imperialists, and the Zionists, Muslims need to supplement their spiritual power that emanates from their faith with the material power that comes from economic development, military buildup, and technological advancements. The quest for material power is a form of jihad, for without it jihad as *qital* would be suicidal.

The fifth purpose of jihad is for Muslims to defend their lives, properties, lands, and what they hold sacred. This is clearly the most basic, or most elementary, form of jihad since it aims at repelling aggression. There is a consensus among mainstream Islamists that it is not only the right of Muslims to defend themselves, but it is their duty to do so. In the view of Fadlallah and the other mainstream Islamists, the Muslims are not just a people, an *umma*, united by a common creed. They are an *umma* appointed by God (or brought forth by God as in Quranic verse 3:110) and entrusted with spreading the message of Islam. If the Muslims allow themselves to be conquered, not only would they lose their independent existence, but they would also forfeit the ability to call for Islam, which is their raison d'être.

While more fiery, Fadlallah's discourse on the purposes of jihad is not fundamentally different from the discourses of his Sunni counterparts. Fadlallah quotes the same verses on fighting that the mainstream Sunni scholar sheikhs quote and interprets them in a similar way. In line with his Sunni counterparts, Fadlallah categorically rejects the notion that jihad aims at coercing non-Muslims to embrace Islam.[124] Fadlallah's treatment of why there can be no coercion in religion is, however, more philosophical than the treatments of his Sunni counterparts. Fadlallah argues that powerful ideas, which are logical, realistic, and perfectly aligned with innate human nature, do not need force to find their way into the hearts and minds of reasonable people. "God forbid that the logic of Allah [the Quran] be a feeble logic that can be suppressed by any other logic," Fadlallah argues.[125] Accordingly, to claim that Islam cannot take hold of the human soul and mind without force is to diminish its intrinsic worth as a divine system of ideas that is superior to all other ideational systems.[126]

In summary, Fadlallah embodies the mainstream Islamist thesis that jihad is defensive and not offensive in nature. Jihad is also not an end in itself,[127] but it aims at protecting Muslims from the oppression and domination of others; and not at oppressing and dominating others. After quoting several Quranic verses, Fadlallah concludes that "jihad in Islam is a defensive movement (*haraka difa'iyya*) against those who want to impose aggression on people, it is a movement in support of the wronged ones and the oppressed."[128] Fadlallah emphasizes that in the contemporary era, the preparations for jihad and its declaration have become the responsibility of the state and not of private individuals and groups.[129] Fadlallah shares the apprehensions of his Sunni counterparts about private individuals and groups, such as Osama bin Laden and al-Qaeda, calling for jihad, and thus implicating their countries and the entire *umma* in dangerous and illegitimate ventures. Fadlallah is not internally consistent on this pivotal matter, though, for he did support the "resistance" of Hezbollah and of Hamas against Israel, while being fully aware that these entities were not states.

The Ethics of War

Fadlallah's treatment of how jihad ought to be pursued, i.e., the conduct of war, is not as detailed as the treatment of Qaradawi and Zuhaili. Fadlallah refers to the rules that govern the conduct of war as the "ethics of war" (*akhlaqiyat al-harb*), a term that we rarely encounter in the discourses of his Sunni counterparts.[130] Nonetheless, Fadlallah fully subscribes to the views of his Sunni counterparts regarding the need to offer the enemy a choice between embracing Islam or paying the *jizya* before hostilities start. Fadlallah adds that this offer should be genuine and not mere rhetoric before engaging the enemy in fighting.

Quoting a prophetic *hadith*, Fadlallah maintains that winning over souls to Islam is always more desirable than acquiring any material gains.[131] He also maintains that civilians should be spared as much as possible the scourges of war. In this regard, Fadlallah produces a *hadith* by Shia Imam Jaafar al-Sadiq, who narrates that the Prophet Muhammad used to address his forces as such before marching to battle, "March in the name of Allah . . . March as partisans of the Prophet of Allah. Do not commit excesses, do not mutilate bodies, do not kill old men, teens, and women and do not cut trees except when militarily necessary. . . If someone approaches you in peace [to learn about Islam] give him sanctuary until he hears the word of God, if he does not accept Islam [of his own free will] let him return in peace."[132] Versions of this often-quoted *hadith* appear in the discourses of most mainstream Sunni Islamists.

Once hostilities start, the Muslims' attention must be focused on winning the battle. Victory may require resorting to deceit (*al-khid'a*)[133] and/or inflicting serious casualties among enemy combatants in order to make them fearful and drive them to surrender. Fadlallah interprets verse 8:66, "It is not fitting for a prophet to hold prisoners until he has achieved supremacy in the land" as a divine rebuke of the Muslim combatants, and indeed of the Prophet himself, at the battle of Badr for getting distracted by capturing prisoners, instead of remaining focused on killing more polytheists in order to frighten the Qurayshites and, thus, deter them from further aggression.[134] In line with the mainstream Sunni Islamists, Fadlallah emphasizes that all tactical matters regarding the waging of war must be left to *wulat al-amr* and their military commanders, as respecting the chain of command is a prerequisite for military victory.[135]

While he emphasizes that it is not lawful to target civilians, for Fadlallah it is difficult to maintain the distinction between combatants and civilians in the contemporary era since the waging of war is highly dependent on the mobilization of the home front to produce and transport the armaments and other material that are crucial for modern warfare.[136] In war, absolute priority must be given to achieving military victory or at least avoiding defeat. If achieving victory (or avoiding defeat) requires the targeting of civilians, then targeting them becomes lawful.[137] The deliberate targeting of civilians is, however, the exception and not the norm; it is a weighty decision that ought to be left to the determination of *wulat al-amr*. But Fadlallah does state that even at the time of the Prophet, long before the emergence of modern warfare, the separation between combatants and noncombatants was not a straightforward matter.

In line with his Sunni counterparts, Fadlallah does not shy away from addressing the circumstances under which it becomes lawful to slay aged men, women, and monks, but not teens. Using examples from the *Sira* of the Prophet, Fadlallah is adamant that if aged men participate in battle physically or provide counsel to the combatants, then they are to be treated as combatants.[138] The same applies to women, although Fadlallah cautions that the killing of women should be seen as a last, extreme resort with lesser punishments, such as imprisonment, being more appropriate in this case.[139] Monks, who are supplicating in high mountains, are to be treated the same way as aged men. As long as they stay away from combat, whether physically or by encouraging or counseling enemy combatants, their lives are to be spared.[140]

Fadlallah's treatment of the issue of the prisoners of war is very much in line with that of the mainstream Sunni Islamists, especially Zuhaili's, whose seminal work *Athar al-Harb* he often quotes. Fadlallah maintains that the principal Quranic verse which provides guidance on the fate of prisoners of war is verse 49:4. The verse specifies only two options regarding the fate of prisoners once war is over: unconditional release (*minna*), and release in exchange for Muslim prisoners or a ransom (*fida'*). Fadlallah notes, in passing, that the mentioning of *minna* before *fida'* in the verse is perhaps intended to encourage Muslims to act mercifully and to unconditionally release their prisoners once war is over.[141]

Just as Qaradawi and Zuhaili do, Fadlallah grapples with the issue of reconciling between verse 49:4 and the practice of the Prophet, which included killing some prisoners and enslaving others. Similar to Qaradawi and Zuhaili, Fadlallah maintains that the Prophet sanctioned the killing of only a handful of prisoners as just punishment for their prior aggression against Muslims. Fadlallah, thus, writes, "If one reflects on the nature of the prisoners of war who were killed, and even their number, One can easily notice that that this was an exceptional measure, carried out for very special reasons that emanated from the extremes to which these individuals went in their enmity toward Islam and Muslims and the grave harm they inflicted."[142]

Fadlallah deals in more detail with the subject of slavery in Islam, noting that the Prophet and subsequent Muslim rulers engaged in this practice because it was customary between warring entities.[143] Enslaving defeated enemy combatants was a just retaliation for the enslavement of Muslims by their enemies and a deterrent against such future acts of enslavement.[144] Fadlallah points out correctly that both the Byzantine and the Persian Empires engaged in slavery and that slavery was not outlawed in the Torah or the Christian Bible.[145] A recurrent theme in the discourses of Fadlallah and the mainstream Islamists is that Islam favored the abolition of slavery but adopted a gradual approach to that. Accordingly, the eventual worldwide abolition of slavery was very much in line with the intents of Islam.[146]

The common voice of mainstream Islamists is that Muslims, whether as individuals or as states, should unequivocally embrace the current international norm that prohibits all forms of slavery, including slavery arising from war. Fadlallah writes clearly that in the contemporary era "there can be no justification or pretext for enslavement; slavery has become a nonissue. It has no meaning in contemporary international and human relations."[147] In the same vein, Fadlallah and the mainstream Islamists contend that Muslim states should abide by prevalent international norms and conventions, primarily the Geneva Conventions, regarding the humane treatment of prisoners of war, emphasizing that these norms conform to the *sharia*.[148]

The Ending of War

Fadlallah's discourse on the ending of war is in line with the discourses of his Sunni counterparts, but not as extensive as those of Zuhaili and Qaradawi. For Fadlallah, war ends either with a temporary peace (*sulh mu'aqat*) or a permanent peace (*sulh da'em*).[149] Fadlallah uses fluid terminology, *sulh mu'aqat* and *hudna* (truce) are delpoyed interchangeably, and the same applies to *sulh da'em* and *salam* (peace).[150] Based on a quick review of the opinions of Shia jurists, while making reference to Zuhaili's *Athar al-Harb*, Fadlallah argues that both methods of ending war and reestablishing peace are consistent with the *sharia*.

The decision to pursue a temporary or a permanent end to war is to be made by *wali al-amr*, who would consult individuals with knowledge and expertise.[151] In Fadlallah's construct, neither the *'ulama* nor those who loosen and bind (in the Sunni tradition) have a real say in decisions about initiating or ending wars. *Wulat al-amr* have absolute jurisdiction in this area as they are the ones to determine the public interest (*al-maslaha al-'amma*). Fadlallah, nevertheless, offers some sensible guidelines to *wulat al-amr*, noting that the Muslim side should not seek or accept an end to hostilities when the Muslims have the upper hand and are confident of victory.[152] Equally important, the decision to end or to suspend hostilities should not be driven exclusively by military calculations but should include political and economic considerations.[153] Fadlallah does not rule out making payments to the enemy to end, or even avoid, a war when the balance of power is heavily tilted against the Muslim side, or if a certain exigency warrants ending or suspending the war effort.[154] The common thread in the discourses of

Fadlallah and the mainstream Islamists is that war, in all its dimensions, is a very serious matter that ought to be handled by those in authority in light of the *sharia* and also in light of the Muslims' public interest.[155]

The Road to Islamic Unity

As noted, the one Muslim *umma* constitutes Fadlallah's principal unit of analysis, and, in line with his Sunni counterparts, Fadlallah romanticizes the *umma*. In a Friday Sermon, he referred to the watchful and vigilant *umma* (*al-umma al-waʿiyya*) that supports those leaders who stand for the cause of the truth (*al-haq*), while dismissing those who stand for the cause of falsehood (*al-batil*).[156] Accordingly, Fadlallah is as preoccupied with the subject of Islamic unity as his Sunni counterparts are, but as a Shia religious scholar, his construct of Islamic unity does not revolve around the restoration of the caliphate, an office historically dominated by Sunni dynasties. Fadlallah and the Sunni mainstream Islamists start from the same point, namely that the Prophet Muhammad established an Islamic state in Medina during his lifetime.[157] For all Islamists, mainstream and radical, this is the model state that all Muslims should strive to bring back to reality. Fadlallah's views on the Islamic state are arguably influenced by his reading at a young age, while a student at *al-hawza*, of al-Mawdudi and Sayyid Qutb, two contemporary Sunni Islamists.[158] What brings Fadlallah even closer to the mainstream Sunni camp is his generally positive view of Islamic history, despite it being dominated by Sunni dynasties. Clearly, in his Friday sermons, Fadlallah made ample references to Imam ʿAli as the rightful successor to the Prophet, the martyrdom of Hussain at Karbala, and the historic persecution of the Shias.[159] This heavily Shia rhetoric is, however, largely absent in his multiple interviews with the press and his academic writings. In *The Book of Jihad*, Fadlallah even makes a positive reference to the famous Umayyad Caliph Umar ibn Abd al-Aziz, also known as Umar II, despite the Shiite animosity to the entire Umayyad dynasty.[160] In the same work, Fadlallah notes, though in passing, that the Shias did fight on the side of unjust Sunni rulers when Islamic lands were attacked by the *kufar* (the Byzantines, Crusaders and Mongols).[161] In one of his Friday semons, Fadlallah narrated that when Imam Ali was warned that the King of the Byzantines (*Malik al-Roum*) could use this internal strife to attack Muslim lands during the battle of Safin with Muawiyya, his response was "in that case, Muawiyya and I would be against him".[162] Fadlallah sees in the diversity of *mazhhabs* a source of richness to Islam, as long as the sectarian identity does not overshadow the common Islamic identity.[163] The thrust of his argument is that those like himself who embrace openness to and dialog with non-Muslims, cannot but embrace, with even greater force and conviction, dialog among the followers of different *mazhhabs* within Islam.[164] This dialog is necessary because the "different mazhhabs are no more than different understandings of the Quran and the sayings of the Prophet."[165]

The theological and juristic differences among the Sunnis and Shias, Fadlallah insists, constitute differences over details and not over fundamentals.[166] Throughout Fadlallah's massive oeuvre, one cannot discern any criticisms of the beliefs of the Sunnis or any insinuation that their understanding of Islam is an erroneous understanding. Fadlallah is very much aware of the theological and juristic differences between the Shia *mazhhab* and the Sunni *mazhhabs*, but he simply chooses not to address these differences since his concerns lie elsewhere. In Fadlallah's worldview, the multiple challenges and threats that the Muslim world faces in the contemporary era do not allow Muslims the luxury to dwell on their past internal differences and mutual animosities.[167] Fadlallah argues that the "existential issues" (*al-qadaya al-masiriyya*) confronting the Muslim *umma* today "necessitate that Muslims freeze their differences, or change the mentality with which they approach these differences, or the style by which they manage them, in order to reach the shore of safety."[168] Clearly, Fadlalah prioritizes his Islamic identity over any other identity, including his Shiism, and expects others to think and act accordingly. In a Friday Sermon, Fadlallah argued, "We must think in an Islamic way and set forth from this base in all our thinking."[169] In another sermon, Fadlallah noted, "We must treat the Islamic world as one unit. The Islamic world, in our consciousness, represents a single unit." Fadlallah then quotes a well-known Prophetic *hadith*, one that also appears in the discourses of his Sunni counterparts, to the effect that the Muslims constitute a single body; when one organ of the body hurts, all the other organs experience the pain.[170] Elsewhere, Fadlallah criticizes those Islamic movements, which "brandish grand Islamic titles," but fail to broaden their popular base to include adherents of more than one *mazhhab*.[171] By and large, his Sunni counterparts hold the same view despite the occasional slips into sectarianism, especially on the part of Qaradawi.

Fadlallah's Vision of Islamic Unity

Were we to drop the references to the restoration of the caliphate that permeate the discourses of the mainstream Sunni Islamists, there would be no fundamental differences between Fadlallah's vision of Islamic unity and that of his Sunni counterparts. Mainstream Sunni Islamists view the restoration of the universal caliphate as the ultimate goal of Islamic unity. They are highly aware, though, of the multiple hurdles that stand in the way of this ultimate goal, and are willing to settle for the short-term, or intermediate, goal of intensifying collaboration among the various Muslim states in the cultural, economic, political and military realms. This is exactly how Fadlallah envisions Islamic unity. Instead of aiming at the untenable goal of unifying the political and religious leadership of the *umma*, Fadlallah focuses on the more achievable goal of ensuring that Muslims adopt a unified position on the pivotal issues that confront them.

The long and the short read of it is that what really matters to Fadlallah is unity of purpose and not unity of leadership. Islamic unity should, thus, manifest itself, in acting in concert to terminate the military presence of the major powers throughout the Muslim world and to renegotiate the economic and political relationship with them; in aiding oppressed Muslim populations worldwide, especially the Palestinians who are struggling against an unjust and oppressive occupying force; in refraining from any alliances with non-Muslim powers that seek to encircle and isolate a Muslim country that has an Islamic government, such as the Islamic Republic of Iran; and in intensifying collaboration among Muslim countries in the scientific, cultural, and economic domains on the bases of parity, acceptance of sectarian differences and mutual respect. Thus, in Fadlallah's dynamic view of the political universe, Islamic unity is more of a process than an outcome. It is a process of continuously mobilizing and aggregating the latent spiritual and material resources of the one Muslim *umma* in order to empower Muslims globally.[172]

For Fadlalah, unity and power are mutually reinforcing dynamic notions. Unifying the Muslim *umma*, along the axes noted above, leads to its empowerment; the more powerful the *umma* is, the more effective it would be in thwarting efforts to divide it along political, economic, cultural, ethnic, or-most dangerously-sectarian lines. This mutually reinforcing relationship between unity and power best manifests itself in the coordination of jihad as resistance efforts throughout the Arab and Islamic worlds. In a Friday sermon from 1988, Fadlallah, thus, argues:

> This is how we wish to lead ourselves throughout our life; to feel that we are part of this great Islamic endeavour. We should not consider the scene of jihad in Lebanon in isolation from the scene of jihad in Palestine, Egypt, Tunisia, Iran, Iraq, or any other country. As Muslims, our stances in regard to jihad, politics and in regard to any other position are integrated. Each stance of power supplies

fresh power to other stances, and the masses advance to supply new power to every situation of weakness. This is how the Islamic spirit complements itself.[173]

Finally, Fadlallah and the Sunni mainstream Islamists agree that Muslim populations globally should be the ones advocating for Islamic unity. Accordingly, all mainstream Islamists emphasize the centrality of awakening, within the souls and minds of Muslims worldwide, their sense of fraternity and of common destiny, as called for in multiple Quranic verses such as 3:110 and 21:92. Awakening in the Muslim public the yearning for Islamic unity globally is one of the most important manifestations of the Islamic awakening (*al-sahwa al-Islamiyya*) that all mainstream Islamists, especially Fadlallah and Qaradawi, emphasize in their discourses.

Conclusion

This last substantive chapter has included a Shii dimension to the discussion on how contemporary mainstream Islamists perceive international relations. Fadlallah is undoubtedly more revolutionary in his approach to international relations than the Sunni scholar sheikhs are. His revolutionary rhetoric aside, however, Fadlallah does not deviate from the core mainstream thesis that peace is the norm in international relations, while war is the exception.[174] Nonetheless, Fadlallah's views on peace and war are more nuanced and more complex than the views of his Sunni counterparts. Fadlallah views both peace and war in relative rather than absolute terms. Peace is desirable on both moral and pragmatic grounds, but it remains a precarious peace. Its preservation depends on the ability of weak powers to strengthen themselves in order to ward off aggression.

Fadlallah's deep-seated suspicions regarding the intentions of the major powers drive him to believe that their leaders and dominant elites do not seek peace for its own sake and are all too willing to engage in limited wars against weaker entities in pursuit of their material interests.[175] In a Friday Sermon, Fadlallah stressed that the major powers are keen on preserving peace only when it serves their interests. He goes on to accuse these insolent powers (*al-mustakbirun*) of "brandishing peace when it serves their interests and brandishing war when it serves their interests."[176]

Equally important, and as noted earlier, Fadlallah has little faith in the ability of international institutions to protect the weak states from the more powerful ones since they are dominated by the major powers.[177] For him, weakness invites aggression, but war is also limited in nature, fought for specific purposes and in accordance to certain rules. Wars and other forms of limited military conflicts are to be terminated whenever the purposes for which they are fought are fulfilled. The heavy rhetoric against the forces of international arrogance or insolence, (*quwa al-istikbar al-'alami*) notwithstanding, Fadlallah does not advocate an open-ended confrontation with any major power, especially the United States.[178] Any military confrontation with the United States is to be strictly confined to those theaters where the United States acts as an occupying power.[179] In Fadlallah's construct, the struggle against the aggression and the hegemonic designs of the major powers, especially those of the United States, is a long term multifaceted struggle that is not restricted to the military arena, for it also encompasses the political, economic, and especially cultural or "civilizational" domains.[180]

The essentially conflictual relationship with the major powers does not, nevertheless, preclude the possibilities of cooperation in the economic, cultural, and scientific fields, as long as this cooperation is in the Muslims' public interest and does not contradict the *sharia*. Nabeel Ali Saleh also argues that Fadlallah is particularly open to dialog and cooperation with European countries, which he views as more balanced than the United States in their relationships with the Arab and Muslim worlds, despite the colonial legacy.[181] While a careful reading of Fadlallah's discourse supports the above claim that Fadlallah had a more positive view of Europe than of the United States (often depcicted as the Great Satan[182]), Fadlallah was dismayed by the positions of the European powers during the July 2006 war between Hezbollah and Israel.

In a Friday Sermon delivered at the height of that war, Fadlallah rebuked the European powers, especially France, accusing them of abandoning their ideals and toeing the US line which unconditionally backed Israeli "aggression."[183] But Fadlallah equally emphasizes that initiatives to reduce the intensity of regional and international conflicts, particularly through dialog, are desirable on both moral and practical grounds. In a nutshell, for Fadlallah, the dynamics of international relations are essentially conflictual dynamics, but these dynamics do not preclude the possibilities of multifaceted cooperation and of long periods of peace.

This chapter has highlighted the similarities between Fadlallah's reading of international relations and the readings of his mainstream Sunni counterparts, whether concerning the underlying principles of international relations, the purposes of jihad and its conduct, the ending of war, or the road to Islamic unity. Fadlallah's views on international relations are closer to those of Bahi and Qaradawi than they are to the views of Shaltut, Abu Zahra, and Zuhaili. The first three scholar sheikhs adopt a critical stance toward Western powers, while engaging in a fair amount of anti-Western polemics. More importantly, they display a strong realist outlook on international relations, as will be further discussed in the concluding chapter. On the other hand, Shaltut, Abu Zahra, and Zuhaili are less critical of Western powers and less inclined to engage in anti-Western polemics. Their emphasis on human diversity, the centrality of peace to international relations, and the growing role of international norms and conventions and of international institutions and international law in organizing international relations bring them close to the liberal-internationalist school of IR. While the discourse of each of the six scholar sheikhs examined in this book exhibits unique features, these discourses, when read together, form a common narrative on international relations. This rich narrative is quite distinct from the narrative of the radical Islamists. The concluding chapter returns us to this common narrative, while also clarifying the main variations within it.

Notes

1 "Mapping the Global Muslim Population," (2009), *Pew Forum*, https://www.pewforum.org/2009/10/07/mapping-the-global-muslim-population/, accessed 26 April 2020.
2 Muhammad Hussein Fadlallah, *Kitab al-Jihad* (The Book of Jihad) (2nd ed.) (Beirut: Dar al-Malak, 1998), 219.
3 Fadlallah, *Kitab al-Jihad*, 330.
4 Fadlallah, *al-Haraka al-Islamiyya: Ma Laha wa Ma 'Alayha*, 32.
5 See, in particular, Fadlallah's early work, *al-Hiwar fi al-Qur'an* (Dialogue in the Quran) (Beirut: Dar al-Malak, 1996).
6 Verses 60:8–9, "As for those who have not fought with you over religion, nor expelled you from your homes, God does not forbid you treat them honorably and act with fairness towards them, for God loves those who act fairly. God, however, forbids you to ally yourself with those who fought with you over religion, expelled you from your homes or contributed to your expulsion. Whoso allies himself with them – these are the unjust."
7 Fadlallah, *Kitab al-Jihad*, 26, 218; *al-Haraka al-Islamiya: Ma Laha wa Ma 'Alayha* (The Islamic Movement: its Strenghts and its Weaknesses) (Beirut: Dar al-Malāk, 2004), 125.
8 Fadlallah compares normalizing Muslim relations with Israel to "legalizing the eating of dead flesh, blood and pork and the drinking of wine." Mohammad Fadlallah, *Iradat al-Quwa: Jihad al-Muqawama fi Khitab Samahat Ayatollah al-Uzma al-Sayyid*

Muhammad Hussein Fadlallah (The Will of Power: Resistance Jihad in the Discourse of Grand Aytallollah Sayyid Muhammad Hussein Fadlallah) (Beirut: Dar al-Malak, 2000), 94. For more on Fadlallah's positions on Israel and the legitimacy of Palestinian resistance, see Mohammad Fadlallah, *al-Mudanas wa al-Muqadas: Amerika wa Rayat al-Irhab al-Duwali* (The Unsacred and the Sacred: America and the Banner of International Terrorism), (Beirut: Riad El-Rayyes Books, 2003), esp. 107–10, 118– 22, 139–41, 135–46, 158, 243, 247–48, 251–53, 277, 280–81, 296–99, 309.
9 The quotes are original.
10 Bahi, *al-Fikr al-Islami al-Hadith*, 119.
11 Jaber Muhaisin 'Ulaywi, *Mahatat Min al-Sira wa al-Masira: al-Sayyid Muhammad Hussein Fadlallah fi Sutur* (Stations from his Life History and Life Journey: Some Words on Sayyid Muhammad Hussein Fadlallah) in Majmou'a min al-Mou'alifin (Various authors), *Muhammad Hussein Fadlallah al-'Iqlaniyya wa al-Hiwar min Ajl al-Taghyeer* (Rationality and Dialogue for the Purpose of Change) (Beirut: Center for Civilization for the Development of Islamic Thought, 2010), 19–21.
12 Jamal Sankari, *Fadlallah: The Making of a Radical Shiite Leader* (London: SAQI, 2005), 45.
13 Fadlallah, *al-Haraka al-Islamiyya ma Laha wa ma 'Alayha*, 329.
14 Sankari, *Fadlallah*, 49.
15 For short biographic information on these Shia *marja's*, see Gerhard Bowering, et al., eds., *The Princeton Encyclopedia of Islamic Political Thought* (Princeton, NJ: Princeton University Press, 2013).
16 Sankari, *Fadlallah*, 49.
17 The radio station is still operational. http://www.albachaer.com/, accessed 17 June 2020).
18 Sankari, *Fadlallah*, 47.
19 Sankari, *Fadlallah*, 47.
20 Qaradawi, *ibn al-Qarya wa al-Kuttab*, Vol. 2, 170–72. The long poem was known as the "*nouniyya*" because the rhyme letter was the Arabic letter for "n".
21 Sankari, *Fadlallah*, 49.
22 Muhammad Hussein Fadlallah, *Uslub al-Da'wa fi al-Quran* (the Way of Calling to Islam in the Quran) (6th ed.) (Beirut: Dar al-Malak, 1998), 44–49.
23 For the history of the ICP and its role in Iraqi politics, see, Tareq Y. Ismael, *The Rise and Fall of the Communist Party of Iraq* (Cambridge: Cambridge University Press, 2008).
24 Sankari, *Fadlallah*, 87–99.
25 This is not the place to analyze this important, but controversial, legislation. It raised the minimum age of marriage to 15 (for both genders) and required a married man to obtain the authorization of a judge before marrying a second wife. Despite the modest nature of these reforms, they were vehemently opposed by the Sunni and Shia religious establishments.

252 | *Contemporary Islamist Perspectives on International Relations*

26 Sankari, *Fadlallah*, 60–65.
27 Of the same age as Fadlallah, Sheikh Shams al-Din's career moved in parallel to that of Fadlallah. He returned to his native Lebanon and advanced within the Shiite religious establishment, becoming the Head of the Lebanese Islamic–Shiite Higher Council from 1978 until his death in 2001. References to his views will be made in different parts of this chapter since they overlap with those of Fadlallah.
28 For the life, thought and political role of Baqir al-Sadr, see T. M. Aziz, "The Role of Muhammad Baqir al-Sadr in Shii Political Activism in Iraq from 1958 to 1980," *International Journal of Middle East Studies* 25, no. 2 (1993): 207–22.
29 Fadlallah, *al-Hiwar fi al-Quran*, 63.
30 Fadlallah underscores a central idea in the discourses of most Islamic thinkers, namely that Islam is the religion that is most compatible with innate human nature (*al-Islam huwa din al-fitra*). Fadlallah, *Uslub al-Daʿwa*, 64.
31 Fadlallah, *Uslub al-Daʿwa fi al-Quran*, 44–49.
32 The centrality to the message of Islam of the prohibition of the use of coercion to convert unbelievers to Islam is emphasized in the opening pages of Fadlallah's *Kitab al-Jihad*, 49–62. See also Mohammad Fadlallah, *al-Ijtihad: Bayn Asr al-Madi wa Afaq al-Mustaqbal* (Jurisprudence between the Captivity of the Past and the Horizons of the Future) (Beirut: al-Markaz al-Thaqafi al- ʿArabi, 2009), 35.
33 Fadlallah, *Uslub al-Daʿwa fi al-Quran*, 50–51, 58, 70, 75–76; *al-Hiwar fi al-Quran*, 84, 146, 148.
34 Fadlallah, *Uslub al-Daʿwa fi al-Quran*, 71; *al-Hiwar fi al-Quran*, 82–84.
35 Fadlallah, *Uslub al-Daʿwa fi al-Quran*, 55–56.
36 Fadlallah, *Uslub al-Daʿwa fi al-Quran*, 84.
37 Shams al-Din, *Fiqh al-ʿUnf al-Muslah fi al-Islam*, 17.
38 There are a few academic studies on Shams al-Din. See, in particular, Rola el-Husseini, "Resistance, Jihad, and Martyrdom in Contemporary Lebanese Shiʿa Discourse," *Middle East Journal* 62, no. 3 (2008): 399–414.
39 Sankari, *Fadlallah*, 122.
40 For al-Sadr's biography and his role among Lebanon's Shias, see Fouad Ajami, *The Vanished Imam: Musa al-Sadr and the Shia of Lebanon* (Ithaca and London: Cornell University Press, 1986). See also Fouad Ajami, "Lebanon and Its Inheritors," *Foreign Affairs* 63, no. 4 (1985): 778–99.
41 Biographic information about Shams al-Din can be found at "Sheikh Muhammad Mahdi Shams al-Din," (n.d.), *Marefa.org*, https://www.marefa.org/%D8%A7%D9%84%D8%B4%D9%8A%D8%AE_%D9%85%D8%AD%D9%85%D8%AF_%D9%85%D9%87%D8%AF%D9%8A_%D8%B4%D9%85%D8%B3_%D8%A7%D9%84%D8%AF%D9%8A%D9%86, accessed 7 July 2010. For an analysis of Shams al-Din views on Jihad, see el-Husseini, "Resistance, Jihad, and Martyrdom."
42 Bob Woodward, *The Veil* (London: Simon and Schuster, 1987), 396–97.

43 For Fadlallah's reference to the assassination attempt, see his Friday Sermon of February 26, 1988, reprinted in Mohammad Fadlallah, *al-Jumʿa: Minbar wa-Mihrab, Tawtheeq li-Khutab al-Jumʿa 1988* (Friday [Prayer]: A Pulpit and a Prayer Niche: Documentation of Friday Sermons 1988) (Beirut: Dar al-Malak, 1996), 95. For the Bir al-ʿAbd explosion and the CIA's alleged responsibility for it, see Hala Jaber, *Hizbullah: Born with a Vengeance* (New York: Columbia University Press, 1997), 69–70; Sankari, Fadlallah, 9, 209; and especially Woodward, *The Veil*, 396–97.
44 Ajami, "Lebanon and its Inheritors," 792.
45 Almost all works on Hezbollah include references to the party's relationship to Fadlallah. See, in particular, Judith Palmer Harik, *Hezbollah: The Changing face of Terrorism* (London: I.B. Tauris, 2004), 61–62, 65; Jaber, *Hizbullah*, 70–71; Augustus Richard Norton, *Hezbollah* (Princeton: Princeton University Press, 2007), 31–32, 118–119; Magnus Ranstorp, *Hizb 'Allah in Lebanon: The Politics of the Western Hostage Crisis* (New York: St. Martin's Press), 28, 36–37.
An-Nahar, (Beirut), June 19 1997, 7.
46 Sami E. Baroudi, "Islamist Perspectives on International Relations: The Discourse of Sayyid Muhammad Hussein Fadlallah (1935–2010)," *Middle Eastern Studies* 49, no. 1 (2013): 107–33.
47 Fadlallah's statement was carried by the Lebanese daily *An-Nahar*, May 13 2009, 9.
48 For coverage of the funeral and eulogies of Fadlallah, see: *As-Safir* (Beirut), 12 July 2010, 7; *As-Safir*, 14 July 2010, 19; Kuwait Times, July 7, 2010, http://www.kuwaittimes.net/read_news.php?newsid=OTU0MjEyMDU5. (Accessed on April 25, 2011).
49 Baroudi, "Islamist Perspectives on International Relations: The Discourse of Sayyid Muhammad Hussein Fadlallah," 109–00.
50 Fadlallah, Friday sermon of February 2, 1988; reprinted in Fadlallah, *al-Jumʿa: Minbar wa*-Mihrab, 74.
51 Muhammad Hussein Fadlallah, *Iradat al-Quwa: Jihad al-Muqawama fi Khitab Samahat Ayatollah al-Uzma al-Sayyid Muhammad Hussein Fadlallah* (The Will of Power: Resistance Jihad in the Discourse of Grand Ayatollah Sayyid Muhammad Hussein Fadlallah) (Beirut: Dar al-Malak, 2000), 39.
52 Fadlallah, *al-Ijtihad*, 24.
53 Fadlallah, *al-Haraka al-Islamiyya: Ma Laha wa Ma ʿAlayha'*, 72.
54 Fadlallah, *Iradat al-Quwa*, 38.
55 Fadlallah, *al-Haraka al-Islamiyya: Ma Laha wa Ma ʿAlayha'*, 14–15.
56 Fadlallah, *Uslub al-Daʿwa fi al-Quran*, 38.
57 Fadlallah, *Uslub al-Da 'wa fi al-Quran*, 38; *al-Haraka al-Islamiyya: Humum wa Qadaya*, 77.
58 Fadlallah, *Kitab al-Jihad*, 114.
59 Fadlallah, *Kitab al-Jihad*, 111.
60 Fadlallah, *Kitab al-Jihad*, 116, 118.

61 For the role of contemporary mainstream Islamists in popularizing the motion of the Islamic state, see Baroudi, "The Problematic Notion of the Islamic State."
62 Bernard Weiss, *The Spirit of Islamic law* (Georgia: Georgia University Press, 1998), 27.
63 Over and again, Fadlallah emphasizes that his support of the Islamic Republic of Iran is not because Iran is a predominantly Shia country. This support, he argues, emanates from Iran's adoption of an Islamic system and its pursuit of an "Islamic line" (*Khat Islami*) in its foreign relations. See Friday Sermon of September 1, 1989, reprinted in Mohammad Fadlallah, *Salat al-Jum 'a, al-Kalima wa al-Mawqif: Tawthiq li-Khutub al-Jum'a 1989* (Friday Prayer, Discourse and Stance: Documentation of Friday Sermons 1989), 388. Elsewhere, Fadlallah contends that every Muslim is entrusted by God with "ensuring the survival of the Islamic state [in Iran] through lending it support and power." He goes on to note that "at this stage, no voice should be louder than the voice of Islam's battle with unbelief and the [Iranian] Revolution's battle with injustice (*al-baghi*) and oppression." Fadlallah, *al-Haraka al-Islamiyya Ma Laha wa Ma 'Alayha*, 170.
64 Muhammad Hussein Fadlallah, *al-Islam wa Mantiq al-Quwa* (Islam and the Logic of Power) (2nd ed.) (Beirut: al-Dar al-Islamiyya, 1981), 39–46. Fadlallah returns to this theme repeatedly in subsequent writings; see one of his opening editorials in *al-Hikma*, reprinted in Mohammad Fadlallah, *Ma' al-Hikma fi Khat al-Islam* (Beirut: Mu'asasat al-Wafa, 1985), 9.
65 Fadlallah, *al-Islam wa Mantiq al-Quwa*, 74–69.
66 For reference to this often quoted verse, see Fadlallah, *Kitab al-Jihad*, 75, 90, Friday Sermon of April 28, 1989, reprinted in *Salat al-Jum'a*, 140, *Uslub al-Da'wa*, 95.
67 Mohammad Fadlallah, *al-Haraka al-Islamiyya: Humum wa Qadaya* (The Islamic Movement: Concerns and Issues, (Beirut: Dar al-Malak, 2001), 162–63, 258.
68 Most of Fadlallah's Friday Sermons emphasize the need to resist injustice and oppression, irrespectively of whether their sources are domestic or international. See Friday Sermon of March 3, 1989, reprinted in Fadlallah, *Salat al-Jum'a*, 13–15. See also Fadlallah, *al-Haraka al-Islamiyya Ma Laha wa Ma 'Alayha*, 136–7, 142–4, 161–5.
69 Fadlallah, *Kitab al-Jihad*, 76.
70 Fadlallah, *Kitab al-Jihad*, 72.
71 Kenneth Waltz, *Man, the State and War: A Theoretical Analysis* (New York: Columbia University Press, 1954, 1959, 2001).
72 Fadlallah, *Kitab al-Jihad*, 34. The same idea is conveyed in Fadlallah's earlier work *Uslub al-Da 'wa*, 45.
73 Friday Sermon of January 1, 1988, reprinted in Fadlallah, *al-Jum'a Minbar wa Mihrab*, 34.
74 Friday sermon of March 4, 1988, reprinted in Fadlallah, *al-Jum'a Minbar wa Mihrab*, 116.
75 Muhammad Hussein Fadlallah, *Ida'at Islamiyya* (Islamic Illuminations) (Beirut: Dar an-Nahar, 2003), 46, 52.
76 Fadlallah, *Iradat al-Quwa*, 168.

77 Fadlallah, *Iradat al-Quwa*, 117–18.
78 Fadlallah, *al-Mudanas wa al-Muqadas*, 53–54.
79 Friday Sermon of March 18, 1988, reprinted in *al-Jum'a Minbar wa Mihrab*, 149; Friday Sermon of August 11, 1989, reprinted in Fadlallah, *Salat al-Jum'a*, 302–03.
80 Fadlallah, *Iradat al-Quwa*, 141–3, 156–62, 185–91, 204–8, 211–4, 244–57, 303–9.
81 Fadlallah, *Ida'at Islamiyya*, 74.
82 Muhammad Hussein Fadlallah, *Fi Afaq al-Hiwar al-Islami al-Masihi* (In the Horizons of Inter-Islamic-Christian Dialogue) (Beirut: Dar al-Malak, 2005), 49.
83 Friday Sermon of August 25, 1989, reprinted in Fadlallah, *Salat al-Jum'a*, 363–6.
84 Fadlallah, *Iradat al-Quwa*, 233.
85 Fadlallah, *al-Haraka al-Islamiyya: Ma Laha wa Ma 'Alayha*, 132–3.
86 See, inter alia, Fadlallah, *Iradat al-Quwa*, 93–112, 185–219, 347–51; and *al-Islam wa Mantiq al-Quwa*, 126–7.
87 Fadlallah, *Iradat al-Quwa*, 86–87. For more criticisms pf the UN, see *Iradat al-Quwa*, 180–1, 235–6.
88 Fadlallah, *Kitab al-Jihad*, 134.
89 Fadlallah, *Kitab al-Jihad*, 72.
90 Fadlallah, Friday Sermon of March 17, 1989. Reprinted in Fadlallah, *Salat al-Jum'a*, 32.
91 Fadlallah, *Kitab al-Jihad*, 187–90.
92 Fadlallah, *Kitab al-Jihad*, 254–55.
93 The verses he quotes are: 4: 139: As for those who adopt the unbelievers as allies apart from the believers – do they truly seek power from the? All power belongs to God."
94 Fadlallah, *al-Ijtihad*, 35. The idea appears several times in Fadlallah's discourse. See his Friday Sermon of April 14, 1989, reprinted in Fadlallah, *Salat al-Jum'a*, 101.
95 Fadlallah, *Iradat al-Quwa*, 104.
96 Fadlallah, *al-Islam wa Mantiq al-Quwa*, esp. 110–12.
97 Fadlallah, *Kitab al-Jihad*, 71.
98 Fadlallah, *Kitab al-Jihad*, 72, 77.
99 Fadlallah, Kitab al-Jihad, 71–81.
100 Fadlallah, *Iradat al-Quwa*, 182.
101 Fadlallah, *Kitab al-Jihad*, 13.
102 Fadlallah, *Kitab al-Jihad*, 112–4.
103 Fadlallah, *Kitab al-Jihad*, 82–83, 96–97.
104 Fadlallah, *Iradat al-Quwa: Jihad al-Muqawama fi Khitab Samahat Ayatollah al-Uzma al-Sayyid Muhammad Hussein Fadlallah*.
105 Fadlallah, *Iradat al-Quwa*, 481.
106 Shams al-Din, *Fiqh al- 'unf al-Musalah fi al-Islam*, 18.
107 Shams al-Din, *Fiqh al-'Unf al-Musalah*, 18.
108 Fadlallah, *Kitab al-Jihad*, 74.
109 Fadlallah, *Kitab al-Jihad*, 134.

256 | *Contemporary Islamist Perspectives on International Relations*

110 Fadlallah, *al-Haraka al-Islamiyya Ma Laha wa Ma 'Alayha*, 165.
111 Fadlallah, *Uslub al-Da'wa*, 94–98.
112 Fadlallah, *Kitab al-Jihad*, 27–29.
113 Fadlallah, *Kitab al-Jihad*, 78–83.
114 Fadlallah, *Kitab al-Jihad*, 90.
115 Fadlallah, *Kitab al-Jihad*, 107–10.
116 Fadlallah, *Kitab al-Jihad*, 94–106.
117 Fadlallah, *Kitab al-Jihad*, 82.
118 Fadlallah, *al-Mudanas wa al-Muqadas*, esp. 21–22, 18–183, 261–3.
119 Fadlallah, *Ida'at Islamiyya*, 90–112.
120 Fadlallah, *Iradat al-Quwa*, esp. 18–19, 75–77 and *al-Mudanas wa al-Muqadas*.
121 Fadlallah, *Kitab al-Jihad*, 74.
122 Fadlallah, *Kitab al-Jihad*, 94–104; and *Uslub al-Da'wa*, 101–4.
123 Friday Sermon of April 21, 1989, reprinted in Fadlallah, *Salat al-Jum'a*, 137–40.
124 Fadlallah, *Kitab al-Jihad*, 52–62.
125 Fadlallah, *Kitab al-Jihad*, 112.
126 Fadlallah, *Kitab al-Jihad*, 107–10.
127 Fadlallah, *Kitab al-Jihad*, 16.
128 Fadlallah, *al-Mudanas wa al-Muqadas*, 156.
129 Fadlallah, *Kitab al-Jihad*, 132.
130 Fadlallah, *Kitab al-Jihad*, 104–6.
131 Fadlallah, *Kitab al-Jihad*, 90–93.
132 Fadlallah, *Kitab al-Jihad*, 103, 324.
133 Fadlallah notes that in most of his raids, the Prophet concealed his destination in order to surprise the enemy. *Kitab al-Jihad*, 129. For the legitimacy of using deceit in battle, see Fadlallah, *Kitab al-Jihad*, 289.
134 Fadlallah, *Kitab al-Jihad*, 306–7.
135 Fadlallah, *Kitab al-Jihad*, 254–5.
136 Fadlallah, *Kitab al-Jihad*, 264–5.
137 Fadlallah, Kitab al-Jihad, 365.
138 Fadlallah, *Kitab al-Jihad*, 215–8.
139 Fadlallah, *Kitab al-Jihad*, 267–9.
140 Fadlallah, *Kitab al-Jihad*, 267–8, 296.
141 Fadlallah, *Kitab al-Jihad*, 310.
142 Fadlallah, *Kitab al-Jihad*, 311.
143 Fadlallah, *Kitab al-Jihad*, 311–6.
144 Fadlallah, *Kitab al-Jihad*, 315–6.
145 Fadlallah, *Kitab al-Jihad*, 311–2.
146 Fadlallah, *Jitab al-Jihad*, 315
147 Fadlallah, *Kitab al-Jihad*, 314
148 Fadlallah, *Kitab al-Jihad*, 314–6, 364–5.

149 Fadlallah, *Kitab al-Jihad*, 349.
150 For references to *hudna* and *salam* as the two conditions of coexistence with non-Muslims (outside of war), see Fadlallah, *al-Haraka al-Islamiyya*, 130.
151 Fadlallah, *Kitab al-Jihad*, 351.
152 Fadlallah, *Kitab al-Jihad*, 350–4.
153 Fadlallah, *Kitab al-Jihad*, 351.
154 Fadlallah, *Kitab al-Jihad*, 350–1.
155 Fadlallah, *Kitab al-Jihad*, 226, 255.
156 Friday Sermon of May 26, 1989, reprinted in Fadlallah, *Salat al-Jum'a*, 205.
157 Fadlallah, *Kitab al-Jihad*, 111–23.
158 Sankari, *Fadlallah*, 69, 80, 117.
159 A perusal of Fadlallah's Friday sermons from 1988 to 1989 reveals references to Imam 'Ali, his sons Hasan and Husain, other Shia Imams, Ahl al-Bayt, and the battle of Karbala in almost every sermon. See, Fadlallah, *Salat al-Jum'a*, and *al-Jum'a Minbar wa Mihrab*.
160 *Fadlallah quotes approvingly* Umar's II famous reprimand to his regional commanders "God sent Muhammad as a Messenger and not as a tax collector." The background to this reprimand (according to mainly Sunni Islamic scholars) is that some Muslim regional governors were reluctant to encourage the local populations to embrace Islam out of fear of losing the *jizya* money. Fadlallah, *Kitab al-Jihad*, 321.
161 Fadlallah, *Kitab al-Jihad*, 136–9.
162 Friday Sermon of February 26, 1988, reprinted in Fadlallah, *al-Jum'a: Minbar wa Mihrab*, 91.
163 Fadlallah, *al-Haraka al-Islamiyya*, 140. Fadlallah, *al-Jum'a: Minbar wa Mihrab*, 91.
164 Fadlallah, *al-Haraka al-Islamiyya: Humum wa Qadaya*, 139.
165 Fadlallah, Friday Sermon of January 22, 1988, reprinted in Fadlallah, *al-Jum'a: Minbar wa-Mihrab*, 70.
166 Fadlallah, *al-Haraka al-Islamiyya: Humum wa Qadaya*, 139–41.
167 Fadlallah, Friday Sermon of March 31, 1989, reprinted in *Salat al-Jum'a*, 60–64.
168 Fadlallah, *al-Haraka al-Islamiyya: Humum wa Qadaya*, 139. See also his Friday Sermon of March 31, 1989, reprinted in Fadlallah, *Salat al-Jum'a*, 60–61.
169 Friday Sermon of March 31, 1989, reprinted in Fadlallah, *Salat al-Jum'a*, 63.
170 Friday Sermon of April 21, 1989, reprinted in Fadlallah, *Salat al-Jum'a*, 128–9. See also Fadlallah, *al-Haraka al-Islamiyya Humum wa Qadaya*, 279.
171 Fadlallah, *al-Haraka al-Islamiyya Ma Laha wa Ma 'Alayha*, 52.
172 Fadlallah, *al-Haraka al-Islamiyya Ma Laha wa Ma 'Alayha*, 165.
173 Fadlallah, Friday Sermon of January 22, 1988, reprinted in Fadlallah, *al-Jum'a: Minbar wa-Mihrab*, 61.
174 Fadlallah, *Kitab al-Jihad*, 217.
175 Fadlallah, *Kitab al-Jihad*, 282.
176 Friday Sermon of May 26, 1989, reprinted in Fadlallah, *Salat al-Jum'a*, 205.

258 | *Contemporary Islamist Perspectives on International Relations*

177 Fadlallah, for example, views the UN Security Council as an agent of the major powers, especially the United States. Friday Sermon of February 26, 1988, reprinted in Fadlallah, *al-Jum 'a Minbar wa Mihrab*, 97–98.
178 Fadlallah's work *al-Mudanas wa al-Muqdas* is principally about the September 11, 2001 attacks on the United States and the US response to these attacks. For Fadlallah's criticisms of the attacks, see, Fadlallah, *al-Mudanas wa al-Muqadas*, esp., 21–31, 344–5.
179 Fadlallah, *Ida'at Islamiyya*, 90–112.
180 Fadlallah, *Kitab al-Jihad*, 226–7.
181 Nabeel Ali Saleh, "*al-'Allama al-Sayyed Muhammad Hussein Fadlallah wa manjahiyath fi Mu'alajat wa Tahleel ba'd al-Qadaya al-Mu'asira 'ala Daou' Mu'tayat al-Fikr al-Islami*" (The Erudite Scholar Sayyed Muhammad Hussein Fadlallah and his Approach to the Treatment and Analysis of some Contemporary Issues in the light of the Givens of Islamic Thought) in Majmou'a min al-Mou'alifin (Various Authors), *Muhammad Hussein Fadlallah al-'Iqlaniyya wa al-Hiwar min Ajl al-Taghyeer* (Muhammad Hussein Fadlallah: Rationality and Dialogue for the Sake of Change) (Beirut: Center for Civilization for the Development of Islamic Thought, 2010), 279–80.
182 For references to the United States as the great satan, see Fadlallah, *Iradat al-Quwa*, 89–90, 134.
183 Friday Sermon of July 14, 2006, reprinted in Mohammad Fadlallah, *Khitab al-Muqawama wa al-Nasr: fi Muwajahat al-Harb al-Israeiliyya 'ala Lubnan Tammouz 2006* (The Discourse of Resisatnce and Victory: Confronting Isarel's War on Lebanon of July 2006) (Beirut: Dar al-Malak, 2006), 14–15.

8

Conclusion: The Mainstream Islamists Within Their Ideational and Historical Milieus

This has been a study of the international relations discourses of six prominent scholar sheikhs from the Arab world, representing the Sunni and Shii denominations (*mazhhabs*) of Islam. It has sought to demonstrate the presence of a moderate-reformist, mainstream, strand of political Islam that offers a contemporary reading of international relations quite distinct from the reading of radical Islamists. True, there are important variations within this mainstream narrative. Nevertheless, it retains its internal coherence due to broad agreement among its advocates on several pivotal themes in contemporary international relations. This concluding chapter reiterates the core argument of the book, while situating the discourses of the six scholar sheikhs in their ideational and historical contexts.

The Book's Principal Argument

As noted in the introductory chapter, Political Islam, or Islamism, represents one of a number of interpretations of Islam, although its many adherents insist that it embodies the correct reading of Islam. Throwing light on the complex relationship between Islam and Islamism, Martin and Barzegar note, "Islamists share the label Muslim with more traditional, liberal, modernist, mystical, and secular Muslims, with whom they may agree on many theological points but with whom they are in disagreement over others."[1] Clearly, there are no rigid demarcation lines between Islamists and Muslims, and Muslims may subscribe in varying degrees to different components of competing Islamist agendas. However and despite its mercuric nature, the term Islamist is indispensable for labeling the political and socioeconomic views of a large number of Muslim scholars who draw primarily on Islam's scriptural sources in analyzing contemporary worldly, i.e., temporal, problems facing modern-day Muslim or majority-Muslim societies, and proposing solutions to these problems that are anchored in Islam.

While maintaining that Islam must guide all aspects of life within the Muslim Community as well as its relations with other communities, Islamists present a plethora of conflicting opinions on both domestic politics in majority-Muslim societies and on international relations. Thus, although united in rejecting the secularization of the state, i.e., the separation of religion from politics, and in demanding *sharia*-based legislation, Islamists disagree on multiple political and socioeconomic issues, including issues of international relations. Consequently, in the context of refuting the ideology and practices of the so-called "Islamic State in Iraq and al-Sham" (ISIS), Lebanese commentator Muhammad 'Ali Farhat wrote, "We are not facing one political Islam. There are several quarreling political Islams, each claiming to offer divine guidance, while alleging that the others are going astray or at best falling short."[2]

In brief, this work has sought to shed light on how a select distinguished group of mainstream Islamists view international relations, and how they depict it to their primarily, but not exclusively, Muslim audiences. Based on a close reading of the discourses of six Arab scholar sheikhs, the book has sought to capture the constituent elements of the image of international relations that they project. This image, the book has argued, revolved around at least six principal interconnected themes, presented below in summary form.

First, for mainstream Islamists, international relations concern relations between Muslim and non-Muslim states, and relations among the latter. Accordingly, relations amongst existing Muslim states that allegedly were once part of a single Islamic state do not fall within the proper purview of international relations, since they concern relations among members of one *umma*. This Muslim *umma*, rather than the territorial nation-state, is the principal unit of analysis for Islamists. Stated more precisely, the *umma* incorporates the capacities of a "modern" territorial nation-state, despite obviously lacking the "sustainable capability to act globally."[3]

This emphasis on the Muslim *umma* as a distinct presence on the international stage distinguishes the discourses of mainstream and radical Islamists from

Conclusion: The Mainstream Islamists Within Their Milieus | 261

those of western IR scholars and secular Arab writers, whose principal unit of analysis is the modern territorial nation-state. Nevertheless, and because Islamists attribute to the Muslim *umma* many of the features of the "modern" territorial nation-state, their analyses of both the internal politics and the international relations of the "imagined" single Islamic state bears considerable similarity to the analysis of state conduct by Western academics and commentators.

For that reason, in analyzing international relations, mainstream Islamists use a range of notions that are widely used by Western and other non-Islamist academics and commentators in analyzing the nation-state and its foreign policy. The meanings mainstream Islamists assign to core IR concepts (e.g., independence, sovereignty, diplomacy, peace, war, treaties, truces, cooperation, reciprocity, humanitarian intervention, and international law) are hardly different from their widely used and "universally" accepted meanings. The only difference, an important one at that, is that mainstream Islamists attribute these features of the modern nation-state to an "imagined" Islamic state, whose existence they assume rather than prove.[4] It is worth reiterating here that the notion of the "Islamic state" is equally pivotal to the discourses of mainstream Islamists and their radical counterparts. Mainstream and radical Islamists, however, differ markedly regarding the internal and external conduct of this "imagined" Islamic state. Broadly speaking, the Islamic state, as envisioned by mainstream Islamists, shares significant elements with the modern nation-state, in its domestic and international conduct, even if it differs from it in form. Any account of Islamists' perspectives on international relations must therefore commence with this pivotal though ambiguous notion of the Islamic state.

In line with the Islamic tradition, Islamists both mainstream and radical view "Muhammad, like Moses, as both prophet and ruler."[5] In this Islamist foundational narrative, the Prophet established a new state in Medina as the bastion of the new religion. To quote Weiss, he also acted as its "lawgiver (mediator of the divine law), judge, statesman, and head of an army."[6] The six scholar sheikhs surveyed here addressed at length the relationship between the establishment of the "Islamic polity" (Islamic state) and the need to defend Islam and Muslims against external enemies and internal violent dissenters (*bughat*), developing constructs of the state, domestic politics, and international relations that were firmly anchored in their interpretations of the Quran and the Sunna of the Prophet. While aware of the division of the Islamic world into separate and often rival nation-states, the six scholar sheikhs examined here built their political and international relations discourses on the notion of the single Islamic state that articulated the interests of the *umma* and allegedly spoke with one voice to the rest of the world.

Second, mainstream Islamists treat peace as the guiding principle (*al-asl al-'am*) in relations between Muslim and non-Muslim states and war as the exception to the norm. This fundamental distinction between war, and more generally violence, on the one hand, and peace, on the other, brings to mind the following profound observation by the renowned German-born American political theorist Hannah Arendt. Arendt writes:

> Violence is by nature instrumental; like all means, it always stands in need of guidance and justification through the end it pursues. And what needs justification by something else cannot be the essence of anything. The end of war – end taken in its twofold meaning – is peace or victory; but to the question And what is the end of peace? there is no answer. Peace is an absolute, even though in recorded history periods of warfare have nearly always outlasted periods of peace.[7]

Without having read Arendt or the Western sources that inspired her thinking, mainstream Islamists subscribe to essentially the same juxtaposition between violence and peace that she draws. In line with Arendt, they adopt an instrumental view of violence, including jihad. The lengthy answers that they provide to the fundamental question of "why Muslims fight" reflect their belief that the violence in which Muslims engage must be justified by serving a higher purpose, namely defending the Muslim community and preserving the freedom of Muslims to practice Islam and to peacefully call for it. Jihad, while exalted in the discourses of mainstream Islamists, remains a means to an end, rather than an end in itself. The quest for peace, on the other hand, needs no justification, as peace is an end in itself.

Peace is compatible with human reason and with innate human nature (*al-fitra al-insaniyya*), although the inclination toward peace differs from one human to another and one community to another. In the mainstream narrative, Muslim communities are more peaceful in their internal and external relations than the non-Muslim ones. Most importantly, mainstream Islamists emphasize that peace is at the essence of the message of Islam. As Qaradawi notes, the words peace (*salam, silm*) and Islam derive from the same Arabic root, and the "Bringer of Peace" is one of God's most beautiful names.[8] Qaradawi adds that the Quran refers to paradise as the "abode of peace," as in Quranic verse 6 128, "They shall dwell in the House of peace with their Lord," and the traditional Muslim greeting is "peace be upon you."[9] Qaradawi concludes that the "Muslim is peaceful in his worship (*'ibadath*) and peaceful in his dealings with others (*mu'amalath*)."[10]

Despite the centrality of international peace in their international relations perspectives, there are important variations amongst mainstream Islamists regarding the best means for its preservation. Shaltut, Abu Zahra, and especially Zuhaili emphasize the centrality of international agreements, international institutions, and international law to the maintenance of international peace. Zuhaili's principal contribution to this mainstream perspective, for example, lies in his emphasis on the compatibility of the *sharia* with international law, particularly international humanitarian law.[11] Broadly speaking, the approach to international relations, championed by these three scholar sheiks, bears some resemblance to the liberal-institutional (liberal internationalist) perspective on IR.

The above statement, to be read with great caution, does not imply that these three scholar sheikhs embrace the liberal perspective on the individual and the state. They do not. Their understanding of individual freedoms centers on the freedom of belief and the freedom to employ one's reason to discover the "eternal truths" about God and the universe. While recognizing the right of non-Muslims to practice their beliefs, they do not recognize it a right to convert Muslims to these beliefs. They do not place all religions on an equal footing, as liberals presumably do, but privilege Islam over other religions, for Islam represents God's last message to humanity. In the same token, freedom of religion does not entail freedom from religion. Islamists do not recognize the right of individuals, whether Muslims or non-Muslims, to openly reject all religions and to advocate atheism or agnosticism.

Equally importantly, they do not subscribe to the liberal view of the state as an arbiter between conflicting interests and conflicting ideational systems, but view the state as the instrument of divine justice. For mainstream Islamists, the state ought to be guided primarily by the *sharia*, rather than by the wishes of its citizens, although they make the implicit assumption that in majority-Muslim states, the majority of Muslims would choose *sharia* rule of their own volition. The idea that Muslims would voluntarily choose human-made laws over the *sharia* is so foreign to mainstream Islamists that they even refuse to give it serious consideration.

Although their views of the individual and the state are obviously not in line with liberalism, Shaltut, Abu Zahra, and Zuhaili subscribe to several tenets of the liberal-internationalist paradigm of IR, particularly regarding the sanctity of international treaties and agreements. Equally importantly, they underscore the need to abide by prevalent international norms and conventions, and more generally by international law, while recognizing the important contributions of international institutions, especially the UN, to the preservation of international peace and the promotion of international cooperation. They also embrace free trade and relatively free movement of capital. A world of closed borders in which each nation or each civilization shuts out other nations and civilizations is anathema to the thinking of the three scholar sheikhs. Abu Zahra and Zuhaili, in particular, argue in detail that the divine division of the world into separate peoples and nations is intended for people to become familiar with and to dialog with each other.[12] Based on a close reading of the discourses of Abu Zahra and Zuhaili, Baroudi, notes, "Religious diversity, like other forms of diversity, is divinely intended for the wellbeing of humanity, and is not per se a source of conflict or war."[13]

Bahi, Qaradawi, and Fadlallah, on the other hand, are skeptical of the effectiveness of international agreements and international institutions in preserving international peace, especially given the foreign policy orientation of non-Muslim major powers. While valuing international peace, they see its preservation as primarily dependent on the ability of Muslims to expand their power base in order to deter aggression. All mainstream Islamists argue in favor of deterrence, which Shaltut refers to as "armed peace" (*al-salam al-musalah*); however, there are more references to its role in the preservation of international peace in the discourses of Bahi, Qaradawi, and especially Fadlallah than in those of the other three scholar sheikhs.

The disagreements among mainstream Islamists regarding the prerequisites of international peace should not be exaggerated. The six scholar sheikhs commonly subscribe to the view that the empowerment, or "self-strengthening,"[14] of Muslim societies would contribute to a more just and peaceful international order since they are aware of the power differential between the major powers on the one hand, and Muslim societies on the other. Skeptical of the intentions of the major powers to varying degrees, they are adamant about the need to rectify this power imbalance not only to ensure that Muslims are better equipped to protect themselves against aggression and defend their core interests, but also to anchor international relations on a more stable and more just base.

Mainstream Islamists subscribe to an agenda of change in international relations that aims primarily at redressing the power imbalances between the rich and developed states, on the one hand, and the poorer, less developed states, on the other hand. They are highly cognizant that the Islamic world is part of the Global South. It shares the Global South's multiple frustrations with the prevalent international order, while subscribing to its aspirations for meaningful change. Abu Zahra is the voice of mainstream Islamists when he emphasizes the inexorable link between international peace and international justice. Mainstream Islamists, including the more radical Fadlallah, do not believe, though, in the effectiveness, or even appropriateness, of violence as a means to bring about the desired changes that would usher a more just and a more peaceful international order. Change is to be achieved primarily through concerted and incremental action on multiple fronts in the political, economic, cultural, and security domains.

Third, for mainstream Islamists, jihad is primarily a defensive activity spurred by aggression, or by an imminent threat of aggression. According to this mainstream reading, Muslims prefer peace to war; but when war is imposed on them by others, they marshal all tangible and intangible resources to repel the aggression. For mainstream Islamists, aggression includes preventing Muslims from practicing their religion or peacefully calling for Islam. This emphasis on the defensive purposes of jihad can be traced back to the thought of 'Abduh, summarized by Yvonne Haddad as such, "Fighting is sanctioned under restricted conditions in order to stop aggression against the truth and its people, as well as to maintain peace. It has never been to force people to convert to the religion nor to take revenge on those who disagree with them."[15]

Thus, despite its exalted status in the discourses of contemporary Islamists and in the broader Islamic tradition, jihad remains a means to an end. Equally important, in the mainstream Islamist view, jihad is a collective duty (*fard kifaya*), not becoming an individual duty (*fard 'ayn*) except in the case of an attack on one's self, property or homeland. Jihad is a highly regulated collective activity that falls under the purview of the rulers (*wulat al-amr*), who generally are solely responsible for declaring or terminating it.

Mainstream Islamists identify the aims, or purposes, of jihad in terms of defending the Muslim community against the aggression of both external enemies, commonly identified as unbelievers (*kufar*), and internal dissenters who, without a just cause, engage in violence against the *wulat al-amr* and/or against the Muslim population at large. None of the mainstream Islamists considered here elevates jihad to the status of a pillar of Islam, equal to profession of faith (*al-shahada*), prayer, fasting, paying alms (*zakat*), and performing the pilgrimage (to those who can). Qaradawi, however, contends that Shia scholars make that judgment, although he does not name any.[16]

While mainstream Islamists focus primarily on fighting external enemies, they also address fighting violent internal dissenters, usually referred to as *bughat*, in their discourses on jihad. Since this is a work on the international relations discourses of mainstream Islamists, it does not focus on fighting internal dissenters when discussing the purposes of jihad. A close reading of their discourses does reveal, though, that they consider this form of fighting as a category of jihad. In *The Jurisprudence of Jihad*, Qaradawi provides a thorough treatment of the juristic bases for fighting the *bughat*.[17] The references offered by the other scholar sheikhs are shorter, but in line with that of Qaradawi. Shams al-Din, whose views were briefly considered in this work, devotes a large part of his *Fiqh al-'Unf al-Musalah fi al-Islam* to refute the arguments of those who endorse the use of violence by armed groups to overthrow governments on the grounds that their rule is un-Islamic, i.e., not based on the *sharia*.[18] However, a full examination of the views of mainstream Islamists on fighting violent internal dissenters warrants an independent book-length study. To return to the main point, Jihad, in the mainstream reading, is defensive, rather than offensive, in nature.

Still, the major emphasis that all mainstream Islamists place on safeguarding the right of Muslim populations to freely practice Islam, and for Muslim *du'at* (preachers) to peacefully call for it, adds a dimension to jihad not commonly found in Western constructs of defensive wars or just wars. For mainstream Islamists, safeguarding the Islamic identity of Muslims is as important as preserving their lives, property, and homeland. In this worldview, taking away from Muslims the right to practice their religion, or better to live their Islam, all their other rights, including the right to life, become of little worth.

Believing that coercing others to embrace Islam is impermissible reflects mainstream Islamists' conviction in the centrality of the religious identity to the human identity. As Baroudi notes, "... for Abu Zahra, Zuhaili and scores of contemporary mainstream Islamists, religion is at the core of an individual and a group identity."[19] Both mainstream and radical Islamists define individuals primarily in terms of their religious identity, which explains the prevalence of the *millet* system under Islamic rule, such as in the Ottoman Empire.[20] The main difference between mainstream Islamists and radical Islamists, in this regard, is that the mainstream ones emphasize that the basic rights of non-Muslims, especially their right to practice their religion, are protected under Islamic rule. Each of the six scholar sheikhs featured in this study devotes considerable attention to the rights of non-Muslim populations under Islamic rule.

Fourth, mainstream Islamists argue that, even when fighting for legitimate purposes, Muslims ought to fight in accordance to certain "rules of warfare" whose origins lie in the *sharia*. Fadlallah refers to these rules as the "ethics of warfare." These rules are designed to limit harm to civilians and to avoid unnecessary cruelty in the treatment of enemy combatants (e.g., torture, mutilation of bodies). In this regard, mainstream Islamists, Zuhaili in particular, underscore the compatibility of the *sharia* with prevalent international norms and conventions that regulate the various tenets of modern warfare. The convergence between the *sharia* and international humanitarian law is a core theme in the discourse of Zuhaili.

Fifth, the notion of a "total war" that is fought until the annihilation of the enemy or one's own annihilation is anathematic to mainstream Islamists. According to the mainstream view, Muslims need not fight their enemies to the bitter end, and the ending of war is not contingent on a clear Muslim victory. The six scholar sheikhs surveyed here present alternative scenarios for ending war, including the possibility of payment to the enemy. They all leave ample room for *wulat al-amr* to use their judgment to terminate unsuccessful, or costly, wars. While discernible in the discourses of the six scholar sheikhs surveyed here, this emphasis on the limited purposes of war and the permissibility of terminating wars without a clear victory is mostly visible in the writings of Abu Zahra and Zuhaili.

Sixth and last, mainstream Islamists underscore the centrality of treaties and international agreements to the preservation of international peace and the facilitation of collaboration in the economic and cultural spheres. Mainstream Islamists argue in detail that the Quran, the Sunna of the Prophet, and, more generally, the Islamic tradition grant those in power (*wulat al-amr*) the authority to conclude a truce (*hudna*) that suspends hostilities or a peace treaty (*muʻahadat salam*) that permanently ends hostilities. They contend that the Prophet always honored the covenants he made with non-Muslims, including the Jews in the environs of Medina, party to the constitution of Medina, and even the polytheists.

In the mainstream narrative, the practice of honoring covenants was scrupulously followed by the rightly guided caliphs. Qaradawi, for example, frequently quotes the example of the second caliph's (Umar's) covenant with the Christian inhabitants of Jerusalem to preserve their churches and not to allow Jews, whom the Christians had earlier expelled from the city, to live in it.[21] In the contemporary era, mainstream Islamists argued that the destructiveness of modern warfare and the virtual impossibility of distinguishing between combatants and civilians intensifies the need to establish a rule-based international order that reduces the risks of war, regulates its conduct when it erupts, and, more generally, defines the rights and obligations of states in times of war and in times of peace. An important contribution of the mainstream perspective, emphasized primarily by Abu Zahra and Zuhaili, lay in demonstrating that abiding by international treaties, conventions, and norms, and more generally by international law, represented a continuation of time-honored practices that were enshrined in the Quran, the Sunna, and the Islamic tradition.

The Ideational Context

This study has been based on two premises. The first premise is that important ideas do not die out or simply fade away but are transmitted from one generation to the next. This was the case with the ideas of the founding generation of moderate-reformist scholar sheikhs (Afghani, 'Abduh, Rida) on interconnected topics, particularly: 1) the compatibility of reason and revelation; 2) the sheer impossibility of detaching the Muslim world from the increasingly interdependent international system and world economy; 3) the need to borrow selectively and judiciously from the West, while preserving, and reinforcing, the Islamic identity of majority-Muslim states; and 4) perhaps most importantly, the possibility, indeed desirability, of long periods of peace and of collaboration with the non-Muslim world, especially the West. The scholar sheikhs of the second and third generations of moderate-reformist Islamists internalized these ideas and expanded on them.

In the process, they collectively produced an impressive body of work on contemporary international relations that, while anchored in centuries-old Islamic tradition, also incorporated prevalent, contemporary concepts and notions about international relations, which were exogenous to this tradition. Most importantly, their body of work targeted the lay public and was not primarily intended for religious specialists or religious students. Thus, even in their more theoretical lengthy manuscripts, the mainstream scholar sheikhs surveyed in this work wrote in an accessible style that lay educated Muslims could comprehend and benefit from.

While discernable in the discourses of the scholar sheikhs of the founding generation, this emphasis on reaching out to the *umma* as a whole, or at least to its rapidly expanding literate segment, became even more pronounced with members of the second and third generations of scholar sheikhs. In brief, the moderate-reformist strand of political Islam exhibits a multi-generational approach to politics, economics, and society that grew in depth and breadth over time to encompass issues of international relations. The core elements of this approach, summarized above, were laid out by the scholar sheikhs of the founding generation. Members of the second and third generations engaged more fully with these themes, providing us with impressive texts on international relations that, while anchored in the Islamic tradition, draw on other, mainly Western, sources, at least in terms of the notions used in analyzing international relations.

The second premise in this work is that despite the origin in Western history and thought of the standard concepts and theories in the field of International

Relations (IR), they can be used effectively to analyze the IR discourses of non-Western scholars, in this case contemporary mainstream Islamists. This means that the core concepts that constitute the principal building blocks of the IR discipline, e.g., independence, sovereignty, diplomacy, treaties, power, violence, and war, have significant applications even outside the Western environment from which they emerged. Equally important, the two principal Western traditions of theorizing about international relations, namely realism and liberalism, can capture important components of the IR perspectives of contemporary mainstream Islamists, even when these non-Western scholars do not directly engage with these theories. It is, thus, appropriate to compare a non-Western scholar's views on international relations to the views of Western realists or liberals, even when the former has not read the seminal works that state and elaborate on the basic tenets of either realism or liberalism.

Accordingly, to argue that there are strong realist elements in the discourses of Bahi, Qaradawi, and Fadlallah—especially regarding their view of the international system as anarchic, skepticism of the intentions of the major powers, emphasis on the centrality of the balance of power to the preservation of peace, and bleak view of human nature—is not to claim that these scholar sheikhs have read Hans Morgenthau, Kenneth Waltz, or John Mearsheimer, to name a few prominent realists. An example would help illustrate my point. To note that the deep skepticism of these three scholar sheikhs about the effectiveness of international institutions mirrors the realist belief "that institutions cannot get states to stop behaving as short-term power maximizers"[22] does not mean that any of the three has read John Mearsheimer's critique of liberal institutionalism. Equally important, Qaradawi and Fadlallah's frequent references to *sunnat al-tadafu'* (law of mutual restraining), which they primarily derive from Quranic verses 2:251 and 22:40, brings to mind the Western realists' emphasis on the principle of the balance of power in international relations.

Baroudi argues that Qaradawi and Fadlallah articulate a non-Western variant of realism, one he calls "Islamic realism" that, while anchored in these two Quranic verses, is predicated on core realist notions regarding the anarchic nature of the international order, the central role that power plays in international relations and the role of human nature.[23] Broadly speaking, the "Islamic realism" of Qaradawi and Fadlallah has more in common with the classic realism of Henry Kissinger, Hans Morgenthau, Reinhold Niebuhr, and George Kennan than with the more parsimonious structural theories of Kenneth Waltz and John Mearsheimer, who primarily focus on the anarchic nature of the international system. In his introduction to *American Diplomacy*, Mearsheimer summarizes

Kennan's views on war as such, "Like most realists, he recognized that war is a legitimate instrument of statecraft, but also that it a destructive and brutal enterprise that sometimes does more harm than good and occasionally leads to national disaster."[24] Kennan's construct of war as an enterprise that ought to be entered into for important political reasons, after much thought and after exhausting other venues, finds its echoes in the discourses of Qaradawi and Fadlallah.

Once more, we have no evidence that Bahi, Qaradawi, or Fadlallah had read the works of the Western realists. The fact, though, that they independently arrive at similar conclusions to those of the Western realists lends credence to the claim that "realism represents a universal mode of theorizing about international relations that transcends cultural differences."[25] While realism is generally seen as a product of Western experiences and Western "secular" thought, Baroudi, based on an analysis of the discourses of Fadlallah and Qaradawi, calls for "research into the likely sources of realism in the three Abrahamic religions."[26]

On the other hand, the optimism that Abu Zahra and Zuhaili, and to a lesser extent Shaltut, pin on the positive contribution that international institutions can make to the preservation of international peace and to the promotion of international collaboration in the economic and cultural brings them close to the liberal institutional perspective on international relations. Abu Zahra and Zuhaili's construct of war as a limited enterprise, in both scope and duration that does not necessarily entail the severance of economic ties with the enemy state, is also in line with the liberal view. Abu Zahra and Zuhaili, thus, maintain that trading with an enemy state is permitted, including in time of war, as long as this trade is not in war-related material. In summary, Abu Zahra and Zuhaili's emphasis on limited war, fought for legitimate purposes in accordance with certain rules of warfare, and brought to an end when its political objectives are achieved, bears important resemblance to the liberal internationalist view of war. More importantly, Abu Zahra and Zuhaili embrace the division of humanity into distinct nations and peoples, viewing human diversity as divinely ordained in Quranic verses. One study has claimed that Abu Zahra and Zuhaili's views on human diversity as part of the human condition mirror those of Hannah Arendt, especially as conveyed in her seminal work *The Human Condition*.[27]

Still, there remain strong realist elements in the perspectives of Shaltut, Abu Zahra, and Zuhaili, especially regarding deterrence, "armed peace," and the necessity of strengthening the military and economic capabilities of Muslim states. These realist elements, however, are not as prominent in the discourses of Shaltut, Abu Zahra, and Zuhaili as they are in the discourses of Bahi, Qaradawi and Fadlallah. Despite the flexibility of the two labels, the realist label fits Bahi,

Qaradawi, and Fadlallah far better than the liberal internationalist label fits Shaltut, Abu Zahra, and Zuhaili.

The Historical Context

In this book, I contend that ideas do not simply evolve out of prior ideas and in response to them, but they also reflect the historical circumstances under which they emerge. Stated otherwise, ideas are not invented de novo, but emerge out of existing ideas (sometimes in a dialectical manner) and in the context of lived experiences. Contextualizing discourses is, thus, indispensable for comprehending them. Accordingly, the discourses of members of the founding generation ought to be read against the backdrop of colonialism, which by the end of the 19th century had placed the majority of the global Muslim population under direct or indirect European rule. One of the multiple sources on this era notes, "As the nineteenth century unfolded it became evident that, owing to their technical superiority in the field of armaments, high explosives and steam transport, the spillovers of the Industrial Revolution, the European powers could readily defeat the peripheral countries they wished to colonize."[28] By the late 19th century, most of the Muslim world had become part of these "peripheral countries," and thus the subject of outright occupation or domination.

Afghani's *Islamic Response to Imperialism* (to borrow from the title of Keddie's famous biography of Afghani) must thus be read against this backdrop of the intensification of European, and especially British, colonialism. As Keddie notes, "Sayyid Jamal al-Din al-Afghani (1838/9–1897) was one of the first figures to restate Muslim traditions in ways that met the important problems brought about by the increasing encroachments of the West on the 19th century Middle East."[29] More specifically, Afghani's anti-imperialist rhetoric was prompted by the British occupation of India, with its large, and hitherto dominant, Muslim population; the imposition in 1882 of the British protectorate over Egypt; and alleged British attempts to weaken and divide the Ottoman Empire, not to mention the British persecution of Afghani personally.[30] But even at the height of British power in the late 19th century, Afghani sensed the multiple vulnerabilities of the British Empire and sought to raise awareness about them. Afghani understood that the majority of the hundreds of millions who lived under British rule were subjugated non-European populations.[31]

Given its relatively small population and limited military power, Britain would not be able to maintain its rule over these non-European populations had they chosen to rise together against its rule, according to Afghani.[32] He was, thus, in favor of Muslim-Hindu cooperation in India in order to free the Indian subcontinent of the British raj.[33] Afghani's repeated calls for resisting British, and more generally European, imperialism did not focus primarily on military resistance but also on political and cultural resistance. Yet we are not aware of Afghani, at any point, openly calling for jihad against British rule. While anchored in Islam, the anti-imperialist, or anti-colonial, discourse of Afghani was not fundamentally different in substance from the discourses of non-Muslim critics of colonialism from the same era, such as Cuban poet, essayist, and advocate of Cuban independence José Marti (1853–1895),[34] Filipino nationalist José Rizal (1861–1896),[35] and Bengali novelist and poet Bankimchandra Chatterjee (1838–1894).[36]

The young 'Abduh was a willing accomplice in Afghani's campaign to resist European, primarily British, domination of Muslim populations. His support for the 'Urabi revolt against the khedive Tawfiq, who reigned 1879–1892, and against European meddling in Egyptian affairs, led to his exile from Egypt[37] and provided the context for his close collaboration with Afghani between 1883 and 1884 in issuing the *'Arwa al-Wuthqa*, while both were in exile in Paris.[38] Returning to Egypt in 1889, the mature 'Abduh distanced himself from his former mentor Afghani, acquiesced to British indirect rule over Egypt on the ground that it would be temporary, and reduced his political activism although he continued to support constitutional rule in Egypt to check the arbitrary power of the British and the khedive[39]. He then devoted his considerable energies instead to educational and religious reform, especially at al-Azhar.[40] At no point, however, did 'Abduh vacillate in his belief that Islam was not just a religion but also a great civilization equal to, if not surpassing, European civilizations. Despite his openness to Europe and embrace of dialog with European intellectuals and activists, 'Abduh categorically rejected colonial claims that the European civilization was superior to Islamic civilization or that Christianity was a more rational or a more peaceful religion than Islam.[41]

Of the members of the founding generation, only Rida lived to see the final dismemberment of the Ottoman Empire at the end of World War I and the abolition of the caliphate, not by Western powers, but at the hands of a Turkish Muslim war hero, whom Rida hitherto had admired, Mustafa Kemal Ataturk.[42] Placing Syria and Lebanon under French mandate and Palestine and Iraq under British mandate, as well as abolishing the caliphate in 1924, were momentous developments that Rida responded to with the belief that the resurrection of the caliphate represented the surest path, or the only path he knew, for the

Conclusion: The Mainstream Islamists Within Their Milieus | 273

restoration of the shattered Islamic unity. As Muhammad Khroubat writes, "Rida lived during a tense period in history, the central Islamic caliphate in Istanbul was collapsing bit by bit, Ottoman rule had receded in the various provinces, colonialism was spreading to encompass the entire Muslim world, and the attempts to swallow the whole of Palestine were proceeding in accordance to planned steps."[43]

Rida spent his later years advocating the restoration of the caliphate, participating in conferences for this aim, and drafting a proposal outlining a vision for the reestablishment of the caliphate.[44] His efforts were fruitless, because of squabbles among Arab leaders as to who would fill this coveted office and a general disinterest among leaders and political and intellectual elites, especially in Egypt, and one can argue among the Arab and broader Muslim public, in the idea of the caliphate. While continuing to voice support to the idea of the caliphate, the Sunni scholar sheikhs surveyed here shifted their focus to exploring alterative ways for restoring the political and cocioeconomic unity of the *umma*.

The Egyptian Shaltut, Abu Zahra, and Bahi wrote in a different international and regional environment. Broadly speaking, their environment was characterized, inter alia, by 1) the end of colonialism and its replacement by more subtle forms of domination and exploitation; 2) the raging Cold War between the US-led Western capitalistic camp and the Soviet-led Eastern socialist, or communist, camp; 3) the development of nuclear weapons, which altered the face of modern warfare, coming on the heels of the very destructive World War II; and 4) the emergence of Arab nationalism, and nation-state based nationalism, as rivals to pan-Islamism in the Arab World. These changed material and ideational realities impacted the thinking of the three scholar sheikhs and their perspectives on international relations in multiple ways.

To begin, all three celebrated the recently achieved political independence of nearly all-majority-Muslim societies but viewed it as incomplete due to the continued political, economic, and cultural subservience of these countries to either the US-led camp or the Soviet-led one. They rejected both capitalism and socialism in favor of an Islamic alternative, but one that they failed to properly articulate. They were not alone in seeking a third way that was neither capitalistic nor socialistic; other scholars from the developing world were also seeking an alternative to both capitalism and socialism that suited the needs of developing countries, while respecting their native cultures and traditions.

The three turbaned scholars also shared a strong aversion to war, especially a war with a superpower, partly out of fear of the destructiveness of nuclear weapons, and more generally of modern warfare, but mainly out of awareness of the immense power gap between the Muslim world and both the United States and the Soviet Union. Their awareness that the respective encroachments of the US-led and the Soviet-led camps on different parts of the Muslim world were primarily in the political, economic and especially cultural realms, and not in the military field, led them to advocate political, economic and cultural resistance, rather than military resistance. The demilitarization of the conflict with the non-Muslim world was a preoccupation of these three scholar sheikhs, as well as of the scholar sheikhs of the third generation. While the three scholar sheikhs of the second generation engaged in this discourse of resistance, Bahi was by far the most polemical.

Equally important, Shaltut and Abu Zahra reconciled themselves with Arab nationalism, with Abu Zahra claiming that there was no contradiction between the quest for Arab unity and the quest for Islamic unity[45]. Baroudi had the following to say regarding Abu Zahra's ambivalent and ambiguous position toward Arab nationalism:

> While other Islamists, such as Sayyed Qutb and even the more moderate Qaradawi, have rejected pan-Arabism. Abu Zahra acquiesces to it (without wholeheartedly embracing it), as he maintains that it did not constitute a threat to the unity of the *umma*. Abu Zahra's stance is that Islam does not forbid identifying with one's kin, country or nation as long as these ties do not undermine the Islamic tie.[46]

Bahi, on the other hand, remained committed to a pan-Islamist agenda throughout his life. His initial lukewarm support for Arab nationalism, more out of pragmatism than real conviction, turned to outright hostility in his later years, because of the association he drew between Arab nationalism and Egypt's experiment with socialism under President Nasser, which he opposed. Similarly to Rida, Bahi grew increasingly conservative in his later years and rather pro-Saudi in his orientation. When he ventured into the politics of the day, which he rarely did, he tended to be critical of Nasser's view of the conservative Arab monarchies and his penchant to intervene in the domestic politics of other Arab countries. In his last published work, *Tahafut al-Fikr al-Madi al-Tarikhi*, Bahi lashed out against the ideology of historic materialism, as embodied in the theories of Marx and his followers. More importantly, he dwelled on the multiple failures of communist systems in the Soviet Union and Eastern Europe, whether in terms of markedly improving the standards of living of their people, achieving equitable distributions of wealth, or protecting the basic political and civil rights of their citizens.[47]

While Shaltut, Abu Zahra, and especially Bahi invariably maintained that their orientation was Islamic—and neither capitalist nor socialist—they harbored far greater animosity toward socialism, and especially communism, than toward capitalism. Their claimed neutrality in the ideological confrontation between capitalism and socialism that characterized the Cold War is thus questionable. For example, a close and holistic reading of Bahi's extensive discourse on capitalism versus socialism/communism reveals that he believed that capitalism could be reformed and could be significantly altered to conform to the *sharia*, while socialism could not. The scholar sheikhs of the third generation lived to see the end of the Cold War and the rise of the United States to a position of international dominance. While they were not averse to the collapse of the Soviet Union and the demise of communism, which they detested, they voiced serious apprehensions about the United States' exploitation of its "unilateral moment" to advance its interests and the interests of its ally Israel at the expense of the legitimate interests of the weaker developing countries, especially Arab and majority-Muslim states.

While Zuhaili maintained his academic orientation throughout his long career, resorting to only limited and specific criticisms of the United States in his late works, Qaradawi and Fadlallah gave vent to their frustrations with the United States as of the early 1990s, utilizing the multiple venues at their disposal—Friday Sermons, television and radio programs, media interviews, the Internet, and published works—to denounce the United States. One can see in their discourse against the United States that Fadlallah and Qaradawi directed their critiques specifically at US foreign policy toward the Arab and Muslim worlds. Their critiques revolved around specific issues concerning the substance of US Middle East policy, with the Middle East broadly defined. To start with, Qaradawi and Fadlallah criticized American direct and indirect support of dictatorships all over the Arab and Muslim world—despite the US pro-democracy and pro-human rights rhetoric which intensified in the wake of the end of the Cold War—as long as these dictatorships toed the US foreign policy line, opened their economies to US businesses and suppressed domestic Islamist movements. Qaradawi and Fadlallah were to give the same examples of US backing of dictatorships: its backing of the Algerian military after it annulled the results of the 1991 "democratic" election in order to prevent the Islamist party, the Islamic Salvation Front, from capturing power; and its support of the regime of Saddam Hussein in his long war with Iran and acquiescence to his remaining in power after the war to liberate Kuwait in 1990.

Equally importantly, the two scholar sheikhs accused the United States of working tirelessly to undermine governments that adopted an Islamic agenda, whether in Iran after the Iranian Revolution, or in Sudan under former president Omar al-Bashir, who ruled between 1989 and 2019. Even more importantly, they accused the United States of exploiting the September 11, 2001 attacks on its territory to launch an unprecedented campaign to discredit Islam by unjustly tying it to terrorism. Both Fadlallah and Qaradawi accused the United States, specifically the George W. Bush administration which they detested, of pressuring Arab and Muslim governments to revamp their educational curricula to deemphasize religious education in favor of secular-liberal education, and more seriously, to promote apolitical quietist interpretations of Islam. Qaradawi, thus, warned Arab and Muslim governments against "yielding to American pressure that is backed by armaments, money, sciences, cunning, and planning, and manufacturing an American Islam, *Islaman Amrikaniyan*, which is less concerned with satisfying God than with satisfying Uncle Sam."[48]

No issue, though, clouded Qaradawi and Fadlallah's, and more generally Islamists' and Arab nationalists', relationships with the United States than did US-alleged unconditional support for Israel in its decades-long conflict with the Palestinians and neighboring Arab states. A recurrent theme in the discourses of Qaradawi and Fadlallah and those of other Islamists is that the United States took advantage of its enhanced international power and status, following the end of the Cold War, to pressure the Palestinians and Arab states to agree to peace with Israel on the latter's terms. While one may argue that Qaradawi and Fadlallah were opposed to the whole peace process with Israel, their criticisms of the United States focused on their perceived US disregard of Palestinian and Arab rights, especially regarding the status of Jerusalem, and the US wholehearted embrace of Israel. For Qaradawi and Fadlallah, in the post-Cold War era and especially after the September 11 attacks, the United States even stopped pretending that it was playing the role of the honest broker and fair arbitrator between the Arabs and Israel.

Generally, those mainstream Islamists who lived to see the end of the Cold War voiced major apprehensions about the US preeminent role in the reconfigured international order. While Zuhaili's criticisms of the US-dominated international order were measured, Qaradawi and Fadlallah did resort to what one may call "rhetorical offensives" against US hegemony.[49] The heavy polemics notwithstanding, their specific criticisms of US Middle East policy were shared by secular Arab nationalists[50] and, one may argue, by broad sections of the Arab public.

It is significant to note that Fadlallah and Qaradawi legitimated armed resistance to the United States only in those theaters where the United States was an occupying power, mainly post-2001 Afghanistan and post-2003 Iraq. They opposed, on both moral and practical grounds, attacks on US territory, like the September 11 attacks, or against US citizens and property. Accordingly, they viewed resistance to American hegemony, mainly in political, economic, and cultural terms, rather than in military terms. At no point, did they openly advocate jihad against the United States, despite their endorsement of armed resistance to US military presence in Afghanistan and especially in Iraq.

Since the reading of international relations of mainstream Islamists is quite different from the reading of radical Islamists, an important question ensues: which of the two camps of Islamists has had a greater sway over the Arab public? Limitations of space and absence of reliable data on the topic preclude a detailed and "scientific" answer to this question. Cursory evidence, however, points out that the mainstream Islamists, especially Shaltut (as Sheikh al-Azhar), Qaradawi and Fadlallah, who had direct access to large segments of the public, appealed to a larger segment of the Arab public than did radical figures such as Bin Laden, Ayman al-Zawahiri, Abu Muhamad al-Maqdisi and other ideologues of al-Qaeda and the "Islamic State in Iraq and al-Sham" (ISIS).

It is true that thousands of radicalized Muslim Arabs left for Afghanistan in the late 1970s and 1980s to fight the Soviet occupation of that country, but that number still constituted a tiny fraction of Arab Muslim populations. Jihadist groups in Egypt drew little public sympathy, especially since their attacks on Western tourists adversely impacted the frail Egyptian economy and hurt the livelihoods of many Egyptians. Qaradawi, in particular, wrote extensively on refuting the ideology and denouncing the practices of the radical and jihadist movements in his native Egypt.[51] The Muslim Brotherhood, the most popular Islamist movement in Egypt and other parts of the Arab world, claimed Qaradawi as one of its own, while distancing itself from the thought of al-Qaeda and other jihadi-salafi movements. ISIS failed to garner significant support from most Sunni Arabs, not to ignore the Shias who detested it, and its hold over territory in Iraq and Syria, brief as it was, was due to the ferocity of its fighters, many of whom came from outside the Arab world, and the brutality of its methods of repression.[52]

In conclusion, it is true that mainstream Islamists do not approach international relations as IR scholars do. They clearly do not provide us with parsimonious and clearly articulated theories of international relations, such as Kenneth Waltz's "structural realism,"[53] John Mearsheimer's "offensive realism,"[54] Stephen Walt's "balancing against threats,"[55] John Ikenberry's "liberal institutionalism,"[56] Daniel Deudney's "republican security theory"[57] and Alexander Wendt's "systemic constructivism,"[58] to name a few prominent theories and their principal proponents. Nevertheless, a close reading of their discourses provides us with penetrating insights into how a select group of non-Western public intellectuals (scholar sheikhs in our case) construed contemporary international relations. Hence in the title of this book, I refer to "Islamist perspectives on international relations," rather than to "Islamist theories of international relations." Analyzing the perspectives of the six scholar sheikhs, who represent the moderate-reformist, mainstream, strand of political Islam, has served at least three interconnected purposes.

First, it has demonstrated the diversity within political Islam and the necessity of differentiating between the views of different Islamists, despite the Islamists' common point of departure, namely that there can be no separation between religion and politics in Islam. Accordingly, it is hoped that this work has contributed to shattering any lingering myths about the monolithic nature of political Islam, while encouraging a nuanced understanding of the diverse, and often conflicting, views of contemporary Islamists. What divides Islamists is seemingly more important than what unites them. Understanding and appreciating the diversity, and indeed the tensions and conflicts, within political Islam should be of interest not just for academics, but also for policy makers, whether from within or from outside the Arab world, who need to deal with Islamist activists and movements.

Second, it has shown that the Quran, the Sunna, and more generally the Islamic tradition are open to diverse, and often, conflicting interpretations, especially when it comes to addressing political and socioeconomic problems, including issues of international relations. As Tariq Ramadan notes, while "Islam's two scriptural sources (the Qur'an and the Prophetic tradition—the Sunna) are recognized by all schools of thought and constitute the bedrock of Islamic belief," there is considerable diversity "in the way the two scriptural sources... are read and interpreted."[59] Mainstream and radical Islamists turn to religion for inspiration and guidance on temporal matters, including matters of individual and group conduct (*mu'amalat*). Based on their different interpretations of essentially the same revered sources, mainly the Quran and the Sunna, they recommend different courses of action for their audiences.

While lacking the "scientific" means to verify this claim, one would expect the conduct of lay Muslims, i.e., those who are not steeped in knowledge of the religion, to vary based on whether they heed to the call of the mainstream Islamists or that of the radical Islamists. This work has been predicated on the notion that there can be no separation between thought and praxis as ideas influence action. Understanding the various, and often contradictory, currents of thought within political Islam is, thus, pivotal for understanding the conduct of lay Muslims and of Islamist movements as diverse as the Muslim Brotherhood, the Nahda party in Tunisia, Hezbollah, and Hamas and indeed al-Qaeda and the now defunct Islamic State in Iraq and al-Sham (ISIS).

Third, this work has attempted to relate the discourses of mainstream Islamists to the two dominant Western traditions of analyzing international relations: realism and liberal internationalism. This "ideational situating" aimed to demonstrate that the stock concepts that constitute the building blocks of the discipline of IR are quite useful in analyzing the discourses of non-Western scholars who address issues of international relations. Despite its Western origins and its Western orientation in terms of the problems that preoccupy it, the field of IR has engendered an incredibly rich repertoire of knowledge. More specifically, the concepts and theories, which are at the core of the IR discipline, can be "intelligently" used to analyze problems in international relations, irrespectively of where they occur, as well as to examine perspectives on international relations, including by scholars from non-Western background. Thus, any work on international relations that consciously or unconsciously sidelines the concepts and theories that are at the core of the field will remain marginal to the discipline and of little interest to IR students. It is hoped that this work, despite its obvious and multiple limitations, has contributed to our understanding not just of political Islam but also of international relations.

Notes

1 Richard C. Martin and Abbas Barzegar, "Introduction: The Debate about Islamism in the Public Sphere," in *Islamism: Contested Perspectives on Political Islam*, eds. Richard C. Martin and Abbas Barzegar (Stanford: Stanford University Press, 2010), 2.
2 Quoted in Baroudi, "On Origins: Arab Intellectuals' Debates on ISIS," 238.
3 Borrowed from Richard Harknett and Hasan Yalcin, "The Struggle for Autonomy: A Realist Structural Theory of International Relations," *International Studies Review* 14, no. 2 (December 2012): 499–521, 505.
4 Baroudi, "The Problematic Notion of the Islamic State."
5 Bernard Weiss, *The Spirit of Islamic Law* (Athens, Georgia: Georgia University Press, 1998), 3.
6 Weiss, *The Spirit of Islamic Law*, 4.
7 Hannah Arendt, *On Violence* (New York: Houghton Mifflin Harcourt Publishing Company, 1969), 51.
8 Qaradawi, *Fiqh al-Jihad*, 424.

9 Qaradawi, *Fiqh al-Jihad*, 424.
10 Qaradawi, *Fiqh al-Jihad*, 425.
11 This is Zuhaili's principal argument in his late work *al-islam wa al-Qanun al-Duwali al-Insani*.
12 See, in particular, Sami E. Baroudi, "The Problematic Notion of the 'Islamic state' in the Discourses of Contemporary Islamists: The Case of Sheikh Muhammad Abu Zahra (1898–1974)," *Middle Eastern Studies* 56, no. 33 (2020): 496–510. doi: https://doi.org/10.1080/00263206.2019.1704269.
13 Sami E. Baroudi, "Hannah Arendt, the Human Condition and the Embrace of Human Diversity in the Discourses of Two Contemporary Islamists: Sheikh Muhammad Abu Zahra (1898–1974) and Sheikh Wahbah al-Zuhaili (1932–2015)," *British Journal of Middle Eastern Studies* (2019), Doi: https://doi.org/10.1080/13530194.2019.1699775, 19.
14 Keddie, "Sayyid Jamal al-Din al-Afghani," in *Pioneers of Islamic Revival*, ed. Rahmena, 11, 28–29.
15 Yvonne Haddad, "Muhammad Abduh," in *Pioneers of Islamic Revival*, ed. Rahnema, 30–63, 41.
16 Qaradawi, *Fiqh al-Jihad*, 76.
17 Qaradawi, *Fiqh al-Jihad*, 1095–130.
18 Shams al-Din, *Fiqh al-'Unf al-Musalah*.
19 Sami E. Baroudi, "The Problematic Notion of the 'Islamic state' in the Discourses of Contemporary Islamists: The Case of Sheikh Muhammad Abu Zahra (1898–1974)," *Middle Eastern Studies* 56, no. 3 (2020): 496–510, 19. doi: https://doi.org/10.1080/00263206.2019.1704269.
20 For the millet system under the Ottoman Empire, see, for example, Richard Antaramian, *Brokers of Faith, Brokers of Empire: Armenians and the Politics of Reform in the Ottoman Empire* (Stanford: Stanford University Press, 2020).
21 Qaradawi, *Fiqh al-Jihad*, 1008–9.
22 John Mearsheimer, "A Realist Reply," *International Security* 2, no. 1 (1995), 82–93, 82.
23 Baroudi, "The Islamic Realism of Sheikh Yusuf Qaradawi (1926) and Sayyid Muhammad Hussein Fadlallah."
24 John Mearsheimer, "Introduction," in *American Diplomacy: Sixtieth-Anniversary Expanded Edition*, ed. George Kennan (Chicago and London: The University of Chicago Press, 2012), xxiv.
25 Baroudi, "The Islamic Realism," 113.
26 Baroudi, "The Islamic Realism," 94.
27 Baroudi, "Hannah Arendt, the Human Condition and the Embrace of Human Diversity in the Discourses of Two Contemporary Islamists".
28 Ali Rahnema, "Introduction," in *Pioneers of Islamic Revival*, ed. Ali Rahnema, xxvii.

Conclusion: *The Mainstream Islamists Within Their Milieus* | 281

29 Keddie, "Sayyid Jamal al-Din al-Afghani," 13.
30 Qalʻaji, *Thalatha min Aʻlam al-Huriya*, 64–71.
31 Qalʻaji, *Thalatha min Aʻlam al-Huriya*, 142–3.
32 Qalʻaji, *Thalatha min Aʻlam al-Huriya*, 134.
33 As Keddie notes, "In the late 1870s and early 1880s he [Afghani] wrote many articles in support of nationalism, including praising the unity of Muslims and Christians in Egypt and of Muslims and Hindus in India." Keddie, "Sayyid Jamal al-Din al-Afghani", 25.
34 For the life and thought of Marti, see, in particular, Alfred Lopez, *José Marti, A Revolutionary Life* (Austin, TX: Texas University Press, 2014).
35 For the life and thought of Rizal, see, in particular, Leon Guerrero, *The First Filipino: A Biography of José Rizal* (Manilla: National Heroes Commission, 1963).
36 For the thought of Bankimchandra Chatterjee, see, in particular, Tapan Raychaudhuri, *Europe Reconsidered: Perceptions of the West in Nineteenth Century Bengal* (Oxford: Oxford University Press, 2002).
37 Qalʻaji, *Thalatha min Aʻlam al-Huriya*, 195–225.
38 Qalʻaji, *Thalatha min Aʻlam al-Huriya*, 75–78; ʻImara, *al-Aʻmal al-Kamila lil-Imam al-Sheikh Muhammad ʻAbduh*, 73–76; Keddie, "Sayyid Jamal al-Din al-Afghani," 19–20.
39 As can be seen from the title of one article by Muhammad ʻAbduh, "al-Umma wa-Sultat al-hakim al-Mustabid" (The *Umma* and the Authority of the Despotic Ruler) in ʻAbduh, *al-ʻArwa al-Wuthqa: Jamal al-Din ʻal-Afghani* (Cairo: Maktabet al-Shurouk al-Dawliya, 2002), both Afghani and ʻAbduh rejected despotic rule, clearly placing the *umma* above the ruler. Reprinted in Qalʻaji, *Thalatha min Aʻlam al-Huriya*, 134–35. For further evidence of ʻAbduh's support of constitutional rule, see, Qalʻaji, *Thalatha min Aʻlam al-Huriya*, 186–7.
40 Qalʻaji, *Thalatha min Aʻlam al-Huriya*, 245–56.
41 Haddad, *Muhammad Abduh*, 35–43.
42 Works abound on this critical period in modern Turkish history. For Ataturk's abolishing of the caliphate, see, inter alia, Serif Mardin, "Religion and Secularism in Turkey," in *The Modern Middle East: A Reader*, eds. Albert Hourani, Philip Khoury and Mary Wilson (Berkeley and Los Angeles: University of California Press, 1993), 347–74; and Mona Hassan, *Longing for the Lost Caliphate, A Transregional History* (Princeton and Oxford: Princeton University Press, 2016), esp. 2, 10–13, 16, 142–5, 161–3, 184, 224, 237.
43 Muhammad Khrubat, "al-Islah al-Siyyasi ʻind al-Sheikh Muhammad Rashid Rida" (Political Reform according to Sheikh Muhammad Rashid Rida), *al-Fikr al-Islami al-Muʻasir* 7, no. 26 (2001), https://citj.org/index.php/citj/article/view/1673/1395, accessed 27 August 2019.
44 Hassan, *Longing for the Lost Caliphate*, 224–5.

45 Abu Zahra, *al-Wihda al-Islamiyya*, 79–116.
46 Sami E. Baroudi, "Sheikh Muhammad Abu Zahra (1898–1974) on International Relations: The Discourse of a Contemporary Mainstream Islamist, *Middle Eastern Studies*, 54, no. 3 (2018), 415–41, doi: https://doi.org/10.1080/00263206.2018.1434 147, 433.
47 Bahi, *Tahafut al-Fikr al-Madi*, esp. 30–56.
48 Qaradawi, *Khitabuna al-Islami fi 'Asr al-'Awlama*, 15.
49 For rhetorical offensives against US hegemony by Arab secular nationalists, see Sami E. Baroudi, "Countering US Hegemony: The Discourse of Salim al-Hoss and Other Arab Intellectuals," *Middle Eastern Studies* 44, no. 1 (January 2008): 105–29. For similar critiques of US foreign policy by Arab Islamists, see Sami E. Baroudi, "In the Shadow of the Quran: Recent Islamist Discourse on the United States and US Foreign Policy," *Middle Eastern Studies* 46, no. 4 (July 2010): 569–94.
50 See Baroudi, "Countering US Hegemony."
51 See, in particular, Qaradawi, *Fiqh al-Jihad*, 1131–69.
52 Baroudi, "On Origins," 220–1.
53 Kenneth N. Waltz, *Theory of International Politics* (Reading, MA: Addison-Wesley, 1979).
54 John J. Mearsheimer, *The Tragedy of Great Power Politics* (New York and London, W. W. Norton & Company, 2001).
55 Stephen Walt, *The Origins of Alliances* (Cornell: Cornell University Press, 1987).
56 John C. Ikenberry, *Liberal Leviathan: The Origins, Crisis, and Transformation of the American World Order* (Princeton, N.J.: Princeton University Press, 2011).
57 Daniel Deudney, *Bounding Power: Republican Security Theory from the Polis to the Global Village* (Princeton, N.J.: Princeton University Press, 2007).
58 Alexander Wendt, *Social Theory of International Politics* (Cambridge: Cambridge University Press, 1999).
59 Tariq Ramadan, *The Arab Awakening: Islam and the New Middle East* (London: Penguin Books, 2012), 73.

Bibliography

'Abd al-Raziq. Ali. *Al-Islam wa Usul al-Hukm* (Islam and the Principles of Governance). Cairo: Dar al-Kitab al-Masri, 1925.
Abu Zahra, Muhammad. *Al-Mujtama' al-Insani fi dhil al-Islam* (Human Society in the Shade of Islam). Jeddah: al-Dar al-Sa'udia lil-Nashr wa al-Tawzi', 1981.
Abu Zahra, Muhammad. *Tahrim al-Riba: Tandhim Iqtisadi* (Prohibiting Usury: An Economic System). Jeddah: al-Dar al-Sa'udia lil-Nashr wa al-Tawzi', 1985.
Abu Zahra, Muhammad. *Al -'Alaqat al-Duwaliya fi al-Islam* (International Relations in Islam). Cairo: Dar al-Fikr al-Arabi, 1995.
Abu Zahra, Muhammad. *Al-Imam al-Sadiq: Hayatuh wa-'Asruh: Ara'uh wa Fiqhuh* (Al-Imam al-Sadiq: His Life and Era: Opinions and Jurisprudence). Cairo: Dar al-Fikr al-'Arabi, 2005a.
Abu Zahra, Muhammad. *Al-Imam Zaid, Hayatuh wa-'Asruh: Ara'uh wa Fiqhuh* (Al-Imam Zaid: His Life and Era: Opinions and Jurisprudence). Cairo: Dar al-Fikr al-'Arabi, 2005b.
Abu Zahra, Muhammad. *Ibn Taymiyya: Hayatuh wa-'Asruh: Ara'uh wa Fiqhuh* (Ibn Taymiyya: His Life and Era: Opinions and Jurisprudence). Cairo: Dar al-Fikr al-'Arabi, 2005c.
Abu Zahra, Muhammad. *Ibn Hazm: Hayatuh wa-'Asruh: Ara'uh wa Fiqhuh* (Ibn Hazm: His Life and Era: Opinions and Jurisprudence). Cairo: Dar al-Fikr al-'Arabi, 2007.
Abu Zahra, Muhammad. *Nazhariyat al-Harb fi al-Islam* (The Theory of War in Islam). Cairo: Wizarat al-Awqaf, al-Majlis al-A'la lil-Shu'oun al-Islamiya, 2008.
Abu Zahra, Muhammad. *Al-Wihda al-Islamiya* (The Islamic Unity). Cairo: Dar al-Fikr al-'Arabi, 2011.

Abu Zahra, Muhammad. *The Four Imams: Their Lives, Works and their Schools of Thought*. Translated by Aisha Bewley. London: Dar al-Taqwa Ltd., 2001.

Acharya, Amitav. *Rethinking Power, Institutions and Ideas in World Politics: Whose IR?* London and New York: Routledge, 2014.

Afsaruddin, Asma. *Striving in the Path of God: Jihad and Martyrdom in Islamic Thought*. Oxford: Oxford University Press, 2013.

Ajami, Fouad. "Lebanon and its Inheritors." *Foreign Affairs* 63 (1985): 778–99.

Ajami, Fouad. *The Vanished Imam: Musa al-Sadr and the Shia of Lebanon*. Ithaca and London: Cornell University Press, 1986.

Al-Bahi, Muhammad. *Al-Fikr al-Islami al-Hadith wa 'Alaqatuh bi al-Isti'mar al-Gharbi* (Modern Islamic Thought and its Relation to Western Colonialism), 5th ed. Beirut: Dar al-Fikr, 1970a.

Al-Bahi, Muhammad. *Al-Islam fi al-Waqi' al-Ideologi al-Mu'asir* (Islam in the Contemporary Ideological Landscape). Beirut: Dar al-Fikr, 1970b.

Al-Bahi, Muhammad. *Al-Fikr al-Islami fi Tatawuruh* (Islamic Thought and its Development). Beirut: Dar al-Fikr, 1971.

Al-Bahi, Muhammad. *Tahafut al-Fikr al-Madi al-Tarikhi bayn al-Nazariya wa al-Tatbiq* (The Demise of Historic Materialist Thought between Theory and Practice). Cairo: Maktabat Wahba, 1975.

Al-Bahi, Muhammad. *Al-Din wa al-Dawla min Tawjih al-Quran al-Karim* (Religion and the State in Light of the Noble Quran). Cairo: Maktabat Wahba, 1980.

Al-Bahi, Muhammad. *Al-Islam fi Hal Mashakil al-Mujtama'at al-Islamiya al-Mu'asira* (Islam and Solving the Problems of Contemporary Muslim Societies), 3rd ed. Cairo: Maktabat Wahba, 1981.

Al-Bahi, Muhammad. *Hayati fi Rihab al-Azhar: Talib wa Ustazh wa Wazir* (My Life at the Encompasses of al-Azhar: as a Student, a Teacher and a Minister). Cairo: Maktabat Wahba, 1983.

Al-Ghannushi, Rachid. *Al-Hurriyyat al-'Amma fi al-Dawla al-Islamiya* (Public Freedoms in the Islamic State). Beirut: Markaz Dirasat al-Wihda al-'Arabiya, 1993.

Al-Ghannushi, Rachid. *Al-Wasatiyya al-Siyasiyya 'ind al-Imam Yusuf al-Qaradawi* (Political *Wasatiyya* in the view of Imam Yusuf Qaradawi). Jeddah: Mu'asasat Ru'a Thaqafiyya, 2009.

Al-Ghazali, Muhammad. *Al-Islam fi Wajh al-Zahf al-Ahmar* (Islam Facing the Red March). Cairo: Nahdat Masr lil-Nashr wa al-Tawzi', 2005.

Al-Khateeb, Motaz. "Yusuf al-Qaradawi as an authoritative reference (Marja'iyya)." In *Global Mufti: The Phenomenon of Yusuf Qaradawi*, edited by Bettina Graf and Jakob Skovgaard-Peterson, 85–108. New York: Columbia University Press, 2009a.

Al-Khateeb, Motaz. *Yusuf al-Qaradawi: Faqih al-Sahwa al-Islamiya Sira Fikriya Tahliliya* (Yusuf Qaradawi: The Jurisprudent of the Islamic Awakening: An Analytical Intellectual Biography). Beirut: Center for Civilization for the Development of Islamic Thought, 2009b.

Al-Mahmassani, Sobhi. *Arkan Huquq al-Insan fi al-Islam* (The Pillars of Human Rights in Islam). Beirut: Dar al-'Ilm lil-Malyeen, 1979.

Al-Nafis, Ahmad Rasem. *Al-Qaradawi: Wakil Allah Am Wakil Bani Ummayya?* (Al-Qaradawi: The Deputy of God; or that of the Umayyads?). Beirut: Dar al-Mizan, 2006.

Al-Qaradawi, Yusuf. *Al-Khasa'es al 'Amma lil-Islam* (The General Characteristics of Islam). Cairo: Maktabat Wahba, 1977.

Al-Qaradawi, Yusuf. *Al-Hulul al-Mustawrada wa kayfa janat 'ala Ummatna* (Imported Solutions and the injustice they did to our Umma). Cairo: Maktabat Wahba, 1993a.

Al-Qaradawi, Yusuf. *Al-Sahwa al-Islamiyya wa Humum al-Watan al-'Arabi wa al-Islami* (The Islamic Awakening and the Concerns of the Arab and Muslim World). Beirut: Mu'asasat al-Risalah, 1993b.

Al-Qaradawi, Yusuf. *Al-Umma al-Islamiyya Haqiqa la Wahm* (The Islamic Umma a Reality not an Illusion). Cairo: Maktabat Wahba, 1994.

Al-Qaradawi, Yusuf. *Al-Quds Qadiyat Kul Muslim* (Jerusalem the Cause of Every Muslim). Cairo: Maktabat Wahba, 1998.

Al-Qaradawi, Yusuf. *Kayf Nata'amal Ma' al-Qur'an al-'Azim* (Approaching the Magnificent Quran). Cairo: Dar al-Shuruq, 1999.

Al-Qaradawi, Yusuf. *Ummatna Bayn Qarnayn* (Our Umma between Two Centuries). Cairo: Dar al-Shuruq, 2000a.

Al-Qaradawi, Yusuf. *Al-Sheikh al-Ghazali kama 'Areftuh: Rihlat Nisf Qarn* (Sheikh Ghazali as I Knew Him: The Journey of Half a Century). Cairo: Dar al-Shuruq, 2000b.

Al-Qaradawi, Yusuf. *Al-Tataruf al-'Ilmani fi Muwajahat al-Islam: Namuzhaj Turkiya wa Tunis* (Secular Extremism confronting Islam: the Models of Turkey and Tunisia). Cairo: Dar al-Shuruq, 2001a.

Al-Qaradawi, Yusuf. *Fi Fiqh al-Aqaliyyat al-Muslima: Hayat al-Muslimin Wasat al-Mujtama'at al-Ukhra* (Regarding the Jurisprudence of Muslim Minorities: The Lives of Muslims in Non-Muslim Societies). Cairo: Dar al-Shuruq, 2001b.

Al-Qaradawi, Yusuf. *Al-Sahwa al-Islamiyya Min al-Murahaqa ila al-Rushd* (The Islamic Awakening from Adolescence to Maturity). Cairo: Dar al-Shuruq, 2002.

Al-Qaradawi, Yusuf. *Ibn al-Qarya wa al-Kuttab* (Son of the Village and the Kuttab), Vols. 1–3. Cairo: Dar al-Shuruq, 2002, 2004, and 2006.

Al-Qaradawi, Yusuf. *Fatawa min Ajl Filastin* (Fatwas for the Sake of Palestine). Cairo: Maktabat Wahba, 2003.

Al-Qaradawi, Yusuf. *Khitabuna al-Islami for 'Asr al-'Awlama* (Our Islamic Discourse in the Era of Globalization). Cairo: Dar al-Shuruq, 2004.

Al-Qaradawi, Yusuf. *Al-Islam wa al-'Unf: Nazharat Ta'siliyya* (Islam and Violence: Foundational Views). Cairo: Dar al-Shuruq, 2005a.

Al-Qaradawi, Yusuf. *Tarikhuna al-Muftara 'Alayh* (Our Slandered History). Cairo: Dar al-Shuruq, 2005b.

Al-Qaradawi, Yusuf. *Fiqh al-Jihad: Dirasa Muqarina li-Ahkamih wa Falsfatih fi Daou' al-Qur'an wa al-Sunna* (The Jurisprudence of Jihad: A Comparative Study of its Rules and Philosophy in Light of the Qur'an and the Sunna), Vols. 1 & 2. Cairo: Maktabat Wahba, 2009.

Al-Qaradawi, Yusuf. *Fiqh al-Wasatiya al-Islamiyya: Ma'alem wa Manarat* (The Jurisprudence of the Islamic Moderate and Balanced Approach: Landmarks and Signposts). Cairo: Dar al-Shuruq, 2010.

Al-Qaradawi, Yusuf. *Min Fiqh al-Dawla fi al-Islam* (The Jurisprudence of the State in Islam). Cairo: Dar al-Shuruq, 2011a.

Al-Qaradawi, Yusuf. *Shumul al-Islam* (The Comprehensiveness of Islam). Cairo: Maktabat Wahba, 2011b.
Al-Qaradawi, Yusuf. *Nahnu wa al-Gharb* (Us and the West) (2005). https://www.al-qaradawi.net/node/5041, accessed 12 April 2012.
Al-Qaradawi, Yusuf. *Al-Baba wa al-Islam* (The Pope and Islam). https://www.al-qaradawi.net/node/1766, accessed 23 April 2012.
Al-Zuhaili, Wahbah. *Haq al-Huriya fi al-'Alam* (The Right to freedom in the World). Damascus: Dar al-Fikr, 2000.
Al-Zuhaili, Wahbah. *Athar al-Harb: Dirasa Fiqhiya Muqarina* (Effects of War: A Comparative Jurisprudential Study), 4th ed. Damascus: Dar al-Fikr, 2009.
Al-Zuhaili, Wahbah. *Al-'Alaqat al-Duwaliya fi al-Islam: Muqarana bil-Qanun al-Duwali al-Hadith* (International Relations in Islam: In Comparison to Contemporary International Law). Damascus: Dar al-Fikr, 2011.
Al-Zuhaili, Wahbah. "Al-Islam wa al-Qanun al-Duwali" (Islam and International Law), ICRC 2005. https://www.icrc.org/ar/doc/resources/documents/article/review/review-858-p269.htm, accessed 12 April 2012.
Al-Zuhaili, Wahbah. *Al-Qanun al-Duwali al-Insani wa Huquq al-Insan: Dirasa Muqarina* (International Humanitarian Law and Human Rights: A Comparative Study). Damascus: Dar al-Fikr, 2012.
Al-Zuhaili, Wahbah. "Kalimat Dr. Wahbah al-Zuhaili Fi Ta'been al-Dr. al-Bouti Rahamahu Allah" (Dr. Wahba Al-Zuhaili's speech at the memorial of Dr. Al-Bouti, May God have mercy on him), https://www.youtube.com/watch?v=PAKB9OztE0g, accessed 10 August 2015.
Alexander, Yonah and Dean Alexander. *The Islamic State: Combatting the Caliphate without Borders*. Lanham, Boulder, New York, London: Lexington Books, 2015.
Arendt, Hannah. *The Human Condition*. Chicago: The University of Chicago Press, 1958.
Arendt, Hannah. *On Violence*. New York: Houghton Mifflin Harcourt Publishing Company, 1969.
Arendt, Hannah. *On Revolution*. New York: Viking, 1970.
Arslan, Al-Amir Shakib. *Al-Sayyid Rashid Rida aw Ikha' Arba'in Sanna* (Sayyed Rashid Rida: The Brotherhood of Forty Years), Vols. 1–3. Mukhtara, Mount Lebanon: al-Dar al-Taqadumiyya, 2010.
Asad, Talal. "The Idea of an Anthropology of Islam," Occasional Papers Series. Washington, DC: Georgetown University, Center for Contemporary Arab Studies, 1986.
Atwan, Abdel Bari. *The Digital Caliphate*. Oakland, CA: California University Press, 2015.
Ayoub, Mohamed. *The Many Faces of Political Islam: Religion and Politics in the Muslim World*. Ann Arbor: The University of Michigan Press, 2008.
Aziz, T. M. "The Role of Muhammad Baqir al-Sadr in Shii Political Activism in Iraq from 1958 to 1980." *International Journal of Middle East Studies* 25 (1993): 207–22.
Baker, Raymond William. *Islam without Fear: Egypt and the New Islamists*. Cambridge: Oxford University Press, 2003.
Baroudi, Sami E. "Countering US Hegemony: The Discourse of Salim al-Hoss and other Arab Intellectuals." *Middle Eastern Studies* 44 (2008): 105–29.
Baroudi, Sami E. "In the Shadow of the Quran: Recent Islamist Discourse on the United States and US Foreign Policy." *Middle Eastern Studies* 46 (2010): 569–94.

Bibliography | 287

Baroudi, Sami E. "Sheikh Yusuf Qaradawi on International Relations: The Discourse of a Leading Islamist Scholar (1926–)." *Middle Eastern Studies* 50 (2014): 2–36.

Baroudi, Sami E. "The Islamic Realism of Sheikh Yusuf Qaradawi (1926–) and Sayyid Muhammad Hussein Fadlullah (1935–2010)." *British Journal of Middle Eastern Studies* 43 (2016): 94–114.

Baroudi, Sami E. "Sheikh Muhammad Abu Zahra (1898–1974) on International Relations: The Discourse of a Contemporary Mainstream Islamist." *Middle Eastern Studies* 54 (2018): 415–41.

Baroudi, Sami E. "Hannah Arendt, the Human Condition and the Embrace of Human Diversity in the Discourses of Two Contemporary Islamists: Sheikh Muhammad Abu Zahra (1898–1974) and Sheikh Wahbah al-Zuhaili (1932–2015)." *British Journal of Middle Eastern Studies* (2019). doi: https://doi.org/10.1080/13530194.2019.1699775.

Baroudi, Sami E. "On origins: Arab Intellectuals' Debates on the ideational Sources of ISIS." *Middle East Journal* 74 (2020a): 220–42.

Baroudi, Sami E. "The Problematic Notion of the Islamic State in the Discourses of Contemporary Islamists: The Case of Sheikh Muhammad Abu Zahra (1898–1974)." *Middle Eastern Studies* 56 (2020b): 496–510.

Baroudi, Sami E. and Jennifer Skulte-Ouaiss. "Mohamed Hassanein Heikal on the United States: The Critical Discourse of a Leading Arab Intellectual." *Middle Eastern Studies* 50 (2015): 93–114.

Baroudi, Sami E. and Vahid Behmardi. "Sheikh Wahbah Al-Zuhaili on International Relations: The Discourse of a Prominent Islamist Scholar (1932–2015)." *Middle Eastern Studies* 53 (2017): 363–85.

Bartal, Shaul and Nesya Rubinstein-Shemer. *Hamas and Ideology: Sheikh Yusuf al-Qaradawi on Jews, Zionism and Israel*. Oxford and New York: Routledge, 2018.

Bayat, Asef. "Islamism and Social Movement Theory." *Third World Quarterly* 26 (2005): 891–908.

Berman, Paul, Jeffrey Herf and Marc Lynch. "Islamism Unveiled: From Berlin to Cairo and Back Again." *Foreign Affairs* 89 (2010): 144–50.

Berman, Sheri. "Islamism, Revolution, and Civil Society." *Perspectives on Politics* 1 (2003): 257–72.

Berridge, W. J. *Hasan al-Turabi, Islamist Politics and Democracy in Sudan*. Cambridge: Cambridge University Press, 2017.

Bhagwati, Jagdish. *In Defense of Globalization*. Oxford: Oxford University Press, 2004.

Bowering, Gerhard, et al., eds. *The Princeton Encyclopedia of Islamic Political Thought*. Princeton, NJ: Princeton University Press, 2013.

Browers, Michelle. *Political Ideology in the Arab world: Accommodation and Transformation*. Cambridge: Cambridge University Press, 2009.

Brown, Nathan J. "*Post Revolutionary al-Azhar.*" The Carnegie Papers, Middle East September 2011 (Washington, DC: Carnegie Endowment for International Peace, 2011). https://carnegieendowment.org/files/al_azhar.pdf.

Brown, Nathan J. *When Victory Is Not an Option: Islamist Movements in Arab Politics*. Ithaca: Cornell University, 2012.

Burchill, Scott and Andrew Linklater. "Introduction." In *Theories of International Relations*, edited by Scott Burchill and Andrew Linklater, 5th ed. New York: Palgrave Macmillan, 2013.

Burgat, Francois. *Islamism in the Shadow of Al-Qaeda*. Austin, TX.: The University of Texas Press, 2010.
Burke, Jason. *Al-Qaeda: The True Story of Radical Islam*. London: I. B. Tauris & Co, 2003.
Byman, Daniel L. and Kenneth M. Pollack. "Iraq's Long Term Impact on Jihadist Terrorism." *The Annals of the American Academy of Political and Social Science* 618 (2008): 55–68.
Caeiro, Alexandre. "The Shifting Moral Universes of the Islamic Tradition of Ifta': A Diachronic Analysis of Four Adab al-fatwa Manuals." *The Muslim World* 96 (2006): 661–85.
Caeiro, Alexandre and Mahmoud al-Saify. "Qaradawi in Europe, Europe in Qaradawi?" In *Global Mufti: The Phenomenon of Yusuf Qaradawi*, edited by Bettina Graf and Jakob Skovgaard-Peterson. New York: Columbia University Press, 2009.
Cragg, Kenneth. *The Qur'an and the West*. Washington, DC: Georgetown University Press, 2005.
Crouter, Richard. *Reinhold Niebuhr: On Politics, Religion and Christian Faith*. Oxford and New York: Oxford University Press, 2010.
Da Lage, Olivier. "The Politics of Al Jazeera or the Diplomacy of Doha." In *The Al Jazeera Phenomenon: Critical Perspectives on New Arab Media*, edited by Mohamed Zayani. London: Pluto Press, 2005.
Dalacoura, Katerina. *Islamist Terrorism and Democracy in the Middle East*. Cambridge: Cambridge University Press, 2011.
Denoeux, Guilain. "The Forgotten Swamp: Navigating Political Islam." *Middle East Policy* 9 (2002): 56–81.
Deudney, Daniel. *Bounding Power: Republican Security Theory from the Polis to the Global Village*. Princeton, N.J.: Princeton University Press, 2007.
Deutsch, Karl W., et al. *Political Community and the North Atlantic Area: International Organization in the Light of Historical Experience*. Princeton, N.J.: Princeton University Press, 1957.
Donnelly, Jack. "Realism." In *Theories of International Relations*, edited by Scott Burchill et al., 4th ed. New York: Palgrave MacMillan, 2009.
Doyle, Michael. "Kant, Liberal Legacies and Foreign Affairs." *Philosophy and Public Affairs* 2 (1983): 205–35.
Doyle, Michael. "Kant, Liberalism and World Politics." *American Political Science Review* 80 (1986): 1151–69.
Drezner, Daniel. *All Politics is Global: Explaining International Regulatory Regimes*. Princeton, N.J.: Princeton University Press, 2007.
El-Husseini, Rola. "Resistance, Jihad, and Martyrdom in Contemporary Lebanese Shi'a Discourse." *Middle East Journal* 62 (2008): 399–414.
El-Sayyed Radwan. "al-Islam fi Zaman al-Inshiqaqat" (Islam in the time of divisions), *Beirut News Arabia*, 2015, http://www.beirutme.com/?p=14371, accessed 27 August 2019.
Enayat, Hamid. "Islam and Socialism in Egypt." *Middle Eastern Studies* 4 (1968): 141–72.
Esposito, John. *Islam and Politics*, 4th ed. Syracuse, NY: Syracuse University Press, 1984.
Esposito, John, ed. *Political Islam: Revolution, Radicalization, or Reform?* Boulder, CO: Lynne Rienner Publisher, Inc., 1997.
Esposito, John. *The Future of Islam*. Oxford: Oxford University Press, 2010.
Euben, Roxanne L. "Spectacles of Sovereignty in Digital Time: ISIS Executions, Visual Rhetoric and Sovereign Power." *Perspectives on Politics* 15, no. 4 (2017)., 1007–1033.

Fadlallah, Muhammad Hussein. *Al-Islam wa Mantiq al-Quwa* (Islam and the Logic of Power), 2nd ed. Beirut: al-Dar al-Islamiyya, 1981.
Fadlallah, Muhammad Hussein. *Maʿ al-Hikma fi Khat al-Islam* (Wisdom in the Path of Islam). Beirut: Muʾasasat al-Wafa, 1985.
Fadlallah, Muhammad Hussein. *Salat al-Jum ʿa, al-Kalima wa al-Mawqif: Tawthiq li-Khutub al-Jumʿa 1989* (Friday Prayer, Discourse and Stance: Documentation of Friday Sermons, 1989). Beirut: Dar al-Malak, 2004.
Fadlallah, Muhammad Hussein. *Al-Jumʿa: Minbar wa-Mihrab, Tawtheeq li-Khutab al-Jumʿa 1988* (Friday [Prayer]: A Pulpit and a Prayer Niche: Documentation of Friday Sermons 1988). Beirut: Dar al-Malak, 1996a.
Fadlallah, Muhammad Hussein. *Al-Hiwar fi al-Qurʾan* (Dialogue in the Quran). Beirut: Dar al-Malak, 1996b.
Fadlallah, Muhammad Hussein. *Uslub al-Daʾwa fi al-Quran* (the Way of Calling to Islam in the Quran), 6th ed. Beirut: Dar al-Malak, 1998.
Fadlallah, Muhammad, Hussein. *Iradat al-Quwa: Jihad al-Muqawama fi Khitab Samahat Ayatollah al-Uzma al-Sayyid Muhammad Hussein Fadlallah* (The Will of Power: Resistance Jihad in the Discourse of Grand Ayatollah Sayyid Muhammad Hussein Fadlallah). Beirut: Dar al-Malak, 2000.
Fadlallah, Muhammad Hussein. *Al-Haraka al-Islamiyya: Humum wa Qadaya* (The Islamic Movement: Concerns and Issues). Beirut: Dar al-Malak, 2001.
Fadlallah, Muhammad, Hussein. *Idaʾat Islamiyya* (Islamic Illuminations). Beirut: Dar an-Nahar, 2003a.
Fadlallah, Muhammad Hussein. *Al-Mudanas wa al-Muqadas: Amerka wa Rayat al-Irhab al-Duwali* (The Unsacred and the Sacred: America and the Banner of International Terrorism). Beirut: Riad el-Rayyes Books, 2003b.
Fadlallah, Muhammad Hussein. *Al-Haraka al-Islamiyya Ma Laha wa Ma ʿAlayha* (The Islamic [Activist] Movement: What Stands for It, and What Stands Against It). Beirut: Dar al-Malak, 2004.
Fadlallah Muhammad, Hussein. *Fi Afaq al-Hiwar al-Islami al-Masihi* (In the Horizons of Inter-Islamic-Christian Dialogue). Beirut: Dar al-Malak, 2005.
Fadlallah, Muhammad Hussein. *Khitab al-Muqawama wa al-Nasr: fi Muwajahat al-Harb al-Israeiliyya ʿala Lubnan Tammouz 2006* (The Discourse of Resistance and Victory: Confronting Israel's War on Lebanon of July 2006). Beirut: Dar al-Malak, 2006.
Fadlallah, Muhammad Hussein. *Al-Ijtihad: Bayn Asr al-Madi wa Afaq al-Mustaqbal* (Jurisprudence between the Captivity of the Past and the Horizons of the Future). Beirut: al-Markaz al-Thaqafi al- ʿArabi, 2009.
Fadlallah, Muhammad Hussein and Ali Fadlallah. *Kitab al-Jihad* (The Book of Jihad), 2nd ed. Beirut: Dar al-Malak, 1998.
Firestone, Reuven. *Jihad: The Origins of Holy War in Islam*. New York and Oxford: Oxford University Press, 1999.
Fishman, Brian. *The Master Plan: ISIS, al-Qaeda and the Jihadist Strategy for Final Victory*. New Haven: Yale University Books, 2016.

Gabon, Alain. "Can Mainstream Sunni Islam Counter the Islamic State? A Critique of Adis Duderija's The Salafi Worldview and the Hermeneutical Limits of Mainstream Sunni Critique of Salafi Jihadism." *Studies in Conflict & Terrorism*. doi: https://doi.org/10.1080/10576X.2019.1657296.

Galal, Ehab. "Yusuf al-Qaradawi and the New Islamic TV." In *Global Mufti: The Phenomenon of Yusuf Qaradawi*, edited by Bettina Graf and Jakob Skovgaard-Peterson New York: Columbia University Press, 2009.

Geaves, Ron. *Aspects of Islam*. Washington, D.C.: Georgetown University Press, 2005.

Gerges, Fawaz. *ISIS: A History*. Princeton and Oxford: Princeton University Press, 2016.

Gerges, Fawaz. *Making the Arab World: Nasser, Qutb and the Clash that Shaped the Middle East*. Princeton and Oxford: Princeton University Press, 2018.

Gilpin, Robert. *The Political Economy of International Relations*. Princeton, N.J.: Princeton University Press, 1987.

Gilpin, Robert. *Global Political Economy: Understanding the International Economic Order*. Princeton, N.J.: Princeton University Press, 2001.

Graf, Bettina and Jakob Skovgaard-Peterson, eds. *Global Mufti: The Phenomenon of Yusuf Qaradawi*. New York: Columbia University Press, 2009.

Guerrero, Leon. *The First Filipino: A Biography of José Rizal*. Manilla: National Heroes Commission, 1963.

Haddad, Mahmoud. "Arab Religious Nationalism in the Colonial Era: Rereading Rashid Rida's Ideas on the Caliphate." *Journal of the American Oriental Society* 117 (1997): 253–77.

Haddad, Yvonne. "Muhammad Abduh: Pioneer of Islamic Reform." In *Pioneers of Islamic Revival*, edited by Ali Rahnema. London: Zed Books, 1994.

Haj, Samira. *Reconfiguring Islamic Tradition: Reform, Rationality, and Modernity*. Stanford, CA: Stanford University Press, 2009.

Hallaq, Wael. *Shari'a, Theory, Practice, Transformation*. Cambridge: Cambridge University Press, 2009.

Hamid, Shadi. *Islamic Exceptionalism: How the Struggle over Islam is Reshaping the World*. New York: St. Martin's Press, 2016.

Harknett, Richard J. and Hasan B. Yalcin "The Struggle for Autonomy: A Realist Structural Theory of International Relations." *International Studies Review* 14 (2012): 499–521.

Hassan, Mona. *Longing for the Lost Caliphate, A Transregional History*. Princeton and Oxford: Princeton University Press, 2016.

Haykel, Bernard. "On the Nature of Salafi Thought and Action." In *Global Salafism: Islam New Religious Movement*, edited by Roel Meijer. Oxford: Oxford University Press, 2013.

Hegghammer, Thomas. "Jihadi-Salafis or Revolutionaries? On Religion and Politics in the Study of Militant Islamism." In *Global Salafism: Islam New Religious Movement*, edited by Roel Meijer. Oxford: Oxford University Press, 2013.

Hirschkind, Charles. "What is Political Islam." In *Political Islam: A Critical Reader*, edited by Frédéric Volpi (London and New York: Routledge, 2011).

Hobbes, Thomas. *Leviathan*. London: Penguin Books, 1968.

Hourani, Albert. *Arabic Thought in the Liberal Age: 1798–1939*. Cambridge: Cambridge University Press, 1983.

Hroub, Khaled, ed. *Political Islam: Context versus Ideology*. London: SAQI in association with London Middle East Institute, SOAS, 2010.
Hurd, Elizabeth. *The Politics of Secularism in International Relations*. Princeton: Princeton University Press, 2008.
Ikenberry, G. John. *Liberal Leviathan: The Origins, Crisis and Transformation of the American World Order*. Princeton: Princeton University Press, 2011.
Ikenberry, G. John. *After Victory: Institutions, Strategic Restraint, and the Rebuilding of Order after Major Wars*. Princeton: Princeton University Press, 2012.
Ikenberry, G. John. *A World Safe for Democracy: Liberal Internationalism and the Crises of Global Order*. New Haven: Yale University Press, 2020.
'Imara, Muhammad. *Al-A'mal al-Kamila lil-Imam al-Sheikh Muhammad 'Abduh* (The Complete Works of the Imam Sheikh Muhammad 'Abduh). Cairo: Dar al-Shuruq, 1993.
'Imara, Muhammad. *Rifa'a al-Tahtawi: Ra'id al-Tanwir fi al-'Asr al-Hadith* (Rifa'a al-Tahtawi: The Pioneer of Enlightenment in the Modern Period). Cairo: Dar al-Shuruq, 2009.
Ismael, Tareq Y. *The Rise and Fall of the Communist Party of Iraq*. Cambridge: Cambridge University Press, 2008.
Jaber, Hala. *Hizbullah: Born with a Vengeance*. New York: Columbia University Press, 1997.
Jackson, Roy. *Mawlana Mawdudi and Political Islam: Authority and the Islamic State*. London and New York: Routledge, 2011.
Jahn, Beate. *Liberal Internationalism: Theory, History, and Practice*. London: Palgrave MacMillan, 2013.
Kamali, Mohammad Hashim. *The Middle Path of Moderation in Islam: The Quranic Principle of Wasatiyyah*. Oxford: Oxford University Press, 2015.
Kaplan, Morton. *System and Process in International Politics*. New York: John Wiley, 1957.
Keddie, Nikki. *Sayyid Jamal al-Din "al-Afghani": A Political Biography*. Berkeley: University of California Press, 1972.
Keddie, Nikki. *An Islamic Response to Imperialism: Political and Religious Writings of Sayyid Jamal ad-Din "al-Afghani"*. Berkeley: Berkeley University Press, 1983.
Keddie, Nikki. "Sayyid Jamal al-Din al-Afghani." In *Pioneers of Islamic Revival*, edited by Ali Rahnema. London: Zed Books, 1994.
Kelsay, John. *Arguing the Just war in Islam*. Cambridge, Massachusetts and London: Harvard University Press, 2007.
Kennan, George. *American Diplomacy* (Sixtieth-Anniversary Expanded Edition with introduction by John Mearsheimer). Chicago: Chicago University Press, 2012.
Kepel, Gilles. *Jihad: The Trails of Political Islam*. Translated by Anthony F. Roberts. Cambridge, MA: Belknap Press, 2002.
Kerr, Malcolm H. *Islamic Reform: The Political and Legal Theories of Muhammad 'Abduh and Rashid Rida*. Berkeley and Los Angeles: Berkeley University Press, 1966.
Kinsella, David and Craig Carr, eds. *The Morality of War: A Reader*. Boulder and London: Lynne Rienner Publishers, 2007.
Kissinger, Henry. *A World Restored: The Politics of Conservatism in a Revolutionary Age*. New York: Grosset & Dunlap, 1964.
Kissinger, Henry. *Diplomacy*. New York: Simon and Schuster, 1994.

Kugle, Scott and Stephen Hunt. "Masculinity, Homosexuality and the Defense of Islam: A Case Study of Yusuf al-Qaradawi's Media Fatwa." *Religion & Gender* 2 (2012): 254–79.
Lav, Daniel. *Radical Islam and the Revival of Medieval Ideology*. New York: Cambridge University Press, 2012.
Leiken, Robert S. and Steven Brooke. "The Moderate Muslim Brotherhood." *Foreign Affairs* 86 (2007): 107–21.
Lieven, Anatol and John Hulsman. *Ethical Realism: A Vision for America's Role in the World*. New York: Pantheon Books, 2006.
Lopez, Alfred. *José Marti, A Revolutionary Life*. Austin, TX: Texas University Press, 2014.
Lynch, Marc. *Voices of the New Arab Public: Iraq: Al-Jazeera and Middle East Politics Today*. New York: Cambridge University Press, 2006.
Lynch, Marc. "Islam Divided between Salafi-Jihad and the Ikhwan." *Studies in Conflict and Terrorism* 33 (2010): 467–87.
Makki, Majd. "Al- Allama al-Faqih al-Sheikh Muhammad Abu Zahra" (The Scholar Jurist Sheikh Muhammad Abu Zahra), *Syrian Scholars Association*. http://www.islamsyria.com/portal/cvs/show/496, accessed 5 July 2016.
Mandaville, Peter. *Islam and Politics*, 2nd ed. London and New York: Routledge, 2014.
Mansfield, Laura. *His own Words: A Translation of the Writings of Dr. Ayman al Zawahiri*. Old Tappan: TLG Publications, 2006.
Mansour, Imad. "A Global South Perspective on International Relations Theory." *International Studies Perspectives* 18 (2017): 2–3.
March, Andrew F. "Taking People As They Are: Islam As a 'Realistic Utopia' in the Political Theory of Sayyid Qutb." *American Political Science Review* 104 (2010): 189–206.
March, Andrew F. "Rethinking Religious Reasons in Public Justification." *American Political Science Review* 107 (2013): 523–39.
Mardin, Serif. "Religion and Secularism in Turkey." In *The Modern Middle East: A Reader*, edited by Albert Hourani, Philip Khoury, and Mary Wilson. Berkeley and Los Angeles: University of California Press, 1993.
Martin, Richard C. and Abbas Barzegar. "Introduction: The Debate about Islamism in the Public Sphere." In *Islamism: Contested Perspectives on Political Islam*, edited by Richard C. Martin and Abbas. Barzegar Stanford: Stanford University Press, 2010.
Mawdudi, Sayyid Abu al-A'la and Muhammad Abu Zahra. "The Role of Ijtihad and the Scope of Legislation in Islam." *Muslim Digest* 9, no. 2 (1959): 15–20.
McCants, William. *The ISIS Apocalypse: The History, Strategy and Doomsday Vision of the Islamic State*. New York: St. Martin's Press, 2015.
Mearsheimer, John. "A Realist Reply." *International Security* 2 (1995): 82–93.
Mearsheimer, John. *The Tragedy of Great Power Politics*. New York and London: W.W. Norton & Company, 2001.
Mearsheimer, John. "Introduction." In *American Diplomacy: Sixtieth-Anniversary Expanded Edition*, edited by George Kennan. Chicago and London: The University of Chicago Press, 2012.
Mearsheimer, John. *The Great Delusion: Liberal Dreams and International Realities*. New Haven: Yale University Press, 2018.

Meijer, Roel, ed. *Global Salafism: Islam's New Religious Movement*. Oxford: Oxford University Press, 2013.
Mendelsohn, Barak. *The al-Qaeda Franchise: The Expansion of al-Qaeda and Its Consequences*. Oxford: Oxford University Press, 2016.
Mitchell, Richard P. *The Society of the Muslim Brothers*. Oxford: Oxford University Press, 1993; first published 1969.
Morgenthau, Hans. *Politics Among Nations, The Struggle for Power and Peace*, 7th ed. New York: McGraw-Hill Education, 2005.
Moussali, Ahmad. *The Islamic Quest for Democracy, Pluralism and Human Rights*. Gainesville: University Press of Florida, 2001.
Nasr, Seyyed Vali Reza. *Mawdudi and the Making of Islamic Revivalism*. New York and Oxford: Oxford University Press, 1996.
Norton, Augustus Richard. *Hezbollah*. Princeton: Princeton University Press, 2007.
Osman, Tarek. *Islamism: What It Means for the Middle East and the World*. New Haven: Yale University Press, 2016.
Palmer Harik, Judith. *Hezbollah: The Changing Face of Terrorism*. London: I.B. Tauris, 2004.
Peterson, Eric. "Christianity and Power Politics Themes and Issues." In *Christianity and Power Politics Today: Christian Realism and Contemporary Political Dilemmas*, edited by Eric Peterson. New York: Palgrave Macmillan, 2008.
Pintak, Lawrence. *Reflections in a Bloodshot Lens: America, Islam and the War of Ideas*. London: Pluto Press, 2006.
Polka, Sagi. "Taqrib al-Madhahib – Qaradawi's Declaration of Principles Regarding Sunni–Shi'i Ecumenism." *Middle Eastern Studies* 49 (2013): 414–29.
Polka, Sagi. *Shaykh Yusuf al-Qaradawi: Spiritual Mentor of Wasati Salafism*. Syracuse: Syracuse University Press, 2019.
Qal'aji, Qadri. *Thalatha min A'lam al-Huriya: Jamal al-Din al-Afghani, Muhammad 'Abduh and Sa'd Zaghlul* (Three Luminaries for Freedom: Jamal al-Din al-Afghani, Muhammad 'Abduh and Sa'd Zaghlul). Beirut: Sharikat al-Matbou'at lil-Nashr wa al-Tawzi', 1994.
Rahnema, Ali. "Introduction." In *Pioneers of Islamic Revival*, edited by Ali Rahnema. London: Zed Books, 1994a.
Rahnema, Ali. ed. *Pioneers of Islamic Revival*. London: Zed Books, 1994b.
Ramadan, Tariq. *The Arab Awakening: Islam and the New Middle East*. London: Penguin Books, 2012.
Randal, Jonathan. *Osama: The Making of a Terrorist*. London and New York: I.B. Tauris, 2004.
Ranstorp, Magnus. *Hizb 'Allah in Lebanon: The Politics of the Western Hostage Crisis*. New York: St. Martin's Press, 1997.
Rida, Rashid. *Al-Khilafa* (the Caliphate). Cairo: Mu'assat Hindawi lil-Ta'lim wa al-Thaqafa, 2012.
Rock-Singer, Aaron. "Scholarly Authority and Lay Mobilization: Yusuf al-Qaradawi's Vision of Da'wa, 1976–1984." *The Muslim World* 106 (2016): 588–604.
Rock-Singer, Aaron. *Practicing Islam in Egypt: Print Media and Islamic Revival*. Cambridge: Cambridge University Press, 2019.
Rosefsky Wickham, Carrie. *The Muslim Brotherhood: Evolution of an Islamist Movement*. Princeton and Oxford: Princeton University Press, 2013.

Rosenthal, Joel. *Righteous Realists: Political Realism, Responsible Power, and American Culture in the Nuclear Age*. Baton Rouge and London: Louisiana State University Press, 1991.
Sabiq, Sayyid. *Fiqh al-Sunna* (The Jurisprudence of the Sunna). Beirut: Dar al-Kitab al-'Arabi, 1973.
Said, Edward. *Orientalism*. New York: Pantheon, 1978.
Salahi, Adil. "Scholar of Renown: Muhammad Abu Zahra." *Arab News* (2001) http://www.arabnews.com/node/216148, accessed 5 July 2016.
Salama-Carr, Myriam. "Negotiating Conflict: Rifā'a Rāfi' al-Tahtāwī and the Translation of the 'Other' in Nineteenth-century Egypt." *Social Semiotics* 17 (2007), 213–27.
Saleh, Nabeel Ali. *"Al-'Allama al-Sayyed Muhammad Hussein Fadlallah wa manjahiyath fi Mu'alajat wa Tahleel ba'd al-Qadaya al-Mu'asira 'ala Daou' Mu'tayat al-Fikr al-Islami"* (The Erudite Scholar Sayyed Muhammad Hussein Fadlallah and his Approach to the Treatment and Analysis of some Contemporary Issues in the light of the Givens of Islamic Thought) in Majmou'a min al-Mou'alifin (Various authors), *Muhammad Hussein Fadlallah al-'Iqlaniyya wa al-Hiwar min Ajl al-Taghyeer* (Muhammad Hussein Fadlallah: Rationality and Dialogue for the Sake of Change). Beirut: Center for Civilization for the Development of Islamic Thought, 2010.
Salhab, Hassan. *Al-Sheikh Mahmoud Shaltut: Qira'a fi Tajribat al-islah wa al-Wihda al-Islamiya* (Sheikh Mahmoud Shaltut: A Reading of an Attempt at Reform and Islamic Unity). Beirut: Markaz al-Hadara li-Tanmiyat al-Fikr al-Islam, 2008.
Salmi, Ralph H., Cesar Abdul Majid, and George K. Tanham. *Islam and Conflict Resolution: Theories and Practices*. Lanham, Maryland: University Press of America, 1998.
Sankari, Jamal. *Fadlallah: The Making of a Radical Shiite Leader*. London: SAQI, 2005.
Sayyid, Bobby. *A Fundamental Fear: Eurocentrism and the Emergence of Islamism*. London and New York: Zed Books Ltd., 1977.
Scheuer, Michael. *Osama Bin Laden*. Oxford: Oxford University Press, 2011.
Schwedler, Jillian. "Studying Political Islam." *International Journal of Middle East Studies* 43 (2011): 135–37.
Sedgwick, Mark. *Makers of the Muslim World: Muhammad 'Abduh*. Oxford: Oneworld Publications, 2010.
Shabbir, Akhtar. *Islam as Political Religion: The Future of an Imperial Faith*. London and New York: Routledge, 2010.
Shaltut, Mahmoud. *Al-Quran wa al-Qital* (Fighting in the Light of the Quran). Cairo: Dar al-Kitab al-'Arabi, 1951.
Shaltut, Mahmoud. *Al-Islam wa al-Wujud al-Duwali lil-Muslimin* (Islam and the International Presence of Muslims). Cairo: Matba'at Dar al-Jihad, 1958.
Shaltut, Mahmoud. *Al-Islam: 'Aqida wa Sharia* (Islam: A Creed and a *Sharia*). Cairo: Dar al-Shuruq, 2001.
Shaltut, Mahmoud. *Min Tawjihat al-Islam* (From the Guidance of Islam). Cairo: Dar al-Shuruq, 2004.
Shams al-Din, Muhammad. *Fiqh al-'Unf al-Muslah fi al-Islam* (Jurisprudence of Armed Violence in Islam). Beirut: al-Mu'asasa al-Dawliya Lil Derasat wa al-Nashr, 1998.

Shavit, Uriya. *Scientific and Political Freedom in Islam: A Critical Reading of the Modernist-Apologetic School*. London and New York: Routledge, 2017.
Sheikh, Faiz. *Islam and International Relations: Exploring Community and the Limits of Universalism*. London and New York: Rowman & Littlefield, 2016.
Shiraz, Maher. *Salafi-Jihadism: The History of an Idea*. Oxford and New York: Oxford University Press, 2016.
Smith, Tony. *Why Wilson Matters: The Origin of American Liberal Internationalism and Its Crisis Today*. Princeton: Princeton University Press, 2017.
Snyder, Jack. "Introduction." In *Religion and International Relations Theory*, edited by Jack Snyder. New York: Columbia University Press, 2011.
Spero, Joan and Jeffrey Hart. *The Politics of International Economic Relations*, 7th ed. Belmont, CA: Wadworth Cengage Learning, 2010.
Spykman, Nicholas. *America's Strategy in World Politics: The United States and the Balance of Power*. Oxford and New York: Routledge, 2007.
Stakelbeck, Erick. *ISIS Exposed: Beheadings, Slavery and the Hellish Reality of Radical Islam*. Washington, DC: Regnery Publishing, 2015.
Tamam, Ahmad. "Abu Zahra, 'alem You'raf Qadrahu" (Abu Zahra, a Scholar Known for His Worth), *al-Multaka al-Fuqhi*, 2008. https://www.feqhweb.com/vb/threads/%D8%A3%D8%A8%D9%88-%D8%B2%D9%87%D8%B1%D8%A9-%D8%B9%D8%A7%D9%84%D9%85-%D9%8A%D8%B9%D8%B1%D9%81-%D9%82%D8%AF%D8%B1%D9%87.2047/, accessed 5 July 2016.
Tammam, Husam. "Yusuf al-Qaradawi and the Muslim Brothers: The Nature of a Special Relationship." In *Global Mufti: The Phenomenon of Yusuf Qaradawi*, edited by Bettina Graf and Jakob Skovgaard-Peterson, 55–84. New York: Columbia University Press, 2009.
Tang, Shiping. "Fear in International Relations: Two Positions." *International Studies Review* 10 (2008): 451–71.
Tauber, Eliezer. "Three Approaches, One Idea: Religion and State in the Thought of 'Abd al-Rahman al-Kawakibi, Najib 'Azuri and Rashid Rida." *British Journal of Middle Eastern Studies* 21 (1994): 190–98.
Tibi, Bassam. *The Sharia State: Arab Spring and Democratization*. New York: Routledge, 2013.
Toth James. *Sayyid Qutb: The Life and Legacy of a Radical Islamic Intellectual*. Oxford: Oxford University Press, 2013.
'Ulaywi, Jaber Muhaisin. "Mahatat Min al-Sira wa al-Masira: al-Sayyid Muhammad Hussein Fadlallah fi Sutur" (Stations from his Life History and Life Journey: Some Words on Sayyid Muhammad Hussein Fadlallah) in Majmou'a min al-Mou'alifin (Various authors), *Muhammad Hussein Fadlallah al-'Iqlaniyya wa al-Hiwar min Ajl al-Taghyeer* (Rationality and Dialogue for the Purpose of Change). Beirut: Center for Civilization for the Development of Islamic Thought, 2010.
Vatikiotis, P. J. *The Modern History of Egypt*. New York and Washington: Frederick A. Praeger Publishers, 1969.
Vatikiotis, P. J. *The History of Modern Egypt from Muhammad Ali to Mubarak*, 4th ed. Baltimore: The Johns Hopkins University Press, 1991.

Volpi, Frédéric, ed. *Political Islam: A Critical Reader*. London and New York: Routledge, 2011.
Wagemakers, Joas. *A Quietist Jihadi: The Ideology and Influence of Abu Muhammad al-Maqdisi*. Cambridge: Cambridge University press, 2012.
Wagemakers, Joas. "The Transformation of a Radical Concept: al-wala' wa al-bara' in the Ideology of Abu Muhammad al-Maqdisi." In *Global Salafism: Islam's New Religious Movement*, edited by Roel Meijer. Oxford: Oxford University Press, 2013.
Walt, Stephen. *The Origins of Alliances*. Cornell: Cornell University Press, 1987.
Waltz, Kenneth. "Kant, Liberalism and War." *American Political Science Review* 56 (1962): 331–40.
Waltz, Kenneth. *Theory of International Politics*. Reading, MA: Addison-Wesley, 1979.
Waltz, Kenneth. *Man, the State and War: A Theoretical Analysis*. New York: Columbia University Press, 2001.
Weiss, Bernard. *The Spirit of Islamic Law*. Georgia: Georgia University Press, 1998.
Wendt, Alexander. "Anarchy is What States Make of It: The Social Construction of Power Politics." *International Organization* 46 (1992): 391–425.
Wendt, Alexander. *Social Theory of International Politics*. Cambridge: Cambridge University Press, 1999.
Wood, Simon A. *Christian Criticisms, Islamic Proofs: Rashid Rida's Modernist Defence of Islam*. Oxford: Oneworld Publications, 2007.
Woodward, Bob. *The Veil*. London: Simon and Schuster, 1987.
Zaman, M. Raquibuz. "Islamic Perspectives on Territorial Boundaries and Autonomy." In *Islamic Political Ethics: Civil Society, Pluralism and Conflict*, edited by Suhail Hashmi. Princeton: Princeton University Press, 2002.
Zaman, Muhammad. *Modern Islamic Thought in a Radical Age: Religious Authority and Internal Criticism*. Cambridge, Cambridge University Press, 2012.

Index

A

Abbasid 85, 88, 152–3
'Abd al-Raziq, 'Ali 64
'Abd al-Raziq, Mustafa 64, 190
'Abduh, Muhammad 4–5, 13, 20, 33–7, 41–51, 53–6, 59, 64, 88, 104–6, 116, 121, 139, 145–6, 166, 190, 199, 265, 268, 272, 281
Abu Bakr 85, 98, 165
Abu Hanifa 55, 67, 74
Abu Zahra, Muhammad 1, 3–5, 21, 23–4, 35–6, 59, 63, 66–81, 83–90, 96–7, 102–3, 110, 121–2, 139, 143, 146, 153, 157, 159, 162–3, 166–7, 169, 170–3, 189, 191–2, 195–6, 199, 201–2, 205, 208, 210, 218, 229, 250, 263, 264, 266–7, 270–1, 273–5
Afghani, Jamal al-Din 5, 17, 20, 33–51, 53, 55–6, 86, 88, 105, 116, 121, 139, 268, 271–2

Ahl al-'aqd wa al-hal 54, 153, 204
Al-Ahbash 194
Al-Assad, Bashar 141–2, 195
Al-'Assal, Ahmad 101, 137–8
Al-Azhar 1, 2, 4, 21, 26, 48, 50, 59, 64–7, 101, 104, 105–9, 127–8, 136–41, 189–91, 221, 272, 277
Al-Bahi, Muhammad 1, 3, 5–6, 21–4, 35–6, 39, 41, 52, 63, 65, 68, 75, 84, 88, 89–90, 101–25, 127–8, 138–41, 144, 148–9, 153–4, 157, 178, 202, 204, 208, 210, 218, 220, 227, 229, 232–3, 250, 264, 269, 270, 273–5
Al-Banna, Hassan 50, 136, 142, 145–6, 158–9, 178, 181
Al-Bouti, Muhammad Said Ramadan 193, 213
Al-Ghannushi, Rachid 84, 138, 146
Al-Ghazali, Muhamad 49, 67, 115, 117, 136, 144–5, 166, 176, 181
Al-Islam al-Haraki 23, 226

Al-Khateeb, Motaz 146
Al-Khoei, Abu al-Qassem 4, 221, 224–5
Al-Madrasa al-Sultaniya 46
Al-Mahmassani, Sobhi 2
Al-Manar 50
Al-Maqdisi, Abu Muhammad x, 1, 277
Al-Maraghi, Muhammad Mustafa 64, 90, 106, 190
Al-Maslaha al-'Amma (public interest) 37, 244
Al-Qaeda x, 16, 25, 34, 241, 277, 279, 288–9, 293
Al-Qaradawi, Yusuf 1, 3–6, 13, 21–4, 39, 52, 65–8, 73–4, 76, 78, 80, 84, 88–90, 101–2, 108, 110, 115–6, 120–1, 128, 133–76, 181, 189–91, 194–5, 202, 204–5, 207–8, 210, 218–20, 222–3, 226–9, 232–3, 236–7, 241, 243–4, 246, 248, 250, 262–7, 269–71, 274–7, 279
Al-Radd 'ala al-Dahriyyin 36
Al-Sadiq, Ja'afar 67, 242
Al-Salaf 34, 44, 56, 145
Al-Salaf al-Salih 15
Al-Tahtawi, Rifa'a Badawi Rafi' 33–4
Al-Zawahiri, Ayman x, 1, 105, 277
Al-Zuhaili, Wahbah 1, 3, 5–6, 21–4, 30–1, 66–8, 73–4, 76, 78, 80, 88–90, 139, 146, 152, 157, 162–3, 166–71, 175, 189–211, 218, 229, 233, 241, 243–4, 250, 263–4, 266–7, 270–1, 275–6
'Alim 193
Ansar 84–5
Antoun, Farah 49, 51
Aqalim 69, 174
Aqtar 69
Arendt, Hannah 74, 80, 262, 270
Aristotle 39, 40
Armed Peace 73, 109, 195, 264, 270
Arms Races 19

Asad, Talal 11
Ash'arite 43–4
Ataturk, Mustafa Kamal 9, 116, 272
Athar al-Harb 22, 163, 196, 198, 199, 212, 243–4
Atwan, Abdel Bari 25
Ayoob, Mohammed 6–8, 15, 35

B

Baker, Raymond William 133, 141, 176
Baroudi, Sami E. 264, 266, 269, 270, 274
Bayat, Asef 9, 17
Bin laden, Osama x, 1, 241, 277
Browers, Michelle 8
Brown, Nathan J 9, 26
Burchill, Scott 2
Burgat, Francois 25
Burke, Jason 25
Burton, Greg 7

C

Caeiro, Alexandre 176–7
Cairo University 64, 66–7, 189, 191
Caliphate 3, 51, 53–6, 83, 85, 88–9, 121–2, 153, 173, 245–7, 272–3
Capitalism 6, 22, 75, 90, 102, 104, 110–3, 116–7, 121–3, 149, 209, 273, 275
Causality 151
Christianity 5–6, 36, 38–9, 51–2, 95, 114, 129, 145, 148, 156, 190, 226, 232, 272
Christians 39, 53, 66, 114, 150, 169, 170, 190–1, 224, 267, 281
Civilians 15, 30, 135, 163, 167, 201, 205–6, 220, 242, 266–7
Cold War 5, 23, 65, 69, 102, 110, 273, 275–6

Colonialism 5, 24, 35, 37–9, 54, 76, 106, 111, 114–5, 122, 143–4, 154, 229, 271–3
Combatants 80–82, 167, 197, 201–2, 205, 234, 242–3, 266–7
Communal spirit 103, 112–3, 118
Constructivist 11
Cooperation 3, 14, 19, 54, 70, 72, 123, 125, 135, 173–4, 209–10, 219, 233, 249, 261, 263, 272
Cragg, Kenneth 84
Crusades 115, 153
Crusading 232

D

Dalacoura, Katerina 26
Dar al-Harb 14, 74, 170, 195, 199
Dar al-Silm 14, 195, 199
Denoeux, Guilain 8
Deterrence 77, 81–2, 238, 264, 270
Deudney, Daniel 277
Diplomacy 14, 18, 202, 261, 269
Doyle, Michael 99

E

Egypt 2, 16, 35, 38–40, 42, 46, 48, 50–2, 55, 63–6, 104, 106, 108–9, 113–4, 124, 134, 136–8, 140–1, 153, 158, 167, 169, 174, 179, 191, 193–4, 239, 247, 271–4, 277
El-Husseini, Rola 252
El-Sayyid, Radwan 190, 193, 195, 211–3, 298
Esposito, John 7, 9, 34, 36–7
Europe 33, 36–9, 41–2, 45, 47–9, 51, 105–6, 111, 116–7, 139, 232, 239, 249, 272, 274

F

Fadlallah, Muhammad Hussein 2–6, 22–4, 39, 53, 68, 89–90, 110, 113, 116, 120, 134, 150, 157, 162–3, 166–7, 169–70, 189, 198, 207, 210–11, 217–50, 264, 266, 269–71, 275, 276, 277
Fiqh 78, 144, 147, 266
Fiqh al-jihad 157, 163, 166
Firestone, Reuven 166
Fishman, Brian 25
Fuller, Graham 7

G

Galal, Ehab 176, 179
Geaves, Ron 155
Gerges, Fawaz 108
Gilpin, Robert 30
Graf, Bettina 139, 142
Great Britain 29, 39, 234
Guizot, Francois 36

H

Haddad, Mahmoud 5, 54
Haddad, Yvonne 265
Haj, Samira 11, 49
Hallaq, Wael 9–10
Hamas 16, 241, 279
Hamid, Shadi 10
Hanafi 55
Hanbali 55
Hassan, Mona 281
Hawza 2, 4, 220–1, 223, 245
Hay'at Kibar al-'ulama 64
Haykel, Bernard 34–5
Hegghammer, Thomas 10

Hezbollah 4, 16, 194, 225, 237, 241, 249, 253, 279
Hirschkind, Charles 6
Hobbes, Thomas 77
Hourani, Albert 33, 35–6, 38–40, 42, 48–9, 54, 56
Hroub, Khaled 6–7, 24, 32
Human dignity 112, 197–8
Human nature 70, 76–7, 102, 112, 116, 151, 155, 157, 160, 171, 175, 203, 223, 231, 241, 252, 262, 269
Hurd, Elizabeth 7

I

Ibn Taymiyya 35, 67, 144, 165–6
Ijtihad 37, 50, 54–5, 158, 224
Ikenberry, G. John 277
'Imara, Muhammad 34–5, 38, 40, 45–6
International humanitarian law 18–9, 22, 171, 190, 201, 205, 210, 263, 267
International law 12, 14, 18–9, 89, 145, 152, 171, 190–2, 196–7, 199, 202, 204–6, 208, 210, 236, 250, 261, 263, 267
International Relations – underpinning principles 6, 63, 67, 142, 195, 202, 217, 226
Islamic Awakening 153–4, 171, 248
Islamic Jihad in Palestine 16
Islamic Research Academy (Majma' al-Buhuth al-Islamiyya) 4, 67
Islamic state 9, 17, 21, 54, 69, 78, 81, 84–5, 88–9, 122–3, 138–9, 143, 152–3, 164, 173–5, 204, 209–10, 227–8, 237, 240, 245, 260–1, 277
Islamic State in Syria and Iraq x, 1, 15–6, 135, 260, 277, 279

Islamic unity 3, 6, 20–2, 34–7, 41, 51, 56, 63, 65, 69, 83–9, 104, 121–5, 135, 154, 171, 173–5, 190, 208–10, 218–20, 245–8, 273–4
Islamism 6–9, 11, 17, 40–1, 193, 259, 273
Iqbal, Muhammad 116, 121

J

Jackson, Roy 38, 48–9, 139
Jahn, Beate 30
Jama'at al-Tabligh wa al-Hijra 16
Jihad 3, 6, 9–10, 14, 20–2, 39, 53, 55–6, 63, 65, 73, 77–8, 104, 110, 119–21, 123–5, 135, 144–6, 150, 156–66, 171, 173, 195, 198, 200, 202–3, 207, 210, 218–9, 224, 226–7, 230–1, 236–41, 245, 247, 249, 262, 265–6, 272, 277
Jizya 80–1, 165–6, 169–70, 190, 207, 242
Justice 70, 73, 76, 79, 81, 84, 119, 145, 147, 151, 152, 156–157, 161, 165, 195, 197–198, 209, 224, 226, 234–236, 240, 263, 264

K

Kamali, Mohammad Hashim 190
Keddie, Nikki 35, 38, 41, 44, 48, 271
Kelsay, John 38
Kemalist 9
Kennan, George 269–70
Kepel, Gilles 28
Kerr, Malcolm 42–4, 49, 54
Khan, Sir Sayyid Ahmad 9, 114
Kissinger, Henry 232, 269
Kufar 66, 207, 245, 265
Kufr 66, 219

L

Lav, Daniel 25, 28
Liberal xi
Liberal Internationalist 17, 19–20, 68, 263, 270–1
Linklater, Andrew 2
Lynch, Marc 134–5, 141

M

Maher, Shiraz 34
Mainstream x, xi, 1, 3, 5, 7, 9–10, 12–4, 17, 21, 23–4, 33, 35, 37–9, 41–4, 47, 49–51, 54–6, 65, 68–72, 75–7, 79–84, 87, 89–90, 102, 110, 112, 120–1, 123, 125, 134–5, 142, 146, 148–54, 156, 159–67, 170–3, 189–90, 192, 198, 200, 202–5, 208–11, 217–20, 223–4, 226–9, 234–49, 259–69, 276–9
Majma' al-Buhuth al-Islamiyya (See Islamic Research Academy) 4, 67
Mandaville, Peter 6, 8
March, Andrew 8, 11
Martin, Richard C. 259
Marx, Karl 102, 108, 110–2, 117, 121, 240, 274 (including Marxist and Marxian)
Marxism 109–10, 116–7, 125, 149
Materialism 22, 65, 110, 113–4, 116, 149–50, 155, 274
Mawdudi, Sayyed Abu al-A'la 86, 138–9, 245
Mazhhab 21, 65, 67, 172, 192, 194, 245–6, 259
Mearsheimer, John 18, 20, 156, 269, 277
Mecca 52, 78, 84, 164, 172, 227, 236–7, 240

Medina 69, 72, 78, 84–5, 103, 143, 152, 164, 172, 227, 245, 261, 267
Meijer, Roel 34
Mitchell, Richard P 179
Moderate-Reformist x, 1, 5–6, 12–13, 15, 21, 33–5, 56, 101, 190, 199, 202, 217–9, 224, 259, 268, 278
Modernists 9–10
Morgenthau, Hans 269
Muawiyah 85
Muhammad, Prophet 11, 50, 70, 72, 78, 79, 84, 103, 141, 143, 151–2, 162, 172, 205, 220, 228, 233, 242, 245
Muslim Brotherhood x, 4, 10, 15, 50, 67, 108, 136–9, 145–6, 158–9, 191, 193, 222, 277, 279
Muslim world 2, 5–7, 22–3, 33–4, 37–9, 48, 52–3, 56, 69, 86, 88, 90, 102, 111, 114–5, 118, 122–5, 134, 144, 149, 153–4, 168, 192–3, 209, 231–2, 246–7, 249, 268, 271, 273–5
Mutual restraining 151, 154–7, 171, 218, 269
Myanmar 10

N

Nasr, Seyyed Vali Reza 20
Normative International Relations 9
Normative political Islam 9
Norton, Augustus Richard 253

O

Oppression 70, 119, 149–150, 152, 155, 162, 164, 198, 204, 226–230, 235, 238, 241
Orientalism 11, 17, 43

Osman, Tarek 9
Ottoman Empire 39, 52, 54, 56, 122, 153, 204, 266, 271–2

P

Palestine 10, 52, 135, 142, 158, 163, 170, 174, 232, 239, 247, 272–3
Palmer Harik, Judith 253
Pan-Islamism 40–1, 193, 273
Peaceful coexistence 14, 65
Political Islam (see Islamism) ix, x, 1, 3, 6–12, 15–7, 24, 34, 56, 145, 190, 217–9, 259–60, 268, 278–9
Polka, Sagi 181
Power x, xi, 2, 5, 8, 14, 18–9, 38–41, 45, 47, 52, 54–5, 70, 73–4, 76–7, 81–2, 84, 86, 88–90, 108, 110–1, 114–7, 119–20, 122–3, 141, 143, 145, 149–51, 154, 156–7, 161–2, 170, 174, 193, 204, 209–10, 218, 224, 226–41, 244, 247–50, 264, 26
Prisoners of War 19, 80, 152, 168–169, 199, 201, 202, 205–206, 243

Q

Qal'aji, Qadri 38, 56–9, 281, 293
Qum 4
Quran xi, 2, 11, 13, 21, 44, 59, 63, 65–6, 69–73, 76–7, 79–84, 86, 94–8, 108, 116, 122–6, 128, 135–8, 143–6, 152, 156–7, 159, 161, 163, 165–6, 170, 175, 182, 185, 193, 196, 198, 203, 206, 208–9, 221–3, 228, 237, 241, 246, 250–3, 261–2, 267, 278, 282, 284–6, 289, 294

Quranic 44, 68–73, 75, 77–9, 81–3, 101, 112, 120, 138, 147–8, 155, 162–3, 165–6, 168–9, 172, 181, 184, 196–8, 203, 206–7, 210–1, 221, 224, 234–5, 238–41, 243, 248, 262, 269–270, 291
Qutb, Sayyid x, 1, 25, 27, 108, 128, 166, 177, 179, 183, 185, 245, 274, 290, 292, 295

R

Radical Islam 13, 15–6, 25, 28, 288, 292, 295
Radical Islamists x, 1–5, 10, 12–6, 20, 47, 75, 166, 168, 218, 250, 259–61, 266, 277–8
Rahnema, Ali 57, 59, 280, 290–1, 293
Ramadan, Tariq 92, 96, 138, 193, 211, 229, 278, 282, 293
Randal, Jonathan 25
Realism xi, 18–9, 23, 29–31, 68, 147, 154–7, 175, 177, 182–3, 218, 229, 231, 269–70, 277, 279–80, 287–8, 292–4
Realist 17, 19–20, 23–4, 27, 29–30, 151, 154–7, 174–5, 183, 195, 199, 218, 231, 233, 241, 250, 269–70, 279–80, 290, 292, 294
Renan, Ernest 49
Riba 66, 84, 91–2, 172, 283, 294
Rida, Rashid 4, 5, 10, 26, 33, 41, 49, 59–61, 116, 139, 281, 286, 290–1, 293, 295–6
Risalat al-Tawhid 43, 46
Rock-Singer, Aaron 175, 177, 293
Rosefsky Wickham, Carrie 10, 27–8, 178, 183, 293
Rosenthal, Joel 183, 294

S

Sabiq, Sayyid 78–9, 97, 104, 107, 128, 294
Said, Edward 11, 28, 43, 294
Salafi 13, 15–6, 25, 27–8, 34–5, 49, 57, 176, 181, 277, 290, 292–3, 295–6
Salama-Carr, Myriam 33, 57, 294
Saleem, 'Abd al-Majid 64
Sankari, Jamal 220, 251–3, 257, 294
Sayyid, Bobby 9, 27, 294
Schwedler, Jillian 7, 26, 294
Secularism 7, 26, 113–4, 122, 149, 281, 291–2
Sedgwick, Mark 13, 28, 49, 59, 60, 294
Shabbir, Akhtar 95, 294
Shaltut, Mahmoud 1, 4, 5, 10, 21, 23–4, 63–85, 87–99, 101–3, 106–7, 109–10, 126–8, 137–9, 142, 145–6, 148, 157, 163, 166–7, 172, 178, 181, 189, 191, 195–6, 199, 202, 205, 210, 218, 229, 250, 263–4, 270, 273–5, 277, 294
Shams al-Din, Muhammad 163, 184, 207, 215, 224–5, 237, 252, 255, 266, 280, 294
Sharia 5, 10, 14–6, 26, 47, 50, 53–5, 64, 66–8, 70, 72, 75–6, 81, 84, 93, 95–6, 98, 118, 133–4, 140, 142–7, 152, 156–7, 161, 169–72, 176–7, 179, 190–2, 196, 199, 201–2, 204–5, 207–10, 223–4, 228–9, 231, 244–5, 249, 260, 263, 266–7, 275, 294–5
Shavit, Uriya 12, 18, 23, 28, 34, 57, 59, 144, 181, 295
Shaybani 74, 96
Sheikh, Faiz 6, 9, 26, 295
Shia 1, 2, 4, 15–6, 21, 23, 35, 41, 44, 54, 65–7, 85, 90–1, 93, 98, 153, 163, 172–3, 182, 194, 198, 209, 211, 217–8, 220–5, 228, 230, 239, 242, 244–6, 251–2, 254, 257, 265, 277, 284

Shiraz, Maher 57, 295
Shumul al-Islam 144–5, 158, 178, 180–1, 184, 286
Shura 37, 40, 47, 54, 61, 84, 153, 209
Slavery 206, 243–244
Snyder, Jack 99, 295
Sunna xi, 2, 11, 31, 43, 70, 72, 75, 78, 80, 83, 92, 97, 116, 120, 122–4, 135–6, 142–6, 151–2, 155–6, 161, 169–71, 175, 198, 208–9, 229, 237, 261, 267, 269, 278, 285, 294
Sunnan Allah 43–4, 75, 120, 142, 151, 156, 171, 175, 229
Sunni 1, 2, 11, 15–6, 21, 23, 35, 41, 43, 54–5, 65–7, 133–5, 153, 169, 172–3, 176, 181, 191, 194, 208–9, 217–23, 226–30, 233, 235–49, 251, 257, 259, 273, 277, 290, 293
Syrian conflict 195

T

Tafrit (laxity) 13
Takfiris 15–6
Tammam, Husam 136, 177, 295
Taqlid 13, 49, 190, 211–3
Tashdid (Excessiveness) 13
Taskhiri, Mohammad-Ali 194
Tibi, Bassam 7, 26, 295
Total war 80, 206, 267
Twelver Shiism 21, 65, 172, 209, 217

U

Uhud, Battle 151, 167, 185
Ulama 11, 43, 53, 64–5, 91–2, 105–8, 126, 134, 142, 166, 208, 244

Umma 9–10, 13, 15, 22, 28, 36–7, 39, 40–1, 45, 50–5, 65–7, 69, 72, 81–8, 115, 120, 122–5, 138, 142, 144–8, 152–34, 157, 161, 163, 171–5, 177, 178, 181–3, 185–7, 196, 200, 203, 208–9, 218, 222–3, 227, 230, 233, 237, 240–1, 245–7, 260, 261, 265, 268, 273–4, 281, 284–5
United Nations 14, 74, 174, 233
University of Cairo 2
'Urabi, Ahmad 45–6, 59, 272
al-'urwa al-wuthqa 35, 46

V

Volpi, Frédéric 8, 26–7, 290, 296

W

Wagemakers 25, 34, 57, 296
Wali al-amr (plural) 204, 208, 244
Waltz, Kenneth 18, 28–9, 99, 156, 183, 204, 231, 254, 269, 277, 282, 296

Wasati 12–3, 49, 142, 146–8, 150, 154–5, 160, 161, 181, 190, 293
Wasatiyya 146–8, 150, 155, 157, 176, 181–2, 190, 211, 228, 284, 291
Weapons of Mass Destruction 206, 273
Wendt, Alexander 29, 277, 282, 296
West 6, 9, 23, 33–4, 39, 47–8, 51–2, 55, 75, 86, 98, 111, 114–9, 122, 125, 135, 149, 150, 154, 165, 168, 225, 229, 232, 271, 281
World Bank 20
World Trade Organization 20
World War I 51–2, 70, 116, 122, 272
World War II 39, 70, 106, 114, 116, 273

Z

Zaman, Muhammad 5, 26, 31, 38, 58, 60–1, 158, 176–7, 183, 213, 288, 296
Zionism 123, 176, 229, 232, 287
Zionists 52, 240